Africa First! *asks what can be d.... .. ..,, ...*
presents the key policy choices and potential benefits ranging
from demographics to digitisation. This is an extremely important
book that I strongly recommend to all engaged in the future of
the continent.

– Sahle-Work Zewde, President of the
Federal Democratic Republic of Ethiopia

A remarkable tour d'horizon, this book is a treasure trove of in-
formation and an invaluable guide to unlocking Africa's future
potential.

– Professor Rita Abrahamsen, Graduate School of
Public and International Affairs, University of Ottawa

Cilliers refuses to adopt a fatalistic attitude . . . or to get stuck in
simplistic models that equate GDP growth with genuine develop-
ment . . . His very practical recommendations, largely focusing
on issues of governance and policy efficiency, are based on solid
empirical evidence and sound argument. This book can make a
difference and will contribute to improving the human condition
on our continent.

– Professor Maxi Schoeman, University of Pretoria

Jakkie Cilliers has a deep knowledge of Africa's current develop-
ment dynamics, theoretically and practically. His writings always
provide extremely useful insights on the possible futures of our
continent. I consider Africa First! a must-read for academics and
policy-makers inside and beyond Africa.

– Dr Ibrahim Mayaki, CEO of
the African Union Development Agency-Nepad

JAKKIE CILLIERS

AFRICA
FIRST!

Igniting a growth revolution

Jonathan Ball Publishers
Johannesburg & Cape Town

Published in South Africa in 2020 by
JONATHAN BALL PUBLISHERS
A division of Media24 (Pty) Ltd
PO Box 33977
Jeppestown
2043

ISBN 978-1-77619-030-0
ebook ISBN 978-1-77619-031-7

Every effort has been made to trace the copyright holders and to obtain
their permission for the use of copyright material. The publishers apologise
for any errors or omissions and would be grateful to be notified of any
corrections that should be incorporated in future editions of this book.

The original research on which this book is based was funded by:

www.jonathanball.co.za
Twitter: www.twitter.com/JonathanBallPub
Facebook: www.facebook.com/JonathanBallPublishers

www.jakkiecilliers.org

Cover design by Simon Richardson
Design and typesetting by Nazli Jacobs
Set in Plantin

To Ulrika

Contents

List of abbreviations and acronyms

ACLED	Armed Conflict Location and Event Data Project
ACP	African, Caribbean and Pacific countries
AfCFTA	African Continental Free Trade Area
AGOA	African Growth and Opportunity Act
AGRA	Alliance for a Green Revolution in Africa
ANC	African National Congress
APSA	African Peace and Security Architecture
Asean	Association of Southeast Asian Nations
AU	African Union
AUDA-Nepad	African Union Development Agency-Nepad
CAR	Central African Republic
Comesa	Common Market for Eastern and Southern Africa
DRC	Democratic Republic of Congo
EAC	East African Community
Ecowas	Economic Community of West African States
EPA	Economic Partnership Agreement
EU	European Union
FAO	Food and Agriculture Organization
FDI	foreign direct investment
GATT	General Agreement on Trade and Tariffs
GDP	gross domestic product
GSP	Generalized System of Preferences
HDI	Human Development Index
ICT	information and communications technology
IFs	International Futures

ILO	International Labour Organization
IMF	International Monetary Fund
IPCC	Intergovernmental Panel on Climate Change
ISS	Institute for Security Studies
MER	market exchange rate
MPI	Multidimensional Poverty Index
Nepad	New Partnership for Africa's Development
OAU	Organization of African Unity
OECD	Organisation for Economic Co-operation and Development
OPEC	Organization of Petroleum Exporting Countries
PPP	purchasing power parity
SACU	Southern African Customs Union
SADC	Southern African Development Community
SDGs	Sustainable Development Goals
SEZ	special economic zone
UCDP	Uppsala Conflict Data Program
UN	United Nations
Unctad	United Nations Conference on Trade and Development
Undesa	United Nations Department of Economic and Social Affairs
UNDP	United Nations Development Programme
Uneca	United Nations Economic Commission for Africa
Unicef	United Nations Children's Fund
UNPD	United Nations Population Division
USAID	US Agency for International Development
WaSH	water, sanitation and hygiene
WHO	World Health Organization
WTO	World Trade Organization
Zanu-PF	Zimbabwe African National Union – Patriotic Front

Author's note

I have been studying Africa for most of my adult life. In 1990 I founded the Institute for Security Studies (ISS) in Pretoria, which played an important role behind the scenes in facilitating discussions and conceptualising the future of a post-apartheid military. When Nelson Mandela was elected as president of a democratic South Africa in 1994, I was spending much of my time in Addis Ababa, working with and for the Organization of African Unity, today the African Union.

Today the ISS is the largest independent institute that deals with broad human security matters on the African continent. We have offices in each of the five continental regions and employ staff from more than twenty African countries. I am fortunate to have worked with the most amazing colleagues at the institute.

In 2015 I stepped down as head of the ISS and accepted a Fulbright scholarship to spend a few months in the US, most of which I spent at the Frederick S Pardee Center for International Futures at the University of Denver, working with Barry Hughes, Jonathan Moyer and others, using their International Futures (IFs) forecasting platform. I use IFs extensively in this book. Additional information on IFs is provided at www.jakkiecilliers.org, including details on the interventions used for the forecasts presented in the various chapters.

Upon my full-time return to the institute, I assumed the role of chair of the ISS Board of Trustees, and I serve as full-time head of the African Futures and Innovation programme in the Pretoria office.

Africa First! draws upon more than a decade of work on the future of Africa at the ISS.

1

The growing gap between Africa and the rest of the world

Optimism should not be mistaken for romanticism; rather it is tempered by realism even as we strive continuously for improvements in the human condition.

– Kofi Annan[1]

Addis Ababa is my favourite city in Africa, probably because of my admiration for the headstrong Ethiopians. I first started travelling there in 1993 to work with the Organization of African Unity (OAU), now the African Union (AU). Over weekends, I used to jog the five kilometres from my hotel, a crumbling Hilton, to the OAU compound as part of a longer training run.

Addis then was a slow, rural town where you had to watch carefully what you ate lest you end up with severe diarrhoea, as happened regularly to many visitors. The public abattoir, nor far from the OAU compound, released a stench that hung over the city. Hyenas were reportedly sighted within the city limits. There were no traffic lights and it cost around 10 or 15 birr (today about US$0.35) for a taxi ride to the OAU in one of the blue Russian-made Lada taxis – all of which had seen better days and were themselves a couple of decades old.

I have been back to Addis probably at least 50 times over the last two and a half decades and have witnessed a transformation that is literally impossible to convey. Today, Addis is almost a modern city, and definitely the most rapidly developing city in Africa. There is so much construction, and the skyline changes from year to year. Instead of only the Hilton and Sheraton, two ridiculously overpriced hotels in the midst of extreme poverty, Addis now has dozens of top-quality and mid-level hotels. It is a thoroughly busy, frantically growing city, and jogging within the city has become a definite no-no. Poverty, beggars, grime and dirt abound, but Addis Ababa is undergoing a massive transformation. Even the herds of goats that used to be a regular feature are seldom seen.

As head of the Institute for Security Studies (ISS), I paid regular visits to many countries across the continent over three decades, travelling from our head office in Pretoria. I can confirm the good-news story of a vibrant and dynamically developing continent, particularly in its cities. Gleaming new airports, bustling streets, traffic jams and youthful vigour and life can be found from Addis Ababa and Lusaka to Nairobi and Lagos. It is a far cry from the stereotype generally conveyed in most Western media.

Africa is undoubtedly experiencing a broad-based improvement in human well-being, which is reflected in a number of health indicators such as rates of infant mortality and life expectancy. In this regard, Africa is catching up with global averages.

However, looking at the bigger picture, one can argue that this is largely because rapid improvements are easier to achieve at lower levels of development, while continued improvements in rich countries are more difficult at their much higher levels. On most other indicators of well-being, the gap between Africa and the rest of the world is actually *increasing*. In the words of my colleague Julia Bello-Schünemann, 'things are getting better, but not everywhere and not for everybody'.[2]

If Africa could have talked itself into development, it would be doing quite well. But only rarely do the many plans and visions translate into reality. These plans and visions include the 1980 Lagos Plan of Action for the Economic Development of Africa, the New Partnership for Africa's Development (Nepad) and recently Agenda 2063, the long-term development vision of the AU.

This book has its origin in the growing gap in average gross domestic product (GDP) per capita between Africa and the rest of the world. GDP per capita is a key indicator of progress since it reflects economic productivity and the relative standard of living. It is a relatively crude measure, as it does not take quality of life into account nor the distribution of economic output among the population. It is calculated by simply dividing the total output of a country in a year by the total population. Because of this simplicity, GDP remains the most popular measure of national economic productivity that allows easy comparisons between different countries.

In 1960, GDP per capita in Africa was about half the global average, and this gap remained relatively constant until the late 1970s. By 1993, however, GDP per capita in Africa had plummeted to less than one-third of the global average. In fact, it actually declined in the 1980s in absolute terms, falling from about US$4 200 per person in 1980 to US$3 500 in 1995.

Thereafter, GDP per capita in Africa steadily improved, but the gap between Africa and the rest of the world is likely to widen to 2040. By 2040, GDP per capita in Africa is projected to be less than one quarter of the average for the rest of the world (in purchasing power parity, or PPP).

Figure 1.1 presents this information in a graph that compares the average GDP per capita in Africa with that in the rest of the world from 1960 to 2040. Up to 2017 the underlying data is from the World Bank and thereafter it is a forecast. Like the jaws of a yawning crocodile, it paints a picture of increasing divergence. I use this graph at the start of most of my presentations on African futures to illustrate the progress made and the challenges that lie ahead.

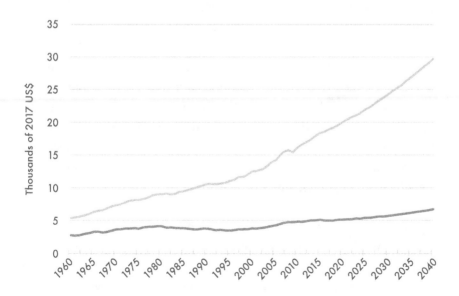

Figure 1.1: GDP per capita in purchasing power parity[3]

The increasing divergence between the trend in GDP per capita in Africa versus the average for the rest of the world correlates with many other indices of human development or well-being, such as average levels of education and various measures of health.[4]

This brings me to the central question of this book: why does Africa continue to slip further and further behind global averages of well-being, and what can be done about it?

My goal is to present a cohesive story about human and economic development in Africa revolving around three essential questions: 1) Where does Africa find itself today in relation to the situation elsewhere in the world, and what explains this state of affairs?; 2) Given historical trends and what we know about the world, where do we think Africa will be in 2040? Is this future really inevitable? 3) What can be done to improve this trajectory and create a better tomorrow?

Clearly something drastic is needed. Doing more of the same is not going to lead to tangible progress. The momentum from a burgeoning population, the continuing growth of China, India and others, the swift pace of technological change and other developments offer truly amazing opportunities for Africa in areas such as electricity generation and access, expansion of mobile broadband networks and better access to financial services. However, if left untapped, Africa could be left further behind as development accelerates elsewhere.

In essence, this book describes and then models a series of fundamental transitions in demographics, agriculture, education, health, manufacturing and governance that are needed in Africa and how to create the capacity or ability to bring these transitions about. At the same time, we must take into consideration the potentially constraining impact that armed violence and climate change could have against the backdrop of a rapidly changing world order.

Governments need to intervene in many areas. They are supposed to improve education, spend on health, build infrastructure, and provide security. But, because resources are limited, the most important policy question is, what to prioritise? What gives the best return on investment?

These choices imply that some degree of trade-off is inevitable – some short-term pain will accompany long-term gain. This is an issue to which I return in the concluding chapter of this book.

Extreme poverty and Africa's marginal role in the global economy

Extreme poverty is declining globally, except in Africa. In fact, the continent is set to miss the headline goal of the UN 2030 Agenda for Sustainable Development – the elimination of extreme poverty – by a large margin.

Although the percentage of extremely poor Africans is set to slowly decline, the actual number is likely to *increase* for almost the next two decades. I explain why in a separate section below, but the main argument is set out in Chapter 7, which also deals with inequality.

The challenge of the growing divergence between Africa and the rest of the world is also reflected in Africa's marginal role in the global economy. In 1960, Africa accounted for three per cent of the global economy. Sixty years later that share has increased to four per cent despite the fact that Africa's share of the global population almost doubled from 9 to 17 per cent. Compare this to East Asia and the Pacific, a region that increased its share of global economic output from about 11 per cent in 1960 to more than 30 per cent today. East Asia's share of the global population, on the other hand, has shrunk from 34 to 30 per cent during this period, pointing to its much more productive economies.

In the future, Africa needs to seize the opportunity offered by renewable energy and the promise of the fourth industrial revolution to rapidly improve productivity growth and to provide many more jobs. But how can that be achieved in a global economic environment where Africa is becoming more, not less, dependent on the export of commodities? And where growth of the manufacturing sector is constrained by the fact that South East Asia has become the world's factory?

Currently, the services sector (banking, recreation, tourism, transport, food) constitutes the largest economic sector by value and is significantly larger than any other sector in Africa, including agriculture and manu-facturing. Whereas agriculture is generally considered the mainstay of Africa's economy, yields per hectare are the lowest globally and improv-ing very slowly. The result is that Africa is becoming more, not less, dependent on food imports.

Furthermore, the impact of climate change is such that it will very negatively affect the Sahel and West Africa, with more variable impacts elsewhere. With very low levels of basic infrastructure, such as safe water and sanitation, Africa's peoples are more vulnerable to the impact of climate change than people living in other world regions.

Africa also has a smaller manufacturing sector than other regions. In fact, Africa's manufacturing sector is declining instead of increasing as a portion of the total economy. This also explains why it has not been a driver of productivity, jobs and innovation as elsewhere. Generally the contribution of manufacturing to African economies peaked around 1988 at below 15 per cent of GDP, and has subsequently declined, giving credence to the view that what Africa is experiencing is so-called premature deindustrialisation, although there are signs of some recent improvements.

The importance of labour and demographics

Economies grow as a result of increases in the contributions of labour, capital and multifactor productivity to the economy. The last-mentioned is generally calculated as the residual or the remaining improvement in the expansion of the economy after accounting for labour and capital, and is sometimes also termed the 'contribution from technology', or total factor productivity.

At low levels of development, the contribution of labour to economic growth is most important. It is often calculated in terms of a demographic dividend. Once countries achieve middle-income status, the contribution of capital gains importance. In high-income economies, technology generally drives improvements in productivity, although the exact contribution and calculation of each of these three components is complicated, country-specific and contested.

Many studies have tried to explain why Africa has remained so much poorer than other regions over successive centuries. The continent is richly endowed with commodities, including large areas of land for agriculture, and is, after all, the birthplace of our species. But it is exactly for this reason – humanity's origins in Africa – that development here progressed at a slower pace than elsewhere. Humans started to multiply only once they managed to escape the high disease burden on the African continent.

Africa's consistently low population densities over thousands of years did not require the cultivation of plants or systematic farming, which lie at the foundation of human development. Consequently, Africa did not until very recently experience the demographic transition that is the result of the competition for resources that drove development elsewhere. Demographics remains at the core of Africa's underperformance and is among the most underappreciated factors in the continent's development prospects.

In the 1950s and 1960s, few analysts predicted the rise of Japan, the Asian Tigers – South Korea, Hong Kong, Taiwan and Singapore – or China. These countries were all very poor at the time. Back then, the next high-growth countries were generally considered to be Brazil and Argentina. Few pundits looked to Asia, and when they did they tended to favour the prospects of Indonesia or the Philippines, both rich in natural resources.

In retrospect, it is clear that the key factor in the development of the Asian Tigers, Japan and China was the rapid increase in the size of the labour force in relation to dependants, although other factors certainly also played a role. The result was that rates of economic growth accelerated.[5] Today, these countries all face the opposite problem of a slowdown in growth, since a shrinking workforce (as a portion of the total population) has to look after a growing ageing population.

It was only around 1987 that the dependency ratio – the ratio of working-age persons to dependants – in Africa started to improve, albeit very slowly. If this idea seems complicated, it is basically about fertility rates. Africa has so many children relative to adults that it is very difficult to provide resources such as schools and basic medical care quickly enough in an environment in which modern medicine ensures that far more children survive than previously. Only once fertility rates drop below 2.8 children per woman does the ratio of working-age persons to dependants stabilise and increase. As these ratios change, growth generally accelerates because of the additional contribution that more working-age persons make to economic growth.

Being the least developed region in the world, Africa shows enormous potential for rapid improvements in labour productivity through the use of modern technology and practices. Some degree of catching-up or even leapfrogging is possible, but to date, labour productivity in Africa has improved much more slowly than elsewhere, largely because average education levels and the quality of the education provided are lower.

Productivity and digitisation

In the aftermath of the 2007/08 financial crisis, labour productivity growth actually slowed in many economies, dropping to an average of 0.5 per cent in 2010–2014 from 2.4 per cent a decade earlier in the US and major European economies. By 2016 the output per hour of work had actually been declining for more than a decade, according to well-known author and investment fund manager Ruchir Sharma.[6]

In theory, the potential for improvements in productivity as part of digitisation and automation is large. With a shrinking labour force as a portion of the total population in most middle- and high-income countries, artificial intelligence and automation first need to offset the reduction in productivity from a smaller labour force as a portion of total population before these countries experience general improvements in productivity.

A second reason for low productivity is the ongoing shift in the structure of the global economy towards services at the expense of manufacturing. Unlike the manufacturing sector, the services sector is only now starting to experience the full disruptive effect of technology. Since the services sector is more labour-intensive, the shift to services is reducing overall productivity. This will change rapidly over time, however.

Artificial intelligence and automation have the potential to reverse the recent declines in global productivity. According to the McKinsey Global Institute, productivity growth could potentially reach two per cent annually over the next decade, with 60 per cent of this increase due to digital opportunities.[7] New 'digital ecosystems' are emerging that combine goods and services in a highly customer-centric manner, shifting the boundary between these sectors.[8] But so far the digital/fourth industrial revolution has not yet improved productivity to the extent anticipated. It is unclear when this will happen and how exactly it will play out in Africa.[9]

The poor performance of two key sectors – agriculture and manufacturing – help to explain the slow growth on the continent.

Agriculture and manufacturing

While average yields per hectare in Africa have steadily improved over time, such improvements trail behind the swift progress elsewhere.

Today, the vast majority of African countries are net food importers, despite the continent having millions of hectares of arable land, with huge untapped agricultural potential. Yet Africa's food trade deficit bill is US$84 billion, and is expected to quadruple to US$350 billion by 2030.[10] Exports are dwarfed by the value of imports. Africa also loses significantly more to postproduction loss and waste than any other region. In fact, Africa loses about 25 per cent of its agricultural production in moving foodstuffs from the farm to the consumer, compared to 15 per cent in the rest of the world.

Clearly, better utilisation of farming is possible, even as agriculture inevitably declines as a share of the national economy as African economies mature. Take South Africa, for example. Although primary agriculture contributes only about 2.5 per cent to GDP, South Africa is one of the few African countries that provide food security, meaning that food imports are dwarfed by exports, with sufficient calories available per person. Considering the total contribution of South Africa's agricultural sector within the value chain, including agro-processing and trade, farming actually accounts for a substantive 14 per cent of GDP.[11]

Looking to the future, the impact of climate change on agricultural yields in Africa is a big uncertainty. Recently, while conducting a long-term forecast on the future of five of the Sahel countries – Mali, Niger, Burkina Faso, Chad and Mauritania – my colleagues and I were struck by the impact climate change has already had and will continue to have in this region. The Intergovernmental Panel on Climate Change (IPCC) notes soberly that the Sahel, where agriculture accounts for more than 75 per cent of total employment, has 'experienced the most substantial and sustained decline in rainfall recorded anywhere in the world within the period of instrumental measurements'.[12]

The impact of climate change will, of course, vary across Africa in terms of changes in temperature and rainfall and the increased variability of weather, with many more extreme events such as floods, tornados and droughts. There is significant potential for technology to increase agricultural production – not through the traditional route of expanding land under cultivation, but rather through the use of more precise farming, including vertical farming. Eventually solar-powered cold storage, accurate weather forecasting, monitoring of soil conditions and access to market information can all play an important role, as could greater efficiencies to reduce food waste. Eventually, farming in Africa may even come to replicate the situation in the Netherlands, which, despite its small land area, has emerged as the second most important agricultural exporter globally behind the United States. However, this will require current practices to change.

A second explanation for the generally slow economic growth of the continent is the fact that the contribution of Africa's already small manufacturing sector is also declining. In fact, Africa is deindustrialising and becoming even more dependent on low-value commodity exports for its foreign exchange earnings. It is the only region globally where the number of commodity-dependent countries (in terms of value of export earnings) increases year on year.[13]

A vibrant manufacturing sector plays a unique role in boosting productivity throughout the economy, thanks to forward and backward linkages that fuel the development of other sectors, such as agriculture and services. 'Manufacturing contributes disproportionately to exports, innovation and growth,' write James Manyika and other authors in a comprehensive 2012 report for the McKinsey Global Institute.[14]

However, Africa appears to be embarking on a low-productivity services and commodity escalator. Africa's services escalator does go upward, but only slowly, while the manufacturing window is closing. In addition, it has become much harder to establish export manufacturers as the entire sector is shrinking worldwide and competition is fierce.

Africa's structural transformation from low-productivity, often subsistence agriculture to low-productivity, urban-based retail services in the informal sector has therefore been growth-reducing rather than productivity-improving. This is largely because the share of workers employed in high-productivity sectors such as manufacturing is declining, resulting in a drop of the average growth output per worker.[15]

Thinking long-term: Forecasting Africa's future

We therefore find ourselves in a situation in which Africa is progressing more slowly than other developing regions such as South America and South Asia. The future is always clouded by uncertainty. However, based on our understanding of where Africa is today and the correlation between variables across different development systems, we have a good sense of where Africa is currently heading.

For long-term forecasting, I use a general time horizon to 2040, which is well beyond the time horizon of the 2030 Agenda for Sustainable Development but significantly shorter than the African Union's long-term development vision, termed Agenda 2063. While I will consistently benchmark progress to 2040, in certain areas, such as climate change, demographics and projected waves of democracy and/or autocracy, the presentation of trends extends over longer time horizons, in some instances to the end of the century.

On current trends it would be safe to refer, by mid-century, to a global economic system that is likely to consist of four centres of power, namely, China, the United States of America, the European Union (EU) and a rising India, that collectively would account for roughly 60 per cent of global GDP. By 2040 the Chinese economy should be about 40 per cent larger than the US economy, which will, in turn, be a bit larger than the EU group of 27 countries (ie, without the United Kingdom). India would then still be about ten years away from having an economy that is comparable in size to that of the USA although it would have doubled its slice of the global economy to around seven per cent of the global total and would be growing quickly.

But it is unlikely that the world of 2040 will perpetuate our current obsession with national economies. The future is likely to see greater regionalisation, particularly in Asia, which may increasingly look inward for growth and development rather than to the rest of the world. Intra-Asian trade surpassed Asian trade with the rest of the world in 2004 and partly protected the region from the impact of the global financial crisis that followed a few years later. And Asia, in particular, is likely to be much more dynamic than Europe or North America. In this future an economically interdependent and integrated Asia will become the most important region globally.[16]

On the Current Path forecast, Africa is likely to remain a peripheral player in this world, although its share of the world's population will increase quickly. By 2040 Africa's population will have crossed the two billion mark and be significantly larger than the population of India or

China. In fact, Nigeria alone would have a population of 330 million by 2040, making it the fourth most populous country globally after India, China and the US. But, because of poor growth prospects, Nigeria will account for less than one per cent of the global economy and is unlikely to emerge even as a global middle power.

Although Africa's population is set to increase from its current 17 per cent of the global population to 23 per cent by 2040, the continent will then represent only four per cent of the global economy. And Asia, knitted together by China's Belt and Road Initiative (an infrastructure superhighway), will have more than double the population of Africa and its economy will be around 12 times larger.

Some prospects, such as demographics, are easier to forecast than others, such as the potential impact of technology or how changes in governance may evolve. The same holds for the forecasts and scenarios as set out in these pages.

Long-term trends are affected by deep drivers such as demographics that are slow-moving but powerful. Others would be education or commodity supercycles, which also unfold over decades. These deep drivers are increasingly well understood in forecasting literature, even though the exact contribution and sometimes the direction of causality remain a subject of debate. When all is said and done, it is much more useful to spend time and effort on systematically exploring plausible futures than on relying on speculation or gut feeling.

Dealing with Africa's diversity: Using country income groups

A book of this nature can hardly do justice to the rich diversity of Africa, its 55 countries (including the Saharawi Arab Democratic Republic, or Western Sahara, which is occupied by Morocco), thousands of languages and many different cultures.

For the most part I use the most recent World Bank groupings of low-income, lower-middle-income and upper-middle-income groups to explore trends.[17] Of 31 low-income countries around the world, 24 are in Africa. African countries account for 21 of the 47 lower-middle-income countries globally and only eight (out of 60) upper-middle-income countries, namely, Algeria, Botswana, Equatorial Guinea, Gabon, Libya,

Mauritius, Namibia and South Africa. Of 80 high-income countries, only one is in Africa, the island state of Seychelles.

These classifications are particularly useful to compare the structure of economies, levels of income, education and access to infrastructure between countries at roughly the same levels of economic development. Where appropriate, I benchmark Africa to the rest of the world within these categories.

Occasionally, I look at regional economic communities such as the East African Community (EAC), the Southern African Development Community (SADC) or the Economic Community of West African States (Ecowas). Since many of these communities have overlapping membership, I define Africa's five geographic regions as follows:

- North Africa: Algeria, Egypt, Libya, Mauritania, Morocco and Tunisia.
- West Africa: Benin, Burkina Faso, Cape Verde, Côte d'Ivoire, The Gambia, Ghana, Guinea, Guinea-Bissau, Liberia, Mali, Niger, Nigeria, Senegal, Sierra Leone and Togo.
- East Africa/Horn: Burundi, Comoros, Djibouti, Eritrea, Ethiopia, Kenya, Madagascar, Mauritius, Rwanda, Seychelles, Somalia, Sudan, South Sudan, Tanzania and Uganda.
- Central Africa: Cameroon, Central African Republic (CAR), Chad, Democratic Republic of Congo (DRC), Republic of Congo, Equatorial Guinea, Gabon, and São Tomé and Príncipe.
- Southern Africa: Angola, Botswana, Lesotho, Malawi, Mozambique, Namibia, South Africa, eSwatini (Swaziland), Zambia and Zimbabwe.

These categories are exclusive in that no country belongs to more than one geographical region.

In the interests of standardisation, all US dollar figures in this book from Iternational Futures (IFs) have been converted to 2017 prices.[18] Unless indicated otherwise, figures and data are either data or estimates taken from IFs for 2018.[19]

Finally, I sometimes compare Africa with two other developing regions, namely, South America and South Asia,[20] which align most closely on a host of development indicators.

Previous studies and the International Futures forecasting platform

The chapters that follow draw on a decade of work on Africa's prospects at the African Futures and Innovation (AFI) programme at the Pretoria office of the ISS.

The forecasts in this book use the International Futures (IFs) modelling platform developed and housed at the Frederick S Pardee Center for International Futures at the Josef Korbel School of International Studies, University of Denver. Additional data on IFs can be found at www.pardee.du.edu or at www.jakkiecilliers.org.

Each of the following chapters compares the IFs Current Path forecast with a set of interventions grouped as a coherent scenario. The Current Path is an integrated forecast (or scenario) of how we think the world will develop. In other disciplines it is also known as the Base Case or Business as Usual forecast. It does not assume any major paradigm shifts, seismic policy changes or transformative events. Rather, the Current Path represents a reliable expectation of how major development systems are likely to unfold, and is a useful starting point from which to design alternative future scenarios.

The details of the modelling and the specific levers pulled within IFs can be found at www.jakkiecilliers.org., which also details the benchmarking of each intervention, as well as the adjustments that have been made in the IFs Current Path forecast for the purposes of this book.

I should admit from the start that the forecasts presented in this book are sure to be wrong in many respects. Beyond our limited ability to understand the evolution of human, environmental and other systems, data from many African countries is poor or even absent. Fortunately, the quality of international data-gathering is improving as the efforts to improve statistical service agencies bear fruit. Governments also recalculate more regularly the overall price structure of their economies. To that end, the AU and various partners have embarked on a *Strategy for the Harmonization of Statistics in Africa (SHaSA)*, now in its second strategic period with a time horizon from 2017 to 2026.[21]

In 2014 alone, Kenya, Nigeria, Tanzania,[22] Uganda and Zambia all completed economic rebasing exercises, which led to significant revaluations of their respective GDPs. Nigeria's (2013) GDP nearly doubled from US$270 billion to US$510 billion and the country overtook South

Africa as the largest economy in Africa when measured in market exchange rates. The increase of about 90 per cent in the size of the Nigerian economy was attributed to the inclusion of new sectors of the economy, such as telecommunications, the burgeoning local film industry (known as Nollywood) and the retail and informal sectors.

The calculations also revised the size of Kenya and Zambia upward by a quarter, and the World Bank recategorised Kenya from a low-income to a lower-middle-income country. Ghana found that its economy increased by 60 per cent when the previous rebase was announced in 2010 – and by another 25 per cent when the latest rebase was announced in 2018. When Zimbabwe rebased its economy in 2018 it also concluded with a 40 per cent increase, much of which was now sadly part of the informal rather than the formal sector. Country classifications also go the other way. In contrast to Kenya, Zimbabwe was downgraded from lower-middle-income to low-income in 1991, but was again reclassified as lower-middle in mid-2019.[23]

The IFs system has the additional advantage of a comprehensive pre-processor – a sophisticated series of algorithms that estimates and fills any data gaps that may exist. In this manner, the model is able to provide a solid foundation for each of the 500 or so variables that are forecast for each country.

In all instances where data is provided without a reference in the form of a footnote, the reader should assume that it comes from IFs.

Chapter 2 presents the Current Path forecast for Africa to 2040 and serves as a broad overview for the 11 scenarios, each in a separate chapter, on demographics, health and basic infrastructure, education, agriculture, inequality and poverty, manufacturing, leapfrogging, trade, security, governance and external support. Chapters 9 and 15 do not have separate scenarios, but compare the impact of key scenarios on the future of jobs and the impact of climate change. Chapter 16 includes the impact of a combined scenario (Africa First!). It shows what could be possible by 2040 and compares those outcomes with the Current Path trajectory.

The book adopts a structured approach to Africa and the analysis builds from one chapter to the next, although some chapters can be read in a different sequence. But what Africa needs is the combined impact of all of the interventions across the different sectors, and hence there is no shortcut to a better future – nor is there to this book: you have to read it all.

2

The continent's current pa

It's no use going back to yesterday, because I
different person then.
      – Alice, in *Alice's Adventures in Wonderland* by Lewis Carroll

Between 1980 and 1990 Africa lost considerable ground; in development terms it was actually moving backwards. Incomes decreased by about 12 per cent and declined by a further two per cent in the early 1990s.

Then, from 1994 until 2008 (when the global financial crisis hit), Africa experienced its most sustained period of growth since independence in the 1960s – an average of 4.6 per cent per annum. During this period the average per capita income increased by 35 per cent.[1] However, the share of Africans living in extreme poverty decreased by only about five percentage points, in part due to the high levels of inequality on the continent and rapid population growth.

By 2010 the United Nations Development Programme (UNDP) could report that 'the past 20 years have seen substantial progress in many aspects of human development. Most people today are healthier, live longer, are more educated and have more access to goods and services.'[2] Almost all countries in the world have benefited from this progress, except three African countries, namely, the DRC, Zambia and Zimbabwe, which have a lower Human Development Index (HDI) score today than in 1970.[3] This positive story, the UNDP report notes, 'paints a far more optimistic picture than a perspective limited to trends in income, where divergence has continued'.[4]

Today Africa's economic trajectory remains positive, but it has been muted by three recent shocks. The first is that North African countries and the Sahel region have been caught up in the turmoil that followed the Arab Spring (2010–2012). The second is that oil exporters have been affected by the sharp decline in oil prices that has accompanied the shale gas revolution in the US. The third is the continuous impact of the global financial crisis of 2007/08. Although Africa's low levels of integration into the global economy provided a degree of protection from the effects of the crisis, in its aftermath global and African growth was significantly slower. For example, Africa's average growth from 2010 to 2017 was only 3.2 per cent.

This chapter discusses the key events and trends that currently shape Africa's development trajectory. It concludes with the summary characteristics of Africa's likely future – the Current Path forecast to 2040 that includes economic size, demographics and income and poverty levels. It provides an essential backdrop to the struggle for development that is examined across different sectors in the chapters that follow.

From Brundtland to the Sustainable Development Goals (SDGs)

In 1983, concern about growing poverty in low-income countries and the extent to which the world had embarked on an unsustainable growth path saw United Nations (UN) Secretary-General Javier Pérez de Cuéllar appoint the World Commission on Environment and Development. It came at a time of deep pessimism about the environment and about Africa's development prospects in particular.

The purpose of the commission, named after its chairperson, former Norwegian prime minister Gro Harlem Brundtland, was to chart and agree on a common sustainable development pathway. The report of the Brundtland Commission was released in October 1987 under the title *Our Common Future*. It popularised the notion of 'sustainable development' by establishing a clear relationship between economic growth, the environment and social equality. The commission presented its results just as the Cold War came to an end with the collapse of the Berlin Wall in 1989.

The Brundtland Report called for an international meeting to map out goals and programmes to pursue sustainable development. It led to the Earth Summit, held five years later in Rio de Janeiro. As an aside, the impact of the Brundtland Report and the Earth Summit continues to resonate more than three decades later, first with the eight Millennium Development Goals that were adopted at the United Nations Millennium Summit in 2000 and more recently with the SDGs 2030, adopted by the UN General Assembly in 2015. To that end, the Brundtland Report served as an important impetus to the developmental vision of the 21st century.

An important tool to assist in achieving this vision of sustainable development was international cooperation and solidarity, including the provision of overseas development assistance, which will be examined in greater detail in Chapter 14. However, instead of increasing in constant dollar terms, aid levels declined steadily from their peak in 1990 to the UN Millennium Summit in New York a decade later. Kenya, Somalia, Sudan and the former Zaïre (now the Democratic Republic of Congo) experienced some of the largest declines.

One of the reasons for this was that a prolonged recession began in 1991 in Japan, a major aid provider. A second reason was the resource pull exerted by transition economies in South Asia that steadily diverted attention away from Africa. But the most important reason was that the dissolution of the Soviet Union freed Western countries from the need to prop up African dictators who had supported the West during the Cold War. With the end of the Cold War, Africa lost much of its previous geostrategic relevance and hence the external motivation for aid.

Aid only started to regain momentum with the Millennium Summit. It was substantially bolstered by the support of international celebrities such as Bono and Bob Geldof who campaigned for greater awareness about poverty and the Aids crisis and also helped to raise funds for relief programmes in Africa.

The post-2000 momentum was marked by various initiatives, such as the Report of the Commission for Africa, spearheaded by UK prime minister Tony Blair, and the European Consensus on Development. The 2005 World Summit in New York also called for increased aid transfers in order to reach the Millennium Development Goals of halving poverty and hunger by 2015.

The impact of the structural adjustment programmes

The Brundtland Report, and the broader context within which the debates around poverty occurred, also had a wider impact. Among other effects, it led to deep introspection by the World Bank and the International

Monetary Fund (IMF) – the two global financial institutions mandated to respond to underdevelopment – about the effectiveness of their structural adjustment programmes.

The oil and debt crises of the late 1970s had created numerous economic problems in sub-Saharan Africa. During the 1980s the World Bank and the IMF responded by creating loan packages for many poor countries that required them to reduce spending on health and education in favour of debt repayment and the liberalisation of the economy through privatisation and other measures.

These measures were not new. The World Bank and the IMF had been attaching conditionalities to their loans since the early 1950s and their policy prescriptions inevitably closely aligned with the free-market economics dominant in the US, the country where their secretariats are located and the largest contributor to both bodies.

In return for budget and balance of payments support, the Bank and the Fund required African governments to adhere to an agreed set of policy reforms geared towards achieving macroeconomic stability. Perhaps the most significant impact of these structural adjustment programmes was the devaluation of Africa's overvalued currencies to more reasonable levels.

The conditionalities, generally known as the 'Washington consensus', put an effective end to national industrial policies that countries as diverse as Ethiopia, Ghana, Kenya, Mauritius, Mozambique, Nigeria, Senegal and Tanzania had tried to implement, albeit with very limited success. Consequently, industrialisation as a development option for Africa was replaced by trade liberalisation, deregulation, the free market and a small state.

The negative impact of these reforms on health, education, poverty and agriculture would resonate for many years and earn both institutions the enduring enmity of many Africans in what has been described as an effective 'race to the bottom'[5] and offered African leaders and activist academics a ready target.

The development framework had shifted away from the state as the main engine and instigator of growth to a reliance on markets and the private sector for resource allocation. Henceforth, the role of the state would be limited to policy-making and regulatory functions. This was based on the inability of many African states – in the view of the Bank and the Fund – to deliver public goods effectively and to limit the abuse of funds.

Whereas development elsewhere had been facilitated through an active role for the state, the corruption and mismanagement by African governments presented the continent with an impossible situation. It had to develop without the guiding hand of government.

Unable to rapidly improve productivity, and with a fast-growing and youthful population, per capita average income levels in Africa peaked in 1980 and declined to 1994 as trade shocks and economic crises took their toll. The percentage of people living in poverty in Africa followed suit and steadily increased.

From 1989 onwards, development assistance from the West – which a number of African states had become addicted to – also shifted ground. The focus shifted to the importance of democracy, good governance and fighting corruption as part of the efforts to correct some of the egregious misuses of public money and abuses of power by a number of African leaders in the years after decolonisation and facilitated by the partisan politics of the Cold War.

Africa's Western development partners subsequently invested in civil service reform and efforts to improve public financial management, and helped to set up anti-corruption watchdogs and public audit bodies. Multiparty elections, decentralisation and other methods to encourage greater citizen participation were equally popular. In the process, democracy became associated with liberal economic policies that envisioned a small state and a dominant role for the private sector in development.

The problem is that poor countries need an activist, developmental state if they are to engineer an escape from poverty.

Alleviating Africa's large debt burden then came to focus the minds of many in the international development community. Africa's debt peaked twice during these years, first at 79 per cent of GDP in 1988 and then slightly lower, at 77 per cent, in 1995. Whereas a general debt-to-GDP ratio of 60 per cent is generally seen as a responsible ceiling that should not be exceeded, the suggested long-term debt-to-GDP ratio for developing and emerging countries is sometimes set at 40 per cent.[6]

In response to the alarming levels of debt in many poor countries the IMF, the World Bank and other creditors began the Heavily Indebted Poor

Country (HIPC) Initiative in 1996, which was reviewed and compre-hensively expanded in 1999. From 2005 HIPC was complemented by the Multilateral Debt Relief Initiative, a debt relief proposal initially advanced by the G8 in June 2005.[7]

Public debt among low-income countries declined from close to 100 per cent in the early 2000s to a median debt ratio of just over 30 per cent in 2013. By 2018 30 African countries had been assisted (out of global total of 36 countries relieved of US$99 billion in debt). As the HIPC pro-gramme has matured, the international community has focused on strengthening the links between debt relief and progress in implementing poverty reduction strategies and macroeconomic and structural reform programmes.[8]

By 1999, the IMF had replaced its structural adjustment programmes with the Poverty Reduction Growth Facility and placed poverty alleviation at the heart of its efforts. The following year, the World Bank admitted that the poor were better off without structural adjustment.[9] Writing for the African Development Bank, John Page notes, 'Structural adjustment had taken place without producing structural change.'[10]

The debate about the role of the state in Africa's development trajec-tory evolved markedly during this period. The mantra of 'good gover-nance' – defined as 'the manner in which power is exercised in the management of a country's economic and social resources for develop-ment'[11] – steadily replaced the need to downsize the state. For donors such as the IMF and World Bank, the focus on good governance was a way to respond to the inefficiency, corruption and predation that had become a defining characteristic of many African governments.

Later the debate would shift again, this time to the need to attract and enable foreign direct investment (FDI) from the private sector as the best means to facilitate growth. In its most recent incarnation the focus is on the importance of domestic resource mobilisation, effectively com-pleting a circle in which the role of African governments is again being recognised as key to the continent's future.

While aid as a portion of government revenues has steadily declined, both remittances and private capital flows have increased significantly in the intervening years. By 2015 remittances (US$39.2 billion) and private capital flows (US$44.4 billion) each approximated aid flows. In current dollars, private financial flows to sub-Saharan Africa increased from less than US$2 billion in 1990 to around US$44 billion in 2015.[12]

The general trend suggests a steady decline in aid dependency in the region. For example, in 2015, 22 out of 54 African countries received more foreign direct investment than aid.[13] Since their economies are growing quite rapidly, middle-income countries are experiencing the sharpest declines in aid as a share of total inward flows, despite the fact that the portion of aid that goes to lower-middle-income countries (compared to low-income countries) has remained relatively constant.

The debate about the potential contribution of the Washington consensus to Africa's recent growth rates remains mired in controversy, but it is undeniable that the lack of policy certainty and high transaction costs have attracted little private investment to Africa outside of the resources sector.[14] And, as we look to the future along Africa's current development pathway, commodities will likely continue to drive growth, with all the attendant risks and opportunities.

Africa's growing dependence on commodities

Much of Africa's recent growth was enabled by the commodities supercycle that started in 1996, peaked in 2011 and is still in a downswing, even though the Arab Spring caused a brief spike in oil prices. Most of the demand behind the supercycle came from the higher primary export volumes that were required to feed Asia's manufacturing and construction boom.

Supercycles are not smooth, and consequently the upward and downward cycles can vary greatly. Furthermore, each commodity class also has its own pendulum, so that shifts in the price of base metals do not generally correspond with those of livestock, agricultural products or oil, which has evidenced most volatility as the Organization of Petroleum Exporting Countries (OPEC) tries to govern oil prices. For example, although commodity prices were depressed for a year after the 2007/08 financial crisis, they subsequently recovered, though only briefly.

Particularly significant is that during the most recent supercycle, the prices for oil, base metals and agricultural produce all started to increase at roughly the same time. It was therefore generally a stronger and more uniform upward and downward cycle than with previous supercycles, lifting economic growth across all regions in the world, including in Africa.

When the United Nations Conference on Trade and Development (Unctad) released its 2019 commodity report, *The State of Commodity Dependence*, it noted that an increased number of countries, 102 out of 189, were dependent on commodity exports. Nine out of ten sub-Saharan African countries are commodity-dependent.[15] Only 82 countries were considered commodity-dependent in 2009/10.[16]

While the number of commodity-dependent countries in Africa has increased markedly in the intervening years, it has generally remained static in other global regions. In addition, the extent to which African countries are dependent on commodities, when measured by the value of exports, has also increased, with most of this exported to Europe and, increasingly, China. Given Africa's increased dependence on trade in commodities, it comes as no surprise that employment levels remain low, for there is little associated effort towards value addition.

It is unclear exactly when the downturn that started after the 2011 peak will bottom out.[17] Based on the duration of previous cycles, it can take anywhere from 5 to 17 years before a general improvement in commodity prices occurs again. On average, full trough-to-trough supercycles take 32 years, but no two supercycles are the same and the length and intensity of each downswing and upswing vary considerably from cycle to cycle. That said, on the 32-year average we should reach the trough around 2027, and, helped by favourable demographics, this will lift African growth rates until the cycle's likely peak around 2043.

In recent years it was largely the demand from China that boosted commodity prices. The world will remain hungry for commodities, even though the resource intensity of growth is declining and Chinese demand for commodities is shifting from iron ore, copper and coal to consumer-related commodities such as meat, dairy and apparel. Just how rapidly China is growing (in spite of moderating rates) is difficult to grasp, but in the four years from 2014 to 2018, China added the size of the entire economy of Africa to its GDP in market exchange rates. The Chinese economy is already larger than the US economy in purchasing power parity and is expected to overtake the size of the US economy in market exchange rates before 2030.

In addition, a new supercycle (ie, from around 2027 onward) would also be driven by the expected demand for commodities from a rising India that is experiencing a steady improvement in growth rates. Although the world appears to have entered a lower growth trajectory since 2007/08[18] the larger global economy will continue to drive a steady demand for commodities. Global GDP will expand by more than 40 per cent by 2030 (from 2018) and by 2040 the world economy will have doubled in size (all figures in market exchange rates, or MER).

The challenges of commodities-dependent growth and debt

There is ample evidence that commodity dependence leads to slow and poor-quality growth over long time horizons without a very deliberate effort at using the income to diversify the economic base.[19] Commodity dependence is therefore also often closely associated with poor governance.

Supporters of the 'resource curse' hypothesis argue that a too-heavy dependence on natural resources impedes rather than accelerates economic growth and investment. It may also hinder the broadening of the economic base (and manufacturing in particular) and the development of the various institutions of government.[20]

Some of the severe risks that single-commodity exporters face are price volatility, the risk of an increase in dependence on natural resources and a decline in other sectors (the so-called Dutch disease), an increased likelihood of undemocratic government, the prevalence of a rentier state (where the state is not accountable to citizens), pressures to spend within a short-term horizon to maintain support, and a greater likelihood of low-quality institutions. The result is an 'observable correlation between resource abundance and political corruption'.[21]

To date, Botswana is the only African country that has successfully developed its resources sector (diamonds) to the general benefit of its populace, yet it too struggles to spread its commodity-led growth beyond a small, privileged elite in a country that has the third-highest level of inequality globally.

Resource-poor economies generally outperform resource-rich countries, with South Korea, Japan and Taiwan often cited as the best examples of the former and Nigeria, Angola and Equatorial Guinea as examples of the latter. South Korea has virtually no natural resources of any value. In 1962 the country exported mostly raw materials such as fish, rice, iron ore and unprocessed silk, while today it boasts a well-diversified export portfolio that includes electronics, cars, ships and other high-end machinery.

By contrast, Nigeria's main exports in 1962 were assorted agricultural products – mostly groundnuts, soybeans and cocoa beans – and crude petroleum. In 2014 crude petroleum and liquified petroleum gases accounted for about 85 per cent of Nigeria's total exports. In 1962 GDP per capita in South Korea was about half that of Nigeria; in 2018 it was about six times larger.

Africans are moving from subsistence agriculture in rural areas to informal jobs in the urban services sector. Investment and jobs are often limited to capital-intensive commodity enclaves such as in northern Mozambique's new gasfields, with little or no forward or backward linkages into the surrounding economy. And the few jobs that are created through these megaprojects do little to provide employment or create local value chains. They provide jobs for a small number of expatriates and generate large streams of revenue for governments, but generally enclave economics do not benefit national economies. Yet commodity-based enclave development is often the norm.

On average, countries with a higher value of resource-based exports tend to have lower growth rates. When a country depends on natural resource exports, it often leads to exchange rate appreciation, making manufacturing products less competitive.

Debt has also resurfaced as a serious challenge. After 2011, when commodity prices declined, commodity exporters such as Angola, Chad, the Republic of Congo, Niger, Nigeria and Zambia were particularly badly affected. Since 2014, rising debt has been driven by a number of other factors, such as internal conflict (Burundi), the impact of epidemics such as Ebola (in Liberia and Sierra Leone) and fraud/corruption (Mozambique and The Gambia). Finally, a larger liquidity crunch, delays in the start of natural resource production and weaknesses in revenue administration contributed to large increases in debt in Benin, Cameroon, Djibouti, Ethiopia, Ghana, Kenya, Senegal, São Tomé and Príncipe, Rwanda, Togo, Uganda and Zimbabwe.[22]

In its 2018 *Regional Economic Outlook* for sub-Saharan Africa, the IMF noted that public debt rose above 50 per cent of GDP in 22 countries at the end of 2016, up from ten countries in 2013. 'Debt servicing costs are becoming a burden, especially in oil-producing countries, and Angola, Gabon and Nigeria are expected to absorb more than 60 per cent of government revenues in 2017,' the IMF said.[23]

It was against this background that the announcements of additional large loans from China (most recently on the margins of the Forum on China–Africa Cooperation held in September 2018 in Beijing) elicited concern that debt levels in sub-Saharan Africa were rapidly becoming unsustainable. Chinese interest-bearing loans increased from almost nothing in 2000 to US$30 billion in 2016 alone. By 2019 the increased concerns about rising debt levels led to an announcement that Beijing would establish an analysis framework on debt sustainability for Belt and Road Initiative projects and improve transparency.[24] Looking ahead, China's focus will increasingly shift to Asia rather than Africa.

To some analysts, it appeared that Africans were having to borrow money from the IMF to repay China, but closer examination revealed that only in Zambia, Djibouti and the Republic of Congo were Chinese loans the most significant contributor to high risk of debt distress.[25]

In addition to the high level of indebtedness of many African countries and the current low commodity prices, the two countries with the biggest potential to drive regional growth and economic integration are merely muddling along on the economic front. South Africa and Nigeria are projected to be among the weakest-performing economies over the next four years. By contrast, the IMF expects Senegal, Rwanda, Niger and Uganda to average move than seven per cent growth between 2021 and 2024.

The third wave of democratisation in Africa

Contrary to the general trend elsewhere, Africa's recent cycle of commodities-led growth was accompanied by unprecedented democratisation. The world experienced various surges in democracy in the past two centuries, with the third wave of democracy cresting between 1989 and

1993 with the collapse of the former Soviet Union and its immediate aftermath.

Prior to that, there was little to distinguish independent Africa from colonial Africa in terms of the quality of governance. The events in the Soviet Union changed things, as pro-democracy movements and reforms washed across the continent.

According to *Freedom in the World*, an annual index published by Freedom House, levels of democracy in Africa increased by 12 percentage points from 1988 to 1994, with 25 out of 54 countries classified as free or partly free.[26] The West had triumphed, or so it appeared, and with the subsequent concerns for elections, human rights and accountability (rather than ideological orientation) came the closely associated belief in liberal capitalism.

However, history has shown that democracy is generally more resilient above certain minimum levels of income and education, when a solid web of institutions and the rule of law are able to constrain the misuse and abuse of state institutions.[27] In countries with low levels of income, democracy is often fragile, largely because the formal institutions, rules and norms upon which it rests and depends for effective functioning are absent or insufficiently developed.[28]

When comparing the average levels of democracy in Africa's low-income and upper-middle-income countries to those of other countries with similar levels of education and income elsewhere in the world, one finds the continent more democratic than one would expect.[29] In fact, improvements in levels of democracy have outpaced improvements in levels of income and education in Africa. Hence, democracy here rests on somewhat fragile foundations.[30]

There are many reasons why levels of democracy are somewhat out of sync with levels of income and education. The conditional engagement by Western donors over several decades created space for civil society, a free press and competitive elections that otherwise would not have emerged – or at least not as rapidly. Moreover, a series of national democratisation conferences in Francophone Africa (Benin, Gabon, Congo, Mali, Togo, Niger and the DRC) served to confront the economic and political crisis that had enveloped these countries and produced a thirst for pro-democracy reforms.[31]

But the most important reason for the relatively high levels of democracy in Africa is simply the lived experience of decades of brutal authoritarianism. Numerous opinion surveys, such as those conducted by Afrobarometer in more than 35 African countries, point to the strong and growing support for democracy on the continent.[32]

For decades the military dominated politics, and often yesterday's liberation heroes became today's autocrats. Muammar Gaddafi in Libya and Omar Bongo Ondimba of Gabon were Africa's longest-lasting modern rulers. Teodoro Obiang Nguema Mbasogo of Equatorial Guinea has been in power since 1979, a reign equalled only by that of Emperor Haile Selassie of Ethiopia. Paul Biya has presided over Cameroon since 1982 and King Mswati III of eSwatini and Yoweri Museveni of Uganda have ruled their respective countries since 1986. José Eduardo dos Santos of Angola was president for 36 years and Robert Mugabe of Zimbabwe for 35 years. When he was toppled by the military in April 2019, Sudan's Omar al-Bashir had been in power for 30 years.

Long-term incumbency often leads to looting of the state and almost inevitably culminates in a violent uprising and turbulent transition. Mobutu Sese Seko of the former Zaïre (DRC) allegedly stole at least US$4 billion while serving as president.[33] More recently, Teodoro Nguema Obiang – vice president of Equatorial Guinea and son of the current president – was accused of embezzling more than US$100 million. Human Rights Watch describes the situation in Equatorial Guinea as one in which the state foregoes investment in health and education in favour of grandiose infrastructure projects that really function as 'conduits for enriching the ruling elite'.[34] These amounts pale when compared to the US$32 billion 'discrepancy' linked to 'quasi-fiscal operations' by Angolan state oil company Sonangol that the IMF found did not appear in the 2007–2010 official accounts, although it subsequently announced that it was now able to trace much of it.[35]

The problem is that, with few exceptions, Africans don't yet benefit from substantive democracy. In many countries, Africans go through the motions of regular elections but incumbent leaders have become adept at interfering in the electoral process, as has been recently seen in countries as diverse as Zambia, Cameroon and Uganda.

Incumbents will even change the constitution to retain the presidency if that is what it takes. In January 2019, outgoing DRC president Joseph Kabila blatantly rigged the presidential and national assembly election held on 30 December 2018 to install himself as the power behind the newly elected president, Félix Tshisekedi.[36]

Leaders in these countries invest significant resources to ensure favourable electoral outcomes by constraining the democratic space. This is done by rigging the registration process, running interference (for instance, by tying opposition candidates down in spurious legal cases or barring public gatherings), misusing state resources to dispense patronage, controlling the diet of information (particularly through the abuse of public media in favour of the ruling party), and, if all else fails, directly manipulating the results or frustrating any subsequent legal challenge.

The situation is further complicated by the fact that competitive politics in a multi-ethnic context generally relies on the mobilisation of ethnolinguistic groupings for political support.

For decades, African leaders have primarily taken their cue from the West in pursuit of their governance and social model. Today, autocratic China is increasingly calling the shots. Since 2000 China has embarked on a vigorous process of courting African states with its offers to build infrastructure financed by Chinese banks as it seeks a new role for its excess capacity, sometimes as part of the Belt and Road Initiative.[37] However, while their leaders increasingly look east, Africa's citizens generally continue to look to the West.

Democratisation and economic growth are buoyed by Africa's unfolding urban transition. The question now is, what kind of urbanisation is taking place on the continent and how does it impact on the political situation?

Africa's slow pace of urbanisation

Historically, urbanisation has gone hand in hand with growth and development. A 2010 analysis by the McKinsey Global Institute found that the shift from rural to urban employment could account for 20 to 50 per cent of productivity growth in Africa.[38]

Yet, by historical standards, urbanisation is taking place very late in Africa. At the time of independence in 1960 less than one fifth of Africans could likely be classified as urban. By 1980 that number had increased to around 27 per cent and, by 2000 to 34 per cent, and it should by 2033 or thereabouts pass the halfway mark. The rest of the world passed that point shortly after the turn of the century. Africa is likely to get to the two-thirds mark around 2070, compared to 2030 for the rest of the world. The impact of climate change may, of course, accelerate this process.

East Africa, including the Horn of Africa, is the most rural part of the continent and is likely to stay that way, with levels of urbanisation around almost 30 percentage points below North Africa, the most urban region. West Africa is experiencing the most rapid rates of urbanisation. Currently, Gabon, Libya and Djibouti are the most urbanised countries, and Malawi, Rwanda, Niger and Burundi the least urbanised, with less than 20 per cent of their populations considered urban.

However, contrary to historical experience in much of the rest of the world, Africans currently don't move to urban areas in response to existing job opportunities in factories (which would increase productivity) but rather to escape the destitution and poverty of rural existence. Consequently, poverty itself is urbanising.[39] Sharp income inequalities in many African cities also mean that the contribution of economic growth to poverty reduction is limited. As a result, Africa has more urban poor than any other region.

Africa's urban population growth is the fastest globally, although from a low base. Each year urban Africa grows by an estimated 20 million people, and by 2040 that number will be more than 30 million every year.[40] Much of the growth is due to the natural population growth in urban areas. The 2016 edition of *African Economic Outlook*, the annual review of the continent's economy put out by the African Development Bank in cooperation with international development bodies, predicted that Africa could see its slum population triple by 2050 as population growth and urbanisation without industrialisation proceeds apace.[41]

The move from rural subsistence farming to urban informal employment in low-end services is positive in that it is moderately growth-enhancing. It is also much easier and less expensive to provide bulk services, such as clean water, sanitation and electricity, to people in denser settlements than to a population spread over vast rural areas. However, the nature and delay in Africa's urbanisation is a significant drag on economic transformation.

Writing for the International Growth Centre in 2016, Paul Collier succinctly summarises the challenge and the opportunity:

> At its best, urbanisation can be the essential motor of economic development, rapidly lifting societies out of mass poverty. At its worst, it results in concentrations of squalor and disaffection which ferment political fragility. To date, African urbanisation has been dysfunctional, the key indication being that cities have not generated enough productive jobs.[42]

Urbanisation has powerful socio-political implications and it has become an important consideration in explaining the rise of populism. Whereas urban populations are more cosmopolitan and often younger, rural populations are generally older and politically more conservative.[43] Consequently, there is usually a marked difference in attitude between rural and urban people. 'The young, regardless of where they live, tend to associate more with urban outlooks,'[44] Auerswald and Joon write.

Like elsewhere in the world, African urbanites also tend to be much more politically engaged than rural people. Inevitably, it is in the capital city that support first goes to opposition parties. In Zimbabwe, the ruling Zimbabwe African National Union – Patriotic Front (Zanu-PF) party has therefore run an extraordinarily violent campaign over several decades to stall and even reverse urbanisation, and to keep the country's population predominantly rural and under its firm control.

Unless leaders are able to reap the benefits of the greater economies of scale offered within an urban setting, Africa's accelerating urbanisation will come with considerable risks. It is very likely that the management of its urban areas will present African leadership with immense challenges in the future.

The Current Path scenario

In this section, I summarise some of the key characteristics of Africa to 2040 along the Current Path forecast within IFs, namely, demographics, the composition of the African economy and GDP, as well as rates of poverty, and compare these to the global development trends.

Let's start globally. Figure 2.1 presents Africa within a global context in terms of population numbers and Figure 2.2 does so in economic terms.

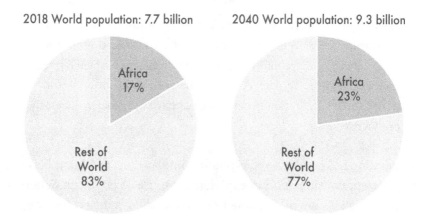

2018 World population: 7.7 billion   2040 World population: 9.3 billion

Figure 2.1: Africa and global population in 2018 and 2040[45]

The IFs Current Path forecast is that Africa's total population will increase from 1 284 million in 2018 to 2 081 million by 2040. At that point the global population will number 9 160 million people, of which 23 per cent will be African, compared to 17 per cent in 2018. In 2018 Nigeria had the seventh-largest population globally. By 2040 Nigeria will be the fourth most populous country globally. Nigeria's population consistently constitutes around 15 per cent of Africa's total population across the forecast horizon.

Compare these population numbers with an expected global economy (at market exchange rates) of US$180.9 trillion in 2040 – almost double its current US$96.7 trillion size – presented in Figure 2.2. Whereas Africa constituted 2.4 per cent of the global economy in 2000, it is currently at 3 per cent (US$2.9 trillion) and will, by 2040, account for 4 per cent (US$7.2 trillion). Nigeria, the continent's largest economy, constituted around 0.6 per cent of the global economy in 2018, and by 2040 should constitute around 0.7 per cent of the global economy.

The IFs Current Path forecast is that Africa's GDP will grow at an average of 4.3 per cent per annum from 2020 to 2040. The average growth rate for low-income Africa is 6.4 per cent, with 4.4 per cent for lower-middle-income Africa and 2.7 per cent for upper-middle-income

Africa. As we will see, these rates would at least have to *quadruple* to get anywhere close to a chance of eliminating extreme poverty by 2030.

Figure 2.2 reflects the extent to which Africa's economy remains marginal globally along the Current Path prospects. By comparison, China accounted for a mere 14 per cent of the global economy in 2018, and by 2040 will have increased its share to 23 per cent, while that of the USA will then likely be at 16 per cent.

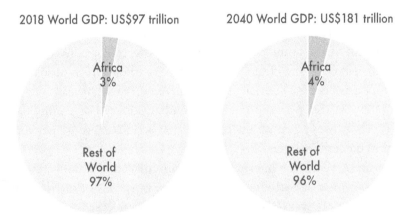

2018 World GDP: US$97 trillion   2040 World GDP: US$181 trillion

Africa 3%   Africa 4%

Rest of World 97%   Rest of World 96%

Figure 2.2: Africa and the global economy in 2018 and 2040[46]

Table 2.1 presents the size of the top six economies in Africa in 2018 and 2040, ranked in order of size. Nigeria retains the top spot. At the moment Nigeria is about the 28th-largest economy in the world, comparable in size to Argentina and Austria. By 2040 Egypt overtakes South Africa for second spot and Angola replaces Algeria as fourth-largest African economy. By 2040 Ethiopia should be the sixth-largest economy in Africa while Morocco drops from its current fifth to seventh position.

2018	2040
Nigeria (US$570 billion)	Nigeria (US$1 295 billion)
South Africa (US$509 billion)	Egypt (US$926 billion)
Egypt (US$337 billion)	South Africa (US$797 billion)
Algeria (US$132 billion)	Angola (US$487 billion)
Morocco (US$138 billon)	Algeria (US$394 billion)
Angola (US$269 billion)	Ethiopia (US$362 billion)

Table 2.1: The six largest economies in Africa, ranked by size[47]

The size of the economy of each country is indicated next to the country name.

Of all the indications of progress, levels of extreme poverty are perhaps the most meaningful in Africa. Poverty has many dimensions, ranging from health and education levels to income and how disempowered people feel. Since poverty also has a subjective side, ie how it makes people feel about important aspects of their lives, the different dimensions to poverty and how it can be measured are part of an ongoing debate.[48]

In recent years, broader measures of poverty have gained increased support, for example the Multidimensional Poverty Index (MPI), which focuses on a set of tangible goods and services without which people might be defined as poor.[49] Different regions also use different measures to more accurately reflect poverty in their member states. For example, the EU typically uses a relative poverty line that is set at 50 or 60 per cent of national median incomes.

For many years, the international community used a single, income-based definition of extreme poverty for the purposes of cross-country comparisons. It was first set at US$1.00, then US$1.25 and more recently US$1.90 per person per day. Each was successively set in purchasing power parity, the latest in 2011 constant dollars. That value was, in turn, anchored in the poverty thresholds used by some of the world's poorest countries, since national poverty lines inevitably increase as national incomes rise. Using the US$1.90 threshold, 36 per cent of Africa's total population is considered extremely poor, a ratio that will decline to 33 per cent by 2030 and 28 per cent by 2040 along the Current Path forecast in IFs.

In addition to the US$1.90 international poverty line, in October 2017, the World Bank announced that it would also be reporting poverty rates using three new international poverty lines, namely, a lower-middle-income threshold set at US$3.20 per person per day, an upper-middle-income line set at US$5.50 per person per day, and US$21.70 for high-income countries.[50]

Although West Africa and East Africa have Africa's largest regional populations of people living in extreme poverty, the use of country income categories is an important step in understanding a growing consensus that poverty is relative – it differs between rich and poor countries, and shows that it is different to be poor in the DRC as opposed to Algeria.

Previously, using the US$1.90 line, North Africa was the only region in Africa that would achieve the goal of eliminating extreme poverty as set out in the 2030 Agenda for Sustainable Development headline goal. In fact, as a group it has already done so (except for Mauritania) with the extremely poor portion of its population at below three per cent. Since the countries in North Africa have all graduated to either lower-middle-income or upper-middle-income status, extreme poverty suddenly 'increases' when the two additional poverty lines are applied. The new poverty lines mean that 18 per cent of the population in North Africa lives below US$3.20 and 48 per cent below US$5.50. By 2040 the percentage of extremely poor people in North Africa would be 10 and 33 per cent, respectively, using these two lines. The World Bank has also made it clear that for the purposes of achieving the headline goal on extreme poverty, it will continue to apply only the US$1.90 line, since shifting the goalposts in so dramatic a manner several years into the SDGs process would not make practical sense.

Using US$1.90, the IFs system estimates that in 2018 Africa was home to 463 million extremely poor people, representing 36 per cent of its total population, and that this number will increase to 587 million by 2040 (28 per cent). If I use the three separate poverty lines for the three country income groups, ie adding the number of extremely poor people in low-income Africa (using US$1.90) to lower-middle-income Africa (using US$3.20) and upper-middle-income Africa (using US$5.50), the numbers are very different. The combined number of extremely poor Africans increases to 637 million in 2018 and 813 million in 2040, or 50 and 39 per cent, respectively, of Africa's total population.

Ten years later, by 2040, Africa will have 785 million out of 2 081 million people living in extreme poverty – 38 per cent of the continent's population. These forecasts imply that if Africa were to use these targets, it would miss by a very large margin the headline target to eliminate extreme poverty by 2030. Technically, ending poverty globally may now be an even greater challenge than before.

Looking at this Current Path forecast on poverty, the impact of Africa's very rapid population growth should be clear. African economies need to grow at an exceptionally high rate to reduce poverty under these circumstances. In fact, while it is impossible for Africa to reach the 2030 target to eliminate extreme poverty when using the single US$1.90 poverty line, the goalposts are now very distant indeed.

More than any other single indicator, the Current Path forecast of the expected increase in poverty for the next three decades underpins the reason for understanding what else needs to be done to change Africa's development prospects. In the next chapter, I turn to the first requirement for change, namely, the importance of a demographic transition.

3
Getting to Africa's demographic dividend

To harness the demographic dividend, we need to put in place
bold interventions to manage fertility and population growth to
be able to accelerate demographic transition, economic growth
and job creation.

– Idriss Déby, President of Chad[1]

The African Union's annual theme for 2017 was 'Harnessing the Demographic Dividend Through Investments in Youth'. In preparation, the
AU Commission in Addis Ababa spent considerable resources to review
progress with the 2006 African Youth Charter[2] and its 2009 – 2018 Plan
of Action,[3] which included a roadmap[4] aimed at unlocking the continent's
youth potential.

The basic premise was that Africa's youthful population would ensure
fast economic growth and that, as a general notion, rapid population
growth was positive for development. If this is indeed the case, it begs the
obvious question: why does Africa, with its youthful populations, not have
the most rapidly growing economies?

When, in October 2018, I presented our research on demographics and
economic growth to staff from the AU in Addis Ababa. I argued that
the Charter, Plan of Action and roadmap skirted the need for a more
rigorous analysis of the demographic dividend, and that they basically
missed the point. In fact, Africa's very high fertility rates were actually
a serious constraint on development, and until such time as the continent
significantly lowered fertility rates, it would not be able to grow economically fast enough to reduce poverty and improve livelihoods. Although
trends were going in the right direction, much more urgent action was
required to speed up Africa's demographic transition.

It was, for some, as if I had let the air out of a very large balloon. Actually, nothing I presented was particularly new or innovative, and it had

all been reflected in mainstream demographic analysis for several decades. As I had expected, one diplomat after the other, including from a country such as Uganda, with its young population and elderly president for life, objected strongly to this attempt at stigmatising motherhood and, apparently, children, muttering darkly that I obviously did not understand the benefits of high fertility rates.

In my presentation, I first made the standard distinction between children (aged 0 to 15) and the elderly (above 64) – the two components of the dependent portion of the population. Forty-three million Africans are born every year, a number that will increase to 53 million annually by 2040. In Africa, the word 'dependants' mostly refers to children, since average life expectancy at birth on the continent is only 63 years, although it is much higher in upper-middle-income than in low-income countries.

Then I pointed to the well-known youthful structure of the African population, with a median age just shy of 20 years, meaning that half the African population is younger than 20 and half are older. The result is a population pyramid that has a very broad base and quickly narrows with each age group.

The contrast is presented in Figure 3.1 in which I compare the population pyramid for the rest of the world with that of Africa.

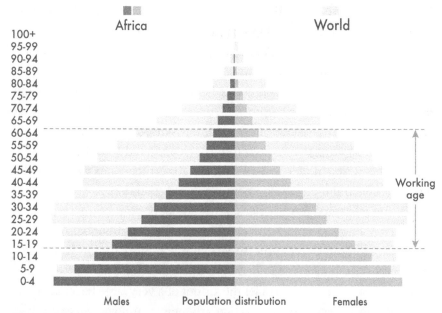

Figure 3.1: Population pyramid for Africa and the rest of the world, 2018

The large cohort of children below 15 years of age means that African countries generally require huge and ongoing investments in education, health and infrastructure that detract from other required improvements.

A large body of research done over several decades by the World Bank and others has found that it is the increase in the size of the working-age population (15 to 64) *relative* to dependants that contributes most to economic growth at low- and even middle-income levels of development. In other words, it is the ratio of working-age persons to dependants that is important, and whether that ratio is changing for the better.

According to the World Bank, in East Asia one-third of the increase in economic growth during its economic miracle can be attributed to a growing labour force. A substantial portion of the remainder was achieved by the determined pursuit of export-oriented policies that provided productive employment for the region's rapidly expanding population.[5] Others estimate that the contribution that an increase in the size of the working-age population makes to economic growth is even higher.[6]

At the moment, 56 per cent of Africa's population falls within this working-age bracket, implying that there are 1.3 persons of working age to every dependant. The ratios in the rest of the world would come to 67 per cent of the total population being of working age, or two persons of working age to every one dependant. The difference of 0.7 is extraordinarily significant given the large numbers involved.

The underlying logic is quite simple. Economic growth is determined by the contribution from labour, capital and technology. At low levels of development, labour makes the biggest contribution to economic growth, and at high levels of development it is technology. So, the larger the labour pool in developing regions such as Africa, the quicker the economy can grow.

The size of the labour force does not necessarily correspond exactly to the number of people in the age bracket 15 to 64, since many would still be getting an education, or would not have a job, but the essential relationship holds even after accounting for these differences.

What history reveals

Several centuries ago, until around the middle of the 17th century, the countries with the largest populations and the most fertile farmland boasted the largest economies. The size of the labour force and the suitability of the land for agriculture were the main engines of growth, even if they seldom made a difference to average incomes and, by modern standards, the vast majority of citizens were destitute.

The industrial revolution in the West upended this state of affairs. The technological breakthroughs of the 18th and 19th centuries transformed the economic structures of the previous centuries by shifting some elements of production from manual labour to machines. Productivity was no longer determined by the fertility of the land or the size of the workforce alone, but also by the unprecedented output of inventions such as the steam engine and the cotton gin.

Workers could produce more output than before. Productivity soared in Europe and North America, although it generally remained stagnant in the rest of the world. This was the start of the 'great divide' that saw Europe, and eventually North America, overtake China and come to dominate the world economy – a global order that has held until very recently.[7]

At some point, technology becomes the most important driver of productivity and improvements in income, overtaking the contributions of labour and capital. When this happens, technology will offset the need for increases in the number of workers to grow the size of an economy. This is already starting to occur in Japan, for example. Clearly, Africa is a long way from this point.

With industrialisation, population structures changed. People moved to cities to work in factories, and birth rates declined, eventually increasing the number of persons of working age compared to dependants. These developments also largely bypassed Africa, for a host of reasons including geography, the continent's high disease burden and the impact of slavery.

Population growth and age structure still remain critical components of economic growth. Even in the 21st century, economies generally do not grow unless their populations also grow. Today, in much of Western Europe, as well as in Japan, countries are experiencing slow economic growth as their populations age. Their population pyramids are no longer triangular but top-heavy as the elderly section of the population grows larger.[8] Once populations start to decline in size, economies also struggle to grow in size, but they can continue to experience steady improvements in income per capita, since the golden rule is that economic growth must simply be more rapid than population growth.

All in all, population structure is very important for economic growth. The relationship between economic growth and population structure is most often operationalised with reference to the demographic dividend or the dependency relationship, of which the latter is simply the inverse of the former.

The impact of the demographic dividend

There are a number of ways to define the demographic dividend, such as median age and rates of fertility. In this book, I prefer to use the ratio of the working-age population (aged 15 to 64 years) to the dependent population, ie children below 15 years of age and adults older than 64.[9]

A country's income generally rises when this ratio improves. The faster the rate of improvement, and the higher the rate achieved, the more rapid economic growth will be.[10] This is particularly true for poor developing countries.

The ratio of working-age persons to dependants in Africa started to improve slowly from the late 1980s, from only 1.1 persons of working age for every one dependant to its current ratio of 1.3. Africa will experience a peak ratio of around two persons of working age to every dependant around 2074. Thereafter the relationship starts to decline.

When the continent reaches a ratio of 1.7 persons of working age to each dependant, as from about 2054, it will enter a window of particularly rapid income growth from the contribution of labour (as opposed to capital and technology) that will last for two decades on the Current Path forecast. Once this demographic dividend has peaked, economic growth will taper off unless an economy has managed to shift gears so that capital and technology are able to compensate for the decline in the relative size of the labour pool and hence for the declining portion of working-age persons to dependants.

China and the Asian Tigers peaked at an extraordinarily high ratio of 2.8 working-age persons to every one dependant in 2010 and 2013, respectively. Africa will not be able to experience the high rates of economic growth achieved by China and the Asian Tigers, however, since the ratio of working-age population to dependants will peak at a relatively low level of two working-age persons to every one dependant.

Unsurprisingly, the ratio of working-age persons to dependants has played an important role in the improvements in prosperity in Japan, China and the Asian Tigers since the 1960s, as well as in the USA and the Nordic countries, although over longer time horizons. In the case of the USA and the Nordic countries, the ratio of working-age persons to dependants did not peak swiftly at the levels of China and the Asian Tigers and then decline, but rather increased slowly and remained in positive territory for an extended period of time. The benefit of a constantly growing pool of working-age persons played an important role in the steady rates of economic growth and improvements in productivity in the USA and the Nordic countries as these countries graduated to high-income status.

Rapid growth in the working-age population relative to the number of dependants does not automatically translate into rapid economic growth, since other facilitators such as an export orientation and a governing elite committed to growth must also be present, but it still has some interesting benefits. Smaller families mean fewer additional schools are needed and the ratio of teachers to pupils can be improved more readily. As a result, parents and the state can invest more resources in those fewer children. Eventually, governments need to provide fewer additional houses, and less bulk water and electricity, and can invest in higher technology, in research and in other measures that are necessary to maintain improvements in productivity even as the size of the working-age population starts to decline.

In summary, an increasing ratio of working-age population to dependants boosts economic growth, since more working-age persons contribute to economic activity. Of course, more than merely the right ratio is required; in addition to having as high as possible a ratio of working-age persons to dependants, the right industrial and other policies should be oriented towards, first, basic education and literacy.

In 2018 half of Niger's population was estimated to be younger than 15, and the population will reach a 16-year median age only by 2026. The country has the lowest median age in the world, and life expectancy

is 62 years.[11] Niger has less than one person of working age to its dependants, and this very low relationship means that the country cannot
grow income per person unless it grows its economy at sustained rates of
around ten per cent per year or more for successive decades. The disproportionate size of the cohort of children makes it difficult to build
enough schools, train enough teachers, and roll out an education (or
health) system able to cope with the massive influx of pupils and simultaneously improve average levels of education for those children already
within the system.

Egypt, on the other hand, with a median age of 25 years and a life
expectancy of 72 years, is on the cusp of achieving an age structure
favourable for rapid economic growth, with a ratio of 1.6 working-age
persons to every dependant – a ratio that is increasing. Given the right
policies and leadership, Egypt should be able to grow improvements in
income levels rapidly. Instead, in April 2019, a desultory number of
Egyptians voted to back a constitutional amendment that allows President Abdel Fattah el-Sisi to remain head of state until 2030. Egypt's
closed political system mirrors its statist and closed economy and means
that it could squander this once-in-a-century opportunity.

Sweden, on the other hand, is about to exit the demographic sweet
spot (median age of 41 and life expectancy of 83). It also has a ratio
of 1.6 working-age persons to dependants, but in contrast to Egypt,
Sweden's ratio is deteriorating. With its advanced technology, open economy and longevity, Sweden is, however, largely able to compensate for
its changing demographics.

Japan has the highest median age in the world, at 47 years (with a life
expectancy of 84 years). The ratio of working-age persons to dependants
is 1.5 and declining, with the result that the disproportionate size of the
elderly cohort is a large burden on the state. The fact that Japan still
manages to grow the size of its economy in spite of its declining population speaks volumes about the high productivity of that economy.

In Sweden and Japan, average incomes are still growing, although
slowly, but both countries have improved income levels very quickly in
previous years, and the slow improvements are therefore from a very high
base. In these countries, longer life expectancy means that people can
extend their working lives beyond 64, thereby expanding the size of the

working-age population. To a degree, a higher retirement age can compensate for the high median age. But, because of the prevalence of non-communicable diseases, such as cancer, in an elderly population, health expenditure is much higher and, as in many rich countries, there is considerable resistance to raising the retirement age.

A demographic dividend provides a structural foundation that can enable rapid economic growth. Since it is the size of a well-educated labour force, rather than the amount of capital or technology, that makes the largest contribution to economic growth at low levels of development, harnessing the demographic dividend is very important for Africa.

Africa's slow demographic transition

Globally, the size of the working-age population relative to dependants peaked around 2010. As a result, the world has entered a structural period of slower growth from which it can emerge only through advances in technology, including capitalising on the digital economy and the fourth industrial revolution, factors that I explore further in Chapter 10.

Africa's youthful population stands out against this global backdrop of ageing populations. Only in Africa is the size of the working-age population as a portion of the total population still increasing. This development is positive, but it is happening slowly and from a very low ratio of working-age population to dependants.

The result is that Africa is likely to experience a real demographic dividend only from the middle of this century onward. Consequently, for the next three decades Africa's dependant youth population will remain a drag on economic growth, although decreasing with every passing year.

Today, most of Africa still finds itself in the early stages of the demographic transition. In other words, the shift from high death and birth rates to low death and birth rates has started, but it is progressing gradually and much more slowly than it did historically in other regions.

Generally, countries (and regions) that have been unable to rapidly progress through the demographic transition are characterised by severe poverty and large disease burdens, as high birth and death rates structurally constrain the ability to reduce poverty and improve livelihoods. The rapid increase in the number of children offsets the increases in income from economic growth.

There are many reasons for Africa's comparably slow demographic transition. Historically, low population density – a function of Africa's high disease burden – translated into low levels of urbanisation and lower rates of income growth. Some of these aspects are explored in Chapter 4, which includes an analysis of basic infrastructure and health.

In recent generations, the continent has also not been able to raise the quality and attainment levels of education, roll out the use of modern contraceptives quickly enough, or transition to economies in which child labour is no longer required.[12] Nor has Africa been able to produce sufficient job opportunities to provide meaningful work for its growing population.

Most African countries are experiencing slow income growth because their populations are very young, although the picture is heterogeneous. A few African countries, including Mauritius, Seychelles, Tunisia, Libya, Morocco, South Africa and Algeria, are much further along in their demographic transition.

Fertility rates across Africa vary significantly. In 2018 they ranged from 7 (in Niger) to 1.4 (in Mauritius). The countries with the lowest fertility rates are the island states of Mauritius and Seychelles, North African countries such as Tunisia, Morocco, Libya and Algeria, and South Africa and Botswana in Southern Africa. The fertility rate for sub-Saharan Africa as a whole is currently estimated at 4.8 children per woman.

In countries such as Tunisia, fertility rates are approaching the level at which population size first stagnates and then starts to decline unless there is significant young, net inward migration and/or changes in fertility rates.[13] Many other countries, for example Mozambique, appear to be stalling in their transition, remaining with very high levels of fertility, while a third group (including Ethiopia) is achieving a rapid decline from very high fertility rates.[14]

Countries with high child mortality rates also tend to have high fertility rates. As children's health and survival improve, family demand for more children slowly declines. Smaller family size improves maternal and child education in a virtuous circle. As female education improves, and as child mortality declines, women have fewer children, which in turn allows for healthier and better-educated children.

The result is that fertility rates are closely associated with income levels, as well as with urbanisation. In Ethiopia, for instance, the fertility rate based on 2016 data was 6.4 children for poor women and 2.6 for the wealthy. The corresponding numbers in Tanzania for the same year were 7.5 and 3.1.[15] Fertility rates in capital cities such as Accra and Addis Ababa are close to replacement levels (understood to be just above two children per woman of childbearing age), while those in rural parts of the DRC are close to seven children per woman.[16]

Life expectancy in many African countries is also low. Whereas life expectancy in North Africa was estimated at almost 74 years in 2018, roughly a year longer than the global average, in sub-Saharan Africa it is 64 years – nine years below the global average. In 2018, 23 African countries, ranging from the Central African Republic (life expectancy estimated at 51.1 years) to Niger (life expectancy estimated at 63.7 years), had a life expectancy below 64 years – the final year at which people are typically assumed to still be of working age.

Lower child mortality rates, higher incomes, the education of women and the availability of contraception all reduce fertility rates.[17] These socio-economic changes are a result of modernisation. Globally, better health care, access to modern medication, structural changes to the economy and a rise in women's status and opportunities have all contributed to a dramatic reduction in total fertility rates and hence in population growth.

In 2018 the global average was estimated at 2.4 children per woman, while that of Africa was 4.5, with large disparities across and within countries. Average fertility rates for Africa's 24 low-income countries were estimated at 5 children in 2018 and are projected to decline to 3.5 children in 2040. That compares to 4.4 children in its 21 lower-middle-income countries and 2.6 in its eight upper-middle-income countries. These rates should decline to 3.3 and 2 children, respectively, by 2040.

The peak and length of the demographic dividend

An important explanation for the dynamism and growth of the US economy over an extended period is that it entered its demographic dividend shortly before 1930 and will only exit it around 2036, having been in this favourable position for more than a century.

China, on the other hand, will spend only 35 years in this fortunate window. This explains why China is unlikely to graduate to high-income status, as reflected in the mantra that China will grow old before it gets rich.

Development takes time. Eventually, India will spend about 60 years in the demographic high-growth range, and by that metric will experience a degree of catch-up with China, which, in spite of its higher peak, is likely to experience it for a shorter duration.

Nigeria progresses to the 1.7 ratio at roughly 2060 in the Current Path forecast. Thirty years later, it peaks at 2.1 and will exit the 1.7 to 1 ratio sometime in the next century. Given this long-term horizon, it is virtually impossible to speculate responsibly on Nigeria's long-term future growth prospects, also because the region is expected to suffer significant impacts from climate change at a time of huge technological advances.

In this context, it is important to remind ourselves that the impact of technology on productivity is expanding every year. While labour is an important component in productivity at lower levels of development, capital and technology are becoming ever more important, which could also reduce Nigeria's growth advantage.

The point is that the level at which countries achieve their peak demographic dividend – and how long they stay there – significantly impacts on economic growth. The longer a country is within this demographic window, the better.

A peak of 2.8 working-age persons dependant (China in 2010) obviously delivers much more rapid economic growth than a peak of 2.2 (India in 2035) or a peak of 2.1 (Nigeria in 2090). This is because the size of the potential labour force relative to dependants is larger. That peak of 2.8 contributed significantly to China's almost 11 per cent rate of economic growth in 2010. According to the IFs Current Path forecast, India is projected to grow at 6.2 per cent in the decade from 2030 to 2040 and Nigeria at less than half that in the 2090s, which is partly explained by its low peak of 2.1.

Looking to the end of this century, the ratio of working-age persons to dependants is set to contract in all regions except in sub-Saharan Africa, where it will peak at a ratio slightly below 2 to 1 only around

2074. At that point, Africa will have a population of 3.2 billion people (of which 2.95 billion will be living in sub-Saharan Africa).

A different way to express this metric is that 66 per cent of the population of sub-Saharan Africa will be of working age, while the global average at that point is expected to be 62 per cent. In this context, a four-percentage-point difference would indicate that sub-Saharan Africa will grow at a greater rate than global averages, but not by much. Also, because Africa will achieve a relatively low worker-to-dependant ratio, it will very likely grow at quite modest rates along the Current Path forecast. None of this is good news for a continent that aspires to catch up with global income averages.

Whereas Europe and Japan are experiencing slow economic growth partly because of their large elderly populations, sub-Saharan Africa is the only region in the world where income levels are growing slowly largely because of its high child-dependency burden.

Sub-Saharan Africa gets to a 1.7 to 1 ratio only by the middle of this century (in 2052), at which point it enters its demographic high-growth period. Only Tunisia, Morocco, Libya and Algeria, the island states of Mauritius and Seychelles, and Botswana, South Africa and Djibouti currently have a ratio of 1.7 and higher.

Africa also has a larger youth bulge (people between 15 and 29) as a portion of the total adult population (ie those aged above 15) than any other global region. It is typical of many poor countries to have a large share of young people relative to the total adult population, and this is also associated with increased risk of conflict and high rates of criminal violence. The problem is compounded when young people lack opportunities in terms of education, training and employment and feel they have no voice and are excluded from the economy and politics. This is covered in greater detail in Chapter 12.

The potential benefits of reducing fertility rates

Generally, a decline in fertility follows a decline in child mortality, with a time lag of several years.[18] The provision of basic infrastructure for water and sanitation, as well as advances in basic health care, reduces infant mortality and eventually leads to reduced fertility rates.

The need to have many children is based not only on the expectation that some children could die before reaching adulthood, but also on the fact that in economies dominated by employment in the agricultural sector (a characteristic of many poor and developing countries), families need children as labour. Child labour was widespread in most agrarian societies, even during industrialisation. As this demand changes, fertility rates decline.

Although many factors impact on fertility rates, a deep driver is female education. In addition, women's increased participation in the labour force, which is closely linked to improved female education and steady improvements in gender parity, also reduces total fertility rates.[19] For example, women who are better educated have more employment opportunities and are likely to want fewer children. Educated women (and men) are also more likely to be better informed about modern contraceptives and the benefits that lower fertility offers in terms of better education for a smaller number of children. Alternatively, where women have a lower social status, lower levels of decision-making opportunities and fewer opportunities outside the household, fertility rates tend to be higher.

While the Middle East and North Africa is not a progressive region in terms of gender parity, in 2015 girls in the region were about five per cent more likely to enrol in primary school than girls in sub-Saharan Africa. From an economic productivity perspective, the investment in female education in North Africa is, however, largely wasted, with the female share of the total labour force roughly half that of sub-Saharan Africa (24 per cent versus 43 per cent). Whereas the labour force participation rate for females is only 23 per cent in North Africa, it is 64 per cent in sub-Saharan Africa.[20]

The use of modern contraceptives is a more immediate driver of total fertility rates than education, although poor access to education among women constrains uptake. Research suggests that the average gap between actual and desired fertility could be as high as two children per woman in sub-Saharan Africa,[21] pointing to a large pent-up demand for the provision of modern contraceptives.

Data from the UN Population Division (UNPD) forecasts that the unmet demand for modern contraceptives in 2018 will be 28 per cent in low-income Africa and 25 per cent in lower-middle-income African countries, with large country-to-country variations. Estimates for the unmet need for family planning in Africa for women of reproductive age (15 to 49 years) who are married or in-union for 2017 range from 12 per cent in Zimbabwe to 41 per cent in the DRC.[22] The potential for rapid uptake of contraceptives, a large impact on fertility and the potential to improve Africa's demographic dividend is therefore large.[23]

Modelling the impact of advancing Africa's demographic transition: The Demographic Dividend scenario

In this section, I explore a scenario called the Demographic Dividend that could set the continent on a demographic trajectory quite different to the Current Path. In designing and exploring this scenario, I do not ask how these policies are motivated or assess the inevitable socio-political challenges that would accompany them. Rather, I look only at the potential impact of successful implementation.

Owing to the slow-moving nature of demographic dynamics, I also take a longer view than I do in most of the other chapters in the book, and look to the end of the century. As with other chapters, the interventions in the IFs system are detailed on www.jakkiecilliers.org, and benchmarked against the historical and expected progress in South America and South Asia as two comparable regions.

The first, and most impactful, intervention is the ambitious roll-out of modern contraceptives, which should be quite easy given the unmet demand mentioned above.

A second intervention is a modest reduction in child and adult female mortality rates from communicable diseases. This intervention imitates a health system better equipped for family planning. A high under-five mortality rate is an important driver of high levels of desired fertility, since high child mortality rates translate into women having more children.

A final intervention is to empower women. Although generally considered the fundamental or deep driver of changes in the number of children that women decide to have, women's empowerment is also the intervention with the least direct impact on demographics. This is because changes in social norms and family structures normally take much longer to impact on fertility than other measures.

The effects of the interventions in the Demographic Dividend scenario are significant. The communicable-disease death rate among women would drop to an average of one death per thousand by 2030, as opposed to nearly two deaths per thousand on the Current Path. The infant mortality rate would fall to approximately 26 deaths per thousand live births by 2030, compared to 36 deaths on the Current Path. Meanwhile, the average fertility rate would drop to 2.2 children per woman by 2050 and to just under two children (1.9) by 2070. On the Current Path, this average is expected to drop to about three children by 2050, and to two children by 2070.

Given the momentum behind Africa's youthful population, the impact of the Demographic Dividend scenario on the size of the global population would be substantial. Instead of a global population peaking at an estimated 10.4 billion people shortly before 2090 (the Current Path forecast in IFs), global population would peak at below 9.8 billion in around 2080, more than a decade earlier, with enormous positive implications for global sustainability.

Meanwhile, the total population of Africa would only grow to 2.8 billion people by the end of the century in the Demographic Dividend scenario, while on the Current Path it is expected to be 3.7 billion people.

The extent to which African countries would benefit from the Demographic Dividend scenario would differ. For example, Zambia, Uganda and Tanzania would gain between six and seven percentage points in the relative size of their working-age population to dependants by 2050. Countries such as eSwatini, Djibouti and Egypt would gain little, and Lesotho, Botswana and Algeria would have a marginally smaller working-age population than previously.

However, with more people entering their productive working age and fewer dependants (mostly children), Africa's overall economy would grow more rapidly until the demographic dividend peaks, which is expected to occur around 2066 instead of 2074.

Since the continent will eventually also have a smaller population, the transition propels substantive increases in average income levels, particularly in those countries with high fertility rates. The average difference in GDP per capita (in purchasing power parity, or PPP) in 2050 in Africa would be US$510, with ten countries experiencing an increase in GDP per capita of more than US$550 per person.

In Angola, average income levels (in PPP) increase by US$693 per person in 2050, and in Tanzania by US$815. In Ghana, the difference is US$690, and in Egypt it is US$322. Tunisia, which has quite a mature population structure, benefits very little, with average incomes increasing by only US$51 per person and in South Sudan the difference is just US$7.

These changes are a function of the extent to which Africa is able to advance the onset of its peak demographic dividend (by eight years), as well as to increase the ratio of persons of working age to dependants, resulting in a larger portion of persons of working age relative to dependants than would otherwise be the case. Instead of peaking at below 2 in 2072, the ratio would peak at above 2.1 in 2066, as reflected in Figure 3.2, which includes forecasts to the end of the century.

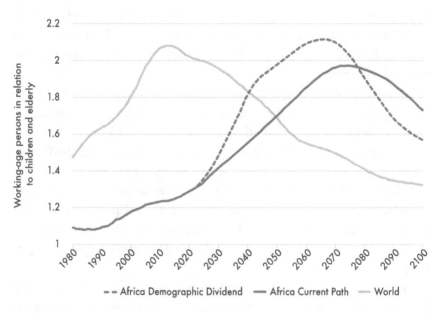

Figure 3.2: Difference in ratio of working age to dependants, Africa vs rest of the world[24]

With more persons of working age and fewer children to educate, the improvements cascade across various indices of human well-being. For example, the number of Africans living in extreme poverty would be 24 million people fewer in 2030 and 129 million people fewer in 2050.[25] With its large and predominantly poor population, Nigeria would have 29 million people fewer in 2050 in the Demographic Dividend scenario compared to the Current Path. This is out of a total population that would reach 372 million people (instead of 404 million on the Current Path) by 2050.

And because individual indicators of human development all improve in the Demographic Dividend scenario, Africa generally narrows the gap between itself and the rest of the world on composite indicators such as the Human Development Index (HDI). [26]

The difference between the Current Path and the Demographic Dividend scenarios by 2063 (the end year of the AU's Agenda 2063 vision) is presented in Figures 3.3a and 3.3b on p 54. In the Demographic Dividend scenario, Africa has a much more mature population structure, with a distinctive bulge along the midriff, compared to the more youthful structure of its population that is evident in the Current Path forecast.

The more lightly shaded area at the centre of each population pyramid indicates no education or incomplete primary education. The darker shading on the outer edge of each pyramid indicates completed tertiary education.

The median years of adult education in Africa would have increased by two months (to 8.8 years), with a concomitant impact on labour productivity.

In the Demographic Dividend scenario, Africa also reduces the gap in average education levels for adults between itself and the rest of the world.

Conclusion: Reducing fertility rates and working towards Africa's demographic dividend

This chapter has explained how Africa's very large number of children currently is a drag on development. Although Africa's demographic profile started to change for the better from the late 1980s, the ratio of working-age persons to dependants has only slowly improved and will continue to do so over the long term.

On the Current Path the continent will enter a demographic dividend only after mid-century. To unleash the potential contained in it at that point will require investments in improved education, eliminating gender inequality in education and boosting female enrolment and graduation rates to those of males at primary, secondary and tertiary levels.

3.3b

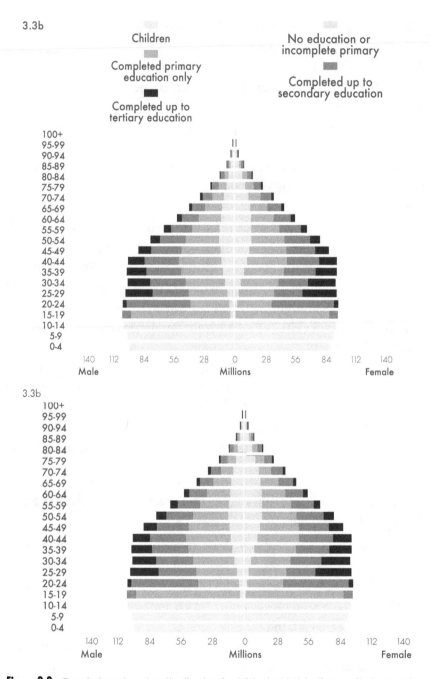

Figure 3.3a: Population education distribution for Africa in 2063 in Current Path scenario

Figure 3.3b: Population education distribution for Africa in 2063 in Demographic Dividend scenario[27]

The empowerment of women lies at the root of fertility rates. As the World Bank notes in an extensive study on African demographics: '[T]he number of children that a couple have depends directly on a woman's position in the household and her bargaining power relative to that of her husband.'[28]

There is a large body of literature supporting the idea that greater inclusion of women can improve overall development outcomes and, potentially, economic growth.[29] A study from the McKinsey Global Institute concludes, perhaps somewhat hyperbolically, that advancing women's equality to a 'best in region' benchmark could add US$12 trillion to the global economy by 2025, while a 'full potential' scenario could add US$28 trillion.[30]

The demographic dividend can be enhanced and intensified through the accelerated roll-out of modern contraceptives and the improved health of women and children by investing in basic infrastructure such as the provision of clean water and improved sanitation. Access to quality education and adequate nutrition are other key enablers that improve human capital.

Finally, in order to fully realise the potential of the demographic dividend, people need job opportunities, which is probably Africa's biggest challenge. This point will be examined further in Chapter 9. That said, people are incredibly ingenious. A larger working-age population will increase economic activity and jobs as people create new opportunities and engage in additional endeavours.

All these interventions to unlock Africa's human capital will require governments, especially those in low-income and lower-middle-income countries, to make family planning a high priority on their developmental agenda. This applies most pertinently to Niger, Somalia, the DRC, Mali, Chad, Angola, Burundi, Uganda, Nigeria, The Gambia, Burkina Faso and Mozambique. In all these countries, the total fertility rate currently exceeds five children per woman. In an additional 23 countries, the average fertility rate exceeds four children per woman. That rural fertility rates are significantly higher than those in urban areas, and differ according to income, complicates these dynamics.

From a societal point of view, this means that Africans need to engage candidly and robustly in public discussions and scholarly analysis on the economic and developmental implications of the continent's large youthful population. Changes in fertility reflect shifts in social and cultural norms that may take time, but while the fertility transition is slow to get started, it can rapidly pick up momentum.

Political leadership in discussing gender inequality, fertility and family size is vital, as are public media campaigns that demonstrate the health and economic benefits of smaller families.

Subsequent chapters will touch on the additional benefits of advancing Africa's demographic dividend, including the prospect for less political turbulence with a declining youth bulge, the lower chance of experiencing a violent political transition (Chapter 12), and the increased chance of being a liberal democracy as median age increases (Chapter 13).

Although the impact of the Demographic Dividend scenario is significant, it is insufficient to reverse the Current Path forecast of growing divergence in average incomes between Africa and the rest of the world. To improve its human capital endowment, the continent requires a consort of structural transitions, including improved health and associated basic infrastructure, as well as education. This is the subject of the next two chapters.

4

Health, water, sanitation and hygiene

> Income and health are two of the most important components of well-being . . .
>
> – Angus Deaton[1]

Homo sapiens evolved in Africa around 300 000 years ago and, although there is evidence of previous waves of migrations going back some 210 000 years, only successfully migrated from Africa relatively recently – some 70 000 years ago. Evidence from human DNA and palaeontology confirms that all humans who have ancestors outside of Africa today are descended from a single small group of migrants and not from previous migrants. They spread along the southern coast of Asia and into Oceania about 50 000 years ago, and into Europe about 40 000 years ago, where they displaced Neanderthals and other dominant populations and eventually emerged as the dominant species across the world.[2]

Homo sapiens gained an initial health reprieve that lasted for several thousand years when the species moved out of Africa into more fertile regions. Large populations (estimated at about 20 million people each around 1 000 years BCE) eventually appear to have grouped in five regions globally: in China, the Indian subcontinent, Egypt, the Fertile Crescent and Iran, and Europe.[3] Perhaps half of Africa's much smaller population was by then concentrated in the fertile Nile Valley.

Having left Africa for cooler regions with fewer insect-borne diseases and 'the many parasites and disease organisms that had evolved in parallel with the human species',[4] *Homo sapiens* multiplied rapidly. The development of agriculture and farming was key to this process, as it increased food production and allowed much higher population densities (and created new diseases). Density led to competition between people over grazing, land, food and status that required political organisation and other aspects of development. As much as it destroyed things, warfare was important in spurring innovation and technological advancement.[5]

By contrast to the situation developing elsewhere, large parts of Africa's interior appear to have had very low population densities, the result of the scourge of sleeping sickness and other vector-borne diseases, such as malaria, which is carried by the female *Anopheles* mosquito. Diseases such as yellow fever and sleeping sickness were endemic, and insect-borne diseases also prevented the use of the horse, ox or camel, thereby reducing the opportunity for progress.[6]

An exception, eventually, was the belt of open savannah south of the Sahara and north of the tropical rain forests in Central and West Africa. Higher population densities here led to these regions experiencing a modest agricultural revolution, although not of the same magnitude as seen elsewhere.[7]

Nature eventually reasserted itself in humanity's new habitat outside Africa. In fact, most of today's most prominent infectious diseases only emerged in the last 11 000 years following the rise of agriculture. Agriculture changed human settlement patterns irrevocably. Larger settlements in the form of permanent villages and towns swept away the spatial limitation on the spread of disease. In particular the introduction of domesticated animals, such as dogs, pigs, cattle, horses and cats, increased human exposure to infectious diseases spread by rats and fleas.[8]

Largely because of Africa's low population densities and the dominant hunter-gatherer lifestyle, the technological developments that accompanied the Bronze and the Iron Ages essentially bypassed the continent, and its development generally lagged behind that of others. Because of its relative isolation from global trade and conquest, Africa was also less affected by the great plagues, such as the Plague of Justinian, which reduced Eurasian populations by a quarter in 541–542 BCE, or the Black Death (bubonic plague), which swept through Asia, Europe and North Africa in the 14th century.[9]

In the meantime, significant African civilisations developed in modern-day Ethiopia (Aksum) and in West Africa along the Niger River. For a while, it seemed that these might come to rival civilisations outside Africa. South of the Sahara, the Bantu people had domesticated cattle and were growing sorghum and millet. They had also discovered how to work iron, but they and other groups were not technologically advanced enough to resist external intrusion. During the centuries of African slavery that followed from around 1500, first Muslim slave traders and later the Atlantic slave trade denuded the continent of much of its stable work-force, and hence its ability to pursue farming. Without sufficient labour and the ability to store foods, it was not possible to identify and cultivate crops and domesticate animals – both prerequisites of farming.

The late 19th and early 20th centuries coincided with imperialism and the colonial division of Africa by European powers. The exploitation and oppression of this era is perhaps best known through Joseph Conrad's novella *Heart of Darkness* (1899), about the cruelty that accompanied the exploitation of the Congo by Leopold II of Belgium.

Two centuries ago there were fewer than a billion people in the world. By 2040 there will be 9.2 billion. The momentum that built up during this period is astounding. It took almost seven centuries for the world population to double to 500 million people – achieved midway in the 16th century. It recently doubled in just 46 years, and reached 7.5 billion people by 2017.

The growth of large cities in much of Europe and elsewhere required authorities to give attention to waterborne sewerage and other measures to combat the spread of communicable diseases. But by the time urbani-sation came to Africa on a larger scale, towards the end of the 19th century, it was partially enabled by imported modern medicine, which permitted the treatment of malaria and other diseases. Much bigger communities of people were able to live in larger settlements across the continent not because of city planning, housing laws, adequate municipal water and sewerage, but rather because modern medicines served to keep infectious diseases under control.[10]

Geography and hence climate arguably also had a second impact in Africa in that large parts of the continent carry a particularly heavy burden of so-called vector-borne diseases. These are illnesses caused by parasites, viruses and bacteria that are transmitted to humans by insects such as mosquitoes, ticks and tsetse flies, which are commonly found in tropical and subtropical regions, such as in Central Africa, and places where access to safe drinking water and sanitation is limited. In temperate zones, such as in much of Europe, parts of Asia and North Africa, seasonal fluctuations in temperature serve as a natural constraint on the breeding cycle of insects and hence on the transmission of vector-borne diseases.[11] In Central, West and East Africa, where *Homo sapiens* origi-nated, their breeding cycle is not disrupted in this manner. As a result, sub-Saharan Africa has a constant high burden of vector-borne diseases, come summer, autumn, winter or spring.

Malaria, the most deadly vector-borne disease, is particularly prevalent in Africa. The continent also accounts for 34 of the 47 countries prone to yellow fever outbreak and about 40 per cent of the global burden of lymphatic filariasis (elephantiasis).[12] Today, Africa is still home to 16 of the 30 countries listed by the World Health Organization (WHO) as hav-ing a high burden of tuberculosis, though none are in the top five.[13]

And then Africa has consistently shouldered between 75 and 85 per cent of the global Aids burden, which peaked in 2004–2005. In each of these years more than 1.5 million Africans died from Aids, although the actual number of people who succumbed to HIV/Aids in the 1960s, 1970s and 1980s will likely never be known.[14]

The recent impact of HIV and Aids

The ancestor of the human immunodeficiency virus (HIV) is the simian immunodeficiency virus (SIV), an infection of African monkeys that has also spread to chimpanzees, is several thousand years old, and may even have been around millions of years ago.[15] That SIV spread to humans is no surprise, for several major human infectious diseases, such as the plague, sleeping sickness, yellow fever, various forms of influenza, Creutzfeldt-Jakob disease and, most recently, Ebola, have done so. Once transmitted to humans, SIV evolved into HIV. Like many other diseases, its African origin is essentially a function of the fact that humanity and its predecessors have a longer and closer relationship with nature in Africa than anywhere else, going back hundreds of thousands of years.

Today, it seems clear that the HIV virus originated in the western equatorial region of Africa (today Cameroon and the DRC) in the first half of the 20th century. By the mid-1970s it had begun to take epidemic proportions. But it remained silent and unrecognised, largely because it affected the immune system, meaning that people were apparently dying from a variety of opportunistic infections and not from a single disease. During the subsequent decade, subgroups of the virus were carried away from the epicentre to infect East, Southern and West Africa. As a result, by the time the epidemic was discovered, it had silently spread across large areas. Its slow-acting, asymptomatic incubation period and the eventual appearance of diverse opportunistic infections defied prompt action until such time as it reached truly momentous proportions.[16]

Because of Africa's poor health systems, bad infrastructure and limited medical research capacity, HIV/Aids remained undetected until it had spread quite widely on the continent. Between 1980 and 2000, life expectancy in sub-Saharan Africa improved by only about 2.5 years, compared to an increase of about 5.5 years globally and close to nine years in South Asia. The Aids pandemic had a dramatic impact on Africa's ability to improve health outcomes relative to other developing regions, with a serious knock-on effect on economic productivity and with disastrous effects on families and communities.

While the first known case of HIV was eventually traced to a man who died in 1959 in the then Belgian Congo, it took another 26 years before the first international conference on Aids was held in Atlanta. By 1982 it was understood that the 'slim disease', a condition previously considered to be a wasting disorder linked to malnutrition, was in fact HIV/Aids. Although Aids is no longer at the top of the global infectious disease agenda, having been replaced by Ebola and Zika, the pandemic has had serious repercussions for life expectancy in Africa.

Then, once it was identified, lack of government capacity and the denialism of influential leaders, such as President Thabo Mbeki of South Africa, led to the unnecessary loss of hundreds of thousands of lives. Mbeki's stance, in the country with the largest Aids death rates globally at the time, would eventually contribute to his being ousted as president in 2008 in favour of a flawed replacement, Jacob Zuma.

While life expectancy in Africa has recovered to a certain extent in the last decade, it still has not properly caught up. In fact, in 2018, the gap in life expectancy between Africa and the rest of the world was about the same as it had been in 1960 – around 12 years – in spite of the fact that the ready availability of medicines should allow Africa to make much more rapid progress at low levels of life expectancy. During the same period South Asia more than halved the gap in life expectancy between itself and the rest of the world – from 12 years in 1960 to five years today.

As much as HIV/Aids dealt sub-Saharan Africa a devastating blow, it came at a time when Africa had shown signs of a turnaround from the declining prospects of the 1980s and 1990s. This change in fortune was the result of various factors, including a determined effort by some in the international community to place poverty alleviation at the core of global concerns – an occurrence that was facilitated by the end of the Cold War.

Africa's approaching health transition

Looking back to the origins of humanity, it is clear that Africa's high communicable disease burden partly explains its particular development trajectory. Recently, and for several decades, HIV/Aids increased this burden and distorted the pattern that saw declining communicable (or infectious) and increased non-communicable diseases in other regions. Africa has a much younger population than other regions in the world. It therefore naturally suffers from a much higher communicable disease burden, including from flu, unsafe water, poor housing conditions and poor sanitation.

The so-called epidemiological transition takes place when improved food security and innovations in public health and medicine result in infectious diseases, such as influenza, being replaced as the dominant cause of death by chronic diseases, such as cancer. This transition is also generally associated with age and income as it relates to lifestyle.

The high costs associated with non-communicable diseases will pose a major problem for many African countries as their comparatively low average incomes translate into limited state budgets and capacity to provide the necessary health care. To give a practical example: providing mosquito nets to every vulnerable person in Africa is one thing, but ensuring that every African has reliable access to insulin, cancer screenings and dialysis is quite another.

Infants and children often die of infectious diseases, while elderly people generally die of chronic diseases. As incomes rise, people live longer, eat more processed foodstuffs, and more readily develop heart disease, high blood pressure, diabetes and cancer. In Europe and North America the transition to non-communicable disease as the main cause of death occurred several decades ago. In Latin America and the Caribbean the transition happened around 1970. In South Asia it occurred around 2000.

In Africa the transition is already completed in North Africa (where it happened around 1980) but is only set to occur around 2034 in sub-Saharan Africa. On the one hand, people in sub-Saharan Africa are living long enough to succumb to non-communicable afflictions, and, on the other, many people in poor countries are contracting the 'diseases of affluence' at younger ages. So, in sub-Saharan Africa the transition is happening at lower levels of income and urbanisation than elsewhere and will present health systems with very large cost implications. And, as explained earlier, whereas the transition in Western Europe and North America came in the 19th century, largely as a result of infrastructure investments, such as closed sewerage systems and clean water supply by public utilities, and later by vaccines and the discovery of penicillin, in Africa different dynamics are at play.

In much of Africa, poor people are moving to cities without the prospect of a job or an improved lifestyle but simply to escape the destitution in rural areas. The result is massive increases in large, sprawling slum cities, some of which are already evident in places such as Lagos, Dar es Salaam and Nairobi.

The result of the approaching double burden of disease, consisting of the increased prevalence of chronic non-communicable diseases and the ongoing battle to deal with infectious diseases, is that there will be more sick adults and that poor countries will have to devote more resources to preventing and treating costlier non-communicable diseases. Pollution and tobacco are also proving to be a huge challenge, as tobacco companies now actively target the next generation of smokers, all of whom are in the developing world.

Still, communicable diseases have a disproportionate and devastating impact on Africa, by any standard. In 2018, about 90 per cent of malaria deaths worldwide occurred in Africa; for HIV/Aids the figure was about 80 per cent. The continent accounts for nearly 50 per cent of all communicable disease deaths worldwide, despite making up only 16 per cent of the global population, as shown in Figure 4.1. In other words, people in Africa are about four and a half times more likely to die from a communicable disease than people elsewhere.

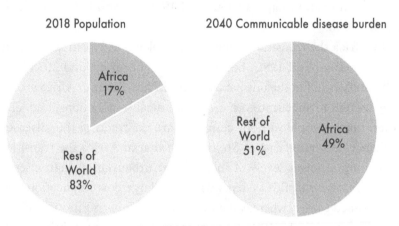

Figure 4.1: Percentage of population and deaths from communicable disease, 2018[17]

This trend is forecast to continue to continue beyond 2040 in the Current Path. By then, Africa is projected to account for about 95 per cent of global malaria deaths, 80 per cent of global Aids deaths and more than 47 per cent of total communicable disease deaths worldwide. It is partly because of this disease burden that average life expectancy at birth in 2018 in Africa is so much lower than that in the rest of the world and is also forecast to remain significantly below global averages beyond the 2040 time horizon.

Addressing Africa's disproportionate communicable disease burden is obviously a high priority, but any progress in this regard will inevitably mean a greater prevalence in non-communicable causes of death. This transition will occur at a point when incomes are still quite low compared to other parts of the world that have already gone through the transition.

Non-communicable diseases are more difficult and expensive to diagnose, treat and manage than communicable diseases. In fact, almost one-third of all deaths in sub-Saharan Africa are already categorised as non-communicable, a share that is forecast to rise to more than 50 per cent by 2040, even in the absence of additional interventions.[18]

Urbanisation and health services

In light of the preceding analysis, a third characteristic that also plays a very important role when discussing health in Africa is the rate and nature of urbanisation.

Africa is urbanising much later compared to other regions, and urbanisation is accompanied by the rapid growth of slum cities without the required basic infrastructure to cope with the influx and natural population growth. The lack of adequate water and sanitation infrastructure in many of Africa's rapidly growing cities doesn't impact much on health. Rather, it is access to modern medicine that is keeping ill health at bay.

According to the Current Path forecast, Africa will become predominantly urban only around 2033 (2036 for sub-Saharan Africa), several decades later than other world regions. This means that Africa remains the most rural continent in the world, although the absolute increase in growth of the urban population is large.

The continent's urban population is forecast to more than double by 2050, adding more than 800 million people to Africa's cities. The UNPD anticipates that, between 2018 and 2035, all ten of the world's fastest-growing cities will be in Africa – and 21 of the top 30.[19] Twelve of these 30 cities are in West Africa, four of which are in Nigeria. The four Nigerian cities alone are projected to add about 200 million people to urban areas in Africa by 2050.

Since most African governments don't have the means to invest in the vast and dense network of transport systems required for such sprawling cities, poorly constructed and poorly maintained roads are crowded with cars and other means of private transport. The result is that the city sprawls out further and further, lowering urban density and increasing the potential cost of providing the required additional infrastructure. Consequently, instead of productivity increasing – one of the main advantages of urbanisation – it actually starts to decrease.[20]

African cities from Nairobi to Cape Town are already known for their slums. Slums and informal townships present a number of problems to African cities, largely because they develop in the absence of planning. Housing units are almost exclusively self-constructed and neighbourhoods are organised independently of the central governing authority.

Some governments even go out of their way to avoid acknowledging that these places exist. Until 2009 the largest slum in Africa was, literally, not even on the map. The space inhabited by Kibera was officially designated by the government of Kenya as a lake next to the Nairobi Dam, that is, until the Map Kibera project kicked off. This free, open-source mobile application has evolved into an interactive community information project that aims to bring together residents of multiple slum communities across Nairobi.[21] It is a great example of human ingenuity and clearly demonstrates the transformative potential of technology in Africa. It also illustrates the chasm between the demand for basic services and the ability of the government to provide them.

Current Path: Access to basic infrastructure

Previous sections have noted that unlike historical pathways elsewhere, African levels of health are not solely dependent on the expansion of water and sanitation infrastructure. Rather, infectious diseases are kept at bay through access to modern medicine. Africa appears to be making the epidemiological transition despite a serious lack of these services. However, this does not mean that poor access to clean water and sanitation doesn't present a major crisis.

Unlike other forms of infrastructure, such as electricity, reliable access to safe water is a basic human right – as proclaimed by the UN General Assembly in 2010. Therefore, access to water, sanitation and hygiene (WaSH) serves as a decent proxy for a government's ability to fulfil the basic needs of its people.[22]

Hypothetically speaking, the centralisation of service delivery points for water, sanitation and health in urban areas should make service delivery easier compared to the challenge of, say, rolling out health care or sanitation in sparsely populated rural areas. However, as discussed, most of Africa's cities are poorly designed, congested and growing rapidly.

It is therefore not surprising that Africa's urban citizens have some of the lowest levels of access to basic services worldwide. In 2018, only about 39 per cent of the continent had access to an improved sanitation facility, while the global average was approximately 70 per cent. For clean water, the rates are only slightly improved, with about 77 per cent of people in Africa having access, while in the rest of the world that figure was more than 97 per cent. In comparison, about 53 per cent of people in South Asia had access to an improved sanitation facility in 2018, and about 94 per cent of the region had access to potable water.

The picture is similar for nearly any other measure of access to infrastructure or services. For instance, in 2018 about 95 per cent of global populations outside Africa had access to electricity. In Africa, the figure was approximately half of that, at 53 per cent (44 per cent in sub-Saharan Africa). The use of solid fuels for cooking and heating instead of electricity is also a major source of indoor air pollution. This lack of access to physical infrastructure and basic services constrains Africa's ability to fully develop its human potential and thus to capitalise on the demographic transition discussed in Chapter 3.

Partly as a result of these differences, people in South Asia can expect at birth to live on average about six years longer and receive more than a full year of additional education relative to their counterparts in sub-Saharan Africa. Infant mortality is about 50 per cent higher in sub-Saharan Africa than in South Asia, and the rate at which African children under the age of five die is nearly twice as high.

WaSH infrastructure supports the development of broader human potential through its strong forward linkages to other important aspects of the Sustainable Development Goals (SDGs), such as poverty, education and gender equality. In other words, improvements in WaSH infrastructure generally translate into sizeable gains in the overall development of a country, since these improve the human capital contribution.

For example, children who do not have adequate access to WaSH facilities have difficulty absorbing nutrients and are more vulnerable to the negative consequences of undernutrition. Malnourished children are highly susceptible to communicable diseases, with diarrhoeal diseases being among the most frequent and severe examples. The United Nations Children's Fund (Unicef) estimates that, of the roughly 1 600 child deaths from diarrhoeal disease each day globally, about half are attributable to a lack of WaSH access.[23] In recognition of this, in 2015 the WHO and Unicef's Joint Monitoring Project recognised access to WaSH facilities as 'fundamental to good health, dignity and quality of life'.[24]

Children who don't succumb to diarrhoeal disease may suffer other lifelong effects, such as stunting, generally recognised as low height for age.[25] Although stunting is commonly described in physiological terms, it also significantly impairs the development of the human brain. According to the WHO, stunted individuals suffer from 'poor cognition and educational performance, low adult wages, lost productivity and, when accompanied by excessive weight gain later in childhood, an increased risk of nutrition-related chronic diseases in adult life'.[26] Put bluntly, stunting is an irreversible condition that inhibits the potential of the affected individual or community for life.

Insufficient WaSH access leaves all children vulnerable, but as they mature, the negative impacts begin to stack up disproportionately against women and girls. Poorly maintained or nonexistent WaSH facilities increase high school dropout rates among teenage girls, for example.[27] This in turn could lead to a large disparity in educational attainment between men and women and significantly diminish economic opportunities for the latter.

In many instances, insufficient WaSH infrastructure also means that women and girls face an increased risk of sexual assault when using these facilities at night, in part due to the absence of decent lighting. In fact, a 2015 study in Khayelitsha, conducted by Yale University, found that simply increasing the number of toilets could lead to a reduction in sexual violence against women and girls. When the 'social cost' of sexual violence, including tangible costs such as medical expenses, legal adjudication and correctional time, as well as intangible costs such as trauma and risk of homicide, is taken into account, erecting more toilets could actually save costs, too.[28]

However, there are immense challenges to advancing access to WaSH infrastructure in sub-Saharan Africa.[29] Even upper-middle-income countries in Africa are struggling to expand access fast enough, in particular to sanitation facilities. Of Africa's eight upper-middle-income countries, only Mauritius, Libya and Algeria register access rates above the global average for countries in this category (about 80 per cent).[30]

In the five remaining upper-middle-income African countries with below-average access levels – South Africa, Namibia, Botswana, Equatorial Guinea and Gabon – about 19 million people were still living without access to an improved sanitation facility in 2018. It is likely no coincidence that four of these five countries, namely, South Africa,

Namibia, Botswana and Equatorial Guinea, rank among the 12 most unequal countries in the world, according to the Gini index, which measures and compares inequality within countries. In South Africa alone, nearly 15 million people live with increased vulnerability to waterborne illness and other negative health consequences due to lack of access to an improved sanitation facility.

Unfortunately, looking to the future, the picture is not likely to improve much. In the Current Path, Africa is projected to fall well short of the SDGs for universal access to clean water and improved sanitation.

On the Current Path forecast, only half of Africa's population are projected to have access to an improved sanitation facility and just over 80 per cent are forecast to have reliable access to clean drinking water in 2030. In 2018, 294 million people in the DRC, Ethiopia and Nigeria alone were living without access to improved sanitation facilities, and 115 million without access to clean drinking water. Those numbers are projected to change to about 335 million and 116 million, respectively, by the time the SDGs are meant to be achieved in 2030.

Modelling the impact of better health and WaSH infrastructure: The Improved Health scenario

Although a coordinated cross-sectoral approach is necessary to overcome the negative impact that poor health outcomes have on development in Africa, a push on the most immediate health and infrastructure priorities would have significant and visible effects on the health situation on the continent. It would also improve productivity and economic growth prospects.

Given how far behind Africa is on these various indicators compared to other regions, the interventions are not calibrated to represent Africa achieving the SDGs by 2030 (Goals 3 and 6 are dedicated to health and WaSH infrastructure, respectively) but merely consist of a determined push on the selected indicators that are benchmarked to an analysis of what is historically possible in South America and South Asia, the two regions most comparable to Africa.

The Improved Health scenario therefore simulates a series of improvements in the provision of basic infrastructure and reductions in the incidence of communicable and non-communicable diseases. These consist of improving access to clean water by 12 percentage points above the 2030 Current Path forecast and by 15 percentage points in the case of improved sanitation.

Advances in treatment and impact are modelled at a 50 per cent reduction in malaria and HIV/Aids infections by 2030, as well as a 10 per cent reduction in the broad category of 'other communicable diseases' by 2030.[31] Already in 2019, some 360 000 children a year in Malawi, Ghana and Kenya are to receive a powerful new anti-malaria drug, Mosquirix, as part of a pilot project that will last for several years.[32]

Due to HIV's ability to mutate rapidly, a preventive vaccine doesn't exist yet, in spite of many scientific advances, but this is surely only a question of time.[33] The scenario almost halves deaths from Aids and malaria by 2030 (compared to the Current Path forecast) and results in a ten-percentage-point reduction in other communicable diseases. The WaSH interventions represent a 60 per cent reduction in the percentage of the population depending on unimproved sanitation facilities and a 40 per cent reduction in the proportion of the population living without clean water when compared to the Current Path forecast.[34]

The Improved Health scenario demonstrates the impact that improvements in one area – basic infrastructure – can have on another sector – health.

The benefits from the Improved Health scenario reduces government consumption on health by US$715 million in 2040, or by a cumulative amount of US$45 billion from 2020 to 2040. But that reduction does not fully offset the increase in government consumption on infrastructure, amounting to US$6.4 billion in 2040, or a cumulative amount of additional US$79 billion from 2020 to 2040.

Technological advances will also help the drive for improved basic infrastructure. For example, since 2011 the Bill & Melinda Gates Foundation has invested more than US$200 million in the Reinvent the Toilet challenge. Although there has yet to be a technical breakthrough, the level of investment and talent that the challenge is attracting is promising.[35] Bill Gates estimates that the market for this new toilet technology could be as big as US$6 billion a year by 2030, more than the current GDP of 16 African countries.

The result of the Improved Health scenario is that there are 887 000 fewer births on the continent in 2040 (cumulatively 8.5 million over the period 2020 to 2040) and an increase in life expectancy at birth of roughly 1.7 years for Africa's 2.1 billion people.

In the Improved Health scenario, about 105 million fewer people rely on unimproved water sources in Africa by 2030, and about 86 million fewer people have to live with an unimproved sanitation facility. Nevertheless, even with the significant push on WaSH infrastructure in this scenario, there are still about 172 million Africans living without reliable access to clean water and more than 500 million living without access to an improved sanitation facility by the end of the SDGs in 2030.

This scenario also reduces the cumulative number of fatalities from Aids and malaria by about 1.4 million and 2.2 million, respectively, by 2030. However, in that same year IFs estimates that Africa will still experience nearly 600 000 fatalities from those two causes of mortality alone.

Although this scenario doesn't get the continent quite to the finish line in time for the SDGs, a push to combat communicable diseases and improve WaSH infrastructure would still have significant benefits for human and economic development. Cumulatively, more than three million fewer Africans will die of HIV/Aids by 2040 and 5.7 million fewer from malaria.

Average life expectancy at birth in Africa is around 1.7 years higher in the Improved Health scenario in 2040, moving the continent closer to the likely global average of 76.3 years. By 2040, there would also be more than 3.3 million fewer children suffering from undernutrition in this scenario relative to the Current Path forecast.

Over the duration of the forecast, the Improved Health scenario increases Africa's GDP growth rate by an average of about 0.1 per cent, which translates into an increased overall GDP – measured at market exchange rates – of US$155 billion in 2040. Furthermore, it drives a US$68 increase in GDP per capita – measured at purchasing power parity – by 2040.

The Improved Health scenario decreases extreme poverty by around 5.8 million people in 2030, and by around 4.6 million people in 2040.[36]

The Improved Health scenario also advances the epidemiological transition – the point at which non-communicable diseases become the leading cause of death in sub-Saharan Africa – by four years, to 2030.

One way of measuring the impact of the Improved Health scenario is to use a standard metric for capturing a country or region's disease burden. Disability-adjusted life years (DALYs) offer a way of accounting for the difference between a current situation and an ideal situation in which everyone lives up to the life expectancy of Japan (the country with the longest life expectancy globally), free of disease and disability.[37] Early death would provide years of life lost, while sickness would translate into years lost due to disability. The two are added together to provide the DALYs – a combined measure of mortality (or death) and morbidity (poor health).

Using Japan as a benchmark, the WHO currently defines standard life expectancy as 81 years for men and 87 years for women. So, a man who dies at 70 would add 11 years to a country's DALYs count, while a woman who died at 70 would account for 17 years. Illness is measured on a scale on which 0 represents perfect health and 1 represents a condition equivalent to death.[38] The DALY is a commonly used, if imperfect, measure of the burden of disease in a society and is generally used to compare the relative disease and mortality burden across countries and regions.

Even relative to other developing regions, Africa stands out in rates of DALYs. In per capita terms, DALYs are about 75 per cent higher in sub-Saharan Africa than in South Asia, and more than twice as high as in Latin America and the Caribbean or in East Asia and the Pacific.

In the Improved Health scenario, Africa suffers from about 60 million fewer DALYs caused by communicable disease by 2040, and 25 million less DALYs from non-communicable diseases. The infant mortality rate also declines by four deaths per thousand live births by 2040 compared to the Current Path forecast.

Average life expectancy in Africa in 2018 was 61 for men and 65 for women. By 2040, the Current Path forecast is that it would have improved to 68 for men and 72 years for women. At that point, average life expectancy in the rest of the world will be 76 and 81 years, respectively.

In the intervening years, the gap between Africa and the average male life expectancy in the rest of the world would have decreased from 11 to 8 years. That of women would have decreased from 12 to 9 years. In the

Improved Health scenario, the gap between the life expectancy of the average African male and female compared to that in the rest of the world would have declined further to seven years by 2040.

So, in terms of life expectancy, Africa is slowly reducing the gap between global averages, and the rate of catch-up increases with the Improved Health scenario. However, we must bear in mind that it is of course much easier to make rapid progress at lower levels of life expectancy, as is evident in much of Africa.

Conclusion: Planning comprehensively and long-term

This chapter has explored the impact of the extended period of time during which humans have interacted with nature in Africa and the resulting high disease burden. It has included an analysis of the impact of the most serious epidemic, HIV/Aids, on the continent and examined the impact of modern medicines (that partly obviate the requirements for functioning basic infrastructure), poorly designed health systems and a lack of state capacity.

It is quite likely that we underestimate the relationship between health and economic growth, and in Chapter 16 I compare the impact of the Improved Health scenario with others. One study found that a one-year increase in life expectancy could be associated with a four per cent increase in GDP.[39] And the UN Economic Commission for Africa (Uneca) found that the impact of the Ebola epidemic had reduced the GDP of Guinea, Liberia and Sierra Leone by between two and five per cent compared to the Current Path.[40]

All this is to say that it is imperative to design health programmes that extend well beyond the health sector itself. In Africa, providing basic infrastructure such as WaSH facilities and electricity reduces the impact of diarrhoeal and vector-borne diseases, as well as the respiratory harm caused by indoor use of traditional fuels such as dung and charcoal. There is also a role for the international community, although installing taps and toilets has historically not been as attractive to donors (and sometimes governments) as, say, eliminating river blindness, but it would have a tremendous impact on livelihoods on the continent.

Demographic growth and technological change can work in Africa's favour, but deferring action will be extremely costly. Delays in urban planning will only result in larger and more dangerous unplanned urban spaces. In addition to provision for roads, railways and ports, urban planning in Africa must emphasise the provision of basic infrastructure such as clean water, improved sanitation facilities and electricity as well as increasing access to, and the general quality of, health and education services.

Africa's health systems are desperately trying to battle, simultaneously, the world's worst communicable disease burden, rising rates of non-communicable diseases and rapid increases in road deaths, personal violence and drug abuse. This is a complex challenge with many moving parts, but a better understanding of the trade-offs in health policy versus investments in providing basic WaSH infrastructure should lead to improved outcomes.

Against this background, improvements in education – the subject of the next chapter – may be among the most important drivers of better health in much of Africa, among its various other obvious benefits. In addition to the role played by education in preventing the spread of communicable diseases such as HIV/Aids, awareness programmes can contribute greatly to communicating the benefits of good hygiene. Such programmes can also instil healthy, lifelong habits around exercise and good eating, which could help to prevent or at least delay the onset of expensive lifestyle diseases such as Type 2 diabetes and heart disease.

5

Rejuvenating education

Education is the most powerful weapon which you can use to change the world.

— Nelson Mandela[1]

Education lies at the foundation of human development and self-attainment. It enables us to lead a self-determined existence, to increase professional performance, and to improve our health. It is the reason why successful modern societies are called knowledge societies.

Education and prosperity go hand in hand. Whereas the average number of years of adult education in low-income countries is just below five, in lower-middle-income countries it is more than seven, in upper-middle-income countries it is almost nine, and in high-income countries it is twelve.

The accepted economic wisdom is that investments in education increase the talent in the labour pool, raise productivity, and boost economic growth and incomes. Let's refer to this as a supply-side model in which parents, governments and others invest in education in the firm belief that it will improve the chances of well-paying jobs for their children (and themselves) and generally a better quality of life.

A study by economists Eric A Hanushek and Ludger Woessmann found that each year of additional schooling is associated with a nearly 0.6 per cent increase in long-term GDP growth rates.[2] And many studies have linked the economic boom in the United Kingdom and the US after the Second World War to the advent of mass public education before the First World War.[3]

But could it not be equally plausible that a growing economy could require and therefore incentivise education? In other words, that demand drives could improve education outcomes? According to this line of reasoning, the potential for better employment drives educational improvements above a certain basic level. China, for instance, only introduced the Law on Nine-Year Compulsory Education in 1986, at which point the Chinese economy was already averaging more than ten per cent growth per annum. At that point, compulsory education could build on adult literacy rates of roughly 72 per cent.[4]

So, beyond basic literacy and primary education (the two generally go together), do subsequent improvements in levels of education precede or follow development? And exactly what type and level of education would Africans require for a future characterised by digitisation and the fourth industrial revolution? What needs to be done and what is practically possible to improve education?

To this end, Wolfgang Lutz[5] and others argue that the concept of the demographic dividend explored in Chapter 3 misses the point. 'The demographic dividend,' they argue, 'is in fact an education dividend.' Their view is that even in South Korea, 'basic education expanded massively among young cohorts before economic growth took off with double-digit rates in the late 1960s.'

History tells both supply and demand stories. Generally, literacy and primary-school education are requirements to graduate from low- to middle-income status. However, whereas in Europe and the US rising levels of education foreshadowed development, in Asia improvements in education beyond primary-school levels generally accompanied more rapid economic growth.[6] In the two decades between 1960 and 1980 the East Asia and Pacific region increased the number of average years of education of its adult population by about 80 per cent, and GDP per capita growth tracked closely at about 85 per cent.

However, in the following two decades (from 1980 to 2000) GDP per capita more than doubled, from about US$3 500 per person in 1980 to about US$7 700 per person. Over the same period the number of average years of education in the adult population increased by just one-third. Of course, coming off a higher base it is not as easy to maintain the previous momentum of improved education as levels approach saturation (or 100 per cent). But could it not also be that educational requirements for the region had largely been met in the first phase of growth, and that the education being provided may not have been well suited to the requirements for further growth?

In practice, the demand model of education therefore complements the supply-side model, but the latter is clearly the more important of the two. In the supply model, educationalists, governments and parents invest in core knowledge and competencies (traditionally termed reading, writing and arithmetic) and complement that core knowledge by trying to anticipate where more specific opportunities lie. In this way the system generally eliminates the problem of a possible time lag in the provision of education by ensuring that supply is readily available.

Instead of (only) trying to forecast what the economy will require, the educational system also needs to respond to job requirements set by the economy, hence the importance of demand. What is in demand today could, of course, change completely by the time students graduate. And in the 21st century demand is changing with each passing decade.

The complexity and level of sophistication of the economy also play a role. In general, all economies require a better-skilled and more highly educated workforce over time. Therefore, going up the technology ladder towards greater productivity requires constant improvements in knowledge levels. Hence the global trend for a decrease in the demand for unskilled labour towards more semi-skilled and skilled labour. But countries that specialise in the production and export of unprocessed commodities do not require a particularly skilled workforce and generally evidence a low-productivity economy.[7]

Furthermore, skilled labour and capital also tend to flow from poorer to richer countries rather than the other way around.[8] This is part of the story of the African brain drain, in which well-educated Africans such as nurses, doctors and engineers often seek employment in high-income countries. In fact, recent data from Afrobarometer confirms that sub-Saharan African nations account for eight out of the ten fastest-growing international migrant populations since 2010, although most migrate within the continent rather than to Europe or North America.[9] This steady exodus means that Africa's education systems need to work twice as hard.[10]

While advancing the average number of years of education in the adult population can give a substantial boost to GDP over the long run, improving the general level of education takes time and the returns take even longer to materialise. A study by the Education Policy and Data Center[11] found that it could take 150 years, or seven generations, to move from 10 per cent adult primary-school completion to 90 per cent secondary-school completion. The average for the countries in the group was nearly 90 years.

At the same time, the example of South Korea demonstrates that rapid progress is possible. Following the devastating Korean War (1950–1953), which split the country into two, a period of rapid economic growth known as the 'Miracle on the Han River' saw mean years of education triple from four years in 1960 to more than 12 years in 2015. By this point, South Korea had caught up with established Western democracies such as the UK and surpassed others such as Sweden. It also included 42 consecutive years of exceptional primary enrolment rates and affirming the importance of getting the foundation right as part of an investment in the future.

Primary education and literacy are therefore prerequisites for economic growth, even at low levels of development. As countries graduate to middle-income status, the educational system needs to provide additional skills and knowledge that responds, in part, to the anticipated future demand.

Recent education trends in Africa

Effective education requires four key ingredients: students who are sufficiently nourished, stimulated and cared for, effective teaching (through professional support, among other things), skilled management and a government and education system that pulls all of this together. Many countries in sub-Saharan Africa do not have these four key ingredients and face a crisis in education, described by the World Bank as a 'low-learning trap'.[12] It is possible to escape from this trap, as shown by South Korea, China and Vietnam, but it requires a tremendous effort, large amounts of funding, political leadership, whole-of-society engagement and the use of modern technology.[13]

The negative consequences of Africa's two recent lost decades during the 1980s and 1990s are difficult to overestimate. Rather than experiencing sluggish growth, Africa experienced a decline in gross domestic income per capita of about 12 per cent between 1980 and 1990 and another two per cent during the 1990s before rebounding by about 30 per cent in the first decade of the 2000s.

During this period, the continent also suffered stagnation or, in some instances, a relative decline in education compared to other regions. During the 1960s and 1970s adults (defined as over 15 years of age) in sub-Saharan Africa were on average better educated than people in South Asia, by a margin of nearly half a year of schooling. By 1995 South Asia had closed the education gap and by 2018 it had surpassed sub-Saharan Africa by almost a year and a half. In 2018 adults in South Asia could expect to receive about seven years of education compared to just 5.6 years in sub-Saharan Africa. Again, while things are improving in Africa they are improving at a slower rate than elsewhere.

This growing divergence in education between Africa and the rest of the world is driven by a number of factors relating to rates of economic growth, policy and government expenditure on education, among others. For the purposes of this chapter, three considerations are particularly relevant. The first is the massive annual influx of more and more children into educational systems that are already struggling to deal with a large number of children and often an inefficient use of resources. This challenge underlines the importance for Africa to accelerate its demographic transition, as discussed in Chapter 3. The second consideration is the inability of many African countries to retain students within the education system, that is, to enable them to progress from one grade to the next and not leave school. The third is about the quality of education, which is discussed separately below.

To understand the challenge of retaining children in school, the education system can be viewed as a long funnel, with various cracks and fissures along the way. Children enter the system at the wider end and graduate with a tertiary or equivalent education at the other end, where the funnel is at its narrowest.

The inevitable goal of educational systems is to increase the pass rates or number of graduates further along in the funnel. Once the funnel has become a straight pipeline with no constraints, we would have a perfect system in which students enter at one end and progress without any leakage to the end.

To this end, policy-makers should first focus on the wide mouth of the funnel in order to maximise primary enrolment and completion rates. In other words, more students should be given the opportunity to progress further along the system past primary to lower and upper secondary level. This will expand the number of students and therefore the width of the funnel, although cracks and fissures will still result in 'leaks' that reduce the progression from one level to the next.

Leaks (pupils who leave the educational funnel) have a knock-on effect. It becomes more difficult to improve outcomes at a certain level if there has been a substantial reduction in the number of students who entered that level compared to the number who completed the previous level, since improvements will require much greater success rates from a smaller pool of students.

As shown in Table 5.1 below, sub-Saharan Africa has a significantly leakier school education funnel than other regions, such as East Asia and the Pacific or North Africa, where the situation is generally better than in other parts of the continent. The situation at tertiary level (not shown) is significantly worse.

	PRIMARY		LOWER SECONDARY		UPPER SECONDARY	
	Enrol-ment	Com-pletion	Enrol-ment	Com-pletion	Enrol-ment	Com-pletion
Sub-Saharan Africa	102	75	57	43	37	29
East and SE Asia	105	103	99	94	87	73
Middle East and North Africa	105	101	96	82	76	64
Latin America and Caribbean	106	105	105	83	81	63
South Asia	108	97	86	61	61	41

Table 5.1: Progress through the education funnel (gross percentages), 2018[14]

The percentages used in Table 5.1 are so-called gross enrolment numbers and can be quite misleading if not placed in context. Gross enrolment rates include all students in a grade irrespective of whether they are at the appropriate age or not. Students who are over-age, including students who are repeating the grade, would therefore also be included in the gross rate. The result is that percentages are sometimes above 100 per cent.

Had I used the net figure, it would have included only students at the appropriate age. For example, the gross enrolment rate for primary school in sub-Saharan Africa in Table 5.1 is 102 per cent but the net primary enrolment rate (not shown in the table) is only 69 per cent, indicating that a large number of children who are supposed to be in school are not, and that the classes are generally crowded by older children. Crowded classrooms have a variety of negative consequences that range from more students per teacher to insufficient desks, books and equipment.

The completion rate is the percentage of students who successfully complete, for example, primary school (75 per cent in sub-Saharan Africa). It represents the ratio between the number of students completing an education level and the number of children or youth in the population at large who are at the expected age to have done so.[15]

Table 5.1 shows the acute drop in completion rates, from 75 per cent for primary to a mere 29 per cent for upper secondary, in sub-Saharan Africa. It is therefore clear that the educational funnel narrows very rapidly in sub-Saharan Africa.

Furthermore, educationalists generally distinguish between official enrolment and school attendance rates and numbers. Table 5.1 uses the former. Attendance rates are sourced by asking households directly, as opposed to using information pulled from official registration data. In the majority of poor countries enrolment rates are significantly higher than attendance rates, as many children who are officially enrolled do not regularly attend school.

Another set of statistics that is used to measure the general level of education in a country looks at the mean level of education of adults. Figure 5.1 presents the mean years of education for each of Africa's five regions in 2018 and compares the figures with those for South and North America. It includes the situation in 2018 and the Current Path forecast for 2040 for each region. The comparison is done for the age group 25 years and older.

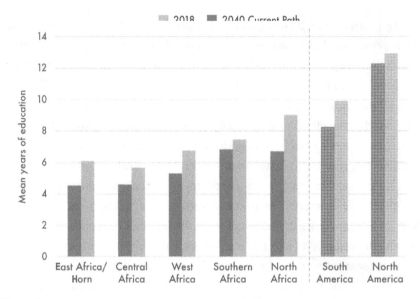

Figure 5.1: Mean years of education (25+ age group)[16]

Currently, East Africa/Horn is the region with the lowest level of educational attainment, but it overtakes Central Africa by 2040, with Seychelles, Mauritius and Kenya doing particularly well. Southern Africa presently has the highest levels of adult education but will be overtaken by North Africa by 2040.

The main reason for Southern Africa's slow rate of improvement is that levels of adult education in South Africa are forecast to remain stagnant while those in Angola could even deteriorate slightly. This forecast for South Africa, the economic giant in the region, is alarming as the country will soon find itself in a demographic sweet spot for growth with a ratio of 1.9 working-age persons to dependants (as discussed in Chapter 3).

South Africa is often used as an example of how to get things wrong. Bad policies, poor governance and corruption in the governing African National Congress (ANC) have kept South Africa from benefiting from its remarkable transition from apartheid. The country is forecast to grow slowly, and slow growth translates into limited revenues to invest in education. The rush to apply imported educational models with limited regard for the local context (such as outcomes-based education), instead of focusing on getting the basics right, means that the country has progressed significantly below its potential.

For two decades after Nelson Mandela was elected president in 1994, the country served as a guinea pig for educational experimentation. For example, the early dismantling of the country's distinctive teacher-training colleges in favour of teacher training at universities dealt teacher education a blow from which it is only now starting to recover. In addition, there was the extensive unionisation of the teaching profession, which has resulted in a situation in which union leadership now practically run schools and determine policy. Effective systems such as independent inspections have been dismantled in favour of self-regulation (ie, by the unions). There have been signs of progress recently, but that is little consolation to a population that was expecting more.

Comparing education in Africa with other regions

At this point, no region in Africa is on a par with average levels of education in South America, and only North Africa will probably surpass South America's 2018 level by 2040. This does not present a pretty picture.

The contrast with average levels of adult education in North America, which was already at above 12 years in 2018, is even more stark. Whereas the average adult in North America has completed upper secondary school, the average adult in three of Africa's five regions does not currently have the equivalent of primary schooling.

The levels of education in Africa among young people aged 20–29 years are often much higher than those of their parents. Africa therefore also has a large intergenerational gap. The literacy and education rates for the youngest population group in poor countries can be up to three times higher than for the oldest population group.[17]

These large differences in outlook and expectations inevitably translate into discontent and even violence. A prime example is the Arab Spring in North Africa, in which the protests were generally led by younger, well-educated groupings, many of whom were unable to find jobs or other opportunities in economies stifled by state bureaucracy and social conservatism.

The gap in adult educational attainment between Africa and other developing regions is set to widen on the Current Path. By 2030, IFs forecasts that people in South Asia will receive about eight full years of education while people in sub-Saharan Africa will get only about 6.2 years.

This widening gap is also evident in Figure 5.1, where Africa's five regions are compared to North and South America.

This trajectory means it is highly unlikely that Africa will be able to meet the primary education target of the SDGs. Target 4.1 is for all girls and boys to have access to 'free, equitable and quality primary and secondary education', as measured by a minimum proficiency in mathematics and reading.[18] In fact, in the Current Path forecast only about two-thirds of African citizens will complete primary school in 2030 while just half of the continent's population will complete lower secondary school.

The low quality of education in Africa

According to Hanushek and Woessmann,[19] there is a stronger correlation between educational *quality* and economic growth than between educational *quantity* and growth. This makes intuitive sense, as attending class does not automatically guarantee that one will learn something!

It is therefore not only the quantity of schooling, as measured by mean years of education at various age levels, that is important but also the quality of education. According to Hanushek and Woessmann, 'expanding school attainment, at the centre of most development strategies, has not guaranteed better economic conditions. What's been missing,' they write, 'is . . . ensuring that students actually learn.'[20] Fortunately, a number of international standardised tests that have been developed in recent years help to systematically measure learning outcomes at primary- and secondary-school level across countries and have been incorporated into the IFs forecasting platform.[21] The result is that it is possible to include changes in education quality in the scenario that follows.

We know that learning starts slowly in poor countries where pre-schooling is mostly nonexistent. In poor countries, even students who make it to the end of primary school often do not master basic competencies. Research has found that the average primary-school student from a low-income country would be singled out for remedial attention on the basis of being below standard should he/she attend primary school in a high-income country![22]

In sub-Saharan Africa, less than half of students meet the minimum proficiency threshold that is used in the standardised testing, whereas the mean for developed countries is at 86 per cent.[23] Or, to put that in comparative context, when it comes to learning outcomes 'the top-performing country in sub-Saharan Africa has a lower average score than the lowest-performing country in Western Europe'.[24] It is therefore not surprising that the World Bank warned in 2017 of a 'learning crisis in global education'.[25] The report presented an analysis of reading, mathematics and science outcomes, with the results for sub-Saharan Africa making disheartening reading.

Although school attendance is generally good in the region, many children suffer from illness, malnutrition or income deprivation. Since teachers are often not particularly well educated themselves, the quality of teaching is poor, while absenteeism among teachers is rife. Many pitch up at school but then don't attend to the class they are supposed to teach. Some even engage in a second (or third) job to support themselves and their families. Since schools are short-staffed, those teachers who do attend to their duties are inundated with administrative tasks.[26]

For the World Bank, the immediate causes of the crisis are fourfold: children arrive unprepared to learn (generally children from poor households learn much less); teachers often lack the skills or motivation to teach effectively; inputs often fail to reach classrooms or to affect learning; and poor management and governance often undermine schooling quality.

Rates of gender exclusion

Advancement towards gender parity in education – bringing the number of female students participating in a given level of education closer to the number of male students at the same level – is an important milestone on the road to improved education.

In sub-Saharan Africa, gender parity in education has improved over time but still trails behind regions such as the Middle East and North Africa. In sub-Saharan Africa the average woman aged 25 years and above has received about 4.6 years of education, compared to 5.8 years for every male. The gap is slightly smaller when extending the cohort to women and men aged 15 years and above, where the mean is at 5.2 years versus 6.1 years, again indicating the extent to which younger Africans are much better educated than their parents.

The global mean for years of female education stands at 7.8 years – a goal sub-Saharan Africa will achieve only in 2052 on the Current Path, at which point the global average will likely have increased to more than ten years. Again, on the Current Path there is no indication of Africa closing this gap under current conditions. Improving levels of educational attainment is a slow process. For example, it took sub-Saharan Africa 14 years, from 2001 to 2015, to increase the average number of years of education of women by one year.

In 2015 in sub-Saharan Africa, 95 girls attended primary school for every 100 boys, a ratio that worsens significantly at secondary-school level (only 90 girls for every 100 boys) and decreases to 73 women for every 100 men who enrol in tertiary education. In four countries (Liberia, the DRC, Mozambique and Niger), adult women have less than half the mean years of education of males.

In South America, the average woman aged 25 and older will have received about the same number of years of education as her male counterpart, while in East Asia, Central Asia and Europe the gap between the mean for male and female levels of education varies between about 0.9 and 0.97 years. So, in these regions women still get less education than men but are rapidly approaching equality. Of the regions explored in this book, only women in South Asia (with a gap of 2.6 years between the mean for men and that for women) face higher barriers to educational attainment. Given the link between female education and fertility, this large difference to a great degree explains Africa's very high fertility rates, as discussed in Chapter 3.

It is clear that it will be very difficult to build enough schools, educate enough teachers, and make large enough investments in the associated infrastructure for sub-Saharan Africa to catch up with the global averages, but something must be done. More of the same will not do the trick.

Before I proceed to the development of an improved education scenario and an analysis of its associated impact, we must first ask ourselves what Africa's future students need to be prepared for.

Africa's future education requirements

A recent study from the African Development Bank found that three main factors constrain more rapid job creation in Africa. First, job creation has not kept pace with the number of graduates from secondary and tertiary institutions. Second, those who finish school are not equipped with the skills required in the available jobs. Finally, young people generally lack the soft skills, social networks and professional experience to compete with older job applicants.[27]

In a study on the future of work in Africa, the Accra-based African Center for Economic Transformation is more specific:

> There is far too little emphasis on relevant training in science, technology, engineering, and math; on technical and vocational education and training; and on higher-order cognitive and analytical skills. Hence, the considerable skills mismatch, with most job seekers lacking the skills that employers require. They may have good paper qualifications but not 4IR [fourth industrial revolution] skill sets.[28]

We will see in later chapters that education in Africa needs to respond to the demand to expand smallholder farming and agribusinesses (Chapter 6), which will allow African countries to enter low-end manufacturing (Chapter 9) and prepare for the rapid expanded use of modern systems and technologies (Chapter 11) as digitisation and the fourth industrial revolution present new opportunities and risks for the future. Generally, the trend is away from a demand for low-skilled labour and towards skilled labour. In fact, in some countries, such as South Africa, the demand for unskilled labour is actually declining.

These requirements differ from country to country and defy easy generalisation. At a broad level, education must equip students with the skills to lead healthy, productive and meaningful lives. As the authors of the 2018 World Bank report on education explain, this means students should for instance know 'how to interpret many types of written passages – from medication labels to job offers, from bank statements to great literature':[29]

> They have to understand how numbers work so that they can buy and sell in markets, set family budgets, interpret loan agreements, or write engineering software. They require the higher-order reasoning and creativity that builds on these foundational skills. And they need

the socioemotional skills – such as perseverance and the ability to work on teams – that help them acquire and apply the foundational and other skills.

The modern trend appears to be towards broader sectoral training, which includes a set of generic business and life skills rather than preparation for a specific job such as being a welder, carpenter or chef. This allows the individual to move more readily from an entry-level job to a longer-term career. In the future, jobs will require ever-higher levels of education and expertise across all sectors, including information technology, security, health care and professional services – and for all types of professions, ranging from administrative assistants and project managers to nurses.

The recent report from the Global Commission on the Future of Work, an initiative of the International Labour Organization (ILO), refers to 'a universal entitlement to lifelong learning that enables people to acquire skill and to reskill and upskill'. Since the world of work 'begins at home', the authors also emphasise the importance of strengthening women's voice and leadership in addressing gender equality and the rural economy, 'where the future of many of the world's workers lies'.[30]

African educators should also balance the need for academic education with vocational training. For example, the 2018 *World Development Report* devotes considerable attention to the need to replicate successful job skills training programmes and the extent to which most Africans aspire to academic versus technical training.

In addition to advocating for technical and vocational training as a parallel education stream from secondary school onward, the World Bank recommends workplace training and short-term job training programmes.[31] It finds that informal apprenticeships are most common in sub-Saharan Africa and offers examples from Benin, Cameroon, Côte d'Ivoire and Senegal where they account for almost 90 per cent of the training that prepares workers for craft jobs, as well as for employment in some trades.[32]

Modern Germany offers valuable examples of teaching innovation. One of the most widely acclaimed German practices is the country's vocational training system at secondary-school level and the partnership that has been established, in law, between small and medium-sized companies on the one hand and publicly funded vocational schools on the other. The system culminates with a certificate issued to the student by a competent body – a chamber of industry and commerce or a chamber of crafts and trades – in around 330 occupations requiring formal training in Germany. This is a win-win partnership of employers, unions and government.[33]

However, what works in highly formalised and developed Germany will not work in most of Africa, where a large part of the economy is informal. In addition to many other challenges, the low quality of education in most sub-Saharan countries means that students may also not have fully mastered the foundational skills of reading, writing, numeracy, critical thinking and problem-solving that are required before entering the vocational training stream. In its 2018 report the World Bank refers to this as 'not just a lack of trained workers; it is a lack of readily trainable workers'.[34] But, still, digitisation and the fourth industrial revolution will require a large cadre of technical skills, and the poor quality of general schooling in Africa implies that great care must be taken to ensure that students who do choose this vocational line of education have sufficient grounding.

Vocational careers are crucial for the future and need to become part of the educational mainstream in Africa. For this reason the scenario that is modelled in the next section includes, among other interventions, an increase in the proportion of vocational to academic students.

Modelling the impact of improved quality, quantity and nature of education across gender: The Rejuvenation in Education scenario

This section sets out the interventions within the IFs modelling platform that represent aggressive but reasonable improvements in the quantity, quality and nature of education across gender in Africa. It measures the impact on various indices of human well-being, including on growth rates, the size of economies, average incomes and inequality. I go on to compare the Rejuvenation in Education scenario with the Current Path.

A first set of interventions improves the throughput along the entire education funnel. It increases intake (or enrolment), survival and graduation rates at primary, lower secondary, upper secondary and tertiary levels, as well as the transition rates between these various levels of schooling. The improvements are staggered over time so that improvements at the next level can build upon that more solid foundation, in line with the presentation of education as a funnel that was used earlier in this chapter.

Next, I improve gender parity in education to achieve rates close to those in East Asia and the Pacific by 2050. A third set of interventions improves the quality of education at primary and secondary levels by about two percentage points above the Current Path by 2040.

The final set of interventions is designed with an eye to skills requirements for the future. This is achieved by boosting the ratio of vocational to academic students in secondary school and the share of science and engineering students at tertiary level.[35]

There are many different ways to measure the impact of the combined Rejuvenation in Education scenario on levels of education. Figure 5.2 compares the mean years of education for adults aged 20 to 29 years of age for the same regions used in Figure 5.1.

Whereas Figure 5.1 used adults over the age of 25, Figure 5.2 is for the age cohort 20–29 years. Once again, I compare the situation in 2018 with the Current Path forecast for 2040, and then add a third column consisting of the forecast from the Rejuvenation in Education scenario for Central, East/Horn, West, Southern and North Africa. These are compared to the situations for South and North America.

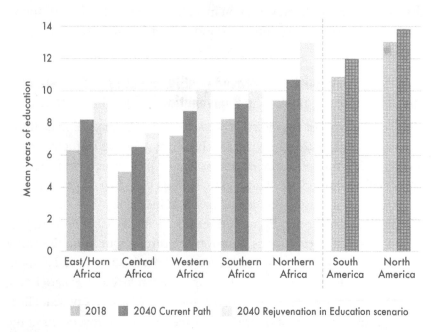

Figure 5.2: Mean years of education for 20-29-year age cohort, 2018 and 2040, for Current Path and Rejuvenation in Education scenarios[36]

The improvements occur across all regions, but with Southern Africa showing the least improvement. By 2040 levels of education for this cohort of young adults are roughly similar for West and Southern Africa while North Africa shows particularly strong growth, surpassing the average for South America by 2040.

The impact of the Rejuvenation in Education scenario is to increase expenditure on education from 5.7 per cent of GDP in the Current Path forecast in 2030 to 5.9 per cent. By 2040 the difference between the Current Path and the Rejuvenation scenarios is 0.4 per cent of GDP. This may not appear to be much but it equates to US$13 billion of additional investment in education in 2030 and US$43.5 billion more in 2040.

These are totals across all levels, primary, secondary and tertiary. Cumulatively, Africa would be required to spend an additional US$340 billion on education from 2020 to 2040. That's a lot of money, but these additional costs are, in time, offset by improvements in the human capital endowment – or, more simply put, as the level of skills improves, Africa's economies start to grow more rapidly and this increase in economic growth accelerates over time.

The average difference in the GDP growth rate is 0.156 percentage points by 2030 (leading to an additional US$30 billion in that year) and 0.38 percentage points by 2040 (an additional US$253 billion in that year). In short, from 2020 to 2040 the Rejuvenation in Education scenario will add a cumulative total of US$1.38 trillion to Africa's economy.[37]

Therefore, through the spending of an additional US$340 billion on education the African economy will by 2040 have increased by US$1.38 trillion. By 2040 average levels of GDP per capita (in PPP) will increase by US$78 per person in low-income Africa, by US$255 for lower-middle-income Africa and by US$380 in upper-middle-income countries. That is an awesome return on investment.

For the first five years or so, primary education receives the largest boost in expenditure, but since primary education levels are close to saturation point, the increased spending soon shifts to lower secondary, then to upper secondary, and eventually tertiary education receives the bulk of increased spending. In fact, by 2040 Africa should have spent about US$15.7 billion *less* on primary education, US$5.9 billion *more* on lower secondary education, US$12.2 billion *more* on upper secondary education, and US$41 billion *more* on tertiary education.

Just imagine the impact if the countries of Africa could simultaneously reduce the size of the annual influx of primary-school children by appropriate family planning interventions, as set out in Chapter 3. Reductions in the number of children entering primary school would soon cascade through the entire education system, meaning more funds could be spent on the smaller cohort of children as they progress from primary to secondary and eventually tertiary levels. In this manner, the Demographic Dividend and Rejuvenation in Education scenarios could reinforce one another in a very powerful way.

Furthermore, improved levels and quality of education would have a small positive effect on reducing inequality (using the Gini index) and would reduce extreme poverty by about 29 million people in 2040 (using the US$1.90 per person extreme poverty threshold).

The Rejuvenation in Education scenario could have a massive impact. But the results will not be achieved without great effort and new ways of thinking. On the one hand, Africa needs to get the basics right. On the other, the sheer magnitude of the challenge requires a very rapid uptake of modern technology to help compensate for deficits in teacher quality and numbers.

From basics to technology

The introduction of tax-funded and generally compulsory primary education in Prussia during the late 18th and early 19th centuries for boys and girls from the age of five laid the foundations for education in the West.[38]

In addition to the basic technical skills, such as reading and writing (mathematics or arithmetic only followed later), the Prussian system served as a basis for the introduction of the Humboldtian (after minister of education Wilhelm von Humboldt) concepts of academic freedom, equality and general knowledge and the subsequent expansion to include compulsory secondary schooling. Its founding concepts are still espoused in 21st-century Germany, and the original philosophy continues to inform education in the West.

Models of education do not change rapidly. Because of colonialism, sub-Saharan Africa has generally followed, and still adheres to, the Prussian model of rote education. This has often been criticised, and rightly so, for being overly rigid and inflexible. But at its core we find the commitment to first teach students how to learn.

In Africa, large classrooms staffed by poorly educated teachers, with the minimum of educational facilities, attended by poor, often hungry children, many of whom have to walk several kilometres every day to school, offer limited policy options. The continent could clearly do with much greater order and a sense of educational purpose, particularly when it comes to improving levels of reading, writing and arithmetic, and teacher attendance, and finding ways to manage the large classes that are typical in so many schools.

We desperately need to find a way to raise the bar, particularly in poorer schools.

Certainly, each African country faces different challenges, but up-skilling teachers and designing teaching and learning methods that are sensitive to local conditions remain central to creating functioning education systems. Against that background, technology in the form of 5G and augmented reality could be the key ingredient to enable the progress modelled in the Rejuvenation scenario.

In just a few years, cellphones, tablets and even computers may all allow three-dimensional holograms as augmented reality becomes com-monplace. Billions of dollars are being spent on research and development by companies such as Microsoft and startups such as Mojo Vision to make all of this practicable. In 2017 spending on education technology invest-ments surpassed US$9.5 billion, up 30 per cent from the year before.[39]

The application of new technologies could replace a teacher in front of a whiteboard (or chalkboard) with apps, gameplay and entirely new ways of teaching. Each student could have an artificial intelligence teaching companion in the cloud that delivers information at the optimal speed for him or her – if the promise of 5G speeds and connectivity examined in Chapter 10 comes to Africa. In this brave new world, students will be able to consume lectures at their own pace, with time in class used for discussing problems or collaborative work.

Instead of students huddling around a teacher in front of an oven to learn how to bake, or around an electric motor to assemble, disassemble and repair it, they will each have their own virtual oven or motor. Using an augmented-reality headset, they will be able to experiment with different ingredients or take the motor apart, study each part, and put it back together – and to do that for any make and model. No one will get hurt and nothing can break (expect for the headset and the data connection). And it can be done at any scale, from large industrial equipment to minute circuitry, and anywhere in the world.

Biology students will be able to dissect virtual animals and view their organs. Medical students will be able to do the same with the human body, while trainee nurses will be able to track blood flow, the digestive system and how muscles work. Already it is possible to use an app to see the workings of the human heart and to study the night sky. Students of history will be able to immerse themselves in Africa's ancient kingdoms, the wars fought in Afghanistan and the construction of the pyramids, guided by their personal artificial intelligence teaching companion.

Augmented reality will make learning more immersive, exciting and effective. It will enable learners in the most isolated and disadvantaged rural areas to see and do things for which they would otherwise never have the opportunity. It is a powerful way to provide individual and flexible learning, connecting theory with the real world. Want to get a child to learn a foreign language or to understand computer coding? Get them to play a game in that language or to experiment with coding.

These advances require vast investments in technology and the minimum in hard infrastructure but could unleash the curiosity that is innate in children and is lost later in life. Einstein famously said, 'I have no special talent. I am only passionately curious.' Curiosity is responsible for all major scientific and technological advances; it is the desire of an individual to understand and explore through experimentation and discovery. In tomorrow's world, understanding technology and coding will be crucial, and augmented reality and artificial intelligence can help us understand computation, sensors, networks, digital printing, genetic engineering and robotics, to name but a few components of that world.

Conclusion: Prioritising education outcomes

At the start of this chapter, I asked what type and level of education Africans generally would require for a future characterised by digitisation and the fourth industrial revolution. What needs to be done to improve education? What is possible?

The chapter has presented a supply-side and demand-side view of the provision of education and found that beyond basic levels of (primary) education and literacy, an education system must evolve to supply many requirements while also being able to respond to changing education demands to help prepare students for future job requirements. The world of work requires more skilled and fewer unskilled workers.

There is clearly a very powerful relationship between citizens' levels of education and the prosperity of nations, but it is quite a complicated one. Duke University educationalist Ricardo Hausmann[40] provides an example:

> In 1998, Ghana's workforce had an average of about seven years of education and its per capita income was about $1 000. When Mexico's workforce first achieved an average of seven years of education – in 1993 – its income was over $10 000, while France's per capita income when its workforce first got to an average of seven years of education (in 1985), was over $20 000. These figures tell us that rich countries are rich not just because of education, and, conversely, that investing in education alone won't make you rich.

Hausmann attributes the ability to translate education and technology into growth to 'collective know-how' – the ability to *apply* knowledge. This, he argues, comes about through imitation and the repetition of tasks – learning by doing. For a country to develop and grow, it needs to provide the opportunity. What he does not examine, however, is the quality of the education provided in Ghana, Mexico and France, and this points to the need to dig deep when considering key relationships.

Our review of the widening gap between education levels and quality when comparing Africa to the rest of the world makes it clear that much more strategic planning, innovation, investment and, most of all, leadership is required to address the continent's education backlog. The picture that emerges from the subsequent review of the general African situation and likely prospects along the Current Path forecast is depressing when compared to the progress being achieved in other regions. Still, it is absolutely crucial to improve the levels and quality of education in

Africa for a more prosperous future. If the continent fails in this dimension, it will fail in all the others.

Education systems are notoriously slow-moving, and those in most African countries particularly so. However, new teaching technologies and methods must be exploited to help meet the challenges of the future.

African countries will not close the gap in average levels of education compared to the rest of the world by using current systems and practices. Technology can fundamentally change the nature of education and enable the move away from brick-and-mortar campuses to electronic or virtual campuses that will facilitate much broader access for both students and teachers.

Finally, it is imperative to find ways to channel many more students towards vocational training programmes, which need to be more broadly integrated into the educational system. The answers here are likely to be found in informal, virtual self-empowerment.

Clearly, children can only be taught if they have enough nutrition, and societies only advance if, beyond basic literacy, there is enough food to feed the nation. This comes from agriculture, the subject of the next chapter.

6

Wanted: A revolution in agriculture

[T]here is no viable alternative to increasing the productivity of
small-scale agriculture if any significant advance is to be made
in solving the problems of absolute poverty in rural areas.
> – Robert McNamara, Nairobi, 1973[1]

Agriculture has been the bedrock of human development, and, in many
ways, farming is the organising principle of civilisation. The clustering
of societies along the great rivers of the world, from the Nile and the
Euphrates to the Yangtze, would not have been possible without the
domestication of animals and the cultivation of crops, which allowed
denser concentrations of people. This historical occurrence, the Neolithic revolution, started more than 12 000 years ago when the pressure
of rising numbers and changed climates forced humans to adapt from
their nomadic hunter-gatherer lifestyle and slowly turn to agriculture to
meet the needs of their growing populations.

The Neolithic revolution led to food being stored in granaries and the
domestication of animals for slaughter, transport and work. It also brought
new infectious diseases, such as tuberculosis, smallpox and measles, due
to the concentration of people in permanent settlements. While this greater
concentration of people did not improve the quality of life for many, it
was key to development.

Hunter-gatherer societies were constantly on the move in search of
food. Farmers, by contrast, needed to remain close to their fields, could
store food surpluses, and generally had more children (in part as a source
of labour but also because many died of disease). Humanity became
sedentary, living in settled villages and towns and practising specialised
methods of cultivation, irrigation and deforestation. They made pots to
preserve foods and developed ways of storing knowledge (writing). Soon
a division of labour followed and communities exchanged goods (trade),

developed rules of property ownership, and learnt how to work metal (the Bronze Age).

None of this would have happened without a secure food supply. In short, food security promotes progress. Without it, meaningful development is difficult, if not impossible, to sustain.

With the notable exception of the Nile River, agricultural development in Africa followed a unique trajectory. Outside of modern-day Ethiopia and some parts of West Africa and the Sahel, the low population density – partly a function of Africa's high disease burden (examined in Chapter 4) – and generally poor soil quality all played a role in constraining agricultural development, although there is some debate as to where and how this took place.

The overall availability of nutrients in soil is initially determined by the nature of the geological parent material, but the parent material in Africa's more ancient soils is poor in nutrients. The most significant exceptions are along great rivers such as the Nile and along the length of the Great Rift Valley in East and Central Africa.[2] And because much of Africa is located in the tropics, with relatively high and stable temperatures and little seasonal change, there is scant relief from the activities of harmful bacteria or disease-bearing animals such as mosquitoes and bats. Africa's high disease burden has kept population levels down compared to other regions in the world.

For these and other reasons, farming seems to have emerged in sub-Saharan Africa several centuries later than elsewhere. One reason could relate to the relative short lifespan of Africa's numerous empires, which all collapsed or were forcibly dismantled by outsiders before the need for organised agriculture could establish itself and spread.[3]

In more recent history, slavery, particularly the Arab slave trade in North and East Africa from the mid-7th century and the Atlantic slave trade from the late 15th century, disrupted agricultural development. Slavery had a devastating impact on the continent, and meant that African societies remained more dispersed and mobile than others. While the Arab slave trade took place over a longer period, it was at least equal to, if not larger than, the Atlantic trade, in which 10 to 12 million Africans were forcibly captured and shipped to the Americas.[4]

In a situation of lawlessness and violence, in which large populations were constantly on the move to avoid capture, agricultural and hence economic development was impossible. With the removal of those of working age, it was often the elderly or disabled who were left behind. In this way, large parts of Africa were denuded of their productive labour force. Farming and herding could therefore not develop in a systematic manner, nor could social, political and economic systems mature to allow for technological and productivity improvements to match those elsewhere.[5]

With the demise of the slave trade from the start of the 19th century, the continuous drain of labour ended. However, it was soon replaced by other forced labour schemes as imperialism and colonialism took its toll. During the Berlin Conference of 1884–1885 Africa was divided between various European states. The continent soon became an increasingly important source of raw materials for the economies of Great Britain, Germany, Belgium, France, Italy, Portugal and Spain. Trade networks linked Africa's agricultural exports to the demands of the colonisers in Europe. These exports had to be supplied at the lowest possible price. Since labour costs were the most important cost consideration, it comes as no surprise that Africans generally received poverty wages on the sprawling colonial farms on which they worked.

Another development was that crops were grown that were unsuited to local conditions and often had disastrous consequences for local economies, for example the raw cotton that was cultivated in West Africa, Angola and Mozambique. Crops such as peanuts and sesame replaced dietary staples such as millet and sorghum. The result was declining food reserves, chronic malnutrition and famine in spite of the development of a sizeable commercial cash crop system (i.e. crops grown for sale rather than for consumption by the farmer) dominated by settler farmers.

With such a firm focus on exports, Africa's colonial infrastructure was oriented towards the coast and from there to markets in Europe. Consequently, the rural and domestic agricultural sector was either destroyed or remained economically marginal.

Despite their relatively short duration, slavery, imperialism and colonialism fundamentally altered agricultural development on the continent. They effectively destroyed intra-African trade and displaced a host of indigenous crops with foodstuffs that were only useful for the industrialising economies in Europe.

Effectively, Africa was forced to export more and more commodities that became worth less and less as the terms of trade (the ratio of export prices to import prices) steadily declined over the long term. According to one estimate, Africa's terms of trade in 1940 had reverted to those it had enjoyed more than a century previously, in 1800, as the continent became poorer compared to all other regions of the world.[6]

After independence

Independence brought many benefits, but few accrued to agriculture. Africa's post-independence leaders generally placed rural and agricultural development at the very end of the queue in terms of resource and budgetary allocation. Production per capita therefore actually decreased from around 1970 and only started to improve some decades later.

In recent years, the continent's average annual agricultural trade deficit (the value of imports minus that of exports) stood at roughly US$100 billion. This is expected to increase to more than US$330 billion by 2030. Agricultural exports remain stagnant while imports increase year on year. By 2040 Africa could be importing more than 30 per cent of its agricultural requirements, which leaves the continent extremely vulnerable to fluctuations in food and other commodity prices. Should a famine occur somewhere in Africa or elsewhere, it will impact on the availability of foodstuffs across the continent.

This dependence on imports is largely the result of low agricultural yields in much of Africa and large post-production losses (the losses that occur between production on a farm and when the produce reaches the consumer). Whereas the average loss and waste of agricultural produce in the rest of the world is roughly 14 per cent, in Africa it is estimated at 25 per cent. In West Africa this rises to more than 30 per cent, meaning that almost a third of food is lost after production. In the developed world most food is simply not consumed but wasted.

It was World Bank president Robert McNamara who, in a famous speech in September 1973 (quoted at the start of this chapter), clearly identified the root of Africa's major problem of rural poverty – the lack of smallholder agricultural development. Having become disillusioned with the US war effort in Vietnam, which he had directed as US Secretary of Defense, McNamara became a passionate advocate for the poor after his appointment to the World Bank in 1968.

McNamara's speech came at a time of relative growth in Africa, although more than 200 million Africans were living in absolute poverty. He pointed out that official development assistance was 'acutely inadequate' to respond to this situation, while government debt was increasing in the worst-affected countries. McNamara advocated for a strategy for rural development with an emphasis on the productivity of smallholder agriculture. By the time he stepped down in 1981, the World Bank had extended its loans threefold.[7] However, the Bank's efforts were scaled down and dismantled after he left, as the focus shifted to other aspects of development.

McNamara's departure coincided with a decline in Africa's fortunes. Income per capita declined from 1980 to 1994 and only returned to its 1980 levels in 2004. Africa was regressing instead of moving forward.[8]

Agriculture today

According to 2016 data from the UN Food and Agriculture Organization (FAO), 17 of the 20 countries with the lowest average cereal yields per hectare are in Africa.[9] At the same time Africa is home to two of the top 12 most productive agricultural sectors in terms of cereal yields. But one of them is tiny Réunion and the other is Egypt, which obviously benefits from having one of the most productive agricultural deltas in the world. After Egypt, the next African state, Madagascar, comes in at 64th position. As recently as 2014 South Africa could be found among the top 40 most productive cereal producers, but the recent drought has pushed the country from the 36th position globally in 2014 to 72nd in 2016.

Despite a few recent success stories – Ethiopia, Madagascar, Mauritania and Sierra Leone all doubled cereal yields between 2000 and 2016 – on the whole the agricultural sector in sub-Saharan Africa is significantly less productive than in other regions. As recently as 1980, agricultural yields in Africa were roughly similar to those in South Asia. But at below four tons per hectare today, average agricultural yields in Africa are two tons below those of South Asia and about one third of South America (see Figure 6.1).

Furthermore, in Africa very little of the land that is under cultivation is irrigated. This means that the vast majority of crop land is dependent on good rainfall, which is increasingly irregular due to the impact of climate change.

Even though agricultural yields per hectare on the continent are improving, the figures reflect a growing gap when compared to averages in the rest of the world. The slow improvement in agricultural productivity in Africa at a time of rapid population growth contributes to the slow rate of poverty reduction. Food security is declining as Africans import larger quantities of food with each passing year.[10]

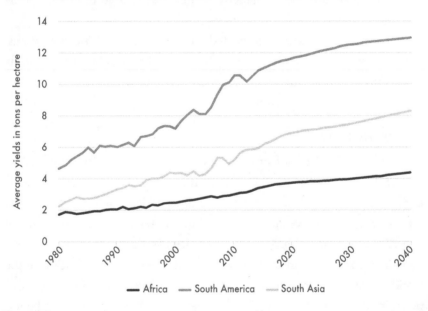

Figure 6.1: Tons per hectare (pre-loss), 1980 to 2040[11]

The contribution of agriculture as a portion of an economy generally declines as countries graduate from low- to middle- and eventually to high-income status. For instance, West Africa has the continent's largest agricultural sector in absolute terms (roughly US$190 billion in 2018 and set to increase to US$226 billion by 2040), but when calculated as a portion of the total economy (ie of GDP), the contribution of agriculture will decline from 24 to 11 per cent.

The Current Path forecast for Central Africa is that the contribution of agriculture to GDP will decline from 22 to 12 per cent from 2018 to 2040. In North Africa agriculture will decline from 17 to 9 per cent, in East Africa/Horn from 32 to 13 per cent, and in Southern Africa from 7 to 4 per cent.

In 2040, however, African economies will be significantly larger than in 2018, with the result that the absolute size of the agricultural sector will, in all instances, also be larger – although only marginally so in Central and Southern Africa.

Obstacles to a revolution in agriculture

According to the World Bank, agricultural markets regularly fail African farmers: the 'pattern of market failures is general and structural, not related to the head-of-household's gender, or to geographic characteristics such as distance to roads or to large population centers'.[12] In other words, African farms are less productive because farmers are chronically unable to access the financial and hence the material inputs that they need.

Take fertilisers, for example. Generally, the soil on the continent is poor in nutrients,[13] and because African farmers use significantly less fertiliser than their counterparts in other regions of the world (prices in Africa are between two and six times the average world price since the continent generally imports fertiliser instead of manufacturing it), soil fertility depletion continues unabated in many countries. Then there is the issue of lack of irrigation, low levels of mechanisation and lack of investment in genetically modified seeds that are more resistant to disease.

African farmers have traditionally followed a practice of land rotation using slash-and-burn practices: they would clear new land and leave the old fields fallow for a year or two to recover. But, as population numbers have increased, shortages of arable land have forced farmers to cultivate the same fields season after season.

A lot of agricultural land is also located in peri-urban areas (for instance in Kenya and Ethiopia) where urban sprawl is driving up land prices and swallowing up some of the best farmland. Elsewhere the absence of infrastructure such as paved roads effectively make arable land economically unsuitable for large-scale production – here the DRC and Angola are two good examples.

The result is that unsustainable cultivation practices in high-density areas are leading to serious soil degradation.[14] Moreover, as average farm size shrinks, the pressure to get more food from less land in order to feed one's family tends to lead to unsustainable farming practices, which further decrease soil fertility.

Traditional farming practices and crops have often been cast aside in favour of more 'sophisticated' techniques, which may work well elsewhere but are poorly suited to Africa's topography. To this end, the Alliance for a Green Revolution in Africa (AGRA) has called for a holistic land management strategy that includes increasing organic matter, moisture retention and other forms of soil rehabilitation in addition to greater use of inorganic fertiliser.[15]

Two findings from the literature on agriculture in Africa highlight its risks and dormant potential.

First, the World Bank notes that 'price risk is the most commonly reported covariate shock, much more so than weather shocks'.[16] Price shocks can come in the form of increases in the cost of inputs such as fertiliser and seeds, a collapse in output prices caused by a change in trade policy or just changes to the prices of other staple goods that influence people's ability to survive.

Second, farmers' inability to access credit and technology, combined with ineffective labour and input markets, makes matters even more complicated.[17] Without access to credit the vast majority of farmers are forced to rely on bumper harvests, which are few and far between and may become increasingly so as the impact of climate change is felt.

The result is that Africa is the most food-insecure region globally. According to a joint statement issued by the World Bank, the FAO, the African Development Bank and the International Fund for Agricultural Development, about 256 million Africans faced undernutrition in 2018.[18] The situation is getting worse in many parts of the continent, the organisations stated, because of the negative effects of climate change on agricultural productivity, natural resource degradation, rapid population growth, increasing fragility and insecurity, and economic stagnation.

Achieving food security

Traditionally, many countries in Africa have had large agricultural sectors but have merely exported raw products without adding much, if any, value. For example, Africa produces 70 per cent of the world's cocoa but is responsible for less than one per cent of chocolate exports. Europe, which grows no cocoa of its own, exported US$19.2 billion worth of chocolate in 2016![19]

Things have started to change, however. Through the Africa Cocoa Initiative, Côte d'Ivoire overtook the Netherlands as the world's largest processor of cocoa during the 2014–2015 season as it moved up the chocolate value chain. And Ghana now processes more than a third of its own cocoa.[20]

But agricultural import dependence is not simply a balance of payments issue. It is also about calories. Hunger, malnutrition and low levels of educational attainment are all well-established causes and symptoms of Africa's underdevelopment and represent significant bottlenecks in the effort to build human capacity and bring about structural economic transformation.[21]

Between 1970 and 1990 Kenya was a net exporter of food, exporting about one per cent of total demand each year. But from 1997 to 2013 the country imported about five per cent of total demand per year. The growing reliance on imported food in Kenya has coincided with a decrease in the number of available calories. In 1980 the average Kenyan had access to about 2 300 calories per day, or about equal to the recommended daily average.[22] By 2000, though, the average Kenyan could expect to access only about 2 000 calories per day, or about 11 per cent less than the recommended allowance.

Insufficient access to calories is a driver of undernutrition and stunting and, together with a lack of access to improved WaSH facilities, can lead to a variety of health problems that force children to fall behind or withdraw from school (discussed in Chapter 4).[23]

If the goal is to transition economies towards higher value-added activities, then a *healthy*, well-educated population is a prerequisite. A lack of access to safe and affordable food can disrupt education and negatively affect other programmes aimed at improving long-term economic productivity.

In order to capitalise on the benefits of having an educated and healthy population, there needs to be an unwavering emphasis on self-sufficiency, as well as on productivity improvements. Herein lies the rub.

The bulk of agricultural production in Africa is already commercially oriented and 'a considerable portion of this market presence is driven by the sale of staple and other food crops, and not necessarily by traditional cash crops'. Furthermore, the World Bank finds 'little evidence of a relationship between increased commercialisation and improved nutritional status'.[24]

Among the few countries to have based their economic development on dynamic small-scale farming are Côte d'Ivoire and Ethiopia, where farming is intensive and efficiently organised. Although estimates differ, agriculture provides a living for about half of the population in Côte d'Ivoire (and up to 70 per cent in Ethiopia) and accounts for an even larger portion of export earnings (84 per cent in Ethiopia).[25] But yields in both counties remain very low by comparative international standards.

It is imperative for African countries to first produce agricultural products for domestic consumption and then to add value to exports. Africa produces about 45 per cent of the world's cashew nuts, yet 90 per cent of that crop is exported for processing overseas. The Africa Cashew Alliance estimates that a 25 per cent increase in raw cashew nut processing in Africa would generate more than US$100 million in household incomes in the sector. As it is, a recent report noted that Tanzania's farmers 'get rock-bottom prices and the country imports its own nuts back after processing to meet buoyant domestic demand'.[26] But like with cocoa efforts to increase prices for raw nuts could actually increase production and collapse prices for processed products, hence defeating the purpose.

The challenge for the future

If African countries prioritise growing staple foods and actively encourage intensive smallholder farming and sustainable practices, that will increase rural incomes, and reduce poverty. This will lead to the much-needed revolution in agriculture that will reduce Africa's agricultural import dependence and improve food security.

A large portion of the continent's labour force is in the informal agricultural sector (a point further explored in Chapter 9). But, instead of increasing employment, improved productivity in the agricultural sector could actually decrease employment, as it inevitably implies a degree of mechanisation. In theory, agro-processing should create more jobs, but this does not always happen.

Furthermore, intensive agriculture is often limited to the periphery of urban centres, ie closer to markets, although road density in Africa is slowly expanding. The implication is that urban growth may constrain the expansion of agriculture.

The potential advantages of agriculture are well known. Boosting the income of farmers helps to stimulate general demand for goods and services in rural areas, which leads to the establishment of new enterprises and the diversification of the economy. This in turn contributes to the broader process of structural economic transformation.[27] Improving agricultural productivity and boosting local demand 'leads to the development of both upstream and downstream activities, the consolidation of value chains and the expansion of agro-industries, which are significant sources of employment and present real opportunities for economic diversification', notes the ILO.[28]

Talking about the importance of agriculture in Africa has been serious business for several decades, but actually *doing* something about it is taken much less seriously. The African Union Development Agency-Nepad – the new name of the Nepad Agency as from 2019 – published its Comprehensive Africa Agriculture Development Programme in 2003, with ambitious goals:

> [T]o allocate at least 10% of national budgets to agriculture, to reach rural growth rates of 6% annually by 2015, integrate and invigorate regional and national agricultural markets, significantly increase agricultural exports, transform Africa into a 'strategic player' in global agricultural science and technology, practice sound environmental and land management techniques, and reduce rural poverty.[29]

The commitment to devote at least ten per cent of national budgets to agriculture and rural development was included in the 2003 Maputo

Declaration that was issued by African heads of state and government and reiterated in the 2014 Malabo Declaration on Accelerated Agricultural Growth and Transformation in Africa. But, according to the FAO, only Malawi has achieved the ten per cent goal, and the average investment is around 2.5 per cent of GDP and declining.[30]

Talk is cheap, and many African governments, NGOs and citizens generally prefer to blame the EU's Common Agricultural Policy for lack of access to its agricultural market instead of looking to the need to focus comprehensively on farming, the production of staple foodstuffs for domestic consumption, advancing regional rather than international trade in agriculture, investing in agriculture research, advancing rural property rights, investing in schooling for agriculture, and generally addressing rural poverty rather than urban elites.[31]

Lessons from elsewhere

A frequently overlooked component of China's success, originating in the monumental reforms enacted by Deng Xiaoping during the 1970s and 1980s, came from rural reforms initiated through the household responsibility system. This transformed the domestic agricultural sector into a market-oriented structure.

The household responsibility system devolved a considerable amount of power to the local level and allowed a far greater level of freedom in selecting which crops to grow and when and to whom they were sold. Land formerly farmed by a collective was contracted to individual households, and with this new responsibility came productivity improvements in the order of 20 per cent above collective-era output.[32]

China subsequently experienced three consecutive decades of steady improvement in agricultural yields. All told, average yields nearly tripled between 1970 and 2013, and this improvement was an important catalyst for economic growth. Meanwhile, the number of available calories per person increased by nearly 70 per cent during the same period. There were some 20 million fewer undernourished children in 2017 than in 1987.

China is not the only large and geographically diverse country to transform its agricultural sector in recent decades. Brazil enjoyed rapid improvements in agricultural production in the decade between 2000 and 2010, and while it has traditionally been a net food exporter, the country improved that position by nearly seven percentage points over this period. Between 1981 and 2016 Brazil more than doubled average cereal yields despite the area of land under cultivation increasing by only about six per cent.

Not only has Brazil's agricultural sector grown in absolute terms but it has also become very diverse. It is the world's largest exporter of both sugar and coffee, second only to the US in soybean exports, and third to the US and Argentina in maize (corn) exports.[33] The genetic tailoring of crops has played an important and often underappreciated role in these changes.

Brazil is now at a stage in development where it can afford to move beyond agricultural production for food security. The country exported approximately 12 per cent more food than it consumed in 2018 and has begun to embrace a 'forest, agriculture and livestock integration' approach to farming that is widely acknowledged to have benefits for both agricultural production and environmental sustainability.[34]

At the other end of the spectrum is Zimbabwe, a country with little food security. In 2005 former president Robert Mugabe famously marked the 25th anniversary of independence by saying, 'We have turned East, where the sun rises and turn our back to the West, where the sun sets.'[35] Like many of his speeches, it was a defence of his disastrous land redistribution programme, which had dealt a huge blow to Zimbabwe's agricultural sector, once the breadbasket of Southern Africa. Instead of implementing a responsible programme of land reform, the ruling Zanu-PF party embarked on a chaotic land grab that eventually destroyed the most productive sector of the country's economy. Between 1960 and 1990 Zimbabwe exported about ten per cent more food than it consumed. By 2018 it was importing close to 26 per cent of total demand.

Modelling a coordinated push on Africa's agricultural sector: The African Agriculture Revolution scenario

A coordinated push in Africa's agricultural sector could unlock profound changes. This scenario, the African Agriculture Revolution, improves average yields in Africa from about 3.7 metric tons per hectare in 2020 to about 5.5 tons per hectare in 2030 and 6.2 by 2040.[36] The scenario also increases the area of land under cultivation of crops by ten per cent between 2020 and 2030, increases land under irrigation by the same percentage, and reduces post-harvest loss by about 15 per cent over the same period.[37]

Globally, irrigated agriculture represents 20 per cent of the total of cultivated land, but it contributes 40 per cent to the total amount of food produced. Sub-Saharan Africa has the lowest proportion of cultivated land under irrigation, at just over three per cent, compared to a global average of 21 per cent.[38] Against this background, the scenario increases the land areas equipped for irrigation by 722 000 hectares by 2040 (around five percentage points).

The impact of the African Agriculture Revolution scenario is impressive. In 2040, Africa will produce a total of 440 million tons of additional food (crops, meat and fish), compared to the Current Path forecast. The scenario drives an increase in the number of available calories per person per day from about 2 600 in 2018 to more than 3 000 in 2040. These available calories help to lower the portion of children suffering from malnutrition by more than one percentage point in 2040, a figure that translates into more than 3.5 million fewer children and a minor reduction in stunting. Finally, it reduces infant mortality by two deaths per thousand live births by 2040.

The African Agriculture Revolution scenario also has major economic impacts. It reduces the number of extremely poor Africans by 128 million people in 2040.[39] GDP per person is US$260 larger in 2040, and there are also impressive aggregate impacts. By 2040 Africa's total economy is about US$387 billion larger than it would otherwise be.[40]

Figure 6.2 compares the size of the agricultural sector by 2040 in the Current Path with the Agriculture Revolution scenario for each of the five regions used in this book. Although the percentage increase is roughly similar, the difference in Central Africa is US$17 billion, in Southern Africa US$26.5 billion, in North Africa US$64 billion, in East Africa/Horn US$62 billion, and in West Africa US$92 billion.

However, these improvements are not a given. Factors that could

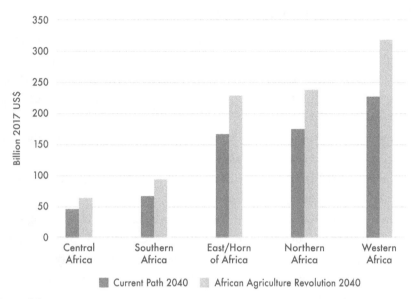

Figure 6.2: Size of agricultural sector in 2040, Current Path vs Agriculture Revolution[41]

impact on their achievability include the utilisation of the water endowment for irrigation and the effect of carbon fertilisation (due to climate change) on crop growth, as well as the possibility of new cultivars and genetically modified organisms that are temperature-tolerant.[42]

The Agriculture Revolution could also – at least temporarily – reverse the long-term declining share of employment in agriculture. More than half of Africa's labour force is engaged in the agricultural sector, although analysts differ about how large such a change would be or how long it would last. For example, a report by the African Center for Economic Transformation finds that boosting agricultural productivity could actually reduce the number of jobs in agriculture.[43] However, the report finds that lowering the costs of raw materials will allow jobs to be created downstream in the much larger agro-processing sector. Productivity improvements could come with upgraded value-chain activities such as logistics, input services, storage and other off-farm activities – all of which will require improved connectivity and basic infrastructure.[44]

The contributions from technology and innovation

When thinking about the future of agriculture (and the improvements modelled in the African Agriculture Revolution scenario), it is important to recognise the rapid improvements that are occurring in this long-neglected sector and the extent to which agriculture is changing all over the world.

Australia, the US and some European nations are experimenting with robotics to remove weeds and harvest crops. A fleet of small robots has even been tested to achieve tasks that were once the domain of large tractors, sprayers and planters.

On high-intensity commercial farms, remote-controlled spraying helicopters are already quite common. Then there is the advent of vertical farming and the fact that in some countries meat will shortly be artificially grown in farming laboratories, or replaced by other, less carbon-intensive products such as soya.

Rather than replacing farm workers, of which there is an abundant supply, agricultural technologies will likely help farmers to reduce inputs such as herbicides, pesticides and fertilisers through greater precision in their use and application. And high-technology devices such as drones could help to inspect fields and monitor herd animals.[45]

While there is a general consensus that inefficient markets and lack of access to credit plague Africa's agricultural sector, the particular ways in which these problems affect farmers vary greatly. Even the World Bank recommends that 'researchers must locate the sources and causes of factor market failures more precisely'.[46] Mobile technology, for one thing, can alleviate the bottlenecks in Africa's credit system and enable farmers to buy farming inputs in a more efficient way.

In Kenya, for example, a company called FarmDrive[47] uses mobile phones, alternative data and machine learning to unlock access to credit for smallholder farmers. This is done, first, by collecting and aggregating various datasets, for instance from individual phone use, social media and agronomic, environmental, economic and satellite data, to produce a credit score for smallholder farmers.

The process involves many incremental steps, such as first determining the exact location of the smallholder farm.[48] Once the location is known on Google Maps, it allows the system to access geospatial information to determine soil quality, weather conditions and market accessibility, and then, using an algorithm, to determine a credit score. It turns out that the best time to engage with farmers is at 10 am (when cows are out grazing), when they have their morning tea and switch on their phones for a while.[49]

Second, FarmDrive offers a decision-making tool that enables financial institutions to develop small-scale agriculture loan products. In this way, the company facilitates a process whereby smallholder farmers can access capital to purchase critical farming inputs such as seed, fertiliser and implements that could increase yields and revenues. In this way, modern technology is opening up opportunities for smallholder farmers that would have been impossible a few years ago. In addition, the services provided by FarmDrive benefit women in particular, as they constitute the majority of smallholder farmers.

In Ghana, Kenya and Uganda, more than 20 000 farms have access to simple and affordable smart insurance contracts (to protect against crop failure or the loss of expensive breeding stock) via their smartphones, using blockchain technology. The system uses high-resolution satellite images to detect rainfall and plant growth data.[50]

The World Food Programme Rural Resilience Initiative (R4) is also helping to implement innovations in finance and insurance to reduce the risk of farming. In 2018, these innovations reached more than 57 000 farmers in Ethiopia, Senegal, Malawi, Zambia and Kenya, helping to increase food and income security by managing climate-related risks.[51] Here, remote sensing by drones can monitor soil moisture content and help to make irrigation systems more efficient. In addition, over the last decade AGRA has invested hundreds of millions of dollars in improved seeds and has doubled maize yields in the 18 countries where it works.[52]

According to the FAO, currently one-third of the world's food (approximately 1.3 billion tons, or US$1.2 trillion a year) is wasted or thrown away. In rich countries, food is generally thrown away by the consumer. In sub-Saharan Africa losses mostly occurs in the distribution process from production to retailing.[53] Using modern technology, it is now possible to reduce losses significantly by tracking inventory and reducing food waste along the chain from farm to retailer or export market. One example is InspiraFarms, which produces affordable, energy-efficient cold storage and processing equipment for on- or off-grid use.[54] Using digital platforms, it is possible to connect smallholders directly to large companies, to provide advice on what, when and where to plant, and to obtain accurate weather forecasts. Companies such as AgroCenta in Ghana and Zenvus in Nigeria are all making a difference in this regard.[55]

Low internet penetration rates and poor access to electricity in rural areas in Africa are the biggest obstacles to applying modern technology in agriculture. However, both these challenges can be overcome by using renewables and the various innovations discussed in Chapter 10.

Conclusion: Aiming at food security and growth

Because cash crops have been prioritised above staple foods, and because of poorly designed and inefficient government support for agriculture, Africa has not been able to seize and exploit the opportunity in this key sector since independence.

There has been some progress, but Robert McNamara's championing of smallholder agriculture remains as valid today as it was in 1973. It is, of course, not only smallholder agriculture that needs to be invigorated but also every level of farming, including medium-scale producers and large-scale commercial farming that is part of export-oriented value chains. Only a comprehensive approach to farming will reverse the trajectory of growing dependence on food imports.

For many African leaders beguiled by the attractions of urban modernity, the challenge of agriculture is that it is simply not politically attractive enough. Furthermore, the direction taken by organisations such as the World Bank has sometimes distracted governments from focusing on agricultural advancement. During the period of structural adjustment programmes (see Chapter 2), there were attempts to reduce the size and scope of government involvement, but agriculture suffered as a consequence. Subsistence agriculture at smallholder level, which largely caters for household consumption, needs targeted and coordinated support from government, which is quite different from the private-sector-led growth model of medium- and large-scale commercial farming.

Yet, with real commitment there is much that can be done, especially by using modern technology. During the production process this includes unlocking access to credit, supporting small commercial farmers, increasing traditional irrigation techniques, using high-yielding varieties and modern inputs such as fertilisers and pesticides, and eventually introducing agricultural machinery to emulate some of the positive aspects of the agricultural revolution (the so-called Green Revolution) in South Asia and South America during the 1950s and 1960s. Such was the success of the Green Revolution in increasing agricultural production that is sometimes referred to as the Third Agricultural Revolution.

The FAO has noted that, over a 25-year time span, the 'maximum attainable yield for rain-fed wheat in subtropical and temperate environments' increased nearly threefold.[56] Globally, cereal yields have nearly tripled since 1961. But the trend of increasing yields may not continue indefinitely, as the effects of climate change are likely to hold significant consequences for agriculture in Africa. Climate change (see Chapter 15) has already contributed to warmer temperatures in the Sahel and a significant drought in southwestern Africa.

Strengthening the supply chain through the direct support of farmers, as well as through investments in infrastructure, transportation and the expansion of the food and packaging industry, could help to substantially reduce food loss and waste in the often-long route from production to consumption.

For a successful agricultural transition, and to expand the local agricultural markets, it is especially important to focus on indigenous crops, such as cassava, cowpea, soybean and yam, as well as on indigenous practices, before looking elsewhere.[57]

The African Agriculture Revolution could potentially have a major impact, ranging from reduced stunting among children and undernourishment among adults to increased incomes and a reduction in poverty. Most importantly, the continent could become less dependent on food imports, with huge attendant advantages.

Challenges such as poor infrastructure, insecure property rights, limiting regulations that prevent investment, lack of access to credit, electricity and modern technologies, and limited labour and capital mobility still plague the agricultural sector. However, all these hurdles can be overcome to a greater or lesser extent by the right kind of leadership, commitment and innovative thinking, and the introduction of modern technology.

To prosper, a country must move up the agricultural value chain. Madagascar, a country that currently survives on exporting unprocessed natural resources such as vanilla and its precious redwood, is also one of the world's poorest nations and is largely dependent on foreign aid. It is one of many examples of what happens when a country does not purposefully pursue the adding of value.

Without adding value to raw products, African countries will also not be able to reduce poverty, which is the subject of the next chapter.

7

Inequality and poverty

For you always have the poor with you . . .

– The Bible, Matthew 26:11

Over the last two centuries the world has witnessed a transition to levels of peace and prosperity that are almost unimaginable by historical standards. Earlier chapters have noted on the remarkable progress in well-being humanity has been able to achieve, but we often don't realise exactly how recent this progress has been.

Until the industrial revolution, poverty was widespread and pervasive. Only a small elite enjoyed decent living conditions. In 1651, Thomas Hobbes famously wrote that, in the absence of a strong central authority (or *Leviathan*, the title of his well-known book), the inevitable inclination of nations is towards civil war, 'where every man is enemy to every man . . . and the life of man, solitary, poor, nasty, brutish, and short'.[1]

The improvement in well-being came off a very low base and accelerated rapidly. Still, even as recently as 1950, three-quarters of the world's population lived in extreme poverty.

During the first half of the past century, *rates* of poverty come down even as global populations continued to increase. Then, from around 1970, the decrease in poverty rates became so rapid that we saw the *absolute number* of people living in extreme poverty also starting to fall in spite of the ongoing and rapid increase in global population.

Until the early 1990s, the number of extremely poor people hovered at above two billion, but from around 1994 it declined precipitously, largely due to rapid progress in China. In the 11 years from 2006 to 2017 the number of people living in extreme poverty actually *halved* to less than 800 million people despite rapid population growth.[2]

These improvements have been so fast that in 2005 the international community was emboldened to adopt a target to halve extreme poverty by 2015 as part of the Millennium Development Goals. In 2015, the goal was set to *end* extreme poverty by 2030. This intention is captured in Goal 1 of the Sustainable Development Goals (SDGs), which refers to 'ending poverty in all its forms everywhere'. Technically, this means that less than three per cent of the population of every country in the world should be living in extreme poverty, using the measure of US$1.90 per person average income.

Because of Africa's rapid population growth, modest rates of economic growth and high levels of inequality, the absolute *number* of extremely poor people in Africa has steadily increased since 1960 and is likely to continue to do so until around 2036 before slowly starting to decline. However, since the early 1990s, the percentage of Africans living in extreme poverty has started to decline. The reason is that even though economic growth in the continent is now slower than before the 2007/08 financial crisis, it is robust enough to reduce the portion of Africans living in extreme poverty, though not enough to reduce the absolute number along the Current Path forecast for the next few decades.[3]

Sadly, Africa will miss the SDG goal of eliminating extreme poverty by 2030 by a very large margin, irrespective of how we define or measure it. In this, the widening gap between Africa and the rest of the world again becomes clear. Things are improving in Africa but much more slowly (and later) than elsewhere.

Globalisation and the sense of relative deprivation

In much of the modern world, globalisation has driven economic growth and played a positive role in the remarkable improvements in human prosperity referred to above. Today, though, the impact is less visible, particularly in high-income countries such us the USA, Japan and Germany.

The pre-financial-crisis period of globalisation appears to have seen a convergence among a group of rich states, the stagnation of middle-income countries and a convergence among poor countries. It is as if hyperglobalisation reached a tipping point with the financial crisis, which temporarily turbocharged income inequality within and between countries.[4]

The last four decades have witnessed steady reductions in income inequality between countries but increases in inequality within countries. In 1975, world income distribution was akin to the two-humped shape of a camel, with one hump (the developing world, particularly Asia and the Pacific) below the international poverty line. The second hump (the developed world) was at considerably higher average incomes. In the subsequent four decades, the poorer countries, particularly in South East Asia, have caught up as the incomes of the world's most poor increased rapidly. The general expectation, which is also reflected in the Current Path forecast, is that global inequality will continue its steady decline but from very high levels, and slowly. Today there is only one hump, as global prosperity has generally improved and incomes have increased.[5]

While the numbers and percentages may tell one story, our interconnected world and access to information seem to have intensified a sense of relative deprivation among large swathes of the global populace, from India and China to the American Midwest and Afghanistan.

In the decade since the 2007/08 crisis, financial benefits seem to have flowed to small urban elites, financial institutions and a handful of large corporations, while little has changed for the middle class. Whatever the reality, the perception is that the poor are getting poorer and the rich richer.

This sense of relative deprivation (that actual improvements in living standards are vastly out of kilter with expectations) is clearly on the rise. In fact, although people in high-income countries have never enjoyed a better standard of living, they seem to feel particularly insecure, scared that they will not be able to maintain their lifestyle and that migrants from poor countries will somehow overwhelm them. The result has been a rise in so-called identity politics in the midst of the most peaceful and prosperous era known to humankind. Ironically, these improvements have largely been created by the very political and market liberalisation that is generally now blamed for creating this perceived increase in inequality.[6]

In spite of the camel now having only one hump, the *sense* is that inequality seems to be expanding between countries, as well as within them. And research by Oxfam underlines the extent to which increases in global wealth largely accrue to the rich.[7] The result is a more turbulent and volatile world in which social protest is becoming the norm, together with a sense that democracy and its various economic underpinnings is not working.

The interplay between inequality and poverty

Economic growth and income distribution (or levels of inequality) are the two key determinants in forecasting national rates of extreme poverty.

As the size of the economic cake grows, there should be more for everyone, even if the division between groups is uneven. Clearly, the more even the distribution of the cake, the more people who will benefit.

So, if economic growth is distributed relatively evenly across a society and takes place more rapidly than population growth, it will raise individual incomes, drawing people out of poverty.[8] In economic jargon this is called 'distribution-neutral economic growth', ie it benefits all people equally and will reduce the percentage of people living in poverty.

However, if the size of the cake does not increase, a more even distribution of the slices could reduce poverty among some, but at some point giving everyone a smaller slice will reach a limit. So, generally the longer the forecast horizon, the greater the contribution made by economic growth relative to income distribution in poverty reduction.[9] A growing economy increases the number of jobs and the amount of money in circulation, and provides more revenue to government to invest in infrastructure, health and education.

The most frequently used measure of inequality is the Gini index, which expresses income distribution from zero to one, with zero corresponding to complete equality (everyone earns the same income) and one to complete inequality (all the income accrues to only one person in society). When comparing regions according to the Gini index, it becomes evident that Africa is quite unequal, and for that reason economic growth does not translate into an equal measure of poverty reduction.

Globally, inequality is worst in Latin America and the Caribbean, followed by sub-Saharan Africa. North Africa is significantly less unequal than sub-Saharan Africa. Southern Africa, where I live, is probably the most unequal region globally and significantly more unequal than Central, West and East Africa/Horn. Levels of inequality in Central Africa, West Africa and East Africa/Horn are all somewhere between the two extremes of relatively low inequality in North Africa and high inequality in Southern Africa.[10]

In fact, inequality in Southern Africa is roughly comparable to that in Latin America, while inequality in North Africa is roughly comparable to that in South Asia. We could therefore expect that economic growth in

North Africa will translate into more substantive rates of poverty reduction than elsewhere in Africa.

That North Africa is so much less unequal than the rest of Africa begs the question of why the Arab Spring would occur in this region and not elsewhere. The reasons, which are explored in greater detail in Chapter 12, come down to the fact that this region has relatively higher levels of education (actually the highest in Africa) and very limited economic, social and political opportunity. Consequently, frustration boiled over.

Countries with low levels of inequality that grow rapidly can translate that growth into extraordinarily rapid reductions in poverty. This is essentially the story of China, although income inequality is also now on the increase in that country.[11] In 1980, China, then a low-income country, had almost a billion people living below US$1.90 daily. By 2018 that number was under two million (less than one per cent of its population) and China had graduated from lower- to upper-middle-income status. Using the US$5.50 extreme poverty line for upper-middle-income countries (pp 34–35), China probably still has more than 300 million extremely poor people.[12] Poverty reduction in India has also accelerated in recent years.[13]

Since the early 1960s, Botswana has consistently grown its economy much more rapidly than Ghana, until very recently. The average growth rate for Botswana from 1961 to 1999 was 10.1 per cent, while for Ghana it was only 2.5 per cent. But because Ghana is significantly more equal than Botswana, poverty reduction in the two countries does not differ as much as one would expect.[14] From 1970 to 1996 poverty came down by 25 percentage points in Botswana and by 14 percentage points in Ghana (using the US$1.90 poverty line).[15] Clearly growth matters, but so do levels of inequality.

The SDGs and measuring extreme poverty

The various goals and targets of the SDGs are described as being 'integrated and indivisible'. Many of them refer to the relationships between economic growth, inequality and decent employment, three of the key factors that determine poverty rates.

SDG Target 8.1, for example, aims for sustained per capita economic growth of 'at least 7 per cent gross domestic product growth per annum in the least developed countries', 34 of which are in Africa. Target 8.5 is about 'full and productive employment and decent work for all women and men'. Target 10.1 commits countries to 'progressively achieve and sustain income growth of the bottom 40 per cent of the population at a rate higher than the national average' and 'to reduce at least by half the proportion of men, women and children of all ages living in poverty in all its dimensions according to national definitions by 2030'.

The SDG goals and targets have led to a global effort to develop the data and associated tools with which the international community can more accurately measure progress. But definitions of poverty differ from country to country, among academics and between agencies. Poverty is closely related to the imbalances in people's opportunities in education, health, level of empowerment and access to technology. It is about much more than just a lack of sufficient income.

In spite of its manifold shortcomings, GDP per capita in purchasing power parity remains the most widely used comparative measure of average standards of living and is often used to make comparisons between countries. It does not take quality of life into consideration, since it is simply a measure of the value of goods and services produced divided by the total population (see Figure 1.1).

Since income is quite a blunt instrument, there have been efforts to flesh out new approaches and definitions. One of these is the Multidimensional Poverty Index (MPI), first mentioned in Chapter 2, developed by the Oxford Poverty and Human Development Initiative and subsequently adopted by the UNDP.[16]

In using GDP per capita, one must be fully cognisant of the fact that poverty in the eastern DRC is quite different from that experienced in Mali or South Africa, for example. Poverty in rural Uganda is also quite different from that in the capital city, Kampala. These imbalances often reflect unequal opportunity. Poverty for men and women also differs sharply, as does poverty experienced by children. Since women tend to be disproportionately responsible for household chores and caregiving, poverty restricts the time that girls can commit to staying in school. It also determines whether families can afford school fees, purchase supplies, or guarantee that their children can attend school when their help is needed at home, either to help generate income or to take care of household tasks.

When the negotiations on the SDGs were finalised, extreme poverty was defined as below a daily income of US$1.90 per person in 2011 prices. It is the most recent incarnation of an international poverty line, originally defined as a dollar a day, and has often been criticised for not really reflecting absolute poverty in middle- and high-income countries.

To compensate for the fact that extreme poverty in richer countries occurs at higher levels of income than in poor countries, the World Bank announced in October 2018 that it would use US$1.90 income per person only for low-income countries (31 countries globally), and would add three additional poverty lines for lower-middle-income (47 countries) and upper-middle-income countries (60 countries), at US$3.20 and US$5.50 respectively, and for the 80 high-income countries at US$21.70. As far as progress towards the SDG headline goal of eliminating extreme poverty is concerned, this will still be measured using US$1.90.

Figure 7.1 presents extreme poverty in Africa from 2015 with a forecast to 2040. It combines IFs data for extreme poverty at US$1.90, US$3.20 and US$5.50, respectively, for low-income, lower-middle-income and upper-middle-income countries.[17]

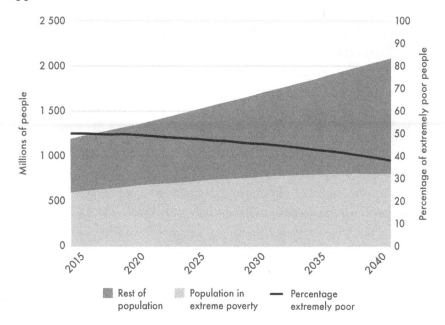

Figure 7.1: Extreme income poverty in Africa, 2015 to 2040[18]

The Bank has also recommended moving away from the household as the primary unit of analysis to individuals, since there is considerable evidence that there are poor women and children living in non-poor households. So, while the main breadwinner in a household may technically not be classified as extremely poor, others in the same household may be living on much lower levels of income.[19]

The impact of the additional poverty lines

The two additional poverty lines (US$3.20 and US$5.50) that relate to Africa compensate for a crucial imbalance by taking into account that the amount of income that a person needs to escape the burden of extreme poverty in low-income Mozambique is quite different from the income that a person in upper-middle-income South Africa would need.

However, using four poverty lines complicates our ability to easily measure and quantify the number of people living in extreme poverty globally, since we first have to forecast the extreme poverty level for each country income group before calculating the extreme poverty level for the continent as a whole. Africa has only one high-income country, the island state of Seychelles. Its population is less than one million, though, so I have ignored Seychelles in calculating the rates and number of extremely poor people in Africa.

The impact of the differentiated poverty rates is to sharply *increase* the number of Africans deemed to live in extreme poverty and, as examined below, to sharply *reduce* the number of African countries likely to achieve the target of eliminating extreme poverty by 2030 if we use all the various income definitions and not only US$1.90.

Using the three poverty lines, the Current Path forecast is that the extreme poverty rate will, by 2040, have declined to an average of 38 per cent, reflected in the right-hand scale in Figure 7.1.[20]

The associated calculations for Africa's low-, lower-middle- and upper-middle-income countries are set out in Table 7.1. In 2018 the population stood at 541 million in the 24 low-income countries, at 612 million in the 21 lower-middle-income countries, and at 115 million in the upper-middle-income countries, and it is expected to increase to 976 million, 963 million and 142 million people, respectively, by 2040. The large differences in population growth are essentially a result of the differences in total fertility rates between these countries.

Currently, roughly 50 per cent of Africans would be classified as living in extreme poverty, that is, after combining the averages for the three country income groups. This rate will decline to 38 per cent by 2040. The number of extremely poor Africans will, however, have increased from 638 million to 796 million.

Country group	2018	2040
Low-income total population (24 countries)	541 million	976 million
Low-income extreme poverty (% of total) using US$1.90	272 million (49%)	335 million (34%)
Lower-middle-income total population (21 countries)	612 million	963 million
Lower-middle-income extreme poverty (% of total) using US$3.20	310 million (51%)	395 million (41%)
Upper-middle-income total population (8 countries)	115 million	142 million
Upper-middle-income extreme poverty (% of total) using US$5.50	56 million (49%)	60 million (42%)
Africa total population	1 284 million	2 081 million
Extreme poverty in Africa	638 million (50%)	796 million (38%)

Table 7.1: Current Path of population and extreme poverty in Africa[21]

The current situation in Africa

In the following countries more than 50 per cent of people were living in extreme poverty in 2018:

■ Low income: Madagascar (76%), DRC (73%), Burundi (72%), Central African Republic (68%); Malawi (67%), Mozambique

(67%), Guinea-Bissau (65%), South Sudan (63%), Somalia (60%), Rwanda (55%) and Togo (54%)
- ▪ Lower middle income: Lesotho (77%), Zambia (76%), Nigeria (76%), São Tomé and Príncipe (67%), Republic of Congo (65%), Senegal (64%), eSwatini (61%), Angola (61%) and Kenya (53%)
- ▪ Upper middle income: Namibia (65%) and South Africa (54%).[22]

The fact that this list includes a number of upper-middle-income countries, such as South Africa and Namibia, points to the importance of inequality in considering poverty. South Africa (with a Gini coefficient of 0.65) is the most unequal country in the world, followed by Namibia and Botswana, Zambia, CAR, Lesotho, eSwatini, Brazil, Colombia and Panama.[23]

African countries also vary widely with regard to the depth of extreme poverty, meaning that many extremely poor people live far below the US\$1.90, US\$3.20 and US\$5.50 income levels per person per day. They are chronically poor, and it will take a long time for extremely poor people in these countries to improve their prospects and to technically reduce poverty rates.

With the newly established additional poverty lines for lower-middle-income and upper-middle-income countries on the Current Path forecast, Africa will only be able to eliminate extreme poverty during the second half of the 21st century.

Although some countries, such as Botswana, have experienced very rapid rates of growth, they have been unable to translate this growth into reduced rates of poverty. This is not the case for all countries, though. Cameroon, Egypt, Ghana, Kenya, Mali, Mauritania, Senegal, eSwatini, Tunisia and Uganda have all been relatively efficient in transmitting income growth into poverty reduction, generally because of relatively lower levels of inequality.[24]

The potential of social grants to reduce poverty

The extent of poverty in Africa, and the various factors that reinforce it, make it clear that there are no quick fixes. Beyond policies for economic growth and redistribution, African governments can reduce poverty by having the right kinds of policies for education, job creation and a social grant system. These policies will have different impacts in the long, medium and short term.

First, in the long term, improvements in education upskill workers and eventually allow for more complex, productive and hence better-paid work. But improvements in education take a very long time to achieve. The Rejuvenation in Education scenario that was modelled in Chapter 5 emulates the impact of an aggressive but reasonable improved education throughput at primary, secondary and tertiary level, improved quality of education and the elimination of gender disparities.

Second, large increases in employment in the formal sector can push up low-end wages and reduce inequality. Being part of the formal sector locks workers into annual wage negotiations, allowing them to qualify for sick leave and other benefits and to be part of pension schemes. (This is discussed in more detail in Chapter 9.)

Social grants have proven to be an effective short-term solution to assist the poor and change levels of extreme inequality. This is demonstrated by the impact of grant programmes in countries as diverse as Brazil, South Africa and India. In their original conceptions, income grants were conditional. Poor people were provided with food stamps or other access to subsidised food, education and transport if they fell below a certain income threshold. The threshold had to be monitored through regular means testing (Is the beneficiary still alive? Does he/she still qualify for the income grant? etc), which is cumbersome and costly.

Brazil, the most unequal country in South America, has been successful in driving poverty reduction on relatively low rates of economic growth by targeting the poorest with social transfer programmes that serve to bolster incomes, incentivise investments in social development, and help the poor to increase their asset base.

Recent years have also witnessed a steady move towards universal, non-means-tested grants in other countries, including South Africa, where the ruling party has placed particular emphasis on redistributive policies rather than on growth. Whereas in 1994 four million South Africans received social grants, that figure has increased to more than 17 million and is set to increase further. Today, social grants in some form or another are paid to 46 per cent of South African households.

But, as we saw when examining poverty levels in different African countries, even with this hugely expensive and expansive grant system, 54 per cent of South Africans still live in extreme poverty.[25] With only 7.28 million taxpayers out of a total population of 56 million, the South African system is ultimately unsustainable without much more rapid economic growth.[26] Social grants at this level can bridge a desperate situation but detract from economic growth prospects. Unlike Asia, where the focus has been on self-sufficiency and self-help, the challenge now facing South Africa is that unconditional social grants have created a culture of dependency, which is proving a severe constraint on improving self-help and entrepreneurship. Without real economic growth, extreme poverty in South Africa is likely to increase as it squeezes out productive government spending in favour of spending on consumption.[27]

Another positive example of using social grants as part of a poverty reduction strategy is India, which is ensuring that every Indian will have a bank account, be linked to the internet and be biometrically identified by a cellphone. The Aadhaar (meaning 'foundation') project started off as a voluntary programme to help tackle corruption and fraud. Today, Aadhaar offers a single, reliable database of the Indian population. It has enrolled more than 1.1 billion Indians on its biometric, digital and physical identity system. Linking bank accounts to biometric identification and cellphones creates a system that can overcome the pervasive corruption that is often part of traditional social grant systems, in which large amounts of cash are doled out to sometimes illiterate beneficiaries by poorly paid officials who are themselves often destitute.

Aadhaar requires that each person go through an enrolment process, during which a facial photograph, ten fingerprints and scans of both irises are recorded, along with the citizen's demographic information (name, address, gender and date of birth). Once the enrolment is completed and the biometric data verified, he/she is issued with a 12-digit unique identification number.

The advantages are clear: service providers can easily verify the identity of a person by submitting the applicant's Aadhaar number, along with biometric data such as fingerprints, to the Unique Identification Authority of India, which will then confirm the person's identity, or not. The system is the gateway to opening a bank account, filing a tax return, or getting a SIM card in India – all necessary processes to participate in social, economic and political life and thus to reduce inequality. Using mobile phone systems, funds (including social grants) can now be transferred directly to individuals, doing away with physical cash payments.

Many African countries are doing the same, but in some, such as Kenya, where corruption is truly endemic, repeated efforts to collect the biometric data of the population and to establish a national ID system have been met with deep suspicion.[28]

A second concept, more radical than social grants, is the idea of a universal basic share. This is an equal payment to all citizens, without any conditions or means testing. While this concept is also under consideration in some rich countries, the debate is particularly interesting in poor, developing countries such as India and in much of low-income and lower-middle-income Africa. The attraction of a universal basic share lies in its simplicity. Instead of having to determine if an individual falls below a certain income level, the payment is simply made to everyone above a certain minimum age.

The problem with a universal basic share payment may actually not be the availability (or lack) of money but rather the tax policies of African governments. Tax rates in Africa are notoriously low, largely because African governments 'forego revenues worth almost a third of those they actually collect'[29] through a bewildering array of tax breaks to donors, special economic zones and tax holidays to big investors – often mining houses. According to an article in *The Economist*, using World Bank data, 'tax collection in Africa resembles an exasperating fishing expedition, in which the big fish wriggle into tax havens and the tiddlers hide in the informal sector'.[30] In addition to low rates of tax, inefficiencies in revenue collection mean that African governments lose large amounts of tax revenue.

Today, the debate around poverty alleviation includes the question of whether various subsidies shouldn't be replaced with direct cash transfers. For example, would it not be more efficient to give farmers money instead of trying to subsidise inputs such as fuel, seed or fertiliser?[31] However, this could create another problem, as direct cash transfers over extended periods of time can lead to dependency (as is the case in South Africa) and reduce the incentive to undertake or seek employment. Why would a farmer try and improve productivity if he/she could live off a government grant? I return to this matter in Chapter 9.

The experiences of different countries illustrate the complexities involved in cash grants. While modern technology can solve most of the issues around payment, the essential challenge of dependency on state grants must also be addressed. The challenge therefore goes far beyond reducing poverty in the short term. The actual question is, how can African economies be transformed to ensure sustained income growth in the long term? Put differently, how do you get people off social grants and into paid employment with taxable incomes?

To this end, social protection policies are best employed in tandem with other economic reform efforts that focus on changing the productive structures. In Egypt, for example, the Takaful and Karama (Solidarity and Dignity) conditional and unconditional cash transfer programme was launched in 2015 and covers 2.26 million households – approximately ten per cent of Egypt's population.

Takaful and Karama was introduced to cushion the impact of the country's ambitious 2014 economic reform programme, which included the removal of energy subsidies, the adoption of a flexible exchange rate and the introduction of new value-added tax. The government has also scaled up its social protection programmes. The Karama (Dignity) part of the programme provides modest unconditional monthly pensions to elderly and disabled citizens, while Takaful (Solidarity) provides conditional family income support aimed at increasing food consumption, reducing poverty and encouraging families to keep children in school while providing them with health care.[32]

These efforts all benefit from the extent to which modern technology now makes feasible a social grant system in which much of the inefficiency and corruption of past programmes can be avoided.

The political and practical challenges for many of the measures set out in this chapter should, however, not be underestimated. In Ethiopia, one of Africa's top performers, efforts launched in 2006 to expand the tax base initially made steady progress but then stalled for several years after the death of Prime Minister Meles Zenawi in August 2012. Zenawi had championed the reforms and insulated them from political interference. When he died, tax reform, modernisation and increased revenue collection ground to a halt, although there were signs in 2018 of a renewed push under Prime Minister Abiy Ahmed. Total taxes collected nearly tripled from US$1.3 billion in 2007 to US$3.8 billion in 2013 and reached

US$7.8 billion by 2017. However, as a share of total government revenue, the contribution from tax grew from 48 per cent in 2007 to 82 per cent in 2016. Therefore, the growth in revenue collection failed to keep up with an economy that, on average, had grown at more than ten per cent per annum since 2000.[33]

The promise of an African welfare state?

In the past, developed countries responded to the problem of inequality and large-scale unemployment with the creation of a welfare state. In such a system, the state plays a key role in the protection and promotion of the economic and social well-being of its citizens.

This was possible because these (mostly Western) states were strong, having evolved through external war and competition, including the extraction of resources from colonies, into a system of governance that was underpinned by a social contract between the elected government and its citizens. In return for compliance and taxes, governments provided services and protection. The experience of the Great Depression during most of the 1930s was particularly important in advancing thinking on new welfare policies.

At the heart of the welfare model are various mechanisms through which the state provides key services such as education and health care and redistributes income from richer to poorer people through a progressive tax system. The welfare model is most developed in the social-democratic system of the Nordic countries. This system, which has created the most advanced, egalitarian and competitive societies in modern history, is rooted in the bitter experience of centuries of war and poverty, crop failures (especially potatoes) and economic upheaval.

The Nordics are all small, open economies that export a large portion of GDP into a highly competitive world. Wage inequality is among the lowest globally yet they have higher sustained economic growth than most, which is largely a function of the fact that, as a group, these countries have lingered for successive decades in the demographic sweet spot for economic growth, with ratios of 1.7 working-age persons to dependants or above (see Chapter 3).

A number of highly developed countries that are very exposed to international competition have therefore managed simultaneously to invest in greater social inclusion and to build globally competitive economies. Admittedly, this social consensus is under considerable political pressure today, even in Sweden, but this may be due to the successes achieved in the past and the political impact of migration, rather than to other factors.

The kind of welfare society found in the Nordic countries, with low inequality and a degree of economic security provided by the state, is good for growth. Since the 1930s economic growth per capita in Sweden and Norway (even if we exclude oil income in Norway) has been higher than in the USA over the same period.

In the long run, a more inclusive/less unequal society eventually also becomes a higher-growth economy. Unlike the USA, with its history as an immigration country, the Nordic countries evidence strong labour unions and strong worker associations that have resulted in wage moderation and assisted in modernisation. The social contract is strong. And, as a result, high-end wages in these countries are lower than they otherwise would have been. The wage differential between the most and least productive enterprises is also much lower than in more unequal countries such as the USA.

Social institutions have been crucial in creating the high-productivity economies of the Nordic countries. They serve as equalising institutions that constrain the growth of inequality by lifting low wages and squeezing down high-end wages. In recent years, though, the impact of technology has been partly responsible for the fragmentation of these labour and employment institutions, and has undercut their role.

There are, of course, also many variations on the welfare state, ranging from conservative to liberal. As people have become more wealthy, their desire for autonomy, to be free from state oversight or interference, has also increased. And then, with the ageing population structure in many Western and some Asian countries, caring for older people suffering from costly, non-communicable diseases has become a big burden. The welfare state is therefore increasingly under pressure, even in the Nordic countries, but only since these countries became extraordinarily productive and wealthy.

In South Africa, Latin America and some parts of Asia, the notion of a welfare state has followed a completely different path, largely moving towards the introduction of conditional and, lately also, unconditional income grants.

To reiterate, there are obviously huge differences between the classic welfare-state-tied benefits to economic activity (evident in developed countries) and the situation in much of Africa, where formal-sector jobs are in scarce supply. The essential question is, however, if there are going to be sufficient jobs in the formal sector, and since improved average levels of education are going to take a very long time to achieve, what are the options for a continent facing such high levels of inequality and poverty?

In addition to the policies discussed and presented in other chapters, for instance around education, the structural transformation of economies and how to provide many more jobs, Africa will also have to use tax revenues to roll out social grants to alleviate extreme poverty. In the next section, I model the potential impact of such efforts and present their impact on poverty and inequality.

Modelling the impact of using tax revenues for social grants: The Social Grants for Africa scenario

To forecast the impact of social grants on poverty reduction in Africa, a first step is to determine how much additional money could be raised for social grants. This is done within the IFs modelling platform by raising taxes on skilled workers and increasing the effective tax rate on firms to 2040. (The exact interventions used for the scenario are available at www.jakkiecilliers.org.)

By 2040, African governments would raise US$171 billion in additional taxes in this scenario, an amount that would have increased with each passing year. This may appear large, but the size of the African economy, in market exchange rates in 2040, is forecast to be US$7.2 trillion. The increased taxes raise government revenues by US$170 billion in 2040.

The next step is to channel the bulk of that additional revenue to low-skilled workers through social grants. In the scenario, by 2040 African governments would transfer US$155 billion in social grants, representing the bulk of the additional government revenues mentioned above.[34] This will take an additional 22 million Africans out of extreme poverty in 2040 and, cumulatively, 300 million Africans over the 20 years from 2020 to 2040. On average, the poverty rate in the three country income groups declines by almost two percentage points by 2040. Inequality comes down in all three country income groups, although the impact is greatest in upper-middle-income countries, largely because these countries have the largest skilled workforce and would otherwise have experienced the biggest increase in income inequality.

This represents a big improvement in the livelihoods of a large portion of the African population. The World Bank's Africa Social Protection Strategy 2012–22 emphasises the importance of safety nets to reduce chronic poverty and to limit the impact of shocks on poor and vulnerable households. New models are emerging, such as a pension scheme for informal workers in Ghana that targets the needs of an increasing elderly population, which, according to UN estimates, is expected to triple to 161 million by 2050 in sub-Saharan Africa. This could also help to tackle the issue of old-age poverty, which is currently accelerating at an alarming rate.

On its own, the Social Grants for Africa scenario does not change the rather dismal extreme poverty forecast that has been explored in this chapter. Under both the Current Path and the Social Grants for Africa scenario, only Gabon, Tunisia, Seychelles, Egypt, Algeria, Morocco and Mauritius eliminate extreme poverty by 2030.[35] By 2040 one additional country, Mauritania, would join this group.

Social grants should therefore not be viewed in isolation from the other scenarios set out in this book. Rather, they should be seen as a measure to reduce absolute deprivation for poor people who otherwise would continue to suffer since they have limited opportunities to improve their dire situation through better education or job opportunities. Social grants are also an important measure that can cushion the impact on the poor and vulnerable of other reforms, such as the removal of fuel and food subsidies.

Conclusion: Reducing poverty through rapid and inclusive economic growth

Generally, poverty reduction requires rapid economic growth, redistributive policies such as progressive taxes, investments in health and basic infrastructure, improved levels of education and investments in agriculture.

Agriculture is usually the sector with the largest potential impact on poverty reduction. This applies particularly to low-income economies, where a large portion of the labour force is often employed in subsistence agriculture.

The IFs Current Path forecast suggests that most African countries will make steady progress in reducing extreme poverty, with the bulk of extremely poor people increasingly concentrated in countries such as Nigeria, the DRC and Madagascar. However, with the right policies and a dedicated effort, more rapid progress is possible.

African governments may need to make a greater effort to introduce large-scale social assistance schemes, something along the lines of the universal basic share mentioned above. In other words, to avoid rising inequality, and to improve human capital, African governments should give cash grants directly to the poor for them to spend on their most important needs, such as education for their children, transport, food, etc. Such measures are much better than subsidies on fuel and other items.

Large-scale social grant programmes appear to be part of the answer to alleviating poverty, and would support human capital development. At the same time, redistributive policies, safety nets and more progressive taxation are all necessary but need to be finely balanced so that they do not compromise an economy's levels of competitiveness. In effect, social protection is an important tool that can be used to cushion the impact of policies that focus on growth. It is possible to be pro-growth and inclusive at the same time.

However, none of this is possible without a huge push to provide Africans with a unique and tamper-proof identity system and the establishment of a national population register in each country. Even the SDGs recognise that some form of official proof of identity is a prerequisite for participation in a modern economy and to access basic rights and services. The advances in digital technology, for instance with biometrics and its incorporation into identity systems, means this can be made available much more cheaply than before. In Chapter 10, I will explore the potential of digitisation and progress that has been made in this regard.

So, if the time has come to give consideration to an African welfare state, the question is: how can the inescapable need to reduce poverty and combat inequality be reconciled with the need for greater productivity in African economies? A welfare society will offset the symptoms of under-development but will not deal with the underlying causes.

To develop, Africa needs to transform its economies to become more productive. Traditionally, that has been achieved through industrialisation, which is the topic of the next chapter.

8
Changing the productive structures

> Africa's defining challenge is to create a pathway to prosperity
> for our people . . . Elsewhere, this has been achieved through
> industrialisation . . . Africa's window to follow that strategy
> is narrowing much more rapidly than previously understood.
> We are running out of time . . .
>
> – President Paul Kagame, opening address,
> 30th AU Summit, Addis Ababa, 28 January 2018

Africa's fast-growing population makes rapid economic growth a pre-requisite to reducing poverty and improving livelihoods. To grow rapidly, an economy needs to improve productivity in agriculture, industry and services. It also has to move labour and capital from a low-productivity sector such as agriculture to a higher-productivity sector such as manu-facturing, and from the informal to the formal sector. Employment in the formal sector improves stability, reduces inequality, and, most importantly, contributes tax revenues that enable governments to roll out health care, education and infrastructure.

The problem is that on current trends, much of sub-Saharan Africa's economic future is likely to consist of a large subsistence agricultural sector in rural areas and low-end, informal services, generally consisting of wholesale and retail trade, in urban areas.[1]

There is no silver bullet to improve productive structures (although digitisation can help), and African countries are also very different from each other. But the common prerequisite is for an activist government that invests in human capital development, encourages labour-intensive (even garden-style) small-scale agriculture, places an unrelenting focus on export-oriented manufacturing, and pursues policies that improve productive capacity.

According to the World Bank,[2] the services sector constituted more than half of economic activity in sub-Saharan Africa by value in 2018, while industry (including manufacturing at 10 per cent) constituted 25 per cent, and agriculture 16 per cent. The forecast within IFs is for a steep increase in the size of the services sector to 2040, with manufacturing as a portion of GDP remaining stagnant, and for agriculture to decline. That forecast is for a slow-growth Africa in which the increase in the size of the population inevitably translates into a larger economy but only slow improvements in average incomes, since the growth of low-end services, evident in much of Africa, does not really improve productive structures.

Low-end services, particularly dominant in urban Africa, were by 2010 only twice as productive as agriculture.[3] Due to its marginally better levels of productivity, the growth in low-end services in Africa has contributed little to improve per capita incomes.[4]

Although estimates differ, Carol Newman and colleagues find that the manufacturing sector in Africa is six times more productive than agriculture. In his best-selling *Kicking Away the Ladder*, the South Korean economist Ha-Joon Chang describes the view that developing countries can largely skip industrialisation and enter the post-industrial phase, in which services increasingly drive employment and productivity growth, as 'a fantasy'. This is because the manufacturing sector has 'an inherently faster productivity growth than the services sector',[5] he argues.

Beyond the various schools of economic theory, authors as diverse as Arthur Lewis, Erik Reinert, Calestous Juma and, recently, Dani Rodrik have written extensively on the importance of early industrialisation – and the significant role of governments and ruling elites in charting this course. Newman and colleagues explain the importance of industrialisation:

> Between 1950 and 2006, about half of the catch-up by developing countries to advanced economy levels of output per worker was explained by rising productivity within industry combined with structural transformation out of agriculture. Industry is the pre-eminent destination sector at early stages of development because it is a high productivity sector capable of absorbing large numbers of moderately skilled workers.[6]

The problem is that, in much of Africa, manufacturing is actually declining while low-end services are growing. Transport, financial, health and recreation services are growing more rapidly than any other sector in terms of their contribution to global GDP across all country income groups, and it is generally expected that the contribution of services will converge at around 60 per cent of average GDP by 2040 across country income groups.

In Chapter 2, I explained that, with a few exceptions, Africa tends to export unprocessed commodities such as coffee and cocoa, and to import processed products and finished goods from the European Union, China and elsewhere. That trend is likely to continue, reflecting the limited value-addition that is characteristic of most African economies.

The law of diminishing returns determines that countries that specialise in supplying raw materials, unprocessed agricultural products or low-end services yield a progressively smaller return for every unit of capital or labour, compared to the provision of value-added goods. For example, a recent study by Unctad on promoting the leather industry in Africa laments the fact that Africa is the largest source of hides and skins in the world but that these exports come with very little value addition.[7] Like coffee (which in Africa largely comes from Ethiopia), 'Italian' handbags and shoes (often made from African leather) demand high prices but are not produced in Africa.

Growth that is based on increasing commodity exports cannot induce structural economic transformation. Instead it has led to high-technology 'bubbles' or economic enclaves with very few linkages to the rest of the economy. Examples include the oil-producing parts of Angola off the coast of Cabinda, parts of oil-producing Nigeria (in the Niger delta), sections of Equatorial Guinea and soon northern Mozambique with its rich natural gas endowment.

Compare this with the activist governments in rapidly developing Asian countries, such as China, South Korea and Vietnam, that pursued growth through the insertion of their manufacturing capacity into global value chains during the 1990s. These countries steadily upgraded their technical capabilities to meet global standards, often by inviting and partnering with multinational companies for the transfer of technology, skills and knowledge.[8]

Today global value chains are again evolving quite rapidly. These offer opportunities for Africa, which is, generally, only peripherally part of this development. First, modern technology offers significant opportunities for industrial latecomers, which can skip over the bricks-and-mortar institutions of yesterday into a world in which banking and sourcing of inputs is done remotely, and in which the degree of financial investment required to embark upon manufacturing is declining. Second, there are also signs of increased manufacturing nationalism (leading to the so-called reshoring of manufacturing back to the 'home' country), with concerns in the US and elsewhere that the rise of Asia has eroded their own industrial and power base. Finally, new technologies permit much greater flexibility and customerisation, with production shifting closer to the consumer. The result is that the complex global value chains that emerged prior to the global financial crisis are now contracting and moving closer to markets. With Africa's large and growing population, these developments are to its potential advantage.

In Chapter 6 I recounted how the transformation of the agricultural sector helped many countries in Asia to alleviate poverty and improve general well-being. Agriculture has served as a stepping stone for many poor countries. Once economies gained some momentum and basic education and literacy had shown sufficient progress, these countries pursued a manufacturing transition that was facilitated by favourable demographics and determined leadership. This eventually led to unprecedented rates of economic growth.

This is the history of the Japanese economic miracle that took place between 1950 and 1990, and was repeated in South Korea, Hong Kong, Macau, Singapore, Brunei, Taiwan and recently China. Countries such as Brazil, Indonesia, Malaysia, Mexico, the Philippines, South Africa and Turkey also experienced substantive growth for several years as a result of industrialisation, but generally not at the rates and not for the extended period seen in the Asian countries.

In Africa, Rwanda and Ethiopia have embarked upon a similar pathway and the results are visible for all to see: they have the most rapid improvements in indices of well-being on the continent.

The contribution of services to growth

The focus that I place on an activist government, going up the agriculture value chain, export-oriented manufacturing and investments in human capital should not be misconstrued. The contribution from services is expanding at all levels of income, and most rapidly in low-income countries. This has become known as the 'servicification' of the global economy and reflects the extent to which services have become an integral requirement for agriculture, manufacturing and other sectors. And, at high levels of development, financial services, computer and software services, and transport and distribution services have all become dynamic requirements for continued growth. But high-value services constitute a very small segment of the large and growing services sector in Africa, much of which is in the informal retailing sector.[9]

At low levels of development, predominantly service-based economies have less ability to export or trade. Lower export earnings mean a weaker ability to buy advanced technology from abroad, which in turn leads to slower growth. According to Célestine Monga, writing for the African Development Bank in 2017, the problem is that at low levels of development, 'most services are low-productivity, subsistence, and even informal activities that may help households escape poverty, but are not sustainable sources of growth'.[10]

India is often considered an example of a country that, until recently, pursued a growth strategy led by the services sector. The contribution of services to GDP overtook that of agriculture in 1975, but the contribution of manufacturing to GDP only overtook agriculture three decades later. India's developmental model has been unique among major economies in the manner in which it has shifted from agriculture to services without major industrial expansion. India's inward-looking economic model has thus relied on domestic markets more than exports, on consumption more than investment, on services more than industry, and on high tech more than low-skilled manufacturing.[11]

The early growth in services, and the fact that India only recently entered a favourable demographic window – the period in which there is a large working-age population relative to the dependent population – are two important reasons for India's lower-than-expected growth over a number of decades. Since 1991, economic liberalisation has unshackled an economy stifled by overregulation, corruption and lack of competition. Furthermore, education levels are improving.

Today India is set for significantly more rapid growth as the ratio of working-age persons to dependants improves, investment in infrastructure has been prioritised, and greater emphasis is placed on expanding its manufacturing sector.

The impact of the diffusion of knowledge

In his widely acclaimed book on the impact of information technology on globalisation, *The Great Convergence*,[12] Richard Baldwin argues that knowledge flows consisting of data, information searches, communications, transactions and video dominate the new globalisation, instead of physical goods and finance flows across borders.[13] For example, in 2016 cross-border flows in data were 45 times bigger than a decade before.[14]

Global flows of knowledge contribute to economic growth and present an opportunity for lagging countries to catch up in this dimension through investment in information and communications technology (ICT). In theory, individuals can participate directly in globalisation by using digital platforms to study, find jobs, showcase their talent, and build networks. In practice, this opportunity is limited to those who are connected to the internet and who have the inclination, knowledge and interest to pursue it.

This caveat aside, ICT-led globalisation and associated knowledge flows are undermining the previous competitive advantage enjoyed by industrialised countries, as well as the outlook for global value chains. The reason for this is that an increased number of jobs in the developed world are now in direct competition with jobs in emerging economies. The cross-border flow of data and knowledge has broken the monopoly that workers in wealthy nations had on the use of advanced industrial-manufacturing intellectual property.

While globalisation has had a disruptive impact in much of North America and Europe, where it has fuelled populist politics, the phenomenon has had a cohesive impact on emerging markets, where the middle class has flourished and millions of people have been lifted out of poverty.

As a result of global knowledge flows, the concept of comparative advantage has been denationalised in countries that were part of integrated trade blocs, such as the North American Free Trade Area (Nafta, now known as the United States-Mexico-Canada Agreement, or USMCA), the EU, and East and South East Asia, where regional value chains have been well established.[15] In response to the impact of this 'new globalisation', industrialised countries have embraced policies to protect their knowledge – excessive use of patent protection being an important example – as well as requirements for minimum labour standards and the like.

Conversely, emerging factory economies have embraced policies that foster knowledge sharing and creation. It is for this reason that China champions globalisation (despite having significant domestic barriers to foreign companies), while the previous advocate of free trade, the USA, now seeks to protect its domestic manufacturing sector from foreign competition. It does so by withdrawing from or renegotiating trade agreements that now include much higher domestic and labour content requirements, thereby raising the bar.

The problem for the US and other high-income economies is that digital communication, the internet and the ICT revolution have broken the monopoly industrialised nations had on knowledge and even on copyright. The result of these changes is that barriers faced by manufacturers and specific industries and services in emerging countries, including in Africa, are constantly being lowered, often quite dramatically.

Trends in robotics, automation, computerised manufacturing and artificial intelligence all appear to reduce the advantage of low-labour-cost locations, but not necessarily to the detriment to Africa. Originally, corporations sought to locate manufacturers in those countries with the cheapest labour. Today rapid growth in multinationals and consumers occurs within emerging rather than developed economies, hence in Vietnam, Malaysia, India and eventually also in Africa. According to one estimate, by 2025 almost half of the world's largest companies will have headquarters in emerging markets and closer to consumer growth.[16] These trends will first benefit the rest of Asia but are also beginning to be felt in Africa.

A variety of digital technologies (particularly in media), new materials (such as bio- or nano-based materials) and new processes (such as 3D printing, not to mention artificial intelligence and robotics) threaten to disrupt existing manufacturing patterns. Collectively, these new trends have caused widespread concern about the nature and availability of jobs in the future (discussed in Chapter 9) and our understanding of economic growth theory.

The future should see the evolution of a more distributed global economy in which manufacturing and services are closely linked and value chains are shorter and closer to the future markets. All offer opportunities for Africa. Generally, new technology decreases the required input costs of manufacturing, and so it will become cheaper to manufacture, particularly for smaller production runs. Technologies such as

3D printing may in due course put an end to the smokestack factory model of production, and perhaps lead to the evolution of something akin to a cottage industry model.[17]

Production is therefore experiencing a shift towards customisation for millions of niche markets, characterised by smaller production runs closer to the end markets, and by greater flexibility.[18] The local manufacturer of, say, a car part or a replacement gear for a machine will pay to download the plan from the cloud and print (or engineer) it using a local 3D printer. This means no more international shipping, tracking or customs clearance is required. Instant gratification.

Ghanaian entrepreneur Bright Simons,[19] president of social enterprise mPedigree, refers to this as the rise of 'Alibaba industrialisation'. He writes eloquently about the 'unsung industrial revolution underway in places like Ghana, Uganda, Senegal and Côte d'Ivoire' that is powered by 'a worldwide revolution in modular design, multi-purpose machinery, efficient small-batch production, global SME–SME [small and medium enterprises] engagement, new forex transfer practices, and the growing strategic transformation of China's late-phase industrial players'. This is a world in which small and medium-sized Chinese suppliers provide large chunks of the industrial jigsaw and 'African hustlers and unconventional industrialists act as shuttle-brokers of the various factors of production between China and Africa'. The fourth industrial revolution and digitisation therefore make it easier for African states to become part of value chains from which they were previously excluded.

One of the unforeseen results of lower barriers to entry is that companies can venture into new areas outside their traditional area of specialisation. Startups can quickly go up the productivity curve to threaten established businesses. It is even evident in something as complex as the manufacturing of cars, where new entrants such as Tesla have been able to blossom.

Manufacturing in Africa

In their 2016 multiyear study of industrial development, Carol Newman and colleagues[20] compared eight African countries with Cambodia and Vietnam, and offered a number of reasons that, taken collectively, explain Africa's lack of industry.

First, there is the widely held belief that the preconditions for industrial development do not exist in Africa, including core infrastructure (such as roads and railways) and human capital (an educated, healthy workforce). Furthermore, there are barriers to entry and the financial sector is not big and sophisticated enough, with small banks and underdeveloped financial markets. Without greater financial depth, many African countries will struggle to develop.

However, at the time of their industrialisation, these conditions also did not exist in Japan, the Asian Tigers or China. Greater financial depth, core infrastructure and a better-educated workforce inevitably develop in response to incentives, policies and effort. Governments are responsible for creating the right incentives to allow physical, human, social and knowledge capital to develop. This, in turn, requires a governing elite committed to economic growth and sufficient government capacity to formulate and implement policy.

Second, few African countries (Tunisia and Mauritius were rare exceptions) have set out and implemented a concerted package of public investments, appropriate policy and institutional reforms to increase the share of industrial exports in GDP. In the majority of African countries, little or no consistent effort has been made to boost non-traditional exports, which mostly consist of commodities.

Third, contrary to successes achieved elsewhere, most African governments have paid little or no attention to making special economic zones (SEZs) work. SEZs have played a large part in the successful industrialisation of Asia. These allow export-oriented industrial agglomerations to benefit from the advantages of being in close proximity to knowledge-intensive institutions, including foreign and domestic companies that are more productive, as well as research institutes and universities, which in turn leads to information and knowledge spillovers.

The provision of improved social services and infrastructure in a limited physical area attracts foreign companies and high-quality staff.[21] In low-income countries, domestic industry generally benefits from positive knowledge spillovers from foreign-owned firms, especially if these are part of the same value chain. Since African governments have not pursued the establishment of local value chains, African firms have not benefited.[22] Instead, manufacturing firms have been dispersed across urban areas (instead of located in close proximity to each other) with limited requirements or incentives to source locally, train locals, and establish local value chains.[23]

African governments also have not invested in high-quality infrastructure in SEZs, and have not promoted these zones or brought in professional management. African SEZs are generally not connected to domestic value chains, since the practice (if not policy) of governments has been to treat them as stand-alone enclaves.[24]

Fourth, even though African governments have created agencies and boards that advocate foreign direct investment, this has been done without real commitment and implementation support, which explains why these efforts have achieved very little.[25] For this reason, most African countries linger at the bottom of indices measuring the ease of doing business and attracting foreign investment.

Finally, a large number of African countries, such as Ghana, Kenya, Mozambique, Nigeria, Senegal and Tanzania, have embarked on investment reforms in an effort to improve the physical, institutional and regulatory environments in which firms operate. However, active efforts to improve the competitiveness of domestic industries, or practical measures to reduce trade friction costs resulting from poor trade logistics, have not accompanied these reforms.[26]

Bad luck has also played a role in Africa's inability to industrialise. When African economies again spluttered into life at the end of the twentieth century, they had to compete with not only the industrial North but also a number of rapidly industrialising countries in East Asia, including China.

Composition of African economies

Current levels and potential for the expansion of manufacturing differ greatly between countries and regions. At roughly 20 per cent of manufacturing value added to GDP, North Africa is the most industrialised region on the continent, and West and East Africa are the least industrialised (both at roughly 12 per cent). On average, the contribution of manufacturing to African economies has steadily declined since independence and has never achieved the manufacturing peak share of 20–35 per cent of GDP that was achieved in Europe and North America. After that peak in manufacturing employment and output in the West, wages increased and employment and output in the manufacturing sector declined. Consumers had more money to spend on services, and growth in this sector therefore accelerated.[27]

Figure 8.1 presents the sectoral composition of selected African economies as reflected in the World Bank Open Data portal, with countries ranked according to the contribution of their manufacturing sector to GDP. The size of the manufacturing sector in Africa ranges from negligible in Mali to 30 per cent in eSwatini – a result of the benefit that the latter country derives from its access to the US market under the African Growth and Opportunity Act (AGOA) and from its proximity to the large South African market.

Africa's economies are dominated by low-productivity services. Generally the contribution from agriculture is lowest among upper-middle-income countries and highest among low-income countries. The contribution from energy and manufacturing is the opposite to agriculture, with low-income countries having the smallest energy and manufacturing sectors.

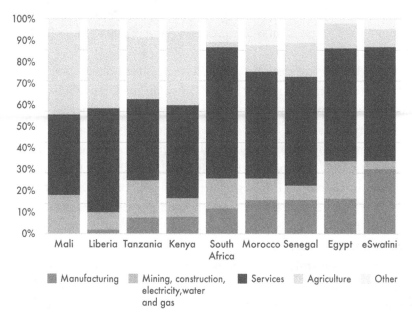

Figure 8.1: Sectoral composition of selected African economies by value added to GDP, ranked by relative size of manufacturing sector, 2017[28]

Sierra Leone has the largest contribution from agriculture to GDP, at 60 per cent, and South Africa among the smallest, at slightly more than 2 per cent. Yet, South Africa, which has an efficient commercial farming sector, is one of the few African countries that is largely self-sufficient in food. Countries such as Sierra Leone, Chad and Guinea-Bissau have very large agricultural sectors as a portion of their economies, but are all net food importers whose import dependence is set to expand significantly.

The energy sector makes the smallest contribution to GDP in Togo, whereas in Equatorial Guinea it constitutes almost 29 per cent of the economy. Other countries where the energy sector makes up a large portion of the national economy are Libya, South Sudan, the Republic of Congo, Angola and Algeria.

The economy of Africa's only high-income country, Seychelles, has the smallest contribution from the raw materials sector. The two countries with the largest contribution from raw materials are Zambia (copper) and Mauritania (mostly iron ore).

The countries with the smallest services sector are Togo, Chad, Sierra Leone and the DRC, at 30–33 per cent. The services sector constitutes more than 60 per cent of GDP in Zimbabwe, South Africa, Cape Verde, Mauritius, São Tomé and Príncipe and Djibouti. In Seychelles it accounts for more than 80 per cent of the economy, largely due to the contribution from tourism.

Over the last two decades, the ICT sector has overtaken agriculture as the third-largest contributor to GDP by value globally and it has become particularly important in high-income economies. Whereas the ICT sector is responsible for only one per cent of the value-add to GDP in low-income countries, it contributes almost eight per cent to GDP in high-income countries. Despite its relatively small contribution to added value, in many instances ICT is a growth multiplier, particularly at higher-income levels, because it facilitates knowledge exchanges, including the effective functioning of regional and multinational value chains that include goods and services.

Africa's upper-middle-income economies trail behind those in the rest of the world in terms of the contribution made by ICT to GDP by an average of two percentage points. In no African country does ICT contribute more than five per cent of GDP, although Mauritius gets closest at 4.8 per cent.

In Nigeria, Africa's largest economy, IFs calculates that agriculture accounts for 24 per cent of added value to GDP, energy for 9 per cent (despite the country's huge petroleum sector), manufacturing for 11 per cent, services for 53 per cent and ICT for 3 per cent.

Industrialisation and growth in Africa

From the preceding analysis, two conclusions are apparent. The first is simply the low levels of manufacturing in Africa relative to comparable regions such as South America and South Asia. From 1999 to 2018 the manufacturing value added to GDP in lower-middle-income and upper-middle-income Africa is around six and ten percentage points, respectively, below the global average for these two country groupings. Thus, on a comparative basis, Africa is significantly under-industrialised.

In a 2017 working paper for the African Development Bank, Bhorat et al describe sub-Saharan African productive structure as 'inherently characterised by lower levels of economic complexity, which informed the notion of limited productive capabilities . . . the African manufacturing sector is marginal in nature and points to limited employment opportunities.'[29]

The second point is the trend towards deindustrialisation in key upper-middle-income economies, particularly in South Africa and Mauritius, and until recently also in Algeria. Among other things, this decline reflects the extent to which Asian and other exporters have successfully penetrated African markets.[30]

The percentage of GDP consisting of services has steadily increased since the 1980s to an estimated 57 per cent, 52 per cent and 47 per cent average for Africa's upper-middle-income, lower-middle-income and low-income country groupings, respectively. Whereas manufacturing and high-end services have grown in East, South East and South Asia, this has not occurred in Africa.

Africa produces about US$500 billion of manufactured goods per annum. Acha Leke, Mutsa Chironga and Georges Desvaux argue that this could be doubled if two-thirds was designated for local consumption.[31] In this context, China's inordinately important role in manufacturing in Africa in recent years (as opposed to exporting to Africa) presents an interesting paradox.[32] For example, the largest ceramic tile factory in Africa was recently built by China in Ethiopia. Nearly a third of the more than 10 000 Chinese companies[33] estimated to be active in Africa are involved in manufacturing. Together they are responsible for more than 12 per cent of Africa's industrial production. Most of them are small, privately owned companies, not state-owned behemoths, and their focus is on serving the needs of Africa's fast-growing domestic market rather than on exports, though with some exceptions, such as in Ethiopia.

The dominance of Chinese firms is even more pronounced in infrastructure, where they claim nearly 50 per cent of Africa's internationally contracted construction market. Why, when they are constrained by the same lack of infrastructure, a poorly educated workforce and other conditions, have such a large number of small, privately owned Chinese companies been able to penetrate the African manufacturing market – often at the expense of local industry or that in neighbouring countries?

Contrary to the general expectation among foreign analysts, most of these companies are oriented towards serving the domestic market rather than exports. They appear to 'represent a long-term commitment to Africa rather than trading or contracting activities':[34]

> 89 per cent of employees were African . . . this suggests that Chinese-owned business employ several million Africans. Moreover, nearly two-thirds of Chinese employers provided some kind of skills training . . . Half of Chinese firms had introduced a new product or service to the local market, and one-third had introduced a new technology. In some cases, Chinese firms had lowered prices for existing products and services by as much as 40 per cent through improved technology and efficiencies of scale. African government officials overseeing infrastructure development for their countries cited Chinese firms' efficient cost structures and speedy delivery as major value adds.

In short, if Chinese companies can enter the manufacturing sector in Africa, why can't Africans?

Some self-defeating policies are self-evident. South Africa, for example, which has a large domestic vehicle manufacturing industry, could stipulate that the government will only procure locally produced vehicles for own use and in that manner support local industry, but it does not. An excessive regulatory burden, including stringent requirements for black economic empowerment, ensures that South Africa's ability to compete against Chinese imports is steadily eroding.

On the other hand, several years ago Nigeria also established a domestic cement industry by offering a four-year licence to import cement on the condition that the licence holder would invest in a domestic cement production plant. Today, Nigeria is a net exporter of cement and the deal has created the richest African, Aliko Dangote.

But the biggest opportunity to grow domestic manufacturing is with intra-African trade (see Chapter 11).

Close to 60 per cent of African imports consist of manufactured goods by value, while the dominant export segment is energy exports such as oil, coal and gas. Many of the imported goods could be manufactured locally and boost the value of intra-African trade. There is great potential to increase intra-African trade in a host of foodstuffs, beverages and cigarettes, rubber and plastics, electronics and non-metallic mineral products.[35]

Replacing imported manufactured goods with goods made in Africa will not be easy, since global value chains have improved efficiencies and reduced prices, making it difficult for new entrants to compete. Still, it remains a crucial step in the transformation of African economies.[36]

Growth in Africa's manufacturing sector requires a stable and facilitating policy framework, government support and incentives.

The entry point for manufacturing traditionally has involved labour-intensive segments of regional manufacturing value chains, meaning that labour costs need to be competitive. Given that Africa suffers from various disadvantages, such as poor physical infrastructure,[37] a high disease burden and poor rule of law, low regulatory and policy quality, and a lack of policy certainty, among others, the general view is that African labour costs need to be cheap enough to compensate for these deficits.[38]

However, a 2017 study on Africa's manufacturing labour costs by Alan Gelb and others[39] concluded that poor African countries have higher labour costs than their average income levels would suggest. The study compared 12 African countries with 17 non-African countries. Only Ethiopia compared favourably. In all other African countries included in the study, labour costs were higher than those of their non-African peers. In this regard South Africa stands out as a middle-income country with particularly high labour costs and a very capital-intensive industrial sector.

Manufacturing labour costs in low-income and lower-middle-income countries Kenya, Tanzania and Senegal – three relatively stable coastal countries with strong business sectors – are higher than in Bangladesh, a country with a comparable World Economic Forum (WEF) competitiveness rating and income levels.

However, one of the effects of the fourth industrial revolution mentioned previously is the declining importance of labour costs in the location of industry, while the trend to locate manufacturing closer to end markets has also been discussed. For these and other reasons, Carol Newman and her co-authors believe that industrialisation in Africa remains possible, although its shape and form will differ from that experienced elsewhere. Writing in 2016, they offer three considerations:

> First, economic changes are taking place in Asia that create a window of opportunity for late industrializers elsewhere to gain a toehold in global markets. Second, the nature of manufactured exports themselves is changing. A growing share of global trade in industry is made up of stages of vertical value chains – or tasks – rather than finished products. Trade in tasks offers late industrializers an opportunity to enter global markets in areas suited to their factor costs and endowments of skills and capabilities. Third, trade in services and agroindustry is growing faster than trade in manufacturers. These 'industries without smokestacks' broaden the range of products in which Africa can compete, and a number of them are intensive in location-specific factors abundant in Africa.[40]

And, eventually, because Africa is growing so much more slowly than other regions, wages in Africa will become competitive and offset the productivity advantage of incumbent industrial producers, including those in East Asia.

Even so, according to a 2017 analysis by the Center for Global Development,[41] most African countries (with the exception of Ethiopia) are still some way from this point. China and other countries in East Asia are, however, restructuring their economies to meet growing domestic demand, which will create space for Africa to compete with countries such as Bangladesh as the low-end manufacturing market of choice for future relocation.[42]

Already the most recent data shows that in selected countries, such as Ghana and Uganda, manufacturing is expanding and contributing to growth. Even low-profile Benin has quietly seen a 50 per cent increase in the size of its manufacturing sector since 2012. In Côte d'Ivoire, a somewhat late but now enthusiastic Chinese trade partner, a growing proportion of industrial added value is contributed by manufacturing. However, a consistent pattern across all these countries has been the steady expansion of capital imports from China.

Modelling the impact of industrialisation: The Made in Africa scenario

This section briefly presents a set of intervention clusters modelled within IFs to emulate industrialisation in Africa with a time horizon to 2040, and compares its impact to the Current Path.

Clear industrial policy and determined government leadership and action are critical if African economies are to grow more rapidly. For this reason, a first cluster of interventions increases investment in the economy. It reflects the determined efforts by forward-looking African governments to set the agenda for industrial development on the continent.

A second cluster of interventions aggressively increases government expenditure on research and development (from the current African average of 0.1 per cent of GDP to 0.4 per cent by 2030), provides export support to the manufacturing and ICT sectors, and modestly raises prices on manufacturing and ICT imports. An increase in expenditure on research and development is a particularly powerful driver of improvements in multifactor productivity.

A final intervention is to improve economic freedom as a proxy for lowering the barriers to entry for foreign companies and making it easier for small businesses to do business.[43]

The exploratory interventions modelled for this chapter (and the book as a whole) were all done at a continental level and were neither tailored to improve the use of labour, capital or multifactor productivity at national level nor to primarily focus on industrialisation in middle-income, as opposed to low-income, economies. At best, the efforts presented here emulate a continent that has committed itself to actively pursuing greater industrialisation, and serves to illustrate potential rather than to map out the specific associated benefits.

Figure 8.2 compares the GDP growth rates in the Current Path with the Made in Africa scenario. The growth rates per country income grouping are presented in Table 8.1 The initial impact of the interventions is limited, but the rates of growth accelerate over the forecast horizon, and since the interventions alter the composition of Africa's economy, they set the continent on a more positive growth trajectory.

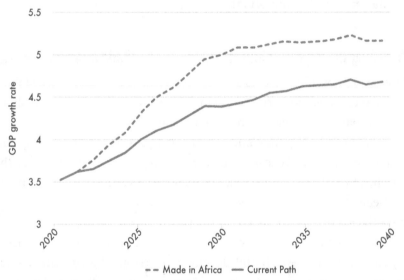

Figure 8.2: Comparing GDP growth rates: Current Path vs Made in Africa, 2020 to 2040[44]

	CURRENT PATH	MADE IN AFRICA	DIFFERENCE
Africa	4.3%	4.7%	0.4%
Low-income Africa	6.5%	6.9%	0.4%
Lower-middle-income Africa	4.4%	4.9%	0.5%
Upper-middle-income Africa	2.7%	2.9%	0.2%

Table 8.1: Average growth rates for country income groups, 2020 to 2040[45]

Compound growth is incredibly powerful. Although the average difference between the Current Path and Made in Africa rate of growth is only 0.4 percentage points from 2020 to 2040, the result is an African economy that will be nine per cent bigger in the Made in Africa scenario by 2040 than it would be under the Current Path (US$7.85 trillion versus US$7.21 trillion in MER).

The Made in Africa scenario is significantly more modest than the wildly optimistic forecast published by McKinsey in a 2017 report, according to which Africa could double its manufacturing output by 2025 'provided countries take decisive action to create an improved environment for manufacturers'.[46]

In the Made in Africa scenario, low-income African economies are forecast to be roughly ten per cent larger in 2040 than they would be in the Current Path forecast (equivalent to US$145 billion) and to increase rapidly thereafter. The economies of lower-middle-income and upper-middle-income countries would be, respectively, ten per cent (US$409 billion) and six per cent (US$90 billion) larger.

The interventions affect the various economic sectors differently. Manufacturing grows from 17 per cent of GDP in 2020 to 20 per cent in 2040 in the Made in Africa scenario, instead of only 18 per cent in 2040 in the Current Path. The contribution of agriculture to GDP declines by half by 2040, but is about 0.75 percentage points smaller in the Made in Africa scenario compared to the Current Path. But, because the African economy grows more rapidly, the agricultural sector is actually US$4.8 billion larger in 2040 than in the Current Path forecast.

The service sector grows rapidly under all scenarios, constituting roughly 59 per cent of the total of value added by 2040, but is marginally smaller in the Made in Africa scenario. The energy sector is slightly smaller as a proportion of GDP in Made in Africa than in the Current Path forecast by 2040. All sectors grow in absolute terms.

Income levels increase substantially in the Made in Africa scenario. By 2040 the average African would have an annual income that is US$227 more than in the Current Path, with the biggest increases on average in upper-middle-income countries, at US$664 (in PPP). The result is a small decline in inequality using the Gini index.

Costs and benefits of a manufacturing pathway

A manufacturing pathway comes with short- to medium-term costs relating to poverty and employment since it diverts expenditure towards higher-value activities against the promise of more rapid and sustainable growth.

The analysis of poverty in Chapter 7 shows that extreme poverty affected 50 per cent of the total African population in 2017 and that it will decline to 38 per cent (although the actual number of extremely poor people will increase) by 2040, using the additional income levels of extreme poverty now used by the World Bank.

In the Made in Africa scenario, poverty levels marginally increase for a decade above the Current Path before more rapid economic growth makes up for this initial increase. For example, by 2030, 17 million *more* Africans will be living in extreme poverty in low-income Africa than would be the case in the Current Path, But, by 2040, 14 million *fewer* Africans will be living in extreme poverty. Thereafter the positive impact accelerates dramatically.

It is unclear if a manufacturing pathway will create more jobs in the short term, but it is certain to increase employment in the medium and long term as rates of economic growth accelerate. Quite likely, the Made in Africa scenario will initially *increase* unemployment slightly before the economy starts growing more rapidly. In contrast, the forecast by the McKinsey report is that an expanded and more productive manufacturing sector could already create 6 to 14 million stable jobs by 2025.[47]

These results point to two important conclusions. The first is the importance of additional measures to reduce extreme poverty, including efforts to directly support extremely poor families through social programmes such as cash grants. The second is that the largest increase in poverty during the initial period of industrialisation will take place in low-income countries, which is why industrialisation should generally be pursued after countries have graduated to lower-middle-income status.

None of these costs should, however, detract from the fact that, eventually, a growing manufacturing sector will have important spillover effects on other sectors. It generally leads to improved productivity in the agricultural sector and incentivises the development of higher-value services.

Conclusion: Promoting and intensifying local production and trade

Since the 1970s, African economies have experienced a limited – as well as limiting – form of structural transformation from low-productivity agriculture to low-end services. Manufacturing and industrial development have never taken off in Africa. In fact, according to some the continent is deindustrialising from already low levels.

By comparison, countries in East Asia grew rapidly and over sustained periods after they had achieved food security, because of the rapid productivity gains that followed determined efforts by activist governments to move labour from low- to higher-productivity sectors of the economy and to invest in the same. Labour typically moved from subsistence agriculture to low-end manufacturing and then steadily upwards to increasingly complex manufacturing products.

Starting from a low base, where the majority of workers engage either in subsistence farming or informal services, Africa has more to gain from structural transformation than other developing regions, but to date it has not managed to achieve this. The primary reason why it is so crucial to grow Africa's manufacturing and high-end services sector is not only because of the potential that manufacturing has to create more formal-sector jobs, but also because it would change the productive structures of African economies and unlock more rapid growth. In fact, James Manyika and colleagues remind us that the contribution of manufacturing to an economy shifts as a nation matures, and that in advanced economies, 'manufacturing promotes innovation, productivity and trade more than growth and employment'.[48] Eventually, more rapid growth translates into more employment.

Digital production – particularly through the impact of artificial intelligence, automation and robotics – will also play a role. It is poised to disrupt the nature of manufacturing and global value chains. I have previously mentioned that the cost of labour is no longer necessarily the primary determinant in the location of production, and the contribution of services as part of regional and global value chains is steadily increasing in importance. Still, since labour remains a key consideration in Africa, it places the continent at a distinct disadvantage. To compensate for Africa's relatively high labour costs, the continent needs to invest in lowering transport and infrastructure costs, ensuring policy certainty and a low regulatory burden, and seeing to the success of trade integration to provide larger markets and rapid digitisation. Collectively, this will attract and grow manufacturing.

In a future in which more goods will be produced and consumed in regional rather than global markets and possibly in a much more distributed manner, Africa has considerable opportunities for industrialisation as well as regional trade (see Chapter 11). However, this will only happen if leaders in key growth-locomotive countries embark on a deliberate effort to go up the manufacturing curve and establish and support SEZs, set clear industrial policies, provide relevant education, and invest in the necessary digital backbone.

SEZs need to be locally embedded. This requires a fine balance – that is, providing tax and other benefits in the interests of export promotion without undercutting local manufacturing firms outside the SEZs. Furthermore, markets should implement import substitution where feasible, and within relevant international legal obligations. On this journey, ICT could play an important role in improving productivity in various sectors.

Without much greater emphasis on actively pursuing structural transformation of the economy towards more highly productive sectors, Africa will not be able to add value to its agricultural sector or develop higher-end services. In the words of Rwandan president Paul Kagame, quoted at the start of this chapter, African economies must be infused with technology, otherwise Africa will remain poor.

The transition from low to higher productivity requires active governments that set up, nurture and support dynamic local industries and services, changing the dominant mode of production – in effect, changing society as a whole. These measures will need very careful, if not surgical, engagement by a competent and modern bureaucracy.

The Made in Africa scenario will, eventually, create many more jobs than the Current Path forecast. This will take a long time, however. Generally, the employment intensity of the manufacturing sector is declining globally when compared to the period when Asia experienced its most rapid manufacturing growth.[49] It is against this backdrop that the next chapter looks at jobs and the changing nature of work in Africa.

9

The future of work in Africa

New forces are transforming the world of work . . . Without
decisive action we will be heading into a world that widens
existing inequalities and uncertainties.

– Cyril Ramaphosa and Stefan Lofven[1]

Africa has a huge unemployment challenge. The African Development
Bank[2] estimates that 10 to 12 million youths, many of them educated,
enter the African workforce annually, yet only three million formal jobs
are created each year. Looking to the future, the IMF[3] calculates that
sub-Saharan Africa has to create 20 million formal jobs per year for the
next two decades, compared to an average of nine million jobs added
annually since 2000. This points to an annual deficit of 11 million jobs.

Currently, most Africans are employed in the agricultural sector, which
is roughly double the size of the labour force employed in the services
sector. The latter, in turn, employs roughly double the number of Africans
employed in the manufacturing sector. Energy and materials and information technology employ significantly fewer people.

The job prospects along the Current Path forecast for Africa are not
good. Between 2000 and 2014, formal employment in Africa expanded by
less than 1.8 per cent annually,[4] but the labour force expanded by 2.6 per
cent per annum. The main reason is that even at a robust 4.8 per cent
annual average growth rate, the African economy was not growing rapidly
enough. In the absence of formal-sector jobs, the vast majority of Africa's
youth are forced into the informal sector, where life is precarious, earnings
are meagre, and there is no social protection.

Due to the large surplus of labour on the continent, economic growth
in Africa is actually more employment-intensive than it would otherwise
be.[5] It is often cheaper to employ more labour than to invest in better
systems or technology. Also, labour productivity is quite low due to the
skills gap, since investments in human capital, particularly in health
(Chapter 4) and education (Chapter 5), are low. The World Bank's

Human Capital Index measures the lost productivity of the next generation of workers as a consequence of underinvestment in health and education. Sub-Saharan Africa is at the bottom of the index's global ranking.[6]

There is an unavoidable tension between employment-intensive growth and productivity-intensive growth. If an economy does not grow, the pressure for more output per worker will contribute to a steady decline in employment or a reduction in average remuneration. Typically, this would happen through the process of automation. To grow employment, Africans need to pay particular attention to measures that can unlock more rapid economic growth. This has already been discussed in previous chapters, pointing to the rather obvious fact that, over long time horizons, more rapid economic growth is generally better at increasing employment than are redistributive policies. Both are required, of course.

In Chapter 8, I briefly examined the phenomenon of premature deindustrialisation (from already low levels) in Africa, and argued that it appears unlikely that Africa will be able to grow employment rapidly based on growth in manufacturing. The analysis presented there is that middle-income countries are apparently experiencing declining shares of industry as a contribution to GDP, and declining shares of industrial employment at an earlier stage of development compared to the history of today's developed countries. But, because manufacturing is important in changing the productive structures within the entire economy, including agriculture and services, I also argued that African countries need to pursue industrialisation aggressively where this is possible.[7]

This trend of premature deindustrialisation complicates the potential impact of structural transformation towards more formal and less vulnerable employment in many African countries. In effect, the opportunity for industrialisation in Africa as a pathway to providing employment and productivity improvements seems to be slipping away. And, since manufacturing is the single most important vehicle through which economies transition to higher productivity, the long-term impact of premature deindustrialisation could be debilitating. The conclusion, as key analysts argue, is that African countries need to look elsewhere for growth, primarily towards tourism, agriculture, natural resource extraction and ICT services.[8]

The problem is that none of these sectors offer particularly exciting employment or productivity prospects. Africa is already overly dependent on natural resource extraction and vulnerable to the associated swings in commodity prices. Commodity dependence is linked to political dysfunction and traps a country at the low end of the value chain. Tourism is employment-intensive but not all countries have the offerings to be able to offer attractive packages or destinations. Nor does tourism offer the kind of learning-driven productivity improvements generally common to manufacturing. And agriculture, where Africa has significant potential, automates even faster than industry.[9]

The dominance of the informal sector in Africa

The formal definition of employment that is used by the ILO and others includes both the formal and informal sectors. Employment data therefore would include the executive of a company who may be earning millions of dollars a year and the teacher in the DRC who earns US$100 per month. It also includes the street vendor who sells packets of peanuts by the side of the road who may be earning 20 or 30 cents per day.

Using the ILO definition, unemployment in Africa was at only 7.9 per cent in 2017, with female unemployment about two percentage points higher than male.[10] Globally, unemployment is highest in North Africa (at 11.7 per cent), particularly among youth and women, and is worse than in sub-Saharan Africa (at 7.2 per cent).

Previous chapters have pointed to the dominance of the informal sector in Africa.[11] But, while the informal sector provides employment for unskilled and undereducated individuals, employment in this context is clearly not 'decent work', which the ILO defines as including 'a fair income, security in the workplace and social protection for families'.[12] Many people in the informal sector live below or just above rates of extreme poverty and have no social protection systems.

On most of the continent, the actual meaning of employment – a situation of having paid work or earning an income – therefore means earning something, anything, but seldom a living wage. Hence, the ILO finds that almost 250 million persons in employment live in extreme or moderate poverty – a number that is expected to rise annually by four million as the working-age population increases.[13]

Estimates of the size of the informal sector and the contribution it makes to African economies differ widely. According to the IMF, the informal sector is responsible for around 16 per cent of GDP in member countries of the Organisation for Economic Co-operation and Development (OECD) but around 38 per cent in sub-Saharan Africa.[14]

Poor countries generally have a larger informal sector than richer countries, and many more people are employed in the informal sector in poorer countries than in wealthier countries. According to the ILO, in 2016, 86 per cent of employment in Africa was in the informal sector (72 per cent excluding agriculture), the highest rate globally.[15] Rates vary widely, however, and informal employment outside the agricultural sector ranges from 34 per cent in South Africa to 90.6 per cent in Benin.[16]

Generally, the existence of a large informal sector is costly for society and constrains sustainable development. Persons active in the informal sector do not contribute much to taxes (since they are not registered to pay personal or company tax) but the informal sector still has to be served by police and requires infrastructure such as roads, water, sewerage, electricity and suchlike. The result is that a large informal sector places an additional burden on service delivery and congests public infrastructure while contributing to neither, except through unavoidable indirect taxes such as value-added and service taxes.

In the absence of a social security net, employment in the informal sector is better than no employment. For this reason, the informal sector plays an important role in Africa, as it provides some level of work and income and hence reduces inequality.

Southern Africa has the smallest informal sector on the continent, with an estimated 40 per cent in informal employment (when agriculture is included).[17] The portion in the rest of the continent is much larger. In this subregion, the informal sector therefore serves as less of a cushion to unemployment than it does elsewhere. With low levels of employment, inequality is generally high. There is probably a historical reason for this, since Southern Africa achieved independence most recently and the ruling parties all stick to an ideology of economic centralism that offers little room for innovation and self-help. As a result, the economic emancipation of its majority peoples has often not yet taken place. Governments promise to provide for their citizens but do so in a manner that fosters dependence rather than empowerment and entrepreneurship. Furthermore, previous systems of mining, education and business that were, until recently, premised on the extraction of maximum profits have left huge inequalities. With low levels of education, employment is particularly low and inequality is exceptionally high.

So what, then, are the prospects for employment in Africa?

Trends in employment

Across all country income groups, the share of employment in services is growing, but the share of employment in both agriculture and manufacturing employment is declining. This applies as much to Africa as to the rest of the world. As explained in Chapter 8, workers in much of Africa are moving out of subsistence agriculture in rural areas into low-end services in the informal sector in urban areas. Working conditions are generally worse in the services sector than in the manufacturing sector and only marginally better than in the subsistence agriculture sector.

The African Agriculture Revolution scenario modelled in Chapter 6 is about the transformation of current traditional agriculture into integrated value chains that link smallholder farmers to retailers using ICT technology and a host of applications, which become the glue holding this complex system together. In this manner, agriculture moves into manufacturing through agro-processing, with significantly higher levels of productivity.

In the short to medium term the African Agriculture Revolution scenario also has a potentially large impact on creating employment. But, over a time horizon of a decade and longer, a manufacturing growth path unlocks more rapid economic growth and eventually also provides more jobs than does agriculture. On top of this, improvements in productivity in agriculture are bound to reduce employment intensity by introducing modern technology into the sector. In other words, there is a clear limit on the potential of agriculture to provide the jobs that Africa so desperately needs, although it certainly would play an important role.

Chapter 8 therefore emphasised the importance of growing Africa's manufacturing sector, not because of the (limited) potential of manufacturing to create jobs in the 21st century, but rather because of its importance in changing the productive structures of African economies and unlocking faster growth.

A larger manufacturing sector has enabling spillover effects. For example, it incentivises high-end services such as financial intermediation, which is crucial for the development of the private sector, and also encourages a more productive agricultural sector and consequently the transition into agro-processing and agribusiness. These changes eventually produce higher growth rates and a more rapidly growing economy that, in turn, creates more jobs in the medium to longer term.

The African Center for Economic Transformation is one of many institutions that hold the belief that both agriculture and light manufacturing are key requirements for the future. In its *African Transformation Report 2017* it argues in favour of 'a dual-track to industrialization – one track that leverages their relative labor-abundance for labor-intensive and export-oriented light manufacturing, and another track that leverages their advantages in agriculture for globally competitive agriculturally based manufacturing.'[18] While an agricultural growth path is appropriate for low-income countries, once these countries achieve middle-income status the importance of a manufacturing growth path generally becomes more important.

However, as a contribution to GDP, or portion of the total economy, the services sector already predominates. In the Current Path forecast, the contribution of services to Africa's economy steadily increases from its current 52 per cent to 59 per cent by 2040 while that of agriculture almost halves, declining from 18 to 9 per cent. This is in line with a global trend towards more service-oriented economies, with job growth particularly in non-routine, low-end occupations such as personal care services. Given the dominance of the services sector, most future employment growth on the African continent is set to come from here, which includes trade, transportation, finance and other commercial services.

These trends are confirmed in an IMF report stating that '[s]ub-Saharan Africa will not be able to transform through manufacturing as East Asia did over the past two decades'.[19] According to the report, the African growth experience over the last 35 years can, in general, be characterised as 'growth in capital-intensive resource- and energy-based industries – which in turn have not generated a sufficient number of jobs.

Africa's manufacturing sector has stagnated in output and employment terms. The latter happened in an environment of an unproductive agriculture sector and an employment intensive, urban-based informal retail sector.'[20] The report's conclusion cautions that most of the new jobs 'were created in sectors with low productivity levels, such as subsistence agriculture and low value-added services. Self-employment has continued to be predominant.'[21]

Given the size of the informal sector and the nature of work in Africa, the key question when looking to the future of work is, will digitisation help to more rapidly formalise African economies and accelerate growth, with all the associated benefits listed above?

Automation and the threat to work

Estimates about the impact of the fourth industrial revolution, robots, the digital economy and automation differ hugely and include alarmist forecasts about the destruction of up to 30 per cent of all jobs globally by 2030. This is highly unlikely. In fact, the rich world, Europe and North America in particular, is enjoying an unprecedented bonanza of jobs. And, instead of the exploitation of low-end workers, wages are generally rising.[22]

With each successive industrial revolution, technology has created many more jobs than it has destroyed. Despite the hype around artificial intelligence, robotics and automation, it is doubtful that the fourth industrial revolution will change this broad trend. The question we need the answer to, though, is: where will these jobs be created – in the developed or the developing world, in Africa or in Asia? Given that the capital- and labour-intensity of manufacturing is declining, ie less capital and less labour are required to produce the same value of goods, it could exert a downward pressure on wages in Africa as the continent struggles to remain competitive. Clearly, a much more appropriate strategy is the consistent upskilling of workers given the job opportunities that are opening at semi-skilled and skilled levels.

Artificial intelligence, robotics and automation will have very different impacts in the developing world compared to the developed world, largely because robotics presents a huge threat to higher-paid routine labour in the more mature economies. As with every previous industrial revolution, new jobs will emerge that will replace the jobs lost to robots and automation. 'Work,' the saying goes, 'fills the time available.'[23]

The largest potential for robot-based automation is in those states with large and well-paying manufacturing sectors, such as Germany, Japan, South Korea, the US and, increasingly, China. The automation of low-wage and light-manufacturing jobs, such as those generally found in Africa, seems much less likely in the foreseeable future. According to the African Development Bank:

> So far, robotisation has had only a small effect on most developing countries, where mechanisation continues to be the predominant form of automation. Despite the hype surrounding the potential of robot-based automation, today the use of industrial robots globally remains quite small and amounts to less than two million units. Industrial robots are concentrated in the automotive, electrical and electronics industries, and in a small number of countries.[24]

According to mainstream analysis, the demand for jobs that cannot easily be replaced by robots, especially those that require non-routine cognitive and socio-behavioural skills, will increase, for example managing teams, nursing and cleaning. However, the demand for routine, job-specific skills, such as required for processing payroll, bookkeeping or assembling goods, will fall. And jobs that combine different skill sets will increase.

A 2017 report by McKinsey estimates that less than five per cent of occupations are candidates for full automation and that the 'correct' lens through which automation should be viewed is that of tasks, not occupations or jobs.[25] Even so, work that requires empathy and judgement (such as nursing and elder care) is harder to automate and thus likely to increase. So, people will have to transition from one set of skills that may be replaced by automation to another where the threat is not as acute. This is clearly less of a challenge in Africa, where employment is less formal and structured than elsewhere.

In Japan and Germany, which have highly paid and scarce workers, many of whom work in automated industries, a higher percentage of additional work could be automated. However, in many parts of Africa new jobs could be created at much lower wages due to the reductions in the capital costs and lower barriers to entry referred to above.[26]

In view of these considerations, and contrary to the trepidation with which the fourth industrial revolution is viewed in Europe and North America, the view from Africa is positive. For one, this is because of the expectation that it will create more jobs in the formal sector. On the basis of extensive fieldwork in 11 African countries, the *African Transformation Report 2017* found that less than a fifth of survey respondents thought the fourth industrial revolution would have a negative impact on jobs. In fact, the vast majority were excited about its positive impact:

> The sectors seen as most positively affected by 4IR [fourth industrial revolution] technologies are software development, information and communication technology (ICT), and infrastructure – not surprising since 4IR will create demand for jobs in these sectors. But agriculture, finance, manufacturing, retailing, and tourism are also seen as benefiting from 4IR; the informal sector is seen as deriving the least benefit from 4IR.[27]

In this vein, a report entitled *The Future of Work*, prepared for the European Commission, concludes:

> The world of work is part-and-parcel of the changing economy, heavily influenced by globalisation, international value and supply chains, more division of labour, and digital disruption. Work is no longer a static concept but an umbrella term for roles performed in a different manner and under different legal arrangements.[28]

Instead of workers being replaced completely by machines, the more likely future is one in which people work next to highly productive machines and use machines (or technology more broadly) to increase productivity. This is already evident in the way ICT is penetrating modern life through the use of smartphone applications to augment or ease the completion of everyday tasks.

Therefore, the impact of the digital economy in OECD countries (where we see the reshoring of the provision of goods and top-end services) will include a trend towards short-term contracts and part-time work, although the vast majority of workers in the EU, for example, are still on full-time contacts. In addition, the Commission believes that automation will reduce routine job opportunities in the formal sector.[29]

Yet, in a certain sense, Africans might find this an easier transition since many in the formal and informal sector often already juggle a number of part-time jobs. According to *The Future of Work* report:

> ['W]ork' is increasingly becoming an umbrella concept for tasks per-formed under different legal, functional and geographic frameworks. Jobs are being broken down into projects that may either be outsourced to independent professionals and experts, or be reconfigured into assignments that assemble physical or virtual teams, across borders and time zones.[30]

The trend towards the so-called gig economy or internet employment, which is characterised by freelance, on-demand work, is the latest manifestation of the greater fragmentation of work. In the gig economy independent workers are hired for short-term tasks, often via online work platforms that pay them for each transaction, or 'gig', they complete. At high levels of complexity and value, the gig economy is about digital technologies enabling geographically dispersed teams, who often come from different countries, to be assembled around a given project.[31] Although still quite small in much of Africa (at less than 0.3 per cent of the active labour force), the gig economy is burgeoning, especially in on-demand services ranging from the delivery of fast food to more sophisticated tasks such as account-ing and editing.[32] But, even in the US, the gig economy accounts for only around one per cent of jobs.[33]

The interesting thing about the notion of the gig economy is that it is already a much wider reality in Africa, although in a different form. Many entrepreneurial Africans in countries such as Kenya already hustle to keep bread on the table by doing any number of jobs, tasks and functions in a seamless and often informally structured work environment.

Eventually it is unlikely that we will witness widespread automation in sub-Saharan Africa. The region's large-scale informal economy and lack of the necessary digital infrastructure currently precludes such a development, since low pay levels means that labour will remain cheap.

Digitisation and job creation in Ghana

In repeated visits to Ghana over the past two decades, I have witnessed the amazing political and developmental revolution that is taking place there, and in many other African states, and been able to consider its potential for job creation and progress.

By African standards, Ghana is small, with a population of around 29 million people. It is more urbanised than most African countries (at around 60 per cent), allowing for a more rapid transition to digital services and making it easier to provide water, sanitation and other services. By 2040 almost 80 per cent of its citizens will live in urban areas – a huge advantage that will allow rapid economic growth. This could eventually allow Ghana to graduate from its current lower-middle-income to upper-middle-income status.

Partly because of higher than average rates of urbanisation, total fertility rates (currently at four children per woman) are declining rapidly and Ghana will enter its demographic sweet spot earlier than most other West African countries, around 2033. Thereafter, the positive ratios of working-age persons to dependants should ensure even more rapid growth rates – provided that Ghana manages to sustain its progress over the past decade towards inclusive, democratic governance.

On a trip to the country in December 2018 I was invited to speak at a conference hosted by the IMF on the future of work in sub-Saharan Africa. The gleaming, brand-new Terminal 3 at Accra's Kotoka International Airport is a far cry from the sorry colonial-era building that served as an international airport for so many years. Officials are smart, courteous and clearly proud of the new facility. Kotoka was built by a Turkish construction company, Mapa Construction, at a cost of US$400 million, and is unpretentious, solid and well maintained (in contrast to many of the Chinese constructions elsewhere).

At the opening session of the IMF conference, held at a swanky Accra hotel, Ghana's vice president, Mahamudu Bawumia, set out the country's plans to leapfrog its development by using information and digital systems. In 2012, Ghana introduced biometric voter registration, and since May 2018 a smart national ID system (dubbed Ghana Card) that uses biometrics has been rolled out (free of charge to all Ghanaians). At some point the Ghana Card will be a requirement to open a bank account, apply for a passport or driver's licence, register a SIM card, buy property, register a business, or even enrol children in school.

Globally, nearly a billion people lack any type of legally recognised form of identification, without which it is impossible to access banking, government benefits, education and many other critical services.[34] Most importantly, a digitised national population registration system linked to the steady increase of electronic forms of payment will allow the state to monitor large portions of the informal sector and incorporate them into the formal economy. This is a huge leap forward in a country that has, until recently, had no comprehensive identity system. It is also occurring at a pace that would astound bureaucrats in China and Western countries where such systems were originally rolled out manually and with great effort over several decades.

In addition to the national ID system, the GhanaPostGPS will provide a unique digital address for each five square metres of land area in a country that previously had no formal system of finding a specific location without local knowledge. Armed with a digital address, small and informal businesses will be able to register for a bank account and access credit. It basically means that anyone with a phone technically has a bank account.

The GhanaPostGPS app comes with other functions as well, such as panic buttons for emergency communication with the police, fire and ambulance services.[35] A unique digital address will allow door-to-door delivery of literally everything. For example, the country will soon start with the delivery of emergency medical and other supplies by drone. Here, Ghana is copying the example of Rwanda, where this has been done for some time. (They used corporate social responsibility funds for the initiative.)

Besides many other benefits, these innovations will improve tax collection, since both informal and formal businesses will steadily be forced to use electronic payment systems that are all part of the formal economy, thereby increasing government revenues. This will, again, enable the state to deliver other services such as education, roads, water and sanitation.

Soon, Ghana will also have a fully digital platform for the payment for all government services, including smart driver's licences and digital car registration. Moreover, the country is busy with the digitisation of land ownership. By the time this book is published, it should have a new base map survey (the first since 1974) that uses blockchain technology to secure and verify the ownership of all land. Furthermore, with the support of the World Bank, the Ghanaian Ministry of Education is adopting modern technology by delivering its lessons through the use of e-learning technology.[36]

Modern technology also allows for better policing of things like mining licences, for example. In many African countries, including in South Africa and the DRC, illegal mining is rife, and is often done by foreigners who mine at night in extremely dangerous conditions. Already 150 drone pilots have been trained to monitor illegal mining across Ghana.

In recognition of these efforts, Google will open its first African artificial intelligence research centre in Accra, bringing together top machine-learning researchers and engineers dedicated to artificial intelligence research and its applications. The centre will work with local universities and jointly with a small number of other centres around the world.[37] This is an example of what is possible in a future Africa where the demand for new services is met and job opportunities for young people in urban areas are unlocked.

The promise of greater economic formalisation in Ghana

Using IFs, I find that the size of Ghana's economy increases by roughly US$1.1 billion dollars (in PPP) over a ten-year period for every two per cent decrease in the size of the informal sector as a portion of GDP. In other words, if Ghana could use digitisation to reduce the size of the informal economy as a portion of GDP by five percentage points (and also to move labour from the informal to the formal economy) from 2020 to 2030, it would gain US$3.3 billion in the size of its economy by 2030.

A larger economy translates into higher average incomes, and the result is an increase of US$129 in average GDP per person above the Current Path forecast by 2030 for Ghana's 37 million citizens. That is an enormous improvement.[38] Other advantages that follow are decreases in poverty and inequality.

This analysis of the potential positive impact of a more rapid formalisation of Ghana's economy corresponds broadly with the gist of an article by Amolo Ng'weno and David Porteus,[39] who argue that the explosion in digital platforms is slowly changing the nature of what it means to be in the informal or formal sector. The result is the incremental formalisation of the former through a process of digital business progression in which each small step is low-cost and low-risk:

> In the short term, it looks like technology is going to create a set of new opportunities in the gig economy: shared-ride drivers, homestay hosts, e-commerce logistics, e-commerce sellers, and small-scale e-commerce producers. These will be supplemented by an army of 'digital translators' . . . As an economy digitizes, more people are needed to help the customer and the citizen transition into the digital economy. Most of these translators work on commission and set their own hours.[40]

On the future nature of work, they write: 'It's time we recognized the truth about the future of work in Africa: it isn't in the growth of full-time formal sector jobs. The future of work will be people working multiple gigs with "somewhat formal" entities.'[41]

Eventually, 'in Africa, as elsewhere, the future of work will depend on the battle between automation and innovation', argues a report by the Mo Ibrahim Foundation: 'While automation leads to a decline in employment in old sectors, innovation makes new sectors or tasks possible.'[42]

Of course the gig economy doesn't only have positive effects. Generally, digitisation lowers barriers to entry and increases competition. In Africa, this could further force down wages and increase the number of people in informal and unregulated work. The danger is that the gig economy could increase precarious or insecure work, with lower job and income security, poorer working conditions and lower social protection coverage than in standard employment relations.

Then again, digital technologies are much more likely to empower individuals, allowing them to access opportunities and markets that they would not otherwise have been able to access, and with significantly lower transaction costs. I will explore this topic further in Chapter 10 as part of a discussion on the continent's ability to benefit from digitisation and to leapfrog into the future thanks to the fourth industrial revolution.

Conclusion: Thinking differently about the future

On the current trajectory, the growth in the African labour force will far outstrip the supply of jobs, leaving many of the continent's citizens destitute, frustrated and dependent on the informal sector to survive. This will make some of them eager to migrate elsewhere in search of opportunities, including to Europe, and desperate to explore any opportunity, even illicit, to survive. These conclusions re-emphasise the importance of an agricultural and manufacturing revolution that would increase growth and employment.

Only if one views employment in Africa through the lens of empowerment and self-employment (much of which currently occurs within the informal sector), digitisation and the fourth industrial revolution does it become possible to think differently about the future of work in Africa. With large numbers of young people entering the labour market, the demand for jobs is huge and steadily increasing. However, previous chapters have also indicated that Africa's labour force generally lacks many of the purported enablers for rapid job creation, such as minimal levels of education and the right skills (Chapter 5), as well as adequate health and the associated infrastructure (Chapter 4).

Even then, a large cohort of young people with improving levels of education who are either unemployed or eking out a meagre living in the informal sector could be destabilising. Young Africans are increasingly connected with each other and the rest of the world through the internet and social media, and will not stop seeking out the opportunities and lifestyles enjoyed by their peers in the developed world.

Chapter 12 deals with the structural drivers of instability, including the combination of youth and unemployment. In a different context, this group coincides with the NEETS – the large group of Africans Not in Education, Employment or Training. Clearly, the orientation of education opportunities towards the actual opportunities or needs within the economy, and vocational training in particular, could assist in lowering the political temperature. In addition, there is the potential for job creation in agriculture, light manufacturing, modern services, tourism and creative industries.

Since much of Africa's growth is going to come from commodity exports, it is equally incumbent upon governments to raise incomes through commodity value addition and to find ways of extending the value chains of the associated capital-intensive projects into the domestic economy. Furthermore, governments have to find ways of enhancing productivity and improving working conditions and regulations to reduce workers' vulnerability.

There will also be an important role for the public sector in creating jobs for social development and through public works programmes, both to improve livelihoods and to enhance skills, never mind the need for social grants, as explored in Chapter 7.

Most concerning is that the vast number of Africans who survive in the informal sector appear to be particularly vulnerable to the hurdles created by the fourth industrial revolution. This underlines the importance of using digitisation to open up new opportunities for this group, such as access to finance, and to bring the informal sector into the mainstream. Every effort should be made to overcome the segregation between the formal and informal sectors through productive linkages and by reforming laws and regulations, most conspicuously by easing the administrative hurdles for registration of businesses, participation in trade and the like.

In this chapter I used the example of Ghana to illustrate how modern technology could potentially formalise its economy more rapidly and the benefits that could accrue from such an approach. I provided an indication of the results using economic growth, poverty and GDP per capita. By following this example, African governments can harness the potential of digitisation to empower ordinary citizens by providing access to finance, education and opportunity.

To provide sufficient meaningful work, the continent needs a shift in mindset from consumption to production and towards innovation, community self-sufficiency and independence. Only this will allow a more speedy escape from poverty compared to the slow progress envisioned under the Current Path forecast.

Only if African governments are able to create a culture of entrepreneurship will the continent be able to reduce unemployment. Attitudes need to change from 'getting education to get a job', to 'getting education to create jobs and opportunities'. Even then, such entrepreneurship and self-employment will make only a small contribution to employment rather than solving the unemployment challenge.

The next chapter builds on these findings to explore the potential of technology to allow Africa to leapfrog towards a better future.

10

Technological innovation and the power of leapfrogging

What's important is that you have a faith in people, that they're basically good and smart, and if you give them tools, they'll do wonderful things with them.

– Steve Jobs[1]

The term 'leapfrogging' has become almost as popular as 'fourth industrial revolution' and 'digitisation' and they are, of course, intimately related. Leapfrogging occurs when we can use technology to radically improve an existing process, such as generating energy, or to solve a particular problem, for example the ability to more efficiently find, hire and pay for transport in a crowded urban environment using mobile phone applications. It can make previous systems and processes redundant, for instance by generating electricity from wave or ocean currents instead of burning coal. Leapfrogging is inherently disruptive, as it either destroys the value of 'old stuff' or presents ways of doing things that were not previously possible.

Leapfrogging is the story of innovation and development. However, we have not yet fully figured out how to leapfrog the provision of basic infrastructure, although there is the potential for progress here (see Chapter 11).

Africa trails globally in every dimension of infrastructure, with the largest deficits being in electricity generation, transport/roads, the provision of clean water and improved sanitation.[2] The drag that poor infrastructure has on economic growth is particularly evident in Africa's low-income and lower-middle-income countries. It is less severe for the eight upper-middle-income countries.[3]

The IMF, in a study of infrastructure spending in several countries from 1985 to 2014, found that an unanticipated 1 per cent increase in public infrastructure boosted GDP by 0.4 per cent the following year but by 1.5 per cent four years later.[4] The Economic Policy Institute concurs, noting in a 2014 report that 'our analysis conforms with a large and growing body of literature persuasively arguing that infrastructure investments can boost even private-sector productivity growth'.[5]

It is very likely, however, that we underestimate the potential for leapfrogging in infrastructure and that we are locked into a particular vision of how things should be done.[6] Once a country has invested in and built an elaborate network of pipes, wires, roads, bridges, buildings and other infrastructure, it becomes very difficult to imagine, or to take the risk of, investing in a different way of doing things. Every piece of existing infrastructure creates vested interests that are often quite difficult to uproot. The result is a tendency towards 'path dependency' in which governments do things in a particular way because that seems to be the way things should be done. Furthermore, since other countries have done things in one way for so long, Africans tend to believe they should follow the same infrastructure and development pathway presented by Europe, the USA and, recently, China.

Can we really imagine the impact of wireless power, automated delivery systems via heavy-lift drones, individual air transport and alternative mass transportation systems that replace cars, buses or trains? What would happen if there was a widespread adoption of atmospheric water generators, which are capable of extracting water from the air during the day and producing electricity at night (wind speed allowing)?[7]

The eThekwini municipality in South Africa's KwaZulu-Natal province recently completed a pre-feasibility study that found that the powerful Agulhas Current, which runs along the steep continental shelf, has the potential to generate 50 400 megawatt hours (or 50.4 billion kilowatts running for one hour). That is roughly equivalent to South Africa's total domestic electricity generation capacity.[8] And South Africa is, by a substantial margin, Africa's largest electricity producer.

Can we even begin to imagine the impact of the wide adoption of contour crafting – a layered fabrication system similar to 3D printing that can be used to rapidly construct buildings and other large pieces of infrastructure, thus doing away with the established bricks-and-mortar approach to construction?[9]

These are all examples of technological innovations that will bring about major changes. Actually, change often starts more modestly, but it creeps up on us. It is only one day when we look back that we realise the journey that has been travelled.

Recently, Volkswagen launched what it referred to as its 'first integrated mobility concept' in Rwanda. To this end it established a modest vehicle assembly plant in Kigali for semi-knockdown vehicle kits imported ready for assembly from South Africa. Most of the vehicles produced here will not be sold, however. Instead, they will be used by mobility services for car-sharing. Initially, employees of companies, government agencies, relief organisations and other institutions will be able to order a vehicle by mobile phone application. As a next step, the service is being extended to private customers who want to reserve a car or book a ride. In this way, Rwanda is pioneering a next-generation business model for point-to-point transport that has already attracted other major players who might not otherwise have been in Rwanda, such as the German technology giant Siemens.[10] It is an example of leapfrogging at quite a basic level.

What distinguishes the 21st century from previous periods is the exponential rate at which scientific knowledge is advancing and our ability to more rapidly translate that knowledge into practical application. Each new generation of technology stands on the shoulders of its predecessors, but today the rate of progress from version to version is driving advancement at rates of change that are sometimes breathtaking. At sufficient scale, technology can have a transformative effect on nations and on the relations between nations, although it is always important to remember that what is technologically possible is not always commercially feasible.

Perhaps the best recent example of technology's potential to literally shift the ground beneath our feet is the way in which the US shale and oil gas revolution has reshaped the global energy market and global politics.

Conventional wisdom has it that US domestic oil production peaked in 1970 at 9.6 million barrels per day and by 2005 had been declining for 35 years. At that point the US was importing just under half of its total petroleum consumption and appeared to be set on growing imports of oil and gas from countries such as Venezuela and Saudi Arabia. To the chagrin of the Americans, Russia was also rapidly emerging as an energy superpower. The situation with natural gas was only marginally better.[11]

Then came the fracking revolution. Hydraulic fracturing involves the high-pressure injection of water, chemicals and sand into shale deposits to release more of the gas and oil trapped within the rock. From 2005, US natural gas production increased year on year for ten straight years and by 2015 the US was the world's largest gas producer. From 2008 oil production followed. By 2018 domestic US crude production was running at about 11.6 million barrels per day, a little ahead of Russia, the world's second-largest producer.

In just a few years the shale oil and gas revolution in the US has changed geopolitics. It reduced the price of energy and thus broke the stranglehold of OPEC on energy production. It also led to a severe slump in the prospects of many oil-exporting countries, such as those in the Middle East, Venezuela, Angola and Nigeria.[12] In the process, the Middle East and Africa lost much of their strategic relevance to the US. But the US has not achieved energy independence, as low energy prices have pushed up domestic demand as consumers flock to gasoline-guzzling sports utility vehicles.[13]

The potential of renewable energy in Africa

Whereas the shale gas revolution in the US is based on a large oil and gas industrial ecosystem that is still difficult to replicate elsewhere, many other rapid advances in technology, such as those linked to renewable sources of energy, require a much smaller technology footprint. They could have a significant impact on Africa.

Hydroelectric, geothermal, solar and wind have the potential to revolutionise electricity access in Africa in a way not dissimilar to fracking in the USA. This revolution is coming to Africa in three forms. The first is through distributed local systems using renewables, mostly solar and wind, and the second is through the improvement and mass installation of electricity storage systems (such as new types of batteries), which is more likely at micro than at bulk level. The third is through new bulk technologies such as ocean current and geothermal power generation.

Power Africa, the initiative started under former US president Barack Obama, already supports 15 geothermal projects with 1 GW potential generation capacity. And, in addition to its large hydroelectric schemes,

Ethiopia has the potential to generate up to 10 GW of power from its geothermal resources. As opposed to the fluctuating energy supply from wind and solar, ocean currents and geothermal can provide stable base-load electricity generation.[14]

There is some disagreement about the share of renewables in global energy supply. In 2017, according to *Global Trends in Renewable Energy Investment*, 12 per cent of electricity globally came from clean sources (wind, solar, biomass and waste-to-energy, geothermal, marine and small hydro). Other estimates are that renewable electricity transmission is around 22 per cent globally, of which 17 per cent is hydropower, about 5 or 6 per cent is wind, and 1 or 2 per cent is solar. The share of fossil energy in the global energy mix (oil, coal and gas) has remained at about 80 per cent for the last two decades.[15]

The Current Path forecast points to a plateauing of fossil fuel use in the 2030s, followed by a steady decline after 2040, with non-fossil fuel sources overtaking fossil fuels just before mid-century and constituting more than 90 per cent of all supply by 2100. Leaving aside for the moment the huge challenge of the environment and climate change (see Chapter 15), this will be a world in which electricity for households will be provided by individual supply or decentralised mini-grids, not from large-scale coal, nuclear or other plants. It will be a world of energy abundance at a time when the lack of electricity is generally considered one of the largest constraints on Africa's development.

In a region with 638 million extremely poor people, electricity is often an unaffordable luxury even where connections exist. The average price for electricity in Africa is about US$0.14 per kWh, compared to US$0.04 in South Asia and US$0.07 in East Asia. Some in the industry cite the actual cost of electricity in Africa as closer to US$0.20 per kWh, largely due to the high cost of running backup generators during regular power shortages.[16]

High electricity prices and intermittent supply act as a strong disincentive to invest in Africa and also impede households from accessing electricity.[17] In 2018, about 54 per cent of Africa's population had access to electricity, in contrast to about 85 per cent in South Asia and well over 90 per cent in the rest of the world, excluding Africa. A rapid electrification of the continent would improve both economic prospects and human development. Affordable, reliable electricity eliminates the need to use traditional fuels inside the home for cooking and heating – thereby reducing the potential for respiratory ailments – and allows children to study longer at night. But many homes in Africa that ostensibly have an electricity connection find the supply inconsistent and the cost extremely high.

Currently, Africa generates very little electricity. The continent had about 168 GW of installed capacity in 2018, but more than half of this was concentrated in three countries: South Africa, Egypt and Algeria. Together, these countries account for only about 15 per cent of the continent's total population. By contrast, China has about 1 770 GW of installed capacity – seven times that of Africa – of which 150 GW is solar, with plans to add another 23 GW per year until 2023.[18] At current rates of growth China's installed *solar* capacity will shortly equal Africa's *total* installed capacity.

However, a number of large hydroelectric schemes are currently being built in Africa. For example, Ethiopia is completing the construction of the Grand Ethiopian Renaissance Dam (GERD) on the upper reaches of the Blue Nile. Once completed, it will be the third-largest hydroelectric facility in the world in terms of installed capacity, capable of generating almost 6.5 GW in peak operating conditions.[19] The idea is to link it to a regional distribution network and sell electricity in the larger Horn of Africa region, as well as to alleviate Ethiopia's own shortages.

The potential for hydroelectric power on the Congo River is equivalent to nearly a quarter of the entire installed capacity of Africa. The DRC plans to start construction imminently on Inga 3, the third of a series of hydroelectric dams connected to the Inga Falls, in 2019. The dam will cost up to US$18 billion. Inga 3 could produce about 11 GW at full capacity, and the full series of dams could eventually yield up to 50 GW at full operating capacity, according to the World Bank.[20]

Inga Falls, the proposed site of the Grand Inga project, is the world's largest waterfall by volume. Here, the Congo River drops an astonishing 96 metres over a distance of less than 15 kilometres. Since the drop is close to the mouth of the river, the water volumes are enormous. This translates into an incredible power-generating capacity compared to most other rivers.

Central Africa's mining sector is interested in the potential of hydro-electric power, particularly for the beneficiation of minerals. But unlike GERD, which has moved rapidly from planning to construction, the Grand Inga project has been perpetually held back by uncertainty, poor planning, delays, inefficiencies and corruption. And, despite being a priority for several pan-African organisations, such as Nepad, SADC and the East African Power Pool, there has been little tangible progress on the project in a country wracked by chronic instability and poor governance.

It's not as if the need is not there. The DRC is one of the most resource-rich countries on earth. It is the leading producer of copper in Africa and contains much of the world's cobalt. In addition, it has sizeable deposits of gold, diamonds and other minerals, including the so-called 3TG metals – cassiterite (tin), wolfram (tungsten) and coltan (tantalum) – that are infamous for being 'conflict minerals'. Other resource-rich countries such as Zambia also suffer from a debilitating electricity shortage.[21]

Wind and solar generation are already having a transformative effect on human well-being in parts of the continent. Kenya recently finished construction of the Lake Turkana Wind Project, the largest wind project in Africa, capable of delivering 310 MW to the grid when fully operational. This is small by international standards, but still is more than the installed capacity of several African countries, including Chad and Liberia.[22]

At the same time, the project is emblematic of the governance failures that hamper technological adaptation and economic growth on the continent. The wind farm was completed in 2017, but only connected to the grid the following year since the connecting infrastructure, which was the responsibility of the Kenyan government, was not in place in time. In the interim, the Kenyan government had to pay royalties (in lieu of electricity sales) to the project's investors.[23]

Already, global investments in solar capacity outstrip the combined investments in coal, gas and nuclear plants as renewable energy costs plummet. China's impact on global solar markets has been well documented, but uptake has also been rapid elsewhere, including in developing countries. This growth, fuelled by rapidly falling prices, has enabled countries such as India, Mexico and Chile to offer electricity from photovoltaic solar at a fraction of the cost (US$0.03 per kWh) of electricity in Africa.

We are only at the start of the solar energy revolution. According to the UN, the greater Sahara has solar potential equivalent to approximately 13.9 billion kWh/year. In 2016, global electricity consumption was 0.02 billion kWh/year.[24] It will require a revolution in electricity storage to unlock some of this potential, but the incentives are substantial, such as diluting Europe's dependence on imported gas from Russia. Beyond the need for technological innovation, the most important impediment is the lack of political stability in North Africa.

Solar energy prices have dropped to less than US$0.05 per kWh in some regions, and levelised costs that can now compete with those of electricity generated by burning fossil fuels. In Africa, solar energy could significantly change the overall picture of electricity supply. Electrifying rural areas would make many other development goals easier to achieve: access to clean water, independent economic activity, the use of electric appliances in general, and access to information via communication technologies. Solar energy could also fundamentally change the political landscape in many countries, leading to a redistribution of political and economic power as cities become less dependent on central governments.

Off-grid solutions could reach consumers in rural areas without the hefty expense of large coal-, oil- or gas-powered power plants linked to the hinterland through massive transmission lines and complex distribution systems. For instance, in sub-Saharan Africa more than 60 per cent of the population live in rural areas, but the region has by far the lowest rural electrification rate worldwide (about 25 per cent). In this context, mini-grids (local power networks that are not connected to the national grid) could provide many opportunities. These technologies can also be deployed much more rapidly than traditional methods of electrification. In fact, in a recent study on the long-term future of Kenya,[25] we saw clear evidence of the dramatic increases in electricity access for these reasons.

Globally, Bangladesh and Laos are widely cited as having expanded electricity access particularly rapidly. Bangladesh increased access by about 50 per cent in roughly 20 years, while Laos increased it by approximately 60 per cent in 25 years. Kenya has moved from about 20 per cent access in 2010 to about 70 per cent in 2018. In other words, Kenya achieved similar rate increases to Bangladesh and Laos in about a third of the time.

Mini-grids and renewables are already bringing about major shifts in how Africa will provide electricity to its people. What could really be transformative is a breakthrough in energy storage technology, since the sun does not shine all day every day, nor does the wind blow constantly. Consequently, electricity grids that include renewables have to allow for large redundancies (surplus capacity) to be able to meet demand on a guaranteed basis. In the absence of progress with energy storage, mini-grids are unable to provide sufficient power for heating and cooling.

The challenge of energy storage

Apart from our dependence on carbon-based sources of energy, a key challenge remains our inability to store excess energy supply at large scale during periods of relatively high production and low demand so that we can access it during periods of lower production and higher demand.

There are some systems that do this, for example the various schemes that use surplus electricity to pump water into an upstream storage dam when electricity demand is low, so that it can be released to generate surge electricity when demand increases. South Africa, Africa's largest electricity producer and consumer by a substantial margin, has two pumped-storage hydroelectricity schemes, one at Palmiet near Grabouw in the Western Cape and a second in KwaZulu-Natal. A third, at Ingula, has been commissioned.

The transition to renewable energy will accelerate dramatically once the challenge of affordable energy storage has been resolved. Huge resources are being poured into this challenge, particularly by vehicle manufacturers such as Volkswagen, Tesla and General Motors. In 2016, Microsoft co-founder Bill Gates launched Breakthrough Energy Ventures, a US$1 billion fund for new energy technologies that prioritises investments in energy storage companies, as well as in nuclear fusion power and geothermal systems.[26] It's just a matter of time . . .

The costs of lithium-ion batteries, currently the leading battery technology in large-scale production, have been falling rapidly as one large production facility after another comes on line.[27] In 2019, Tesla announced a new modular energy storage system (the Megapack) with a proposal to build an energy storage park in California, to consist of 449 Megapack modular units with a total capacity of 1 200 MWh. Each Megapack unit can store 12 times more power than its predecessor, the Powerpack 2, launched just two years earlier, illustrating the rapid progress in battery storage capacity.[28] Meanwhile, China is building a so-called virtual power plant, with a 720 MWh storage capacity.[29] Progress in smart metering, intelligent management of use and mini-grid solutions are also all powering ahead.[30]

And then there are the massive investments being made in fuel cell technology, using hydrogen gas, that could emerge as an alternative to batteries. China alone spent US$12.4 billion on supporting fuel-cell-powered vehicles in 2017 and will continue with its massive subsidies for fuel cells until at least 2025, although its subsidies for battery-electric vehicles are expected to be phased out five years earlier. Another advantage of fuel cell technology is that surplus electricity can be used during off-peak times to produce hydrogen from water, which can then be stored to generate electricity during peak demand or used in off-grid energy applications. China loses an estimated 150 GW of renewable energy generating capacity every year because it cannot be integrated into the grid.[31]

Among other things, distributed energy from renewables will facilitate the rapid expansion of communications and the internet.

Mobile phones and access to the internet: A big leap for Africa

To date, the most ubiquitous example of leapfrogging in many parts of Africa is the use of cellular telephones in areas that don't have fixed telephone lines. This obviates the expense and complication of connecting every telephone to a copper wire.

When the price of mobile technology fell through the floor – prices dropped by about 40 per cent globally and nearly 60 per cent in Africa in the last five years of the 20th century alone – so did demand for costly fixed telephone lines. This led to rapid improvements in the proportion of the population with access to a telephone without much additional cost to the consumer. It also allowed governments to focus on other priorities.

Africa (and also South Asia) has been able to leapfrog over expensive and time-consuming technologies and achieve a degree of catch-up with other parts of the world. Moreover, mobile networks are largely built by the private sector, illustrating the potential of African markets to attract foreign investment under the right conditions. The continuation of these investments has increased mobile phone and internet access in sub-Saharan Africa at rates that would have seemed unthinkable a few decades ago.

In 2000, fixed telephone lines were still relatively rare in the developing world, with a global access rate of about 15 subscriptions per 100 people, and only 38 per 100 people in Europe and Central Asia. Sub-Saharan Africa meanwhile, had access rates that were significantly lower than other developing regions. People in sub-Saharan Africa were more than 90 per cent less likely to have access to a fixed-line telephone than people in East Asia or Latin America, and even 50 per cent less likely than people in South Asia. In 2000, only 14 out of every 1 000 people in sub-Saharan Africa had a fixed-line telephone subscription. That gap continued to widen until about 2005, when there was a clear shift away from fixed lines and toward mobile subscriptions.

Sub-Saharan Africa has managed to start closing the gap between itself and the rest of the world in terms of access to telephony since mobile technology became widely available. Young Africans in urban areas are well connected, with about 80 per cent owning their own mobile phone and most using it daily.[32] Older Africans don't do so well. While more than half of households in Morocco, Mauritius, South Africa and Seychelles have internet access at home, in Liberia, the DRC, Congo, Guinea-Bissau and Eritrea that number is less than three per cent.[33] Although Africa still trails the rest of the world in terms of mobile subscriptions, the gap is much narrower now than it was when fixed-line technology dominated the world of personal connectivity, again illustrating how modern technology allows countries to leapfrog.

Although only about half of Africans own a mobile phone, another 15–20 per cent who do not own a phone have access to one, making the mobile phone access rate about 65–70 per cent. Generally, Africans have better access to mobile phones than to financial services, electricity or improved sanitation.[34]

The world has become significantly more connected over the last 15 years. At the height of demand for fixed telephone lines in East Asia, there were roughly 23 subscriptions per 100 people – or a little less than one per household. In Latin America it was closer to one out of every two households. Today, there are more than 100 mobile subscriptions per 100 people in those two regions, and sub-Saharan Africa and South Asia are rapidly approaching that level as well.

Cellular phone penetration has specific and increasingly well-documented economic advantages. On average, GDP grows between 0.7 and 1.4 per cent for every 10 per cent increase in fixed lines, and an additional 10 per cent penetration of mobile phones increases GDP by around 0.8 per cent per annum.[35]

This is not only about allowing people to speak to and text each other. According to a study on the relationship between broadband access and economic growth in OECD countries in 1996–2007, a ten percentage-point increase in broadband penetration 'raised annual per capita growth by 0.9–1.5 percentage points'.[36] Increased cellular phone penetration guarantees further innovation and additional investment.

In 2013, Google unveiled Project Loon, a plan to send a fleet of balloons into the stratosphere that could beam back internet service to people on earth. In mid-2018 Loon announced its first partnership with Telkom Kenya, Kenya's third-largest telecommunications provider. From 2019, Loon balloons will start sending 4G internet coverage to deliver its first commercial mobile service. Other tech giants such as SpaceX, Facebook and SoftBank-backed startup Altaeros all have similar plans involving satellites, drones and blimps, respectively.[37]

M-Pesa and innovation in mobile banking

Not only does cellular technology rapidly expand access to a communication device and information; it also spawns new innovations. A good example is the development of mobile money through the well-known M-Pesa service (*pesa* means 'money' in Kiswahili). M-Pesa is a mobile money service that was launched in 2007 in Nairobi. It allows users to store and exchange money on their mobile phones. By 2017, there were

30 million users across ten countries, and the service processed more than six billion individual transactions in 2016. Its example has spawned an entire mobile banking industry.

Even more impressive than these figures, though, has been the impact of the service on people's livelihoods. A study by Tavneet Suri and William Jack[38] estimates that M-Pesa has lifted nearly 200 000 households out of poverty since its inception. The improvements have been more significant for female-headed households, and have helped about 185 000 move from agriculture to some other business venture. Access to mobile money has helped borrowers to navigate uncertainties caused by drought, adverse health conditions and other unforeseen events.

The mobile money service has also driven an increase in savings rates of more than 20 per cent, because its more secure method of storing money instils confidence in people that the future is worth investing in. Africa today has more mobile money subscribers – 100 million – than any other region in the world.[39]

Mobile phones and social change

Beyond their direct impact on economic growth and prosperity, internet access and mobile phones have also become tools for social transformation: they allow small-scale farmers to link up with markets; citizens can report (and video) instances of the abuse of state power; election officials can report results instantaneously (and observers can document and submit examples of electoral abuse); and citizens can identify crime incidents. For example, shoppers in Dubai regularly post photographs on the internet of the latest luxury purchases by African leaders, and the alleged money-laundering perpetrated by family relatives and other close associates of Equatorial Guinea's President Teodoro Obiang Nguema Mbasogo has been disseminated to a wide audience.[40]

In today's world, it is much more difficult to hide and conceal wrongdoing, as Wikileaks proved so dramatically in 2010. In South Africa, whistleblowers released troves of emails that documented the extent to which an Indian family, the Guptas, had conspired with former president Jacob Zuma and others to defraud the South African government of hundreds of millions of dollars.

The impact of internet access and mobile phone technology on elections and government accountability, and potentially on the spread of democracy, has been profound. For example, after no candidate received the required 50 per cent in the first round of presidential elections in Ghana on 7 December 2008, a runoff was held between former foreign minister Nana Akufo-Addo and former vice president John Atta Mills on 28 December. Some 9 million votes were cast but eventually fewer than 31 000 votes separated the winner from the loser (a margin of less than 0.4 per cent, with 73 per cent of registered voters casting ballots). Despite a history of coups and social turbulence in Ghana, the country and the region accepted Mills' victory. The reason for this unprecedented transition was that civil society had been able to harness new technology and digital media to place 4 000 trained election monitors armed with mobile phones and an SMS-based coding system to check, report and tabulate results. Furthermore, a parallel civil society system could verify official tallies and ensure a highly credible result.[41]

This pattern has been emulated in various forms across the continent, reducing the ability of incumbents (and others) to manipulate and distort results to their own advantage. These efforts have not always been successful, however, as the December 2018 elections in the DRC showed.

The story of transformation thanks to the internet is likely only starting. The next generation of 5G networks will have almost no delay and be at least a hundred times (possibly a thousand times) faster than current networks, allowing driverless cars to make decisions through the cloud, medical robots to become more common, and doctors to perform more complex operations remotely.[42]

Formalising the informal sector

The preceding sections have presented a range of ways in which technology could allow Africa to leapfrog. In addition, the 2019 report on Africa by the UN Economic Commission for Africa finds that, in the long term, government revenue on the continent can be increased by 12–20 per cent of GDP through the rigorous pursuit of revenue collection that is possible through digitisation. Leveraging digital systems to increase revenue collection through e-taxation has increased revenue collection in Rwanda by six per cent of GDP. South Africa uses online tax payments to reduce by 22 per cent compliance costs and the time to comply with value-added tax.[43]

Technology also enables the documentation of vital events in a person's life (live births, adoptions, legitimations and recognitions, deaths, marriages, divorces, separations and annulments) that are fundamental to having a legal identity and guaranteeing human rights and access to public services. It can provide access to finance and information about health, and offers a way to educate and connect people.[44]

A study of seven focus countries (Brazil, China, Ethiopia, India, Nigeria, the UK and the US) by the McKinsey Global Institute found that 'extending full digital ID coverage could unlock economic value equivalent to 3 to 13 per cent of GDP in 2030'.[45] As we saw with the example of Ghana in Chapter 9, digitisation could also allow for unexpected advantages, such as the more rapid formalisation of the informal economic sector.

This is an unexplored avenue for the potential of leapfrogging and the contribution that digitisation could make to government capacity and to economic growth. Normally, as GDP per capita increases, the size of the informal sector decreases, or, put differently, the informal sector gradually 'formalises'. This is positive because workers in the formal sector in African countries are four to five times more productive than those in the informal sector.[46]

At low levels of development, the informal sector is generally significantly less productive than the formal sector. But typically the productivity gap between the informal and formal sector reduces as countries move up the income ladder. It can also become more criminal: whereas informality is survivalist at low levels of development, it is often more nefarious at higher levels of income. So, at higher levels of income, productivity in the informal sector could, in select instances, be comparable to that in the formal sector since the primary orientation here is often not survival but regulatory avoidance.

While it is possible to imagine a growing informal economy alongside a growing formal sector, disproportionate growth in the informal sector hinders long-term inclusive growth. As a result, the reverse is more likely (and has also been observed widely), namely, that the size of the informal sector generally declines as economies develop and grow.

Informality hinders development, although in a low-growth environment the informal sector can provide an alternative means of survival for poor people. To this end, goal 8 of the SDGs explicitly refers to the formalisation of micro, small and medium-sized enterprises. For the ILO, the transition to formality is 'a central goal in national employment policies'.[47] In fact, reducing the size of the informal sector has distinct advantages as long as it does not detract from economic activism, is carefully managed, serves to incentivise employment and does not stunt growth.

Modelling the impact of improved electricity access, ICT and digitisation: The Leapfrogging scenario

The Leapfrogging scenario presented in this section illustrates the combined impact of the structural shifts I believe to be under way in various dimensions.

The first shift is towards an energy solution that includes more solar, wind and energy storage that is used in decentralised mini- and off-grid solutions. To model such a scenario, I reduced the capital cost-to-output ratio for renewables and electricity transmission losses (emulating advances in high-voltage, direct-current transmission technology) and increased electricity access.[48]

The second set of interventions is the even more rapid roll-out of mobile broadband and general improvement in ICT. In spite of rapid uptake, Africa trails significantly behind other regions in this regard.

In a third intervention, I emulate the impact that digitisation could have on more rapidly formalising the informal sector, generally through the provision of digital identification and unlocking access to banking, government benefits, education and other critical services. To do this, I reduce the size of the contribution of the informal sector to GDP by six percentage points over a ten-year period from 2020 to 2030 and the size of the informal labour force by about ten percentage points. This emulates the impact of digitisation of the economy and the formalisation of large chunks of the informal economy. In addition, the intervention modestly improves the effectiveness of governments because digitisation increases the ability to raise taxes, provide services and oversee regulatory implementation. All of these scenarios imply greater investment in the ICT sector, in particular broadband and associated infrastructure.

The results for a selected number of countries are depicted in Figure 10.1. It is presented as the percentage increase in the size of the economy in 2040 when comparing the Leapfrogging scenario with the Current Path. Increases are generally in the range of two to three per cent, with 3.2 per cent in Chad to 1.1 per cent in Algeria and 0.3 per cent in South Sudan. Because the various economies are quite different in size, the actual dollar numbers are much more impressive, but for comparative purposes the percentage difference is more accurate. For example, the Nigerian economy will, in 2040, be US$139 billion larger than in the Current Path. The corresponding figures for Egypt and South Africa are US$49 billion and US$77 billion, respectively. In the case of Guinea, the IFs forecast is for an increase of US$4.3 billion and for Malawi US$7.9 billion.

These improvements also translate into more income. The average African will experience an increase in annual income equivalent to US$438 per person by 2040, ranging from an additional US$249 for every citizen of Algeria, US$201 for every Liberian, US$378 for every Eritrean, US$404 for every Beninese, US$656 for every Ghanaian, and US$1 067 for every South African.[49]

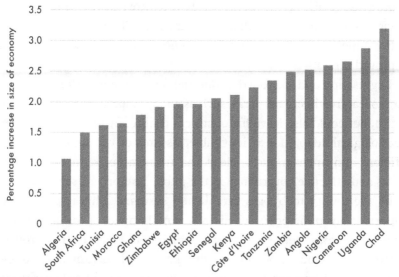

Figure 10.1: Percentage increase in the size of the economy in 2040 for selected countries, Leapfrogging vs Current Path scenario[50]

Leapfrogging is not only about improving growth, infrastructure and income. The Leapfrogging scenario will also reduce poverty in Africa by almost three percentage points – equivalent to 62 million people in 2040. This is largely because of the increased size of the formal sector, with more persons in formal employment. The scenario also slightly reduces inequality.

Conclusion: Harnessing technology for the future

Technological innovation and the notion of leapfrogging are imperative to Africa's future. They will shape development on the continent in ways that are almost impossible to anticipate.

A wealth of innovations is already available for electricity provision through off-grid solutions, using wind and solar energy, to bring power to remote locations across the continent. Electricity consumption per person in large African countries, such as Ethiopia, Kenya and Nigeria, is less than one-tenth of that in Brazil or China. In poorer countries like Mali, a typical household uses less electricity in a year than a Londoner uses to boil a kettle each day. And nearly 600 million people in sub-Saharan Africa lack access to electricity altogether, with the result that whole communities literally live half their lives in the dark. Attention is shifting to more intractable solutions, such as how to provide water and sanitation services to communities such as those in rural Chad, where 97 per cent of the population – just shy of five million people – lacks access to an improved sanitation facility.

Digitisation and the fourth industrial revolution will allow the continent to leapfrog in crucial areas, such as energy supply, infrastructure and health, but could also leave the continent trailing further behind. Where technological adaptation is inevitable, its impact will be magnified by efficient and open markets, clear and transparent regulatory frameworks and effective governance in the public and private sectors, as well as by the ability to bypass established systems. This is particularly important given the potential environmental impact of the large hydroelectric schemes mentioned above, which could lead to the rerouting of rivers and flooding of valleys, with a severe opportunity cost to biodiversity. Environmental pressure groups have raised the alarm over several proposed hydropower projects in Africa, and governments will need to carefully balance environmental sustainability with economic development.

A strong focus on technology can provide leapfrogging opportunities for low- and middle-income countries, but governments must not lose sight of 'traditional' developmental issues, such as governance, infrastructure and skills. According to economist Saadia Zahidi: 'With opportunities for economic leapfrogging, diffusion of innovative ideas across borders and new forms of value creation, the fourth industrial revolution can level the playing field for all economies. But technology is not a silver bullet on its own. Countries must invest in people and institutions to deliver on the promise of technology.'[51]

Many areas of leapfrogging are not examined in this chapter, of which health and education are the most important (see Chapters 4 and 5). General improvements in medical science could curb malaria, Aids, tuberculosis and other diseases that currently ravage large populations in Africa. In the next few decades, the world, including Africa, could move towards dramatic reductions in mortality (the condition of being mortal and dying) and morbidity (being sick or unhealthy), with large implications for population trends.

There is also enormous potential for harnessing technology in the fight against organised criminal activity on the continent, as game wardens at the Maasai Mara National Park in Kenya and Tanzania have discovered. By using an infrared camera that can detect the body heat of poachers and animals up to three kilometres away, wardens have been able to significantly deter poaching in the park. In partnership with the World Crime Technology Project, a platform run by the World Wide Fund for Nature (WWF), authorities installed static cameras around the perimeter of the park, along with vehicle-mounted roaming cameras to detect activity in the surrounding area.

In other parts of Africa, rangers are using drones to significantly expand their ability to surveil parks, at a fraction of the cost of fixed-wing aircraft or helicopters. The same technology could eventually be rolled out to monitor remote borders such as those in the Sahel.

In and of itself technology is, of course, neither good nor bad, and it can also be used by criminals, terrorists, governments and the private sector to further their own interests.

194 — **AFRICA FIRST!**

Last but not least, there are truly globally transformational ideas, such as the effort by Jack Ma, founder of China's Alibaba Group, to establish an Electronic World Trade Platform (eWTP). Ma launched the platform, which is designed to level the playing field for small and medium-sized businesses by allowing them to trade without tariffs and to bypass established systems, in Kigali in October 2018.[52]

Generally, a well-designed digital trade clearance platform could have enormous benefits for regional trade and growth. This is the topic of the next chapter.

11

Trade and growth

Small countries are doomed to poverty unless they have open
markets and free societies. And yet, the typical African country
is small, with closed markets. That is a disastrous combination.

– Paul Collier[1]

Historically, the value of Africa's total trade (ie imports plus exports)
expressed as a percentage of its GDP has been high compared to the rest
of the world but is obviously low in absolute terms given the small size of
the African economy. In 1960, when many African countries were gaining their independence, total exports (ie between African countries
and from Africa to other countries) represented about 23 per cent of the
continent's GDP but steadily declined to 1971. Then, in line with global
averages, exports started to increase, and skyrocketed as growth in China
accelerated to peak at 41 per cent of GDP in 2008.

After several years of contraction and stagnation, global economic
growth has resumed its upward trajectory since the 2007/08 financial
crisis, although there is now more of a trend towards regional rather than
global trade, and expansion is slower than in the past. The problem,
however, is that the bulk of Africa's exports still consist of commodities
as opposed to higher-value items.

For these reasons, the trend in Africa's portion of global trade, as
reflected in Figure 11.1, shows a decline until the start of the 21st century, then increases (largely the result of global growth and commodity
demand from China), remains robust through the 2007/08 financial
crisis (as trade volumes elsewhere declined) but then eventually starts to
decline after 2012 as the Chinese economy starts to rebalance and the
commodities boom ends.

Looking back on those years, the financial crisis of 2007/08 halted and
even temporarily reversed the previous rate of increases in trade and
globalisation. In its aftermath, Africa's exports have declined more rapidly
than global averages.

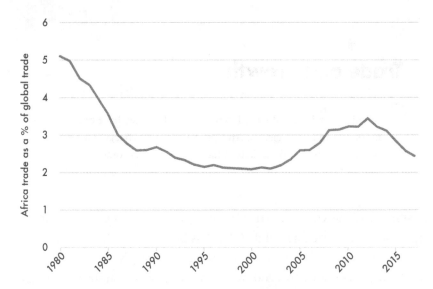

Figure 11.1: Africa's trade as a share of global trade, 1980 to 2017[2]

In interpreting Figure 11.1 the vertical axis is important, for it indicates that Africa's small portion of global trade is proportional to the small size of African economies. Africa's share of world trade by value has more than halved, from above five per cent in the 1980s to less than 2.4 per cent in 2017.

From GATT to the decline of multilateralism

A significant development in global trade was the General Agreement on Tariffs and Trade (GATT), signed by 23 countries in Geneva in 1947. Subsequently, the international community undertook a series of negotiations to expand and broaden the impact of trade. Eventually the so-called Uruguay Round of negotiations, which led to the establishment of the World Trade Organization (WTO), resulted in substantive trade liberalisation in agricultural products, which are typically the mainstay of the economies of developing countries, including many in Africa. WTO members agreed that the next round of negotiations, the Doha Round (also dubbed the development round), would look to the needs of poorer, developing countries.

The Doha Round commenced in 2001 but has not been concluded. It remains stalled (if not discontinued) as a result of the intractable differences between developed and developing countries on issues such as the support provided to domestic agricultural production and industrial market access. And then there is the matter of the size and impact of state-owned enterprises, such as those in China. Developed countries in the West argue that Chinese subsidies distort market forces and run counter to the private-sector ethos that has underpinned global trade liberalisation.

In the 23 years since the Uruguay Round, the WTO's only success has been the conclusion of the Trade Facilitation Agreement, which came into force in 2017.[3] The organisation has been unable to make progress on its core mandate on developing the rules that govern international trade. In fact, under Donald Trump's presidency the future of the WTO may be under threat as economic nationalism and protectionism in the US run their course.

With the rules-based trading system at an impasse, the trend in recent years has been towards regional agreements and the emergence of so-called plurilateral negotiating structures, which allow some countries to agree on specific issues beyond WTO rules but are insufficiently inclusive to be called multilateral agreements. Examples include the Comprehensive and Progressive Agreement for Trans-Pacific Partnership (CPTPP), which came into effect in December 2018, and the negotiations among Asia-Pacific countries on the Regional Comprehensive Partnership (RCEP), which will, once ratified, be the largest trade agreement globally by value. The CPTPP was signed by 11 countries, including Canada, Australia, Vietnam and Japan but excluding the USA and China. The RCEP is an agreement between the ten member states of the Association of Southeast Asian Nations (Asean) and the six Asia-Pacific states and would therefore include China, India and Japan, although India appears to be hesitant about opening its market to a flood of Chinese goods without substantial concessions in return. Signature of the RCEP is scheduled for 2020.

The impact of preferential access

A number of efforts have been made to help integrate developing countries into the global economy and to unlock the potential inherent in export-driven growth by granting least-developed countries (LDCs) 'special and differential treatment'.[4] Typically, these agreements provide access to large domestic markets, especially those of the EU and the US.

The legal basis for these trade preferences is the Generalized System of Preferences (GSP), which provides for exemption on the basis of a list of criteria such as low levels of per capita gross national income and economic vulnerability to external shocks.[5] The two most important measures that relate to Africa are the EU's Everything But Arms initiative and the US's African Growth and Opportunity Act (AGOA) – the latter also under threat during the Trump presidency.[6] AGOA provides 39 countries with tariff-free access to the US market for 6 500 products, ranging from oil and agricultural goods to textiles and handicrafts. In 2015, AGOA was extended to 2025.

These are not trade agreements negotiated between two partners but unilateral concessions made by one party for the benefit of another. As such they are subject to unilateral change (goods may be taken off the eligibility list or the entire arrangement can be cancelled), meaning that the beneficiary countries have no recourse to remedies or dispute resolution. Since they grant non-reciprocal market access and hence deviate from the central free-trade ethos of the WTO, these types of arrangements require a waiver from WTO members.

In the case of AGOA, the trade surplus is broadly in Africa's favour, but most exports to the US are in oil or petroleum-based products (around 67 per cent), not in value-added goods. For example, AGOA allowed duty-free entry of apparel into the US market from some African countries. In response to this opportunity, African exports to the US increased rapidly after the start of AGOA in 2001, but the advantage was eroded from 2005 when quota restrictions on apparel from China and other Asian countries were phased out in terms of the WTO's Agreement on Textiles and Clothing.[7] Lasting progress in expanding exports requires that preferential access should be complemented by domestic reforms, such as improved access to imported inputs through reduction of tariffs, a lighter regulatory burden and enhanced access to infrastructure (such as through the creation of effective SEZs), and flexible exchange rate regimes that lead to competitive exchange rates.[8]

Preferential access has, however, been important in supporting value-added exports, such as the example of apparel exports from a handful of African countries to the US, but it was not responsible for the very sharp increase in exports that occurred in Africa in the years immediately prior to the global financial crisis (see Figure 11.1). In recent years, this demand has tapered off sharply as China's demand for commodities has declined. However, it will likely again be lifted by demand from India as the global commodities cycle swings into positive territory in a few years' time.

The EU has a comprehensive and progressive trade dispensation consisting of several layers. The first and most extensive is the Everything But Arms initiative, which was introduced in 2001. It grants LDCs duty- and quota-free access to the EU single market for almost all their exports, except arms and armaments. Currently, 22 of Africa's low-income and lower-middle-income countries benefit from it. Countries in North Africa and South Africa are excluded since none have LDC status. The scheme has no expiry date and it includes access for processed agricultural products and textiles.[9]

The next level in the EU layer is the so-called Standard GSP, which applies to low- and lower-middle-income countries. The Standard GSP reduces EU import duties for about two-thirds of all product tariff lines and currently applies to Kenya and Nigeria. Cape Verde is currently the only African country to benefit from GSP Plus. This third layer is a special incentive arrangement for sustainable development and good governance that further slashes tariffs when countries implement 27 international conventions related to human rights, labour protection, protection of the environment and good governance.[10]

As the EU concludes trade agreements with other developing countries and lowers its tariffs from them, the preferences granted to Africa inevitably erode over time.[11]

In recent years the EU has been negotiating Economic Partnership Agreements (EPAs) with the African, Caribbean and Pacific (ACP) group of countries, including key sub-Saharan subregions. The intention is to eventually conclude a free trade agreement between the EU and the ACP group as a follow-up to the existing Cotonou agreement, which expires in February 2020.

EPAs are not unilateral concessions and go beyond conventional free trade agreements to include sustainable development and poverty reduction goals. They are controversial for two reasons. First, they include explicit language on human rights, democratic principles, the rule of law and good governance that are, of course, resisted by countries that do not meet these requirements. Second, in addition to the advantages that an EPA affords for trade with the EU, each EPA stipulates that countries in the same region provide at least the same advantages to each other as they do to the EU, as an incentive to grow regional trade. This is, however, less of a stumbling block than the requirement that future trade agreements between ACP countries, or with other developing countries, automatically also apply to the EU (so-called most favoured nation status).[12]

By mid-2019 only the EPA with six SADC states[13] had been ratified and progress with the others had stagnated amid concerns that the EPAs may be detrimental to intra-African trade should such trade not benefit from some type of additional incentive or advantage. The requirement to provide the EU with most favoured nation status as part of an EPA is of particular concern. Moreover, some national governments now balk at the realisation that the agreements would initially reduce tariff revenues from trade with neighbouring countries, making them hesitant to sign – a challenge that will also face these countries under the African Continental Free Trade Area (AfCFTA).[14]

Since they are not classified as LDCs, the states of North Africa are not members of the ACP group. Most are connected to the EU through bilateral association agreements, some of which are being renegotiated.[15]

Africa's shifting trade relations with the rest of the world

In 1970, Europe represented nearly 70 per cent of Africa's total trade, with this share declining to about 45 per cent by 2014 as trade with emerging markets improved. Africa's trade with North America has also declined significantly, falling from a peak of nearly 30 per cent of total trade in the late 1970s to roughly seven per cent in 2014. Whereas Africa's trade with the US quadrupled in value from 2002 to US$100 billion in 2008 it fell back to just US$39 billion in 2017.[16] By contrast, African trade with countries and regions considered to be in the Global South has increased over the last four decades, particularly with China.[17] As China and India rise, they are dragging Africa along with them, for the continent has been able to maintain its relative trade position with both, but with an increased commodities content as opposed to higher-value goods and services.[18] Soon Africa will be trading the majority of goods and services with non-Western partners.

Today, China is Africa's largest single-country trading partner in both exports and imports (see Figure 11.2). But when the EU is considered as a single trading bloc, it dwarfs China. Therefore, in Figure 11.2 the EU accounts for 39 per cent of Africa's exports and 37 per cent of its imports. The EU is followed by China, responsible for 14 per cent of exports and 19 per cent of imports. Next is the US and India. Saudi Arabia appears as an important import destination due to the provision of oil, and Switzerland as an important export destination due to the high value of gems and precious metals for jewellery manufacture.

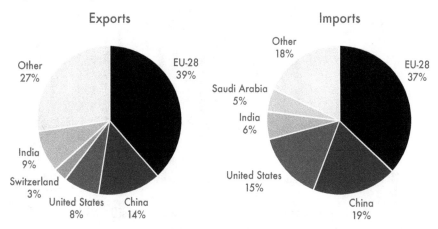

Exports

Other 27%
EU-28 39%
India 9%
Switzerland 3%
United States 8%
China 14%

Imports

Other 18%
EU-28 37%
Saudi Arabia 5%
India 6%
United States 15%
China 19%

Figure 11.2: African exports and imports share with main partners, 2017[19]

The trends are, however, quite different from the 2017 snapshot. China-Africa bilateral trade steadily increased from US$10 billion in 2000 to US$222 billion in 2014 before contracting in 2015. Crude oil, mineral ores, tobacco and wood contribute over 90 per cent of China's imports from Africa, which is in sharp contrast to its more diversified export profile to Africa, largely consisting of value-added goods, with an ever-widening trade imbalance in China's favour.[20]

Then, from 2017 to 2018, trade between Africa and China expanded by 20 per cent, from US$170 billion to US$205 billion. Standard Bank forecasts that bilateral trade should surpass US$300 billion in the next three to five years, but the associated widening trade imbalance that started in 2015 (see Figure 11.3) could be unsustainable.[21] More than

40 African countries currently run a trade deficit with China, and for some, such as Kenya, it is huge. The largest volume of China-Africa trade is with South Africa (which is also the largest African investor in China), while trade with the DRC, Mozambique and Zambia is growing most rapidly.[22]

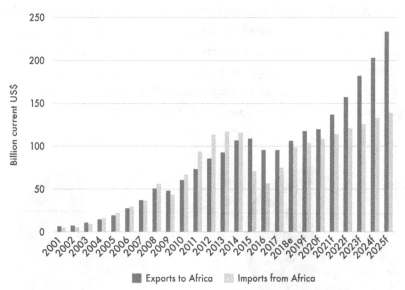

Figure 11.3: China-Africa trade from 2001, with a forecast to 2025[23]

Perhaps more important than total trade is its composition.

The share of manufacturing in total African exports was close to 30 per cent two decades ago but declined for several years before again increasing from 2012 to around 27 per cent by 2016. Generally, the value of commodity exports has increased in line with the commodities supercycle discussed in Chapter 2.[24] Africa's trade with the EU is, however, more balanced than with other regions. The continent 'only' imported 72 per cent manufactured goods from the EU in 2017, while its exports comprised 62 per cent primary goods, mostly energy.[25]

After recovering from the 2007/08 financial crisis, manufacturing as a portion of Africa's trade increased from 2012 to around 27 per cent by 2016. However, apart from Senegal and Togo, the share that manufacturing represents in total exports has again declined, including from countries such as Botswana, South Africa, Madagascar and Namibia that have a relatively high share of manufactured exports.[26]

Clearly, a system of unilateral concessions (such as AGOA or Everything But Arms) is welcome but is not a sustainable basis upon which Africa could or should expand its trading relations with the rest of the world. It implies temporary relief that can be revoked at any point. Although it appears as if preferential access does improve access to, say, the American or European market, it is much less clear whether these improvements are durable and result in lasting improvements in export performance once countries exit from preferential access. Rather, other factors such as the demand for commodities from China dominate. Andrew Mold from Uneca argues that there are three reasons for this state of affairs:

> The design of those preferential agreements is partly to blame, with strict rules of origin and unnecessarily tough phytosanitary and product standards. In addition, African firms have displayed a lacklustre response to the opportunities. However, the Achilles heel of these agreements has been their impermanence – they are concessional and can therefore be suspended or simply not renewed (requiring as they do a special dispensation through the World Trade Organization).[27]

The power of geography is particularly strong when it comes to trade, and it is natural that countries first trade with their neighbourhood rather than with countries that are further away. As a result, the natural market of the North African countries inevitably lies within the Mediterranean basin given the potential for sea transport of high-volume goods and the fact that the Sahara forms a natural barrier to the south. Algeria and Egypt, and to a lesser extent Libya, are already significant exporters of liquefied natural gas to primarily European consumers. In addition, initiatives such as the Mediterranean Solar Plan could eventually help the EU to meet its renewable energy pledge as the pressures of climate change mount globally.[28]

Already, exports to the EU dominate the trade relations of countries in North Africa, including Libya, Tunisia, Morocco, Algeria and Mauritania.[29] The EU envisions a Euro-Mediterranean free trade area, with Euro-Mediterranean partnership countries consisting of Algeria, Egypt, Israel, Jordan, Libya (negotiations are currently suspended), Morocco,

Syria, Tunisia, the Palestinian Authority and Turkey. In 2016, the region represented 9.4 per cent of total EU external trade but progress is hampered by politics, instability and the very low level of intra-regional trade in North Africa.[30]

Intra-African trade and efforts at advancing regional integration

Because agriculture is such a large component of Africa's economy (it has fluctuated around 18 per cent of GDP over several decades), Africans obsess about access to agricultural markets in the developed world, particularly Europe. For decades, no meeting on trade in Africa would start without reference to the extent to which agriculture in the EU benefits from large subsidies, as well as the regulatory hurdles in Europe that effectively bar most agricultural imports.[31] Then there are the massive subsidies for commercial farmers in the US, most of which go to large producers of corn (maize), soybeans, wheat, cotton and rice.[32]

In fact, access to agricultural markets outside Africa has served as an effective lightning rod to divert attention from other, more important matters relating to trade, namely, schemes that would incentivise value-added exports, low-end manufacturing and the beneficiation of the continent's vast mineral exports. And, above all, Africa has until recently done little to increase intra-regional trade, even for foodstuffs.

Yet the advantages of regional integration in Africa were recognised even before the establishment, in 1963, of the OAU, the predecessor to the AU. The Southern African Customs Union (SACU) is the oldest customs union in the world, having recently celebrated its centenary. SACU was, of course, not originally intended as a vehicle for regional integration but rather as a means for Great Britain to facilitate commercial integration and tax management in its various Southern African territories. Then there was the Union of South Africa-Southern Rhodesia Customs Union, established in 1949, and in 1967 the EAC. The latter two arrangements eventually failed and were disbanded, although a new effort is being made with the EAC. The impact of these first regional economic communities was limited and halting, although today SACU accounts for more than 50 per cent of the continent's entire intra-regional trade and SADC[33] for approximately 70 per cent.

Later, the 1980 Lagos Plan of Action, which was essentially Africa's response to the World Bank's structural adjustment programmes, and the Treaty Establishing the African Economic Community of 1991 (generally known as the Abuja Treaty) elaborated on the specific economic, political and institutional mechanisms needed to achieve Africa's economic integration.

Neither of the above made much progress but the tradition of grand schemes continued. Since 2001, the New Partnership for Africa's Development (Nepad, recently renamed the African Union Development Agency-Nepad, or AUDA-Nepad) has provided an overall integration and development framework for the continent, which again assumes regional integration as one of its core objectives. The most recent grand visions are Agenda 2063 and the AfCFTA.

The AfCFTA comes into effect on 1 July 2020, but it is not the only initiative towards economic integration in Africa. The associated benefits have driven repeated attempts at regional integration, to the extent that it is possible to count up to 14 overlapping regional economic communities in Africa, ranging from the 21-member Common Market for Eastern and Southern Africa (Comesa) to the three-member Manu River Union. In fact, Africa has a spaghetti bowl of regional structures, although the AU recognises only eight. In addition to AfCFTA, the Tripartite Free Trade Area, which includes Comesa, the EAC and SADC, is, for example, also making progress towards its goal of greater trade integration.

To varying degrees, the various continental schemes, such as the Lagos Plan and the AfCFTA, view the various subregional economic groupings, such as SADC, the EAC and Ecowas, as building blocks towards greater cooperation, or as implementing agencies for the continental scheme.

Generally, levels of trade in all of Africa's regions are significantly below those of other regional blocs such as the Asia-Pacific Economic Cooperation (APEC) and the EU.[34] For example, the comparative data for intra-regional trade for 2017 is as follows:

- Intra-Africa trade 16.7 per cent
- Europe 68.1 per cent
- Asia 59.4 per cent
- Americas 55.0 per cent.[35]

Trade volumes between African states are low in part because governments depend heavily on income from tariffs. High tariffs serve as an effective tax on trade and invariably reduce volumes. Carlos Lopes, the former head of Uneca in Addis Ababa, estimates that 'the majority of businesses on the continent pay an average of 6.9 per cent tax on cross-border transactions. The cost of the transactions, added to the cost of production, has a huge impact, not only on the competitiveness of the businesses but also on the quality of life of consumers.'[36]

Hefty tariffs invariably inhibit trade flows across borders and often also contribute to smuggling and the growth of the shadow economy when borders are not well policed. Vast amounts of money can be made smuggling items such as petroleum and cigarettes across borders where prices differ substantially between countries. This is particularly characteristic of economies in North Africa, West Africa, the Sahel and Central Africa.

In addition to the various structural reasons for Africa's poor growth, such as a declining demographic dividend (until the late 1980s) and its role as a proxy battleground during the Cold War, bad governance, poor policy and lack of implementation of agreements all played important roles. Structurally, the continent did not develop regional value chains, does not substantively trade among its members and hence has not formed part of the global value chains in goods and services that have developed between parts of Asia, North America and Europe since the 1990s.

Outside Africa, analysis is no longer fixated solely on the growth and structural change in individual economies, but rather uses the lens of global value chains – the complex networks that tie the flows of goods, services, capital and technology together across national borders – to evaluate the strength of economies.

In fact, global value chains are also changing. First, goods-producing value chains are becoming less trade-intensive and trade in cross-border services is growing more rapidly than trade in goods. Second, goods-producing value chains are becoming more regionally concentrated, especially within Asia and Europe. Companies are increasingly locating their production facilities in closer proximity to demand. This could, in time, offer advantages to Africa, with its rapidly growing population and expanding number of consumers.[37]

The need for connecting infrastructure – and the challenge of non-tariff barriers

Organisations such as the World Bank, the African Development Bank and Uneca regularly issue reports that quantify the extent to which Africa's lack of connecting infrastructure, such as road and rail, between neighbouring countries increases transport costs and creates delays. Poor infrastructure reduces the competitiveness of business and undermines much-needed investment flows.

In some East African countries, for example, transport costs are estimated at about five times more than countries in Europe and North America.[38] The large number of landlocked states means that many, such as Ethiopia, Uganda, Rwanda, Burundi and South Sudan, are dependent on their neighbours for access to the sea.

According to the African Development Bank, Africa has an annual infrastructure funding gap of US$130–170 billion, with an annual financing gap of US$68–108 billion.[39] Africa has an average of 204 kilometres of roads per 1 000 km², of which only a quarter is paved. That density lags far behind the world average of 944 kilometres per 1 000 km², of which more than half is paved. Most of the continent's paved roads can be found in a single country, South Africa.[40]

Anyone who has had to travel around West and Central Africa can testify to the dire need for better connecting infrastructure. Whether by road, through ports or on buses, planes or trains, it is difficult to get around – though it is significantly easier than even a few years ago.

However, there has been substantial progress recently in building and financing infrastructure projects. This is largely spurred by the excess capacity to build infrastructure that is now available from China as part of its Belt and Road Initiative, which will connect China tightly to the rest of Asia, Europe and even Africa.

Modern technology will also offer a way to replace costlier forms of more basic infrastructure. A number of African countries already use drones to transport blood and other vital medicines to rural hospitals, bypassing poor, often unpaved roads. But doctors, nurses and patients are all still dependent on roads and bridges to get to those hospitals, and even the advent of mass air transport may not sufficiently compensate for the requirement to transport large volumes of heavy cargo over long distances.

To this end, the AU launched the Programme for Infrastructure Development in Africa and its Priority Action Plan (PIDA-PAP), which is being championed vigorously by the AUDA-Nepad, the AU Commissioner for Infrastructure, Energy and Tourism, the African Development Bank and Uneca.

The PIDA-PAP is a kind of infrastructure master plan for Africa that regurgitates many previous ambitions, some of which date from colonial times, but has seen some implementation.[41] The current PIDA-PAP portfolio from 2012 to 2020 numbers in excess of 400 projects in 51 cross-border programmes in transport (235 projects), energy (54 projects), ICT (113 projects) and trans-boundary water resource management (9 projects).

In November 2018, a PIDA-PAP workshop at Victoria Falls[42] revealed that the capital cost of delivering the plan was estimated at US$68 billion, or US$7.5 billion annually – relatively modest compared to the infrastructure funding gap calculated by the African Development Bank. Of the more than 400 projects, 26 per cent are moving from concept to pre-feasibility or feasibility phases, 16 per cent are currently being structured for tendering, and 32 per cent are either under construction or are already operational, reflecting slow but steady progress.

But so-called non-tariff barriers are arguably an even larger constraint to trade in Africa and African trade with the rest of the world. These consist of onerous regulatory procedures, expensive visa requirements, corruption and inefficiency, and include import prohibitions, quotas, export subsidies, export restrictions and technical barriers to trade (such as regulations, standards and assessment procedures), as well as food safety and animal and plant health standards.[43] Whereas free trade agreements are subject to long, drawn-out negotiations, the removal of non-tariff barriers results from unilateral and bilateral cooperation. Exactly how powerful is presented in a study done by the Stellenbosch-based Trade and Law Centre (Tralac), which found that reducing the time it takes to move goods across borders by just 20 per cent would be more economically advantageous for Africa than removing all import tariffs.[44]

The 2018 World Bank ease of doing business index still has only seven countries from sub-Saharan Africa in the top 100, namely, Mauritius, Rwanda, Kenya, Botswana, South Africa, Seychelles and Zambia, although efforts to remove impediments to improved trade are readily identifiable elsewhere. The Tripartite Free Trade Area website lists examples of 25 non-tariff barriers to trade, ranging from import bans and product classification to corruption. Progress in eliminating these barriers is slow, however.[45]

In an effort to regularise such standards, the WTO's Agreement on the Application of Sanitary and Phytosanitary Measures came into force in 1995. The agreement provides uniform rules for all laws, regulations and requirements regarding how a product is produced, processed, stored or transported to ensure that its importation does not pose a risk to human, animal or plant health. Sanitary measures are aimed at safeguarding human and animal health, while phytosanitary measures are intended to protect plants. Imported goods should be from disease-free areas, should be inspected prior to export, and should not exceed maximum levels of pesticide or insecticide use. The agreement is also meant to prevent countries from using rules and regulations simply to block trade, stating explicitly that the measures cannot be employed in 'a manner which would constitute a disguised restriction on international trade'. But, although importing countries are encouraged to use existing international standards, they are nevertheless allowed to adopt stricter regulations if they can justify their actions scientifically.

In theory, non-tariff barriers should be easier to overcome than, say, the lack of roads and railways. However, this is often not the case given the extent to which many countries (and agencies) are dependent on the income from such measures and are often subject to pressure from domestic interest groups to provide protection from cheaper imports.

Perspectives on the promise of the AfCFTA

Against this rather concerning background, much hope has been placed in the AfCFTA as a vehicle to boost trade in value-added products and to increase economic growth.

The decision to establish the AfCTFA was taken at a summit meeting of the AU in January 2012. The intention was to create a single market for goods and services as originally envisioned in the 1991 Abuja Treaty. The original target date of 2017 was missed, but after a high-level signing ceremony in Kigali on 21 March 2018 momentum has built up rapidly. Following signature, each country has to follow its national legislative processes and then deposit the instruments of ratification or accession with the AU Commission. Once the milestone of 22 ratifications has been reached, the AfCTFA will be operational from 1 July 2020. Full implementation should take place by 2034 at which point the full 97 per cent tariff liberalisation would be achieved.

The immediate next step is a conference of state parties, the establishment of an AfCFTA secretariat in Accra, an African Trade Observatory and various technicalities. The agreement is a framework that covers trade in goods and services, investment, intellectual property rights and competition policy. Once negotiations on trade in goods and trade in services are finalised, rules-of-origin negotiations have to be concluded, as well as negotiations on tariff concessions. Then 'behind the border' trade issues on competition policy, intellectual property rights and investment will follow, which will serve to deepen the AfCFTA.[46]

The AfCFTA provides for a single market for goods and services, as well as a common market with free movement for capital and business travellers. It does not yet include digital trade and e-commerce. Countries joining the AfCFTA must commit to removing tariffs on at least 90 per cent of the products they produce. They can compile a list of sensitive products (amounting to an additional 7 per cent) that are to be temporarily exempted, leaving a 3 per cent exclusion list.[47]

The agreement also provides for a Dispute Settlement Body (DSB) to respond to the dumping of foreign products at a lower price than the normal value. It also allows for Special and Differential Treatment to provide flexibility for states at different levels of economic development, and makes provision for Infant Industry Protection, allowing states to impose measures to protect strategic infant industries.[48] Trade facilitation will be funded by the AU, member states and external investors, and will address transport infrastructure, customs clearance, technical assistance and capacity building.[49]

The AfCFTA has the potential to unlock significant value-added trade in goods and services. Medium- and high-technology manufactures account for 25.4 per cent of intra-African trade but only 14.1 per cent of African countries' exports to developed countries. This means that intra-African trade has relatively higher industrial content than does African countries' trade with the rest of the world (this is similar to other regions), which speaks to the advantage of regional trade over international trade. In other words, African countries first need to trade their manufactured (and agricultural) produce with each other until their products and services are competitive before they will really be able to expand their participation in global value chains.

Many obstacles remain to the implementation of the AfCFTA. The most obvious is simply the ambition and diversity of its members. The AfCFTA would include countries with much bigger levels of income disparity than in blocs such as Asean and the Caribbean Community (Caricom).[50] Agreeing on tariff liberalisation schedules, given the high levels of inequality in the region, is going to require steadfast respect for Special and Differential Treatment by all concerned.

An important feature of the AfCFTA is that it will build on rather than replace Africa's several existing regional free trade areas. For example in Southern Africa, the SACU and SADC free trade areas will continue. The general principle will be that where these regional free trade areas offer better trade terms than does the AfCFTA, the former terms will apply. The same principle will apply to the Tripartite Free Trade Agreement.

There have been a number of scenarios on the potential impact of the AfCFTA. Uneca estimates that it has 'the potential to boost intra-African trade by 52.3 per cent through the elimination of import duties, and by over 100 per cent through the elimination of non-tariff barriers'.[51] In a paper released in February 2018, Unctad modelled two scenarios reflecting full and partial elimination of tariffs and concluded:[52]

> In both long-term scenarios, the largest employment growth rates are found in manufacturing industry followed by some services and agriculture subsectors. All sectors grow, with the exception of a stagnant mining sector. This is in line with the CFTA objective for structural transformation and industrialisation.[53]

According to Unctad, the short-term revenue losses due to tariff reductions will be wiped out over time as trade increases and countries grow more rapidly. It concludes that 'with adequate flanking policies and social safety measures, the AfCFTA has an immense potential to promote equitable and inclusive growth'.[54] Under the scenario for the full AfCFTA implementation, in which all tariffs are eliminated, the nett welfare gains are about US$16.1 billion and GDP growth happens, on average, 0.97 per cent more rapidly than it would otherwise. Total employment improves by slightly more than one per cent, intra-African trade is forecast to grow by one third, and Africa's total trade deficit is cut in half.

During the African Economic Conference 2018 in Kigali, the African Development Bank indicated that it expected the AfCFTA to boost intra-African trade by up to US$35 billion per year, reflecting a 52 per cent increase in trade by 2022, and a US$10 billion decrease in imports to Africa.[55] The recent *African Economic Outlook* for 2019 presented a scenario in which, if current bilateral tariffs are eliminated, Africa would gain US$2.8 billion in real income and intra-African trade would increase by 15 per cent. Additionally, removing non-tariff barriers could increase total real income gains by US$37 billion and intra-African trade by 107.2 per cent.

To reach such a deep level of integration, further progress needs to be made on rules of origin, free movement of persons, financial governance frameworks and regional public goods (infrastructure and regional bodies).

Finally, in its estimate of the impact of the AfCFTA the UN Department of Economic and Social Affairs (Undesa) finds:

> [T]ariff revenue losses may also be outweighed by the additional revenues from growth to be generated by the AfCFTA, which would broaden the tax base and boost revenue collection from other sources. Growth in Africa is expected to accelerate by 0.3–0.6 percentage points by 2040 (depending on the liberalisation approach or scenario adopted), when compared to the baseline scenario. All African countries would experience an increase in their GDP with the AfCFTA reforms, whatever the scenario . . . However, these forecasts are likely to substantially underestimate the economic benefits of the AfCFTA, as they do not take into account the impact of liberalisation in other areas such as services and investment.[56]

Modelling the impact of regional economic integration: The Africa Free Trade scenario

Since the IFs forecasting platform does not currently include a bilateral trading model, I have to rely on three proxies to emulate improved trade. The first is enhancing the quality of government regulations, the second is expanding roads as a proxy of general better transportation infrastructure, and the third is to use an additive factor to multifactor productivity, a powerful driver of economic growth within IFs. I calibrate the impact in accordance with the lower end of the impact of the AfCFTA scenarios done by Unctad, Uneca and Undesa referred to above. Collectively, these three interventions simulate regional integration and its commensurate impact.

There could be major gains if the implementation of the AfCFTA starts in 2025 and tariffs are reduced over the subsequent ten-year period. The cumulative increase in the size of the African economy from 2020 to 2040 is US$3.3 trillion. This growth translates into 2.4 per cent fewer people living in extreme poverty by 2040, which is equivalent to 50 million people (using the US$1.90 poverty line). GDP per capita in 2040 is on average US$426 more for each of Africa's 2.081 billion people.

Since more intra-African trade benefits Africa's manufacturing sector, the services and manufacturing sectors could, on average, be 0.7 and 0.4 percentage points larger in 2040 than in the Current Path scenario. The contribution of the agriculture and energy sectors declines marginally as a portion of the total African economy but not in absolute values, since by 2040 the African economy is significantly larger than it would otherwise be. By 2040 Africa's GDP growth rate is 1.13 percentage points above the Current Path and the total African economy is US$685 billion larger (in market exchange rates).

By 2040 the value of Africa's exports has increased by US$148 billion and that of imports declined by US$124 billion, with the greater part of the increase in exports benefiting Africa's 21 lower-middle-income countries.

South Africa, an upper-middle-income country with the continent's most diversified economy, gains more than double (US$27 billion) the amount from additional exports in 2040 compared to the next country, Egypt (US$14 billion in 2040). Other countries that gain more than

US$5 billion from additional trade in 2040 are Nigeria, Angola, Morocco, Ghana, Algeria and Tanzania. In general, the current account improves, government debt goes down (by about 1.5 percentage points) and household savings rates improve.

Conclusion: Advancing Africa's trade

This chapter has set out the reasons why African countries need to deepen the preferential trade agreements within the region to grow trade and develop and diversify their economies (particularly by entering the manufacturing sector and going up the value-add ladder). Most African economies are simply too small and fragmented to build competitive productive capacity at scale, or indeed to offer sufficiently large markets to attract substantive foreign investment without such agreements.[57]

Since trade potential in goods inevitably diminishes with distance, African countries are best served by first trading with other African countries, although the natural trading relationship for North Africa is with Europe and the Middle East rather than with sub-Saharan Africa given the intervening reality of the Sahara.

A focus on low-end manufacturing should not, however, be assumed to disregard the important changes that are occurring in the nature of trade elsewhere in the world. Flows of services and data now play a larger role in international trade than goods. Goods-producing value chains are actually declining in importance. Furthermore, most trade is now in so-called intermediate inputs, not final goods and services, as items repeatedly cross national borders with value being added at each step. As a result, global value chains are becoming more knowledge-intensive and low-skilled labour is becoming less important as a factor of contribution compared to capital and technology.[58] The demand for labour is increasingly moving away from low-skilled to semi-skilled and skilled.

Examples of these processes are often demonstrated with reference to vehicle manufacturing along the border between the US and Mexico, and to the way in which mobile phone manufacturing in Asia consists of an intricate cross-border production network. But for the time being Africa is not yet able to look at trade within regional or global value chains, for production is largely done nationally, not regionally, and

Africa is generally not part of world trade, except for its role in supplying commodities.

The extent to which Africa will be able to leapfrog to higher-end value in trade will depend on the investments made in selected, well-targeted infrastructure able to support competitive industries and sectors in industrial parks and export-processing zones linked to regional and global markets, as well as investments in appropriate technology and education. For example, Ethiopia, globally one of the fastest growing economies in the last decade, has the ambition to enter low-end manufacturing. But the average Ethiopian adult (over the age of 15) received about 2.8 years of schooling in 2017. By contrast, the average adult in other low-income African countries received about 4.7 years of schooling, or nearly twice as much. Structurally, Ethiopia needs to unlock this constraint, the first and most severe blockage in its education pipeline, if it wants to improve its human capital endowment.

Digital technologies can help overcome Africa's large infrastructure deficit but will likely dampen trade in goods while further fuelling the growth in trade in services.

The major obstacles to regional trade in Africa are often political and are shaped by the short-term pain (loss of tariff income) that is required before the long-term gains (higher growth) set in. Regional integration will eventually grow tax revenues as more rapid growth accelerates increases in government revenues, but it will be difficult to get domestic buy-in on the loss in tariff income.[59]

Trade integration can help African countries to prioritise investment in sectors where they have a comparative advantage. It could foster the establishment or promotion of industries in which African businesses have the potential to trade regionally and eventually globally. Additionally, regional integration would improve the diversification of goods and the technology content of Africa's exports.[60]

In other words, trade liberalisation works to the benefit of countries only when they actively manage levels of openness to trade.[61] For this reason, the policies and support of a national governance that invests in the quality of institutions and provides policy certainty are important.[62] China is the poster child when it comes to how it has successfully managed access to its large domestic market, protected and nurtured its infant industries, and demanded technology transfer from foreign companies. Today, it is the world's factory.

Going up the product and services complexity curve requires that national and regional value chains be established in which cities, regions and national economies can collaborate on a cost-competitive basis in bringing diverse skills together to produce ever more valuable products and services.

Initiatives like the AfCFTA are therefore crucial for growth and prosperity in Africa, with the potential to trigger a virtuous cycle of expanded trade on the continent that will, in turn, drive the structural transformation of economies. Detailed negotiations are likely to take a long time, however, and a number of uncertainties remain, for instance regarding tariff schedules.[63] For this reason, the EAC, SADC, Ecowas and the Tripartite Free Trade Area need to simultaneously press on and pursue trade facilitation reforms and trade integration. Eventually, the biggest challenge for African integration will be how extremely unequal partners such as South Africa and Botswana, both upper-middle-income countries, can be integrated with surrounding low-income countries such as Mozambique, eSwatini and Lesotho.

Expanding trade in Africa requires peace and stability, and this is the topic of the next chapter.

12

Prospects for greater peace

Across time and space, the more peaceable societies also tend
to be richer, healthier, better educated, better governed, more
respectful of their women, and more likely to engage in trade.

– Steven Pinker, *The Better Angels of Our Nature*[1]

There is no magic wand to end armed conflict in Africa by 2020, which
is the target year set by the AU towards its Agenda 2063 vision of
'an integrated, prosperous and peaceful Africa'.[2] Structurally, inclusive
economic development, coupled with substantive electoral accountability,
offers the best prospect for greater peace and stability. Generally, countries become more peaceful as they become more prosperous, and
democracy is the most stable form of government. Both trends are evident in Africa, though developing more slowly than one would want.
This is why most of the chapters in this book try to model how Africa's
development prospects can be improved.

It will take time for Africa to become more peaceful and less violent,
in part because of the slow rate at which the structural changes that are
needed for stability take place. For example, conflict-affected countries
typically have much younger populations than more stable regions, and
population structure shifts very slowly. Levels of education are often
lower, and many countries are not democratic. It may even be that 'for
the poorest countries, development may actually stimulate violence'.[3] In
this context, the resurgence of ethnic nationalism and a 2019 failed coup
attempt in Ethiopia, one of the most remarkable development success
stories of the 21st century, certainly come to mind.

Death rates spiked globally during the two world wars, but thereafter
there was a downward trend. In Africa, the end of colonialism during
the 1950s and early 1960s was a turbulent time, even though the number
of fatalities due to armed conflict declined for several years.[4]

Sustained political violence within countries invariably reflects so-
called deep drivers of conflict. These include history and the impact of

a legacy of armed violence, a youthful population structure and associated social dynamics such as high levels of unemployment and inequality, and instability associated with political transitions. In fact, there is considerable evidence that the causes of violence evolve over time, so what drove instability a decade or more ago may have changed today.[5] That said, leaders and actors are always important since they serve to animate a situation that accentuates (or diverts) the momentum towards violence. In the end, each country is unique, or to paraphrase Leo Tolstoy in *Anna Karenina*: stable countries are all alike; every unstable country is unstable in its own way.

Also, there is a clear limit to the value of broad analysis without much greater attention to local history, detail and context. For example, much analysis searches for the broad religious or global drivers of terrorism, such as foreign funding and the influence of external actors. But the reasons why people join armed jihadist groups and become violent is often primarily local, varied and related to personal experiences, such as abuse suffered at the hands of government, and circumstances.[6]

Cyclical conflict trends and the need for peacekeeping missions

Conflict data on Africa is inevitably incomplete and therefore often contentious, but the quality of data is improving and it is more readily available than ever before.[7]

When examining conflict data from the two largest publicly available data providers, the Uppsala Conflict Data Program (UCDP) and the Armed Conflict Location and Event Data Project (ACLED), it is evident that conflict in Africa follows a cyclical pattern. Generally, the most violent period in Africa since independence in the 1960s coincided with the run-up to the end of the Cold War in 1989, when Africa served as a proxy battleground between the former Soviet Union and the US and its allies. During the 1970s and 1980s, levels of conflict in Africa rose much more quickly than the global average.

Thereafter, instances of armed conflict and fatalities steadily declined, with the period 2004–2006 being more peaceful than any other in Africa's recent history. Violence accelerated again after 2010 with the Arab Spring and the rise in violent Islamist terrorism. It seems to have peaked in

2014–2015 before starting to decline again. Today it is the Middle East, not Africa, that has the highest conflict burden of all world regions, if one weighs the risk of being a fatality by population size.

Repeat violence, or recurring historical conflicts, are a huge problem in Africa. According to a report for the Peace Research Institute Oslo (PRIO), 'Globally, cycles of war tend to repeat themselves in the same countries. Apart from inhibiting development they also spill over into the neighbourhood.'[8] Repeat violence is usually caused by unaddressed grievances, which means that lasting peace, or at least greater stability, will not be achieved until these grievances are addressed. Indeed, the seeds of the next war are often sown during the preceding war.[9] Doing this takes a long time, requiring peacekeepers (the standard international response to endemic conflict) to remain in-country for many years.

Given that only inclusive economic growth can produce the resources required to alleviate these root causes, conflict-torn countries in Africa are caught in a Catch-22 situation. Poor countries are more violent, and because of this they cannot grow rapidly enough to alleviate the stresses and grievances that lead to instability.

Moreover, being situated in a conflict-ridden region is a major risk factor, and neighbouring countries are very likely to experience the spill-over effect of the instability.[10] According to the *World Development Report 2011*, a 'country making development advances, such as Tanzania, loses an estimated 0.7 per cent of GDP every year for each neighbour in conflict'.[11] For example, more than 250 000 refugees from Burundi have spilled over into Tanzania since the start of Burundi's political crisis at the end of 2014. This is in addition to the impact of the violence in the DRC, with which Tanzania also shares a border across Lake Tanganyika. Furthermore, neighbouring countries that are in turmoil regularly offer safe havens for rebel groups and insurgents that operate across borders.[12]

Over the last two decades, Africans have increasingly taken the lead in making peace through mediation and diplomacy. Clearly, preventing conflict is where the focus should be, but once conflict has erupted the introduction of peacekeepers remains the most important and effective means to respond to conflict. Based on extensive research, the PRIO holds that the risk of conflict recurrence drops by as much as 75 per cent in countries where UN peacekeepers are deployed.[13]

Côte d'Ivoire is often used as a recent example of successful peace-keeping (though there are many previous examples). On 30 June 2017, the UN Operation in Côte d'Ivoire (UNOCI) concluded its mandate, some 13 years after it was established. It was a turbulent ride, for resurgent post-electoral violence in 2011 had led to the deaths of approximately 3 000 people. But, eventually, the contribution that UNOCI made to stability and the country's economic recovery enabled the withdrawal of the peacekeepers.

From 2012 to 2017, Côte d'Ivoire averaged growth in excess of eight per cent per year. The government of President Alassane Ouattara has placed particular emphasis on making the country attractive to private-sector investment, which has come at some cost to the fiscus. The measures include various exemptions from value-added tax, reductions in customs duty, tax exemptions on profits and the like as the government seeks to increase trade and attract opportunities in agriculture, industry, mining and services. Such measures inevitably imply a degree of short-term pain, but eventually more rapid economic growth, if accompanied by appropriate redistributive policies, unlocks more job opportunities and better wages.

In the longer term, fundamental political, social and economic reforms are often required to ensure durable peace. At least some of these measures have been put in place in Côte d'Ivoire. However, even after more than a decade of peacekeeping it will still take several years to decisively break the cycle of violence.

Africa itself has limited ability to fund and sustain expensive peace missions, such as those required in the DRC, CAR, Mali and Somalia, and looks to the UN either to undertake peace missions itself or to support the efforts by Africans. In spite of its unwillingness to assume direct responsibility for peacekeeping in Somalia, where previous efforts ended so ignominiously, and the failure to respond to or prevent the 1994 genocide in Rwanda, the UN remains the most important player in this regard. But there are any number of conflict situations in Africa where the UN is unwilling or unable to deploy, which leaves the ball in Africa's court. The result has been a clear trend towards peacekeeping in Africa by

Africans and a strong desire from the continent to move towards a system whereby peacekeeping missions in Africa are funded through a system of assessed contributions from UN member states instead of the current messy and complex system of voluntary contributions.

Armed conflict and fatalities are declining

Over time, the nature of political armed violence in Africa has changed. Today, most conflicts in Africa happen within rather than between states. Furthermore, terrorism is playing a more important role. Whereas in 2010 only five countries experienced sustained activity from violent Islamist extremism (Algeria, Mali, Niger, Nigeria and Somalia), that number had grown to 12 countries by 2017 (Algeria, Burkina Faso, Cameroon, Chad, Egypt, Kenya, Libya, Mali, Niger, Nigeria, Somalia and Tunisia).[14]

The link between transnational organised crime and terrorism is also growing, and the allegiances between Africa's domestic violent radicals and those in the Middle East have shifted from al-Qaeda to Islamic State.[15] But, generally, we have probably seen the peak in imported Islamist terrorism. In the Sahel, the most affected region, violent extremism is again driven by deeply domestic matters, particularly poor governance and neglect, rather than influences from elsewhere. The world's attention also seems to have shifted to other matters such as geostrategic competition, trade wars, cyber-attacks and fake news, fear of migrants and the resurgence of nuclear threats.

Two considerations inform the belief that we have seen the end of large-scale terrorism of the exported variety. The first is the reduction in the flow of money from Saudi Arabia, which for several decades funded fundamentalist Islam elsewhere to divert attention from its domestic repression. The second relates to the defeat of the Islamic State in Iraq and Syria, where it has lost the territories that once provided it with a relatively safe haven, although with the potential to find new breeding grounds, including in Africa. In fact, a number of copycat insurgencies have borrowed its nomenclature, such as in northern Mozambique and the eastern DRC, but it remains uncertain how serious these challenges will prove to be in the longer term.

The effect of limited government capacity

Unlike other regions, Africa experiences a high level of conflict between various armed groups and factions that are fighting each other instead of the state. The UCDP refers to this as 'non-state conflict'. This type of violence is mostly due to absent, weak and unconsolidated governance. Simply put, in areas where the government is not able to provide stability, political, economic or social competition between tribes, herders and pastoralists, and between local militias and traditional groups, becomes more readily violent.

Related to this is the fact that conflict in Africa is becoming more complex because the numbers of conflict actors have increased. Rebel (and extremist) groups often split into further groupings, which complicates efforts at mediation or reconciliation. Therefore, attempts to craft inclusive peace agreements invariably fall short of their stated goal to include all key protagonists, for no sooner do mediators get parties to sign an agreement than a group splits off and a new faction emerges with additional demands, while commentators and interest groups readily agitate for the maximum inclusion as part of agreements. Actually, the problem with most peace agreements is not that they are not inclusive enough, as is frequently claimed, but that they are not implemented.[16]

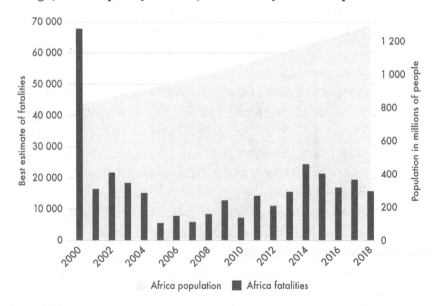

Figure 12.1: Total African fatalities from all armed conflict, 1989 to 2017[17]

Figure 12.1 presents the total number of fatalities from armed conflict events in Africa since 2000 (bar graph and left-hand y-axis) compared to Africa's increased population size (line graph to right-hand y-axis) from 816 million to 1.3 billion in 2018.[18] The periods that saw the highest number of fatalities, excluding the Rwandan genocide, were in 1990–1991 (not shown), 1999–2000 and 2014–2015.[19] The almost 68 000 casualties in 2000 include 47 989 from the last year of the Ethiopia-Eritrea border war.

The general trend of falling fatality rates also holds for the broader category of political violence, which includes deaths from protests and riots. When total fatalities are adjusted for Africa's rapid population growth to represent the ratio of fatalities per million people in the population, it is clear that the fatality rate has steadily declined over long time horizons, although slowly.

The Eritrean-Ethiopian border war (in and around the town of Badme in 1999 and 2000), the impact of the large-scale conflict in the DRC (generally known as the Second Congo War, or Great War of Africa, which wound down from July 2003 having involved nine African countries and nearly 20 rebel groups) and the surge in fatalities associated with Boko Haram in Nigeria in 2014–2015 are also evident in Figure 12.1.[20]

With the exception of these three conflicts, the absolute number of fatalities from armed conflict has slowly declined over time and is limited to a handful of countries. The seven countries that experienced the highest number of fatalities due to armed conflict from 2009 to 2018 are Nigeria, DRC, Somalia, Sudan, Libya, CAR and South Sudan.

Inevitably countries with large populations, such as Nigeria, Ethiopia, Egypt and the DRC, tend to record a corresponding high number of fatalities from armed conflict. Therefore, a better way of looking at the conflict burden is to rank countries by their per capita fatality rates (or the risk to any given individual of being killed during armed conflict). When we take population size into consideration, the seven countries where citizens were most at risk (when measured as fatalities against population size for 2009 to 2018) are the CAR, Libya, Somalia, South Sudan, Sudan, DRC and Mali. Both measures necessarily obscure subnational discrepancies. For instance, people in the north of Nigeria are significantly more likely to experience violence at the hands of Boko

Haram than are people living in Lagos, who may be more at risk from crime.

Country with most fatalities	Country with most fatalities per capita
Nigeria	Central African Republic
DRC	Libya
Somalia	Somalia
Sudan	South Sudan
Libya	Sudan
CAR	DRC
South Sudan	Mali

Table 12.1: Country ranking, total fatalities vs fatality ratio to population

This list includes countries with quite small populations (CAR, Libya, Somalia and Sudan) that have an extraordinarily high casualty burden. Also evident is the extent to which violent Islamist extremism is driving fatality counts. Should Africans or the international community manage to bring stability to these countries, it would have a disproportionately positive impact on continental levels of armed conflict.

An increase in riots and protests

In sharp contrast to the declining impact of armed violence, Africa is experiencing an increase in incidents of anti-government social violence, including riots and violent protests.

While larger-scale armed conflict, with its associated fatalities, is likely to continue its steady long-term decline, it is less clear what the short-term impact of the increase in social instability and protests will be. As is the case elsewhere in the world, democratic African governments are less repressive and tend to use less violence against civilians, meaning that fatalities during protests are not high even if the number of protest events may increase.[21]

According to ACLED, the number of non-violent protests and violent riots in Africa has increased twelvefold since 2001 and at a great rate after the start of the Arab Spring in December 2010. The Arab Spring eventually impacted a belt of North African countries from Morocco to Egypt, as well as Somalia, Nigeria and Sudan. Only Tunisia emerged from that period with significantly improved levels of democracy, but it is struggling with slow growth and an untransformed economic system.[22]

The number of riot and protest events peaked in Egypt in June 2013 with the one-year anniversary of the inauguration of Mohamed Morsi as president, when millions of Egyptians called for his departure. These events culminated in the coup d'état or Second Egyptian Revolution during which General (now President) Abdel Fattah el-Sisi assumed power. In Libya the Arab Spring destabilised the grip that Muammar Gaddafi held on his country. Eventually Gaddafi's efforts at suppressing the revolt led to intervention by the North Atlantic Treaty Organisation (NATO) under a UN Security Council mandate that in turn ignited an active civil war, with devastating effects on the region.

Riot and protest events also peaked in Nigeria in 2015 during the country's closely contested national elections, when the incumbent Goodluck Jonathan lost to Muhammadu Buhari. Riots and protests have also increased in Ethiopia, Tunisia, Algeria, Kenya and Sudan in recent years. In 2019, large-scale protests erupted in Algeria and in Sudan, where thousands of people took to the streets to demand the end of two of Africa's longest-ruling heads of state, Abdelaziz Bouteflika, president of Algeria since 1999, and Omar al-Bashir, president of Sudan since a coup d'état in 1993. Both were eventually forced from power by the public display of anger and resistance.

These extraordinary increases in the number of riots and protests probably also reflect the extent to which social media and internet access have expanded in recent years, making communication and the distribution of information easier and quicker.

The nature of violence and instability seems to change as countries transition to democracy. Whereas political change is often associated with large-scale violent rupture, lower-intensity riots and protests are more prevalent in democracies, with South Africa and Kenya offering two good examples.

By comparative African standards, South Africa is very democratic and protests are the order of the day. Since the country has undergone a fairly recent political transition from apartheid to democracy, it is inherently more prone to civil conflict, particularly given its very high levels of inequality and unemployment. In recent years, the political crisis associated with slow growth, corruption and patronage under former president Jacob Zuma gathered speed, explaining the increase in protests across the country. The transition to President Cyril Ramaphosa in 2018 has the promise to reverse this trend but the country remains unsettled.

However, it is Ethiopia where the most riots and protests took place (calculated per million people for the period 2011 to 2017) and Somalia where they were most fatal. In 2016 Ethiopia experienced an extraordinary increase in the number of riots and protests as the Oromo and eventually also the Amhara ethnic groups started protesting against the perceived dominance of the minority Tigray ethnic group. Whereas Tigrayans make up only about six per cent of Ethiopia's population, they have long been accused of holding inordinate economic, political and security influence. The sense of discontent was worsened by the impact of an acute drought and then floods in the highlands of Ethiopia, particularly in the Amhara and Oromia regions.

The first reaction from the Tigrayan-dominated government was to institute a national state of emergency in 2016, accompanied by brutal repression. But, eventually, in March 2018 Prime Minister Hailemariam Desalegn stepped down to make way for a much younger replacement, Abiy Ahmed, from the Oromo ethnic group. Abiy has embarked on a raft of reforms, including ending the state of emergency, releasing political prisoners, reforming the security agencies, reaching out to Eritrea, and opening up the economy, with far-reaching implications for Ethiopia and the region. His regional peacemaking efforts saw his being awarded the Nobel Peace Prize late in 2019. That the reforms did not go down well with all concerned became apparent in June 2019 when the army chief of staff and others were assassinated during a failed coup attempt.

Generally, riots and protests appear to have become less deadly, meaning that there are fewer fatalities per event when measured over time.

For example, while Africa experienced an average of eight fatalities per riot/protest event from 2001 to 2003, this average declined to three from 2015 to 2017, although wider access to social media reporting may also have played a role.[23]

The steady rate of urbanisation is clearly associated with the increasing number of riots and protests, since these are overwhelmingly urban phenomena. Although average rates conceal vast country-level differences, Africa was on average only 34 per cent urban in 2001, but this increased to 42 per cent by 2018. Africa is significantly less urbanised than other regions in the world, so the potential for swift urbanisation could prove to be politically destabilising, a trend that will increase the opportunity for riots and protests since the region is also undergoing changes in regime type and is democratising (see Chapter 13).

North Africa, the location of the Arab Spring, is significantly more urban than sub-Saharan Africa. In 2010, 53 per cent of people in North Africa lived in urban areas, compared to 35 per cent in sub-Saharan Africa. With a large portion of people in towns and cities, that population concentration facilitated the kind of crowd and mass dynamics that eventually ejected Zine El Abidine Ben Ali from his presidency in Tunisia, forced a rotation in the governing elite in Egypt, and culminated in civil war in Libya.

Structural drivers of violence in Africa

The structural drivers of violence in Africa are complex and country-specific, although there are a number of common themes that relate to poverty, democratisation, regime type, population age structure, repeat violence, the 'bad neighbourhood' effect and poor governance. Even then, violence typically requires politicisation and triggering event(s), such as the decision by the young Tunisian fruit seller Mohamed Bouazizi to self-immolate on 18 December 2010 – the event that is generally accepted as having started the Arab Spring.

For such a spark to ignite widespread violence and unrest, societies need to be afflicted by very high levels of social tension and discontent. In this instance, tension was largely the result of limited social, economic and political opportunity in North Africa and the Middle East, against a backdrop of relatively high levels of education. In addition, North Africa experienced a downturn in economic growth before the Arab Spring that inevitably increased the sense of relative deprivation.[24]

While the debate about causation and what drives violence is very contentious, some things are fairly obvious. In Southern Africa, the extraordinarily high level of inequality in countries such as Namibia, Botswana and South Africa presents a potential threat to stability. The big democratic deficits in Equatorial Guinea and eSwatini will certainly present problems in the future if left unattended. Efforts by leaders such as Obiang Nguema Mbasogo (Equatorial Guinea), Mswati III (eSwatini), Paul Biya (Cameroon), Yoweri Museveni (Uganda) and Idriss Déby (Chad) to constantly extend their terms in office, or to effect dynastic succession, present obvious challenges as pressure mounts without prospects for either democratic change or generational succession.

However, there is no scholarly consensus so far on the direct causal link between factors brought about by climate change, such as desertification, and the outbreak of conflict in Sudan (Darfur) and Mali, although it is clear that specific events such as droughts sometimes lead to violence and that climate change serves as a general conflict accelerator. One example would be the drought that occurred in Ethiopia before the 2016 riots and protests.[25] In many countries in the Sahel, a region with a particularly rapidly growing young population, conflict between herders and farmers causes more fatalities than terrorism, and the role that climate change plays in intensifying the competition over scarce resources is clear.

As climate change alters the nature of resource dependence, it will have consequential effects on states with large natural resource benefits. A report by Cullen Hendrix and Idean Salehyan found:

> Water shocks may lead to social conflict via their effects on resource competition, poor macroeconomic outcomes, and reduced state capacity . . . deviations from normal rainfall patterns have a significant effect on both large-scale and smaller-scale instances of political conflict . . . wetter years are more likely to suffer from violent events. Extreme deviations in rainfall – particularly dry and wet years – are associated with all types of social conflict (violent and nonviolent,

government-targeted and non/government-targeted), although the relationship is strongest with respect to violent events, which are more responsive to abundant rather than scarce rainfall.[26]

African countries will experience widely different effects from climate change in the coming decades (see Chapter 15), which will strain the ability of large regions to support local populations under current developmental conditions. Some areas of the continent are likely to become warmer and drier, and will therefore experience more frequent and severe droughts close to major population centres, particularly in the Sahel. Other parts of the continent may experience widespread drought and, potentially, famine without proper government intervention, while still others could have more extreme rains, which could also adversely affect crops and food security.

Current evidence on the impact of climate change and conflict is country- and region-specific. For example, while the evidence from East Africa is that socio-political factors are more important than climate change,[27] our work on the future of the five Sahel countries points to a more direct link between climate change and conflict as herders are being forced to move earlier and further south in search of grazing, which intensifies competition with pastoral communities.

Improved security prospects

The changes in Africa's growth prospects during the last two decades signify a structural transformation in the continent's fortunes. Although the road ahead is long and will be characterised by many setbacks, over time economic growth and improvements in general living conditions are very likely to translate into stability. The reason for this is actually not that people are more content with improved standards of living but rather that the capacity of governments to provide or enforce security increases as countries develop.

Stability depends not only on the nature of the government, ie democratic or autocratic, or on rapid (or no) economic growth, but more importantly on whether the government has the capacity and the means to provide or enforce security. Poor countries have limited capacity because they have low tax revenues, underfunded and weak institutions, and low-quality officials, which constrains the state's ability to govern or enforce security. In this sense, Africa was trapped in a vicious circle: many countries were unstable because they were poor, and because they were poor they were unstable.

Furthermore, and contrary to popular belief, government spending on security in Africa tends to be quite low when compared to the level of insecurity on the continent and when compared to other regions, such as the Middle East. And spending is often skewed towards providing security for the president or the governing elite. Given the continent's long history of coups d'état and interference by the military in government, security spending is often also divided between a number of competing and overlapping security services so that the president can ensure that no single agency poses a threat – part of the age-old game of divide and rule. At the same time, many areas of Africa are unpoliced and national and local government representation is thin or nonexistent. Institutions are weak, and because of the high levels of poverty, rent-seeking is high.

While the level of resources within a country impacts on state capacity, it is generally not the absolute level of wealth (or the absence thereof) that fuels discontent but rather the distribution of the limited resources within and between groupings. Therefore, civil wars generally happen more frequently in countries with a large population with one or more dominant ethnic, linguistic or religious groupings compared to countries that may have a more evenly balanced ethnic composition.[28] Recent research on the factors that underlie ethnic strife underlines that nearly 80 per cent of the continent's major ethnic groups have never participated in any civil war. The origins of most ethnic conflicts, it found, can generally be traced to the existence of precolonial states and the extent to which insecure postcolonial leaders privileged particular ethnic groups above others.[29]

Hence, conflict in Africa is not directly driven by ethnic divergence, as is often assumed, but rather by historical grievances, including the ongoing mobilisation of identity for political and economic participation and influence. It is for this reason that the comprehensive 2018 World Bank/UN report *Pathways for Peace* highlights: 'Exclusion from access to power, opportunity, services, and security creates fertile ground for mobilising group grievances to violence, especially in areas with weak state capacity or legitimacy or in the context of human rights abuses.'[30]

Regime type and regime dissonance

The character or nature of the governmental system of a country also impacts on the probability of violence.

Africa currently finds itself in a double bind. Because authoritarian governments have generally been an unmitigated disaster, there is strong support for democracy. The problem, however, is that when leaders eventually are pressurised in this direction, they accede to the trappings of electoral democracy but do not allow the development of substantive democracy. Varying levels of electoral democracy can be found in, for instance, Zimbabwe, the DRC, Uganda, Ethiopia, Rwanda and Algeria, where the process (or semblance) of elections takes place regularly but where there is no real choice, freedom of opposition or true debate, although there are signs of potential change in a number of these countries.

A significant amount of research underpins the finding that only when there are proper elections, in the sense of being free and fair and offering prospects for change in leadership, can democracy lead to improved human development. This is because electoral competition incentivises politicians to provide public goods and services. Improved government effectiveness (and hence better service delivery) can therefore be associated with substantive democracy but generally not with mere electoral democracies.[31]

At this point, most African countries are so-called anocracies[32] – countries that have elements of both autocracy and democracy. In these mixed or intermediate regimes, regular competitive elections take place but the legislature has little effective control over the executive branch of government. Thus, anocracies are

> characterised by institutions and political elites that are far less capable
> of performing fundamental tasks and ensuring their own continuity.
> Anocratic regimes very often reflect inherent qualities of instability or
> ineffectiveness and are especially vulnerable to the onset of new

political instability events, such as outbreaks of armed conflict, unexpected changes in leadership or adverse regime changes (eg a seizure of power by a personalistic or military leader in a coup). Anocracies are a middling category rather than a distinct form of governance.[33]

Examples of anocracies include Côte d'Ivoire, Zimbabwe, Tanzania, Algeria, Burundi and The Gambia.

Anocracies or intermediate regime types are more unstable than full autocracies, which are in turn less stable than consolidated democracies. The relationship takes the form of an inverted U, with intermediate regime types six times more likely than democracies, and 2.5 times more likely than autocracies, to experience new outbreaks of civil conflict. More than half of anocracies experience a major regime change within five years and 70 per cent within ten years.[34]

Anocracies with factionalised party systems, in which one ethnic (or other) grouping is advantaged, are particularly vulnerable to political instability. Still, it is generally political mobilisation that turns diversity into violence. Someone needs to start organising.

Finally, research at the Institute for Security Studies points to two important, albeit tentative, outcomes in terms of violence as it relates to regime type. First, if a country is significantly more democratic than other countries at similar levels of income and education, such an imbalance increases opportunities for corruption and the risk of acute episodes of violent protests and demonstrations. Examples include Mozambique (low income), Kenya (lower middle income) and South Africa (upper middle income). Second, if a country is significantly less democratic than could be expected given its levels of income and education, the pressure for political participation and accountability is likely to grow, with Equatorial Guinea and eSwatini serving as textbook examples to watch. Such pressure could lead to instability and even a violent rupture, particularly around leadership renewal. Other examples include North Africa before the Arab Spring but also possibly Ethiopia (low income), the Republic of Congo (lower middle income) and Libya (upper middle income).

Youth and unemployment

Given its current median age of 19 years (18 for sub-Saharan Africa), Africa has an exceptionally youthful population, although fertility rates differ significantly across regions and countries. Large youth bulges, defined as the presence of a large population between 15 and 29 years of age relative to the total adult population, are robustly associated with an increased risk of conflict and high rates of criminal violence in poor countries, particularly when young people lack opportunities in terms of education, training and employment and feel they have no voice.[35]

However youth bulges appear to be more closely related to low-intensity conflict than to civil war.[36] Sub-Saharan Africa is the youngest region globally, with roughly 48 per cent of its adult population between 15 and 29 years of age. Even by 2040 that number is forecast to have come down by only five percentage points. In the Middle East and North Africa the proportion of youth to adult population is declining from its current 36 per cent to 32 per cent by 2040. By contrast, Europe's youth constitute less than 20 per cent of its adult population, a portion that will have declined by about one percentage point by 2040.

Generally, higher education levels are associated with lower conflict vulnerability, but this depends on the size of the youth bulge, levels of employment and the degree of urbanisation.[37]

Many of these correlations were evident in North Africa at the time of the Arab Spring and are current in Algeria and Sudan.[38] In the next five years or so, Uganda, Chad, Niger, Somalia, Mali, Angola, Malawi, Zambia, Mozambique and Burkina Faso will have the largest youth bulges in Africa and therefore will be particularly at risk of violence and conflict, since all these states also have high levels of unemployment, among other contributing factors.[39]

A causal link between youth unemployment and violence in developing countries is widely assumed, particularly crime, gang violence and domestic violence, but solid evidence remains insufficient.[40]

Poor governance and high levels of inequality

In Chapter 13, I will argue that at low levels of income and development, the nature of the governing elite is more important for economic growth

234 — **AFRICA FIRST!**

and for positive development outcomes than the extent to which countries are democratic or authoritarian. Therefore, countries that are fortunate enough to have a developmentally oriented governing elite grow much more rapidly, particularly if there is a cohesive governing party or coterie of leadership with a clear focus on development.

The difference between stable and unstable poor countries is often a political elite that distributes services effectively (particularly among different ethnic groups), develops sustainable institutions, minimises corruption, and encourages the development of the private sector, while focusing on equitable growth. To this end, the Ibrahim Index of African Governance (IIAG) defines governance as 'the provision of the political, social and economic public goods and services that every citizen has a right to expect from their state, and that a state has the responsibility to deliver to its citizens'.[41]

The IIAG measures a country's overall governance performance across four sub-components, namely, safety and rule of law, participation and human rights, sustainable economic opportunity and human development. Countries that score the worst in the overall governance index are Somalia, South Sudan, Eritrea, CAR, Sudan, Libya, DRC, Chad, Equatorial Guinea, Angola and Burundi. All of these countries were allocated a score below 40 out of a possible 100.

High levels of inequality often point to a government that largely looks after the interests of specific sectors or elites or is unwilling to undertake the necessary measures to address inequality. This is reflected in the high inequality scores of South Africa, Botswana, Namibia, Equatorial Guinea, Lesotho, Comoros, Zambia and the CAR.[42] Today, governments in Southern Africa are dominated by former liberation movements that largely focus on nominal redistribution rather than growth. Their inability to grow their economies (a function of their continued pursuit of economic policies originating from the former Soviet Union in the 1960s) means they have also been unable to change the patterns of inequality inherited from colonialism, white settler dominance and apartheid.

With no prospects for political, generational and policy renewal that could impact on these structural imbalances, the promise that is inherent in regular free and fair elections is now also being frustrated. This is perhaps best reflected in the trend towards leadership rotation within a particular party or family, such as the change in the top leadership in Zimbabwe. In 2017, Robert Mugabe, 93, was replaced by the slightly younger Emmerson Mnangagwa, which brought little substantive change to a country that has levels of income much lower than when its white minority government declared unilateral independence from Britain in the mid-1960s. In Gabon, Ali Bongo Ondimba assumed power in 2009 from his father, who had controlled the country since the 1960s. Eventually, without leadership and political renewal, countries inevitably grow below their potential and consequently social problems fester.

Perceptions of the distribution of wealth between groups and the levels of equity in a society play an important role and fuel discontent. But, as discussed in Chapter 7, inequality changes very slowly.

In Central Africa, the recent downturn in global commodity prices has exacerbated an already fragile situation. There, as elsewhere, governments are unable to deliver the most basic services, yet the political elites have been exceptionally creative in designing strategies to retain their hold on power through 'personalised presidential systems supported by patronage networks sustained mainly through elite bargaining and collusion with traditional rulers'.[43]

Besides a history of conflict and chronic underdevelopment, those countries in sub-Saharan Africa that suffer severe inequality, rely heavily on primary commodities, and have a large youth bulge and an oppressive regime are virtually assured of future instability and even a violent rupture. Even then, growth in itself may be insufficient to forestall instability. This was demonstrated in Ethiopia in October 2016, when a national state of emergency was instituted after a decade of remarkable economic growth. Growth had, in fact, widened discontent in a country that many felt was being controlled by a small ethnic elite.

Modelling the prospects for greater peace: The Silencing the Guns scenario

The IFs forecasting platform uses historical data from the Center for Systemic Peace to initialise its forecasts on governance. The algorithm that drives the forecast on instability in turn relies on many of the drivers and correlations that are discussed in this chapter.[44]

The intervention used in the Silencing the Guns scenario is a general multiplier that reduces Africa's risk of violence and instability roughly to the level of South Asia by 2030. It does this by improving the contribution that social capital makes to multifactor productivity within IFs. The impact of average growth rates, when comparing the Silencing the Guns scenario to the Current Path, is depicted in Figure 12.2.

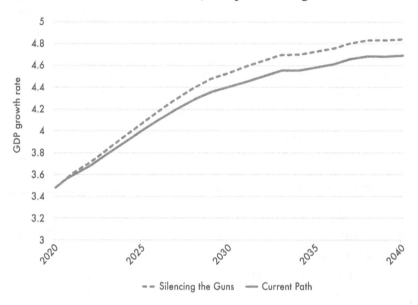

Figure 12.2: Average GDP growth rate for Africa (five-year moving average), Silencing the Guns vs Current Path[45]

More stability translates into bigger inflows of FDI. Thus, in 2040, Africa would attract half a billion dollars of additional investment in the Silencing the Guns scenario than in the Current Path forecast for that year. Stability translates into lower levels of corruption and more effective and capable governance, all of which will improve the investment climate on the continent.

Governments would also be able to roll out more electrification schemes, provide better water and sanitation, and offer more health care services for more citizens, and tourism can also flourish. The results are improvements in health and health care, for example a small reduction in infant mortality rates. By 2040, 162 000 fewer children would suffer from malnourishment compared to the Current Path forecast. Furthermore, fewer Africans would seek to flee their home countries, resulting in lower levels of refugees and migration.

More stability and foreign investment translate into a bigger economy and improved economic growth. In the Silencing the Guns scenario, the African economy is US$147 billion larger than in the Current Path forecast in 2040 (in market exchange rates). The cumulative gains from 2020 to 2040 are even more impressive, amounting to US$974 billion. In 2040 each African would have an additional US$95 in his/her pocket compared to the Current Path forecast, and 15 million fewer Africans would live in extreme poverty. Cumulatively, 104 million fewer Africans would live in extreme poverty from 2020 to 2040.[46] In addition, democracy levels are likely to increase and governance will improve.

Conclusion: Focusing on conflict prevention

The complex and country-specific structural drivers of conflict in Africa are interlinked with factors such as the impact of radical ideology – currently fundamentalist Islamism – poor education, low levels of development and geopolitical competition. Yet, we are likely to see further changes in the nature of instability in the 21st century since levels of education and literacy are increasing, as are levels of political freedom, while trade and travel all connect us more closely than before. Armed conflict and associated deaths are likely to continue to decline, while social protest, riots and urban discord are likely to increase.

Poor governance and lack of inclusive economic development lie at the heart of Africa's instability challenge. For instance, in West Africa and the Sahel political violence is driven by a sense of marginalisation and exclusion from the political centre. Africans need to confront this reality instead of succumbing to the militarised approaches to combating terror that, with much more resources, have failed in Afghanistan.

Generally, states in sub-Saharan Africa are younger and poorer (in terms of income) than most of their peers in the international system. Colonialism and its legacy severely disrupted their natural evolution, and political violence has been a central feature of the region's colonial and postcolonial history.

While armed conflict is often more prevalent in rural areas, riots and protests are becoming an overwhelmingly urban phenomenon, particularly since the share of Africa's urban population living in slums is steadily rising. Political violence in Africa is already largely urban-based, and instability in Africa is likely to affect cities and the unpoliced and unplanned urban sprawls rather than rural areas.[47] Clearly, conflicts over land, property rights and services for urban residents need to be addressed through integrated urban development strategies.[48]

Against this backdrop, the gains in peace and stability over the past two decades are impressive. These include significant multilateral, regional and bilateral efforts and investments in conflict prevention, peacemaking, peacekeeping[49] and peacebuilding. Much remains to be done, however, such as ending the extent to which conflict is instigated and fuelled from neighbouring countries.

Africans have to further expand and capacitate the structures that form part of the AU's African Peace and Security Architecture (APSA). To be effective, however, these institutions need to adopt different practices from those of the recent past, when the organisation looked the other way as elections were being stolen in Zimbabwe, the DRC and elsewhere.

An approach premised on longer-term stability requires setting clear standards for governance, accountability and the provision of security. Africa needs to move from its focus on conflict management to substantive conflict prevention and a focus on the structural drivers of violence. Few investments can compete with the provision of education, for example, as a means to drain the swamp of ignorance that allows radical ideologies to flourish.

Clearly, violence, instability and armed conflict in Africa will remain a major concern that requires an ongoing and dedicated response from the AU, its member states and the international community, for the provision of continued aid and humanitarian assistance to poor countries, for peacekeeping in fragile ones and towards the promise of the SDGs.

Efforts to silence the guns by 2020 are important, but Africa will likely remain turbulent not only because it is poor and young, and because African governments have limited capacity to provide security, but also because it is growing and dynamic. Many African countries are experiencing a political awakening that is uncharacteristic of a continent that has long suffered at the hands of foreign intervention and autocratic exploitation by its own elites.

Unlike elsewhere in the developed world, Africa is not experiencing a democratic regression. Protest has become a more acceptable public behaviour in many countries, since there is an increased number of electoral democracies, although the quality of democracy is thin. This is reflected in the changing nature of violence in which the ballot, not the gun, is slowly becoming the main source of political contestation. This is the theme of the next chapter.

13

Good governance, democracy and development

> Politics matters more in emerging [countries] . . ., where
> institutions are weaker and new or ageing leaders can have
> a clearer impact on the economy's direction and therefore
> on the mood of the markets.
>
> – Ruchir Sharma, *The Rise and Fall of Nations*[1]

Democracy is generally understood to have advanced in three global waves over the last two centuries. Each wave raised the previous high-water mark and locked in increasingly larger proportions of the world's population, although each wave was followed by a modest ebbing.

The first wave began in the early 19th century but ebbed in the years leading up to the Second World War. At its peak there were 29 democracies, but it is important to remember that the number of sovereign states was significantly lower than today's tally of 195 countries. During the Second World War, the number of democracies fell to just 12 by 1942.

The second wave began with the end of the Second World War when the number of independent states also increased rapidly. This wave peaked in 1962 with 36 recognised democracies, dropping to 30 by the mid-1970s. During this wave, rapid decolonisation swept first across North Africa, affecting Eritrea, Ethiopia and Libya. Sudan gained its independence from the United Kingdom and Egypt in 1956 and later that year Tunisia and Morocco theirs from France. In sub-Saharan Africa, Ghana (previously the Gold Coast) became independent in 1957, quickly followed by most of the British, French and Belgian colonies.

It was perhaps no surprise that the third wave of democracy began in Portugal, with the Carnation Revolution of 1974. The country was burdened by its vast colonial empire, a stagnant economy and 48 years of authoritarian rule. In the following year virtually all of Portugal's colonies achieved independence, a hasty and chaotic affair that affected Cape Verde, Guinea-Bissau, Mozambique, Angola and São Tomé and Príncipe.

The end of Portuguese colonial rule accelerated the liberation wars that led to the end of colonial rule in Rhodesia (now Zimbabwe) in 1980 and South West Africa (now Namibia) in 1990. However, the key event that would change the levels of democracy in Africa was the collapse of the Soviet Union in 1991. This ended a series of proxy wars in Africa and, as a result, also Western support for a number of unsavoury regimes intended to counter Soviet expansion. In 1990 it would also allow the start of a negotiation process that, four years later, would see Nelson Mandela elected as president of South Africa, then Africa's largest economy with its most powerful military.

The third wave led to a rash of democratic transitions in Latin America in the 1980s and shortly thereafter in several Asia-Pacific countries, while the dissolution of the Soviet Union allowed a number of countries in Eastern and Central Europe to establish representative systems of government.

These events all need to be borne in mind when considering Figure 13.1, a line graph that uses data from the Varieties of Democracy project (V-Dem) to present average levels of liberal and electoral democracy in Africa and the world for the period 1960–2017.[2] V-Dem is a large and complex effort at conceptualising and measuring democracy over time. It makes a distinction between five types of democracy. In addition to liberal and electoral democracy, it also measures participatory, deliberative and egalitarian democracy.

Of this fivefold typology, liberal democracy is the most mature and developed type, with protection for individual and minority rights against the tyranny of the majority,[3] while electoral democracy is the least substantive. The index on the left-hand y-axis in Figure 13.1 (see overleaf) is from 0 (complete absence of democracy) to 1 (full liberal or electoral democracy in all countries).

Neither average levels of electoral democracy nor levels of substantive democracy changed much in Africa until 1989. By contrast, global averages steadily improved. Then, in just five years, from 1989 to 1993, the level of democracy in Africa (and globally) increased sharply, although the increase in electoral democracy is more pronounced than for liberal democracy.

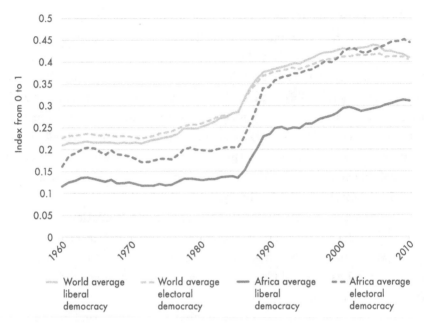

Figure 13.1: Average levels of electoral and liberal democracy in the world and in Africa, 1960 to 2017[4]

This is to be expected, as it is easy to adopt the trappings of democracy. However, it requires much greater effort (and more time) to establish a clear separation of powers between the executive, judiciary and legislature, a truly competitive political environment, a free media and independent oversight mechanisms that have some teeth.

In the years since 1993, the gap between levels of electoral and substantive democracy in Africa has grown larger, meaning that more African countries hold regular elections and provide for varying degrees of civil liberties, but that these changes are not always substantive.

Many analysts hailed the Arab Spring of 2010 as either the start of a fourth wave of democratisation, since it originated in the region with the lowest levels of political and economic inclusion globally, or proof that the third wave had not yet fully run its course. Sadly, the situation in Libya, Egypt and a number of countries in the Middle East and North Africa today is worse than before. To date, only Tunisia has emerged from this turmoil with substantially higher scores on the various V-Dem measures of democracy.

Then, in 2018 and 2019 (not evident in Figure 13.1 since the data is until 2017[5]), a new wave of popular protest started, most prominently in Ethiopia, followed by Sudan and Algeria, as citizens challenged long-standing parties and rulers. These events indicate that democratisation in Africa is indeed still on an upward trajectory. I will pursue this line of reasoning in devising a subsequent scenario.

In contrast to developments in Africa, the rise of terrorism, populism and the influence of an authoritarian China have turned the early optimism about a rising tide of democracy into a degree of democratic pessimism. In fact, a report by the Pew Research Center[6] cites global dissatisfaction with democracy, as anti-establishment leaders, parties and movements have emerged on either side of the political spectrum.

So, the recent trends in Africa stand in sharp contrast to developments elsewhere. Outside Africa, democratic setbacks have affected countries as diverse as Brazil, Hungary, Russia, Serbia and Turkey. This is evident in the decline in the average levels of liberal democracy globally from 2012 (see Figure 13.1). In addition, the future of democracy in the developed world is likely to evolve in uncertain ways. In 2016 the Economist Intelligence Unit described the rise of populism in the West (and elsewhere) and the extent to which democracy in the West was in apparent retreat: 'An increased sense of personal and societal anxiety and insecurity in the face of diverse perceived risks and threats – economic, political, social and security – is undermining democracy, which depends on a steadfast commitment to upholding enlightenment values (liberty, equality, fraternity, reason, tolerance and free expression) . . .'[7]

Roberto Foa and Yascha Mounk go so far as to question the durability of the world's affluent, consolidated democracies. Writing in the *Journal of Democracy*,[8] they note that 'trust in political institutions such as parliaments or the courts [has] precipitously declined . . . as has voter turnout, party identification has weakened and party membership has declined'. In these societies today 'voters increasingly endorse single-issue movements, vote for populist candidates, or support "anti system" parties . . . Even in some of the richest and most politically stable regions in the world, it seems as though democracy is in a state of serious disrepair.'

Foa and Mounk refer to the 'structural problems in the functioning of liberal democracy'.[9] Having no experience of life without democracy, and no memory of the struggle to secure and sustain it, young voters in the industrial democracies of the West are not engaged in traditional party politics. Voter turnout is falling, political party membership has plummeted, and support for distinctly undemocratic regime forms is on the rise. Instead of its consolidating, democracy in the rich West may be under threat of 'deconsolidating'.[10]

Today the relative decline of the West, in particular the transactional leadership style of the Donald Trump presidency, has led to a commensurate weakening of the global impetus towards democratisation outside Africa. As the vacuum in leadership by established liberal democracies becomes evident in the face of challenges such as migration and globalisation, the example (and influence) of successful authoritarian development models such as China increases, backed by its increasing economic muscle. In addition, Western influence within institutions such as the UN Security Council and the International Criminal Court and support for civil society and pro-democracy advocacy groups are declining in line with the reduction in Western economic dominance. This trend is accelerated by the very obvious discord among the Western partners.

But by 2019 the Economist Intelligence Unit noted that 'for the first time in three years, the global score for democracy remained stable',[11] and that it was not deteriorating. The unit's 2019 report points to improvements in voter turnout and membership of political parties, although warning that 'the rise of engagement combined with a continued crackdown on civil liberties is a potentially volatile mix, and could be a recipe for instability and social unrest in 2019'.[12]

The V-Dem data used in Figure 13.1 coincides with data from other sources, such as Freedom House, indicating that whereas in 1988 only 17 out of 50 African countries on which it reported could be classified as 'free' or 'partly free', in 2018 32 out of 54 African countries were either 'free' or 'partly free'.

The state of democracy in Africa

The steady improvements in the levels of electoral and liberal democracy in Africa, particularly since 1989, mean that democracy is now the dominant form of government on the continent. However, the quality of the electoral democracies is often weak and the associated procedures are regularly flaunted as incumbents cook the books to stay in power and obstruct the chances of opposition groups to campaign or even to stand in elections.

Benin is an example of an African country where democracy has deteriorated significantly in recent years. When the country voted for a new parliament in April 2019, not a single opposition candidate could take part after electoral authorities ruled that only two parties, both loyal to President Patrice Talon, met the requirement for participation – and a new electoral law meant that a party had to pay US$424 000 to field a list for the 83-member parliament.[13]

Another way to measure democracy in Africa would be to classify countries as 1) authoritarian (or non-democratic), 2) electoral (or thin) democracies, or 3) liberal (or substantive) democracies. In 2018, Freedom House[14] classified ten out of the 54 African states as 'free' (roughly equating to liberal democracy), 22 as 'partly free' (roughly equating to electoral democracy) and the remaining 22 as 'not free'.

The ten free countries are Benin, Botswana, Cape Verde, Ghana, Mauritius, Namibia, São Tomé and Príncipe, Senegal, South Africa and Tunisia, in total home to only 133 million people, or ten per cent of Africa's population. The 22 'partly free' countries that meet the minimum criteria to be classified as electoral democracies represent an additional 47 per cent of Africa's population. The remainder, roughly 42 per cent of Africa's total population, live in countries that Freedom House considers to be 'not free'.

Based on this analysis, 58 per cent of Africans live in countries that could be considered democratic, even if the quality of that democracy is uneven. Hence the introductory statement that democracy is today the dominant form of government in Africa, both in terms of the number of countries (32 out of 54) and the proportion of total population (58 per cent). Should Nigeria, with its 195 million people, move from being 'partly free' to 'free', the scales would tilt decisively in favour of democracy in Africa.

The V-Dem and Freedom House measures of democracy are not perfect but do provide a way of getting to grips with the challenge of quantifying the depth and extent of democracy in Africa and how it changes over time. A number of additional insights are evident from a deeper analysis of the data presented in Figure 13.1. The first is that the average levels of electoral democracy in Africa are slowly approaching (and even exceeding) the global mean. This convergence is occurring despite the fact that the average level of GDP per capita in Africa is much lower and diverges from the global average (ie levels of income in Africa are growing more slowly than the global mean). In other words, countries now transition to democracy at steadily lower levels of income than before.

Historically, the reason for this trend towards earlier democratisation is likely the dominance, until recently, of the liberal-democratic West, which provided significant amounts of development assistance to Africa (see Chapter 14). Furthermore, in an interconnected world in which citizens can compare their domestic situation with people in other countries, there was an accompanying global example (or push) for democracy as the most desirable governance model. Proof of this support can be found in data gathered by Afrobarometer, which has done extensive and repeat surveys on attitudes to democracy in Africa over many years.[15]

The Afrobarometer findings show that the demand for and support of democracy in Africa is strong and continues to expand. The push for greater democratisation comes from a citizenry that has lived through decades of authoritarianism. Although electoral democracy has hardly delivered better results, the process of being consulted and having the power to effect changes in leadership reshapes the dynamics of power and the perception of accountability. Africans are tired of autocrats and 'big men'.[16]

Finally, as mentioned in Chapter 12, most African regimes are of a mixed (and hence unstable) type. They are neither fully autocratic nor fully democratic but include some democratic systems and practices that coexist with undemocratic systems and practices. These mixed regime types (or anocracies) are more susceptible to abrupt regime change and governance setbacks than countries that are either fully autocratic or consolidated liberal democracies.[17]

While the prevalence of regular elections in Africa is on an upward trajectory, incumbents who cling to power and block executive rotation or replacement present a worrying trend. Denis Sassou Nguesso of the Republic of Congo, Yoweri Museveni of Uganda and Paul Kagame of Rwanda all recently amended their country's constitutions to allow for unlimited presidential incumbency, among other changes. In the DRC, outgoing president Joseph Kabila and his party simply ignored the actual results of the December 2018 elections, clearly won by Martin Fayulu of the Lamuka coalition, and installed a puppet in the form of Félix Tshisekedi, who was duly inaugurated as president on 24 January 2019.[18] As in other regions, the process of democratisation in Africa is turbulent and progress seldom linear.

Levels of democracy in Africa have improved over time, however, despite the absence of many of the supposed preconditions for democratic consolidation. Nic Cheeseman lists these as 'a coherent national identity, strong and autonomous political institutions, a developed and autonomous civil society, the rule of law, and a strong and well performing economy'.[19] Taking a decidedly pessimistic view of democratisation in Africa, Cheeseman argues that since 1990 democratisation has taken place against the odds in a number of poor and unstable countries where the preconditions for democracy did not exist. According to him, democratisation in Africa essentially rests on weak foundations, which opens the possibility of a regression to lower or more 'appropriate' levels, while a façade of regular elections hides the reality of no or only little change in the balance of political and social power and hierarchy.

Indeed, democracy generally operates better above certain minimum levels of income and education, when the web of institutions and the rule of law are able to constrain the misuse and abuse of state institutions.[20] Whatever the exact relationship between democracy, income and education, the indices tell an optimistic story of increased levels of democracy in Africa over time. This is certainly good news in Africa, for, once established and in conjunction with minimum income levels and education, democracy is the most stable form of governance. Thus Glaeser et al find:

> Averaging across the starting years 1960, 1970 and 1980, the probability of a well-educated democracy remaining a democracy twenty years later is 95 per cent. The probability of a well-educated dictatorship becoming a democracy within 20 years is 87 per cent.[21]

But, the essential question for this book is whether democracy is making a difference to the objective living conditions of Africans.

Is democracy making a difference to Africa's development prospects?

In the long term, that is, over successive decades, democracy has a number of developmental benefits over other regime types: through elections, it provides a mechanism to hold the power of the elite or special interest groups in check; it ensures the separation of state powers into different branches of government and the protection of human rights and the rule of law, which in turn creates confidence for the pursuit of long-term investments. However, such substantive (or liberal) democracy only emerges over time and requires significant resources to mature.

At a global level, China's authoritarian post-1978 developmental model is often quoted as proof of a positive relationship between autocracy and development at low levels of income. Its track record is sometimes contrasted to the much poorer progress of India, the world's largest democracy, which has struggled to gain economic momentum. Then there are the Asian Tiger economies (Hong Kong, South Korea, Singapore and Taiwan), which all experienced rapid progress without democracy; they democratised only after achieving middle-income status, providing further support to the Chinese model.

In Africa, the most commonly quoted examples of successful authoritarian regimes are Rwanda and Ethiopia. In recent years, these two have made more developmental progress than virtually any other African country. They benefited from rapid growth in the size of their working-age population relative to dependants, improvements matched by solid, if unspectacular, advances in primary education and literacy.

On both these measures, Rwanda comes off a higher base than Ethiopia, making the improvements in average levels of income of Ethiopians even more impressive. As discussed in Chapter 3, economic growth generally follows rapidly declining fertility rates and subsequent improvements in the proportion of working-age persons to dependants. In addition, the advancement of primary education and improved general literacy levels are important preconditions for turning this larger workforce into productive human capital – areas where Ethiopia still faces many challenges.

These two countries are, however, notable exceptions in a sea of many poor authoritarian countries. This positive outcome has been highly contingent on chance (and personality) and the nature of the governing elites. In both countries, the burning goal for betterment was shaped by a national trauma – the genocide of the Red Terror in Ethiopia under Mengistu Haile Mariam that lasted until 1978, and the Rwandan genocide of 1994.

In the wake of these traumas, governing elites in the two countries intervened decisively in the economy in favour of productivity, often exerting considerable short-term pain for the sake of achieving long-term gain – policy choices and implementation that are much easier in an autocratic than in a democratic setting. Both have clear pro-growth policies and stick to them. In each country, a determined, pro-development governing elite is united in its vision of escaping debilitating poverty and underdevelopment.

At an average rate of nearly ten per cent per year over the past decade, Ethiopia has achieved the most robust GDP growth of any country globally, surpassing countries like China, Qatar and Rwanda. Over that same period, average incomes in the country nearly tripled, and the proportion of people with access to electricity, for example, doubled.[22] But then the wheels started coming off.

In 2015 Ethiopia held parliamentary elections, as well as elections for its regional assemblies. The ruling Ethiopian People's Revolutionary Democratic Front (EPRDF) gained 500 of the available 547 seats but the process and the political environment fell short of being considered substantively free and fair. Shortly afterwards, the government announced its intention to expand the city limits of Addis Ababa into the surrounding Oromia province.

The plan triggered widespread resentment and the suspicion that the EPRDF was aiming to enhance federal authority at the expense of the nation's largest ethnic group, the Oromo, who were poorly represented in government. Protests began in November 2015 in Ginchi, a small town in Oromia about 80 kilometres southwest of Addis Ababa, and although the government formally abandoned the plan to expand the capital in January 2016, tensions continued to simmer.

In October 2016 the crisis reached a tipping point. A heavy-handed response by the security forces during an annual cultural festival in Oromia on 2 October triggered a stampede that killed dozens, possibly hundreds, of people. Three days later, the government blocked mobile phone access to social media. Then, on 9 October 2016, the government declared a nationwide state of emergency that restricted freedom of movement, freedom of assembly and access to social media, and suspended due process for arrest and detention.[23]

In the weeks and months that followed, more than 10 000 opposition members, the majority of them from the Amhara and Oromia regions, were rounded up and detained.[24] Tensions simmered throughout 2017, with armed clashes between ethnic groups becoming commonplace in several regions. By the end of 2017, there were as many as 400 000 internally displaced persons in Ethiopia's Oromia and Somali regions.[25] In February 2018 Prime Minister Hailemariam Desalegn resigned in response to the escalating unrest.

Violence escalated until, in April 2018, Abiy Ahmed Ali, the chairman of the Oromo Democratic Party, was elected as both chairman of the EPRDF and prime minister. He launched a sweeping political, economic, social and foreign policy reform programme in an effort to undercut the discontent that had led to the violence.

The above suggests a possible answer to the democracy/development quandary. Ethiopia ran into trouble because a small ethnic group, the Tigrayans, were perceived to benefit from economic growth. This points to the dangers of ethnic favouritism and the importance of balanced development. To reiterate: at low levels of development, the nature of the governing elite is much more important for economic growth than the institutional setting (whether democratic or not). The main reason for this is simply that institutions are usually much weaker and less developed in low- than in middle- and high-income countries. Finally, for all its other benefits, democracy is not the answer to economic stagnation, inequality and corruption in poor countries, although it helps to hold individuals accountable and to give constituents greater political participation.

Democracy generally only contributes to growth at more advanced levels of development where a more competitive political system reinforces a competitive economic system. Today, the latter is a prerequisite for growth in high-income countries. At low levels of development, democracy may actually constrain growth or have a negligible impact, as is arguably the case with India. Since democracy in low-income countries is invariably of a low, procedural type (ie electoral, not liberal), it makes little contribution to improvements in well-being or even to the way in which the country is governed.

In their study on the relationship between democracy and human development, Glaeser et al find that the electoral democracy/human development relationship is maximised when '(a) elections are clean and not marred by fraud or systemic irregularities, (b) the chief executive of a country is selected (directly or indirectly) through elections, (c) suffrage is extensive, (d) political and civil society organizations operate freely, and (e) there is freedom of expression, including access to alternative information'.[26] These five components interact with each other, and the absence of one severely mitigates the impact on development prospects, although clean elections have the strongest correlation with positive outcomes on human development.[27] These five components lie at the heart of substantive, or liberal, democracy.

The same sequence holds for so-called good governance, a general term that is difficult to operationalise in an objective manner but is often used in conjunction with broad notions of democracy. Many books have been written about what is meant by good governance, but suffice to say that these definitions often share many of the characteristics of democracy and include reference to participation, the rule of law, equity and inclusiveness, accountability, transparency and responsiveness.[28]

Good governance, like democracy, accompanies and generally follows, rather than precedes, development. Therefore, 'the full set of institutional improvements associated with the idea of good governance becomes feasible for countries only *after* substantial economic transformation has occurred'.[29] Yet, in the eyes of many donors, policy-makers and, often, the general public in Africa and the West, democracy, good governance and development all go together and should be pursued in that order, despite the fact that this reverses the historical developmental sequence that is evident from events elsewhere.

Once again, there are examples of where development has taken place despite a lack of good governance. In the 1960s, for example, the starting conditions in the high-growth economies of South East Asia (such as China, Indonesia, Malaysia and Vietnam) and Africa were similar in many respects: there was widespread poverty, hunger, poor infrastructure, bad health and poor quality of education. Despite having strong neopatrimonial political systems (politically corrupt patron-client relations), as was the case in many African countries, these economies grew rapidly and saw reductions in levels of extreme poverty.

All of them had a governing elite that was strongly committed to economic growth. They started their transformation process with a focus first on agriculture, basic education and literacy, and underwent a rapid demographic transition that enabled them to achieve a demographic dividend while embarking on low-end industrialisation.

Certainly, these are very broad conclusions and they do not mean that good governance standards do not improve development outcomes. Good governance serves as a force multiplier on all development aspects. African countries with stronger institutions and/or better governance indicators, particularly in terms of government effectiveness and regulatory quality, generally fare better.

On the negative side, there is considerable evidence that the introduction of competitive politics and economic liberalisation in fragile settings can be costly in terms of violence and loss of human life.[30] The problem is that we don't know how else to legitimise a government. This has been most evident in so-called post-conflict fragile states such as South Sudan, Somalia, CAR, Chad, Côte d'Ivoire and the DRC. In the absence of other mechanisms to make government accountable to its citizens, civil society, regional organisations and the international community have generally insisted on creating governments of national unity and, shortly thereafter, competitive elections, which often undid much of the progress previously made in ending the conflict.

The challenge is the use of a single mechanism, elections, as a means to determine the 'will of the people' where the institutions required to support such a system are absent. The result is a choice between violent and disruptive elections, which are often a sham, or the continuation of the status quo that gave rise to the governance crisis in the first instance. No country demonstrates this challenge better than Somalia – Africa's pre-eminent failed state – and recently South Sudan.

The realities of neopatrimonialism in Africa

Many academics have commented on the apparent resilience of neo-patrimonialism as part of Africa's democratisation processes. The term is widely used to describe a system of politically corrupt patron-client relations that has dominated politics in Africa, particularly in the category of 'not free' and 'partly free' countries. Neopatrimonialism can exist at the highest national level down to community level in small villages.

Pierre Englebert and Kevin Dunn find that the degree to which authoritarian neopatrimonial regimes have been able to adapt to the formal trappings of electoral democracy is one of the most remarkable characteristics of contemporary African politics: 'Thus, to a large extent, neopatrimonialism has proved compatible with democracy rather than having dissolved in it. It has endured and reproduced despite a generalised change in the formal rules of politics.'[31]

Cheeseman is one of many academics who accept the resilience and widespread occurrence of corruption and inappropriate patron-client relationships. He argues that 'patrimonialism itself is not the problem: what matters is the type of patrimonialism that emerges'.[32]

One approach is to distinguish between centrally managed patrimonial relations, so-called developmental patrimonialism,[33] and decentralised, competitive patrimonial systems. The former is evident in Ethiopia and Rwanda, where elites provide coherence and order in the political system, take a longer, developmental view of public provision, and generally provide better outcomes over the medium and long term.

More decentralised or competitive neopatrimonial systems, as in Kenya and Nigeria, show the opposite outcomes. Here, competition is simply about personal benefit, and politics is about who governs and not about policy or improved livelihoods. Issues around personality, affiliation and identity predominate. It is particularly damaging if the national constitutional dispensation is of the winner-takes-all variant, which gives the electoral victor wide discretionary powers to appoint, approve and reward.

While politics is exceptionally competitive and robust in Kenya and Nigeria, electoral democracy does not really deliver improved livelihoods. However, the two countries may in due course reveal the potential for political experiments to disperse power. Nigeria has a steadily expanding federal system, while Kenya recently introduced a county system that provides for a significant devolution of power – an example now being copied in Mozambique and Angola. We do not yet have firm evidence of whether decentralised systems advance accountability or merely increase the opportunity for corruption, but what is clear is that much greater community activism is required for such efforts. And it is crucial that the delimitation of municipalities or counties be based primarily on their potential for financial viability and their capacity to manage those matters for which they are responsible.

In the absence of civil war or some other calamity, it is almost inevitable that both Nigeria and Kenya will grow given the expansion of the working-age population, rising levels of education and rapid rates of urbanisation. However, this growth is unlikely to promote sustainable, broad-based human development outcomes without a change in political culture or the emergence of decisive, forward-looking leadership.

The problem with the twofold distinction between centralised and decentralised patrimonial systems is that countries with centralised patrimonial systems do not necessarily produce better outcomes. Other factors may come into play. In fact, a number of relatively recently liberated countries in Southern Africa, such as Namibia, Angola, Zimbabwe, Mozambique and South Africa, would probably fit into the category of a centralised patrimonial system, since former liberation parties still dominate politics, but generally with disappointing results. In South Africa, where the governing ANC did not come to power through the extensive political indoctrination and associated broad-based people's war that took place in Namibia, Mozambique and Zimbabwe, a liberal constitution, active civil society, entrenched Bill of Rights and independent judiciary have barely been able to constrain the ANC's neo-patrimonial inclinations.

Eventually the degree to which centralised patrimonial systems can advance development is heavily dependent on the quality of the top leadership. Strong, visionary leaders such as Paul Kagame (Rwanda), Thabo Mbeki (South Africa) or Meles Zenawi (Ethiopia) can have a significant impact on development outcomes while they are in power. But there is no guarantee that they will not succumb to the attractions of office – as was the case with Yoweri Museveni in Uganda and eventually also Kagame. Both Museveni and Kagame are now seeking to extend their terms in the belief that their leadership is indispensable for the future of their respective countries. In South Africa, Jacob Zuma succeeded Thabo Mbeki for two subsequent presidential terms and literally bankrupted the country.

Booth's view is that the centralised or developmental patrimonial state is the result of very specific conditions – and never of peaceful multiparty elections. He presents two examples of such conditions: a) where the leadership consists of national liberation forces after war, as still evident in many countries in Southern Africa; and b) in the aftermath of a severe crisis or shock to the system involving large-scale violence, as experienced in Rwanda and Ethiopia.[34]

Cheeseman comes to these issues from a slightly different perspective, namely, the extent to which democracy in Africa is inclusive or competitive. He uses the examples of Côte d'Ivoire and Kenya to argue for the need for greater inclusion, and cites Ghana and Senegal as two examples of political competition driving progress. He notes that 'while elements of competition and inclusion strengthen multiparty systems, too much of either can be fatal to the process of democratisation'.[35] The most notable examples of 'excessive inclusion' are governments of national unity or where there are power-sharing arrangements. Since such governments are largely premised on the need for conflict management, they are often unable to sustain or promote economic growth.

Following instances of electoral violence in Kenya and Zimbabwe in the mid-2000s, regional actors helped craft governments of national unity. While these produced a measure of political stability, they also engendered paralysis of governance and economic performance.[36] Lack of development in turn leads to social instability, and in these circumstances a government of national unity sometimes unwittingly plants the seeds for the next crisis.

Cheeseman therefore argues that 'excessive inclusion is therefore just as bad for democracy and development as excessive competition'.[37] But the point at which inclusion becomes excessive remains unclear and subjective.

The role of leadership in development

Our understanding of the relationship between democracy, development and governance is clearly still incomplete. As is the case with violence, actual outcomes are determined by specific national conditions.

What is clear, however, is that leadership, government capacity and intent are particularly important. It is possible to argue that the winner of the August 2016 elections in Zambia or Gabon made little difference in the short or medium term, since neither government has the capacity to deliver improved development outcomes due to an incapable civil service and a lack of policy space because of the dependence of both countries on single commodities (a function of the choices made by previous elites as well as the dictates of the global economy).

Therefore, given the lack of government capacity, poor leadership and absence of a clear development goal, these two countries will likely bumble along. Burgeoning populations will push up economic growth rates, and the trickle-down effects from the wealth that accrues to a small political elite at the high table of patronage will improve living standards – but among a very small middle class.

Intent and leadership can make a major difference, both negatively and positively. A good example is President John Magufuli of Tanzania – nicknamed 'The Bulldozer' for his apparent no-nonsense approach to corruption and waste. However, the impact of his 'government by gesture', as *The Economist* termed it, remains unimpressive: 'Mr Magufuli's zeal may be admired, but his party, which has ruled Tanzania since independence, is thuggish and undemocratic: it suppressed dissent during the elections [in 2015] and then cancelled a vote held in Zanzibar after the opposition probably won it.'[38] In 2018, in a remarkable display of ignorance, Magufuli stated that Tanzania's women should 'give up contraceptive methods' and that he sees 'no reason to control births in Tanzania'.[39] Actually, with a total fertility rate of almost five children per woman, Tanzania's very high fertility rates preclude reasonable income growth.

This is a discussion that reverts to leadership, and to the unity and capacity of the ruling party and government to deliver, rather than to the extent to which they are inclusive or exclusive, elected or non-elected. Of course, as countries advance along the development trajectory the need for greater inclusion becomes a more important driver of future development. Diversified economies require innovation and knowledge production to sustain growth, which is quite different to the requirements of an undiversified, single-commodity-based economy largely dominated by informal activity.

Eventually, strong authoritarian leaders, as one finds in Rwanda and previously Ethiopia, who are at the helm of an organised party with a firm grip on the country, politics and development (ie centralised patrimonial systems), are likely to deliver more rapid results in low-income countries. The problem is that this only happens in exceptional cases. Usually the dependence on a single key figure more readily undoes progress, as it has done in Uganda, Angola, Zimbabwe, Egypt, Sudan, South Sudan, Equatorial Guinea, eSwatini, Libya and Algeria.

It is easy to underestimate the challenges of governance in Africa and the time horizon required to improve development outcomes. It is also easy to overestimate the ability of political leaders or democratic systems to improve on issues such as poverty reduction.

Modelling the impact of more democracy: The Fourth Wave of Democracy scenario

Whereas the push towards elections, human rights and accountability was, for many years, perceived as largely a donor agenda, it is now driven by Africans, particularly young Africans. This is also reflected in Afrobarometer's findings on the strong support for democratisation on the continent. This trend is, however, increasingly associated with protests and violence. 'Over the past decade, mass uprisings in Africa have accounted for one in three of the nonviolent campaigns to topple dictatorships around the world,' write Zoe Marks, Erica Chenoweth and Jide Okeke.[40] These mass uprisings have been more successful in Africa than anywhere else, having succeeded in countries as diverse as Burkina Faso, Côte d'Ivoire, Madagascar, Mali, South Africa, Tunisia, Zambia and, most recently, Algeria and Sudan.

The likely development is that the global waves of democratisation of the past will become less pronounced, although a regional wave in the Middle East (which is clearly headed for massive governance changes) is inevitable. That, in turn, means that national and regional dynamics will play a more important role in the future.

I model the continuation of a positive trend towards more democracy (the Fourth Wave) within the IFs forecasting platform using a measure of regime type that was originally developed as part of the Polity IV project on regime types. The Polity measure roughly equates to the concept of 'thin' or electoral democracy also used by V-Dem, in addition to their measure of liberal or substantive democracy.[41]

Waves have crests and troughs, and the Fourth Wave scenario is assumed to have started in 2010 with the Arab Spring and to last ten years to 2020 before levelling off. From 2030 a slow democratic regression will set in that lasts until 2051 before the onset of the next (or fifth) wave of democracy that, in turn, will last until 2058 before plateauing.

The history and forecast of the subsequent mean levels of electoral democracy for Africa and the global average are presented in Figure 13.2 and forecast to 2063, the final year of the AU's Agenda 2063. The scale on the left-hand side of the graph has been normalised to represent a score of 0 to 1, which is similar to that used for the data from V-Dem presented in Figure 13.1 instead of the -10 to +10 range that is normally used when presenting the Polity data. The dashed line presents the changed level of democracy in Africa in the Fourth Wave of Democracy scenario.

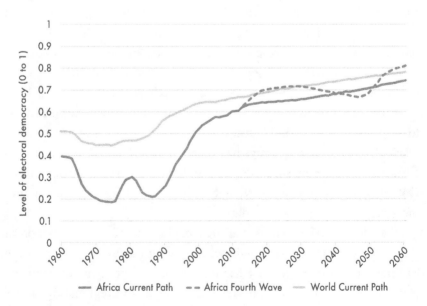

Figure 13.2: The Fourth Wave of Democracy scenario using Polity IV data[42]

The big outlier on democratisation is clearly China, and the question is, when will China adopt or succumb to greater political liberalisation to match the substantive economic liberalisation of the last four decades? Eventually, a competitive economic system requires a more competitive political system, particularly once a country gets to upper-middle-income status. China was formerly classified as low-income, but the World Bank classified it as lower-middle-income as from 1999 and as an upper-middle-income country as from 2010. For these reasons, the trend towards greater political control under President Xi Jinping seems an effort to defy gravity and escape the impact of its large democratic deficit.

Each African country will experience democracy more or less differently, but generally democratic backsliding is much more likely among low-income and lower-middle-income countries during the period of democratic regression from 2031 to 2051, and is unlikely to affect upper-middle-income countries.

Since democracy advances accountability and transparency, more democracy should translate into lower levels of corruption, although modestly so. To this end, the Fourth Wave scenario includes an intervention that links a ten-percentage-point decline in corruption (using Transparency International's Corruption Perception Index) with the crest of each democratic wave. Therefore, by 2031 there will be a ten-percentage-point decline in corruption above the Current Path forecast that then reverses by 2051, and so on. Within IFs, corruption is a powerful driver of improved development outcomes, and much of the effect of the Fourth Wave scenario can be traced back to these changes in levels of corruption rather than to the impact of greater levels of democracy.

The combined impact of the Fourth Wave scenario is that, by 2040, the combined GDP of Africa's 24 lower-income countries will be US$31 billion larger than it would have been otherwise (a difference of 2.1 per cent from the Current Path forecast for 2040) and that 7.2 million fewer Africans will be living in extreme poverty. Lower-middle-income countries will experience an increase of US$56 billion (a difference of 1.3 per cent) in the collective size of their GDP and 3.4 million fewer Africans in this group of 21 countries will be living in extreme poverty.

Africa's upper-middle-income countries will have a combined GDP that is US$27 billion larger (a difference of 1.7 per cent). Around 530 000 fewer Africans will be living in extreme poverty in these eight countries. The total impact of the Fourth Wave is that it reduces the number of Africans living in extreme poverty by roughly 11 million people by 2040.[43]

GDP per capita would also improve by an average of US$47, US$76 and US$193 for low-, lower-middle- and upper-middle-income country groups. In considering these amounts, it is important to bear in mind that by 2040 there will be almost a billion Africans living in low-income and lower-middle-income Africa, respectively, and 142 million in upper-middle-income Africa. The countries that would benefit the most would be Seychelles, Mauritius and Botswana. Those that benefit the least would be the CAR, Somalia and South Sudan.

Conclusion: Promoting democracy, state capacity and human development

Africa faces a unique challenge. It is generally more democratic when compared to the average for countries at similar levels of education and income and is democratising rapidly. The continent therefore faces the double challenge of development and democratisation. Technically, what poor African countries need is not necessarily a democratic state, although that is highly desirable for many reasons, but a developmental state in which the 'political and bureaucratic elite has the genuine developmental determination and autonomous capacity to define, pursue and implement developmental goals'.[44] The challenge is that this requires either a developmentally oriented governing elite or substantive democracy – ideally both. While the latter is a more desirable path than the former, it takes longer to achieve and is fragile at low levels of development.

The problem is the extent to which neopatrimonialism has been able to coexist with the processes of democratisation in Africa and the degree to which the core notions of electoral democracy, such as clean elections and freedom of speech, are often frustrated by incumbents. It is not that African leaders are more corrupt or self-serving than leadership elsewhere. It is essentially that the institutions that should serve as a check on the abuse of power are weak. In some instances, such weakness is accentuated by a tradition that places particular emphasis on respect for elders and traditional structures. Only real progress towards substantive democracy is likely to undo this. Here, modern technology is playing an important role in allowing for the establishment of parallel monitoring systems during elections, and it is clear that, with each passing year, civil society in Africa is better able to hold governments accountable, to monitor elections, and to guard against abuse. This is illustrated by recent events in Sudan, Algeria and Ethiopia, among other countries. Africans are taking it upon themselves to hold their leadership to greater account. In the meantime, every effort needs to be made to hold on to the gains that have been achieved, such as regular elections, ongoing electoral reform, establishing a tradition of robust election monitoring by locals and foreigners, and rigorous adherence to term limits. In the absence of developmentally oriented elites, greater accountability and modern technology have to play an important role.

By itself, democratisation in Africa has clearly not altered the living conditions of most Africans. Many people still endure high poverty levels and social marginalisation. In addition, in key countries nominal democratisation has not resolved deep-seated problems around ethnicity, regionalism and class. That will only change with progress towards substantive democracy. Fortunately, regular elections and the growing depth of civil society in Africa mean that progress towards substantive democracy is more probable than the reverse.

That said, democracy should be pursued as a common good in itself – for the contribution that it makes to individual and collective self-actualisation. It is the only regime type that allows for greater self- and collective fulfilment for the citizens of states, irrespective of geography, religion or culture. According to the World Values Survey, the desire for free choice and autonomy 'is a universal human aspiration'.[45]

As much as democracy, good governance and civic rights contribute to human well-being, the African continent does not exist in isolation. In fact, Africa has been buffeted by global shifts in power and influence, most recently by a sense of competition between the West and China. The way in which that contestation plays out may have important ramifications globally, and the next chapter therefore looks at Africa's external relations.

14

External support: Aid, remittances and foreign direct investment

In the 19th century, the world was Europeanized. In the 20th century, it was Americanized. Now, in the 21st century, the world is being irreversibly Asianized.

– Parag Khanna[1]

From 1960 to 2018 the international community provided a cumulative amount of more than US$2.3 trillion in aid to Africa.[2] Asia and the Middle East, the other two regions that have historically received large amounts of aid, trail significantly behind Africa in total aid receipts. Africa and its people have received more aid than any other region in the world.[3]

Today, Africa gets about 32 per cent (US$59.7 billion in 2017) of total global aid, slightly more than the amount that goes to Asia, but since the latter has almost four times the population of Africa, Africans receive much more aid per person than Asians, although the ratio is shifting in favour of Asia.[4]

Approaches to the provision of aid have undergone significant changes since the end of the Cold War. There was the 2000 UN Millennium Summit, which put aid to Africa in the spotlight, the Report of the Commission for Africa, spearheaded by then British prime minister Tony Blair, as well as the European Consensus on Development. Collectively these efforts paved the way for the 2005 World Summit in New York that called for increased aid transfers in order to reach the eight Millennium Development Goals set in 2000 to, among other aims, halve poverty and hunger by 2015.

Actually, the push to halve poverty by 2015 was met five years ahead of the deadline, largely on the back of rapid economic growth and pro-poor policies in China. Aid played an important but limited role in this achievement.[5] The number of people living in extreme poverty fell from 1.9 billion in 1990 to 836 million in 2015. The target of halving the portion of people suffering from hunger was narrowly missed, however, as were a number of other Millennium Development Goals.[6]

A key development on the road to 2015 was the 2011 Busan Partnership for Effective Development Cooperation, which established, for the first time, an agreed framework for development cooperation that included traditional and new donors from the South, civil society organisations and private philanthropy. The Busan commitments also unlocked greater efficiencies as donors agreed to untie aid to allow recipients to use their aid dollars to procure from the cheapest suppliers and not those prescribed by donors.

These and other reforms saw a steady shift in aid from upper-middle-income countries to low-income and lower-middle-income countries, where the majority of extremely poor people are to be found. Since North African countries long ago graduated to middle-income status, by 2017 more than 90 per cent of aid to Africa went to sub-Saharan Africa.[7]

In the wake of Busan there has also been improved harmonisation of aid modalities between donor countries and the aid that is provided through multilateral agencies such as those of the UN. The average ratio is that around 70 per cent of aid is provided bilaterally and the balance through multilateral channels. Bilateral aid is provided directly from a national agency such as the US Agency for International Development (USAID) or the Swedish International Development Cooperation Agency (SIDA) to the country or region concerned. Multilateral aid is provided through organisations such as the UNDP, the World Bank and the African Development Bank that are able to provide grants as well as concessional loans at below market rates.

Aid from China is not included in these statistics, and sources differ widely in their calculations of its size. The China Africa Research Initiative estimates that China provided US$3 billion globally in 2015 followed by a significant reduction to US$2.253 billion in 2016. It is likely that the bigger portion of this amount went to Africa, but there is disagreement about how much of this would really qualify as aid and not as commercial loans.[8]

Calculations of aid flows also generally exclude contributions from private sources, such as the Open Society Foundations set up by billionaire George Soros and the Bill & Melinda Gates Foundation. The OECD's own large-scale survey on global private philanthropy estimates flows of US$7.96 billion per annum, which is equivalent to around five per cent of government aid flows. Slightly less than a third of private donations goes to Africa.[9]

So, aid to Africa from China and private sources is probably in the same ballpark.

I explained earlier that the larger portion of the estimated US$58.6 billion in aid that Africa received in 2017 (or US$51.8 billion once repayments on loans are deducted) went to low-income countries, accounting for around ten per cent of the GDP of low-income African countries, where most aid is directed. If that aid were to have been distributed equally among African countries, it would equate to about 2.5 per cent of GDP.

Aid serves as an important avenue through which external partners can augment government ability to meet key needs. For example, aid boosted government revenues in low-income Africa by an astounding ten percentage points in 2018. Hence, in a country such as Ethiopia, donors provided US$600 million in health funding in 2015, accounting for roughly half of the total health spending in the country.[10] Here, aid has enabled the country to make rapid improvements in reducing rates of maternal and infant mortality. This, in turn, has accelerated Ethiopia's demographic transition and will have an extraordinarily positive impact on its long-term future development prospects.

The importance of aid for poor countries

Aid will remain important for low-income countries in Africa for at least the next two decades. In the typical poor African country, the role of the state is key to provide security and maintain order, to provide basic infrastructure, including health care and access to safe water, to provide education, and to create an appropriate regulatory framework to facilitate growth. Then, as countries develop, the role of the private sector increases in importance to unlock sustained employment growth and improvements in incomes. In the process, foreign direct investment (FDI) becomes an important tool through which governments can unlock additional private-sector capacity and grow the economy more rapidly. However, the virtues of the private sector in financing infrastructure development (where Africa has its largest need) are often overstated, particularly in its potential to provide basic services such as water, sanitation and electricity to poor people in poor countries.[11]

In the Current Path forecast, Africa would receive US$100 billion net aid in 2030, increasing to US$128 billion in 2040. Most of the increase will (and should) go to low-income countries that are expected to experience a doubling of aid to US$82 billion by 2040, although as a portion of GDP the contribution of aid to these countries will decrease from its current 10 to 5.9 per cent. The reason for the decline in aid as a portion of GDP is, of course, due to the rapid economic growth that most of these countries will experience, in part because they all have young, growing populations.

The expected near doubling of aid in constant dollar amounts would be significantly larger if developed countries met the SDG target of 0.7 per cent of gross national income (GNI) for aid contributions.[12] This is unlikely, and the increase in the amount of aid within IFs is driven by the rapid growth in the economies of donor countries rather than any increases in the aid as a percentage of GNI by donors. Much more realistic is to expect that aid, as a portion of the GNI of rich countries, will remain stable or, more likely, moderately decline.

Future trends regarding aid

The US remains Africa's single largest bilateral aid donor but provides significantly less aid than the EU and its member states. The trend is similar to the weakening of US trade relations, as examined in Chapter 11. For example, from 1995 to 2006, aid from the US to Africa came close to the total of all other donors combined.

Ten years later, in 2017, the US was still the largest single aid provider to the continent, disbursing roughly US$11.2 billion in that year, but followed by the EU with US$6.9 billion (but excluding bilateral aid provided by EU members) and the World Bank's International Development Association with US$6.3 billion. The US is followed by the UK and Germany as the largest bilateral donor to Africa.[13]

However, the picture changes quite substantially if we compare aid from the EU *and* its member states to aid from the US. In 2017 the former amounted to €23.9 billion compared to the €12 billion from the US, ie almost double.[14]

Prior to the shale energy revolution, America's dependence on imported oil to fuel its massive economy determined its relationship with oil-producing countries such as Nigeria and Angola. Then, after 9/11, its focus shifted to the war on terror that culminated in the disastrous Western interventions in Iraq and Libya. Lately, it has also started to draw down its military engagement on the continent. Apart from a continued, if declining, interest in combating terrorism, the US will retain an important role in providing humanitarian support, but it is increasingly distracted by its global competition with China, internal divisions and trade disputes with friend and foe alike.

It took 18 months for President Donald Trump to appoint Tibor Nagy to run the Africa division in the State Department as assistant secretary of state for Africa, although there are now various efforts to reinvigorate US-Africa relations, generally in reaction to Chinese engagement. Nagy assured the US Senate that he would effectively use the new bipartisan Better Utilization of Investments Leading to Development (BUILD) Act (passed in October 2018) to help boost the development of African countries, largely through support for private investment.[15] The new US International Development Finance Corporation (USIDFC) will be able to invest up to US$60 billion in Africa, focusing on small and medium-sized enterprises and support to local companies.[16]

BUILD is part of the Trump administration's Prosper Africa initiative, which former National Security Advisor John Bolton claimed 'will support US investment across the continent, grow Africa's middle class, and improve the overall business climate in the region',[17] Launched in December 2018, Prosper Africa is largely aimed at helping US companies to navigate the US bureaucracy and to benefit from its various programmes and services. Its primary aim is therefore to open markets for American businesses, and hopefully to contribute to goals such as 'grow Africa's middle class, promote youth employment opportunities, improve the business climate, and enable the United States to compete with China and other nations who have business interests in Africa'.[18]

It is unlikely that Europe will follow the US in disengaging from Africa. Europe remains connected to Africa through shared histories, shared languages and physical proximity. The EU has also been diligent in nurturing a collaborative and consultative relationship with Africa that is quite unique among Africa's partners. Whereas the US is cautious, if not dismissive, of regional organisations such as the AU and the various regional economic communities, the EU often sees them as its primary point of engagement. Decades of European investment in building the capacity of the AU, as well as relationships of aid and trade, have created a network of friendship and collaboration that remains important for both parties, in spite of the rise of populism and anti-migrant rhetoric in many of the EU's member states. For instance, without European assistance, the AU's much-vaunted APSA would not have been able to establish its three-brigade-size capability for conflict prevention and management in Southern, West and East Africa. Since 2006, the EU has spent more than €1 billion of its aid commitment to support APSA and various peace support missions in Africa.

The EU's intention to move beyond a donor/recipient relationship towards a more mature engagement was first captured in the comprehensive Joint Africa-EU Strategy (JAES) of 2007, which was adopted by the heads of state and government of the AU and the EU at the second EU-Africa Summit in Lisbon. JAES is implemented through multiannual action plans that define the priority areas of cooperation. The most recent (third) plan outlines four strategic areas from 2018 onwards: investing in people (education, science, technology and skills development); strengthening resilience, peace, security and governance; migration and mobility; and mobilising investments for sustainable structural transformation. Subsequently, at the 5th African Union-European Union Summit, the partners agreed that economic investment, job creation and trade were common priorities, requiring a joint commitment.

In line with this goal, in 2017 the EU launched an ambitious programme of investment mobilisation in Africa, called the External Investment Plan (EIP). It includes a new guarantee mechanism whereby aid is used to mobilise private capital flows through so-called blended arrangements and the provision of guarantees to mobilise additional resources for investment in Africa.[19] This was followed, in 2018, by the announcement of a new Africa-Europe Alliance for Sustainable Investment and Jobs.

Considerable attention is being given to efforts such as Aid for Trade and various so-called blending frameworks – the latter use grants to mobilise additional financial support to the region in the form of loans or equity.[20] Aid for Trade uses a portion of aid (US$13.3 billion of US$59.7 billion total aid to Africa in 2017)[21] to build trade capacity in poor countries and to improve trade diversification and help economically marginalised groups. According to the 2019 joint report on Aid for Trade by the WTO and the OECD, there have been 62 030 projects in Africa, but progress with economic and export diversification in Africa has been slower than elsewhere.

Leveraging foreign direct investment for Africa

FDI is essentially a long-term investment made by a resident of one economy or country in another – a definition that distinguishes it from more volatile foreign portfolio investments. There is a general consensus that FDI is the best way to stimulate economic and industrial development, since it typically implies a degree of technology transfer from a multinational (or mother) corporation to an affiliate in the host country.[22] For this reason, FDI is typically discussed as consisting of a *stock* of investment that has been built up (or that is depleted) through annual *flows*.

For several years, the debate about how to help Africa has been dominated by efforts to find a way to complement aid with loans from the private sector, including from firms, pension funds and sovereign wealth funds, as enthusiasm for aid has declined. The advantages appear self-evident: globally, insurance companies, pension funds and sovereign wealth funds have more than US$100 trillion in assets under management.[23] Africa needs a very small fraction of these savings to plug its large infrastructure financing gap, for example. The private sector is also often quicker to bring projects online and doesn't impose the conditionalities associated with the large multilateral lending agencies such as the World Bank and the IMF.

Private-sector investment is, however, not a substitute for efforts by national governments to reduce the continent's large infrastructure deficit, nor can it replace the contribution from the public sector (from a country such as China) or multilateral development banks. Historically, most private financing in Africa has occurred in the information and communications, renewable energy and transport sectors, not in core infrastructure. The reason is self-evident: returns on large infrastructure development often take decades to materialise and may even require ongoing subsidies.

Most research and efforts to encourage private-sector investment for infrastructure gloss over the shortcomings, such as much higher interest rates than those of other creditors, while maturities (lending periods) are typically also significantly shorter. Most private financiers also lack a development mandate, looking instead to maximise profit, and are reluctant to invest in the early stages of infrastructure development where the need is most severe. They inevitably tend to cherry-pick the projects that they are prepared to fund and are generally risk-averse. At the same time, the amounts of concessional financing available to Africa have declined. The result is that, in 2017, only 2.8 per cent of infrastructure commitments in Africa by source came from the private sector. In addition to national governments, which provided roughly 42 per cent of funds for infrastructure, Africa generally has to look to institutions such as the World Bank and the African Development Bank, or to state-backed lending from a country with deep pockets (and spare construction capacity in search of projects) such as China, to fund its infrastructure deficit.[24]

China also has other advantages when it comes to building infrastructure in Africa: it largely operates on a government-to-government basis (instead of the private-sector-to-private-sector approach of the West); it has significant finances to invest since it has consistently had a positive balance of trade since 1990; and it has massive overcapacity (and lots of domestic experience) in building infrastructure such as roads and railways. None of this is readily available from the US or Europe.

This does not mean that private investment in infrastructure does not occur. It is just that the associated return on investment needs to be high enough to attract the private sector. This typically happens only in the case of oil, gas and other commodities. For example, in June 2019 the US energy firm Anadarko Petroleum Corporation[25] gave the go-ahead for the construction of a US$20 billion gas liquefaction and export terminal in Mozambique – the single largest liquid natural gas project in

Africa at an amount equivalent to almost half of total FDI to Africa in 2018.

FDI flows to Africa peaked at 3.5 per cent of GDP in 2007, declined with the global financial crisis, and by 2017 had recovered to 3 per cent of GDP or US$42 billion, compared to US$476 billion that went to developing Asia. But then the African economy is only 14 per cent the size of developing Asia.[26] Historically, Africa has received less FDI as a percentage of GDP than a region such as South America. For several years China started to buck that trend, but its attention is shifting to its immediate region as it focuses its efforts on the Belt and Road Initiative.

To access capital markets in the West, countries need an internally accepted sovereign credit rating on its creditworthiness. In mid-2019 the only African countries with a sovereign credit rating by all three key international rating agencies (Moody's, S&P and Fitch) were Angola, Egypt, South Africa and Morocco, so it is perhaps no surprise that the majority of FDI goes to these countries.[27] These considerations are, of course, much less important in the case of state-backed loans from a country such as China – although such loans are seldom offered at concessional rates.

In addition to being the largest national provider of aid to Africa, the US also leads on the stock of FDI that has built up from any single country, although recent inflows have declined. Investments by South Africa in the rest of Africa have also expanded rapidly. However, when comparing the stock of FDI from all the EU member states with the US and China, the EU accounts for 40 per cent, the US for 7 per cent and China for 5 per cent.[28]

Overall, FDI to Africa has slowed in recent years, largely due to the impact of the Arab Spring and declining oil prices, which led to economic stagnation in Libya, Egypt and Tunisia, and placed the economies of countries like Angola and Nigeria under tremendous strain. Domestic policies have also played a role in South Africa, traditionally a large recipient of FDI, where investment confidence was undermined by a raft of controversial policies on land reform and investment agreements.[29] Against this background, state-led infrastructure investments from China have become particularly important.

China's growing footprint in Africa

FDI growth rates from China to Africa were up 25 per cent from 2010 to 2014, followed by 13 per cent from South Africa and only 10 per cent from the US. Africa is the third-largest destination for Chinese investment, after Asia and Europe, although investment in sub-Saharan Africa slightly declined in 2017, following a drop in aggregate Chinese investment.[30]

In a comprehensive study on China in Africa, the McKinsey Global Institute concludes that 'the Africa-China opportunity is larger than that presented by any other foreign partner – including Brazil, the European Union, India, the United Kingdom, and the United States'.[31] The authors set out two scenarios. In the first, revenues of Chinese firms in Africa grow from US$180 billion to around US$250 billion in 2025. The second scenario sees Chinese firms in Africa expand aggressively in both existing and new sectors, achieving revenues of US$440 billion in 2025. Together with the proposed increases set out by the UK and steady improvements in stability in North Africa, growth in FDI flows to Africa could realistically return to levels of around 15 to 20 per cent per annum over the next five years.

The IFs Current Path forecast is that inflows from FDI to Africa will increase from the current 3.1 per cent of GDP per annum to around 3.7 per cent by 2040, ie roughly equivalent to the size of the African economy as a portion of the global economy. This will continue a trend that has seen FDI flows overwhelmingly go to Asia. Africa has already benefited significantly from China's remarkable economic transition over the last two decades, first through its demand for commodities, second by China's positive balance of payments (ie it had funds to invest) and finally from the Belt and Road Initiative. Africa was not part of the original scheme, and was only included in 2015 as it and other regions clamoured to benefit from potential investments in infrastructure.

Investments inevitably require collateral, pointing to another advantage for China, which has proven flexible in accepting 'non-traditional' collateral. In fact, China's willingness to accept airports, harbours and future commodity exports (or even mines) as security has raised alarm bells in the US, which sees this as a ploy for China to lay its hands on strategic infrastructure. This complaint is, however, seldom a concern in Africa, although there have been any number of instances in which

African governments have been induced to enter into expensive prestige projects (such as the airport in Lusaka) and apparently overpriced railway lines (such as the Mombasa–Nairobi standard-gauge line). And then there is the Chinese habit of trying to tie countries, for example Angola and South Sudan, into agreements in which it pays for commodities by offering the services of Chinese companies.

But there is also clear evidence that Beijing is concerned about the ability of key African governments to service their loans from China. A more serious concern, often repeated in the mainstream media, is that many of the large Chinese construction (and other) projects apparently provide little work for locals. This was clearly the case in the past, but extensive recent field research in Ethiopia and Angola[32] would indicate that national labour participation is substantially higher than generally assumed in Western media, that wages in Chinese firms abroad are largely similar to other firms in the same sector, and that Chinese firms contribute as much to training and skills development as do other companies in the same sector.

Then there is the issue of quality, which is often quite poor, and the extent to which China is 'exporting corruption' in the way it uses development assistance to buy influence (and contracts) from African leaders. Nor are these companies able to be held to account domestically in China through shareholder activism or public disclosure. The problem with the quality argument, borne out by many travels across Africa, is that Africans generally get what they pay for (low quality at low prices) and that an argument can be made that much is of 'appropriate' quality. German precision standards on building a road or culvert are hardly applicable in rural Congo. Eventually, Africans get what they negotiate as part of the initial agreements and what they subsequently hold their partners to account for, including the use of local labour and technology transfers.

This brings us to the most important difference in Chinese versus Western practices, namely, that large Chinese loans do not come with a requirement to discuss matters around the rule of law, good governance or human rights, as is done by the IMF and the World Bank. China simply does not share the views and approaches of the West in terms of the rule of law, corruption and what have generally become known as standards of good governance.

The advantages listed above are not unique to Africa. China has run a year-on-year positive trade balance for decades, with the result that total overseas lending from China's two largest state banks amounted to US$675 billion at the end of 2016 – already more than twice the size of World Bank loans. A very modest portion of this goes to Africa.[33]

At the time of writing, Chinese lending to Africa is likely to decline amid concerns about high debt levels. In fact, Africa is steadily moving down the Chinese list of priorities as its economy transitions away from infrastructure investment and commodity dependence towards domestic consumption.

The change could have an important impact in Africa, for China has become the biggest single-country funder and builder of infrastructure projects in Africa, having spent about US$11.5 billion per annum since 2012.[34] China is therefore the largest contributor in helping to fill Africa's gap in infrastructure, which the African Development Bank estimates at anything between US$130 to US$170 billion annually.[35]

In addition to the visible, large, state-led infrastructure companies from China active on the continent, McKinsey estimates that there are more than 10 000 privately owned small Chinese companies operating in Africa. This number is substantially more than official data from China's Ministry of Commerce. McKinsey concludes that China's engagement in Africa is 'unparalleled' and that the true picture is understated, with total financial flows around 15 per cent higher than official figures convey.[36]

Although there is a dearth of data on the precise nature and scale of China's investments and overseas lending, including in Africa,[37] there is a clear danger that through the combined impact of China and others, a number of African countries could again find themselves in a debt trap similar to that of the 1980s. In January 2019 the IMF assessed that about 17 low-income African countries were in, or at risk of, debt distress. Loans from China played a role in only a few, however.[38]

Debt can be a severe constraint on growth. In a wide-ranging study on the relationship between debt and growth, Carmen Reinhart and Kenneth Rogoff conclude: 'When external debt reaches 60 per cent of GDP, annual growth declines by about two per cent.'[39] On average, Africa's low-income and lower-middle-income countries consistently had debt levels in excess of 60 per cent of GDP from the mid-1980s for almost two subsequent decades, levels that clearly contributed to slow growth. Looking ahead, without preventive measures, rising debt levels could again constrain Africa's growth.

Infrastructure is not the only (Chinese) game in town. To ease the long-running pressure on the naira after it started steadily losing value against the US dollar in 2015, Nigeria began selling Chinese renminbi (yuan) to local traders and business. The move has made it easier for local businesses in Nigeria to trade and engage with their Chinese counterparts without the need to first convert their local currency to dollars. After the 2015 drop in global oil prices, Nigeria faced a major dollar shortage and its foreign reserves dwindled. Setting up the renminbi as an alternative trading currency eases all of this, although China's conditions and requirements for funding and loans have also hardened of late.[40] A number of other African countries have subsequently followed suit.

To safeguard its growing investments, China has expanded its direct and indirect role in peace and security in Africa, as Europe and the US did in previous decades. In addition to a naval base in Djibouti, the inaugural China-Africa Defence and Security Forum, held in June/July 2018, established an overarching framework for China's security programmes in Africa. In February 2019 China announced that it had provided US$180 million to fund peace and security efforts in Africa and that it was already the largest supplier of weapons to sub-Saharan Africa. China's role in support of the AU and numerous African armed forces is steadily expanding, as are its efforts at mediation.[41]

The third, and much smaller, flow of external funds to Africa is through remittances.

Remittance flows to Africa

Data on remittances needs to be treated with care since such flows mostly occur through informal channels and are driven by the international migrant population, for which data is also not always reliable. Unlike aid and FDI, remittance flows do not affect government revenues, since remittances generally consist of money sent home by migrants, but rather serve to support the livelihoods of poor families.[42]

Generally, migrants have a positive economic impact in hosting countries and are often less likely to be involved in crime. According to the

IMF, each one per cent increase in the share of migrants in the adult population of advanced economies can increase GDP per capita by up to two per cent in the long term. But anti-migrant sentiments have become an important domestic policy issue in most Western countries.[43]

The average annual growth figure for remittances is around five per cent. Nigeria, with its large diaspora, is the largest recipient of remittances in Africa (US$22.3 billion in 2017). As a percentage of GDP, Liberia is the biggest recipient of remittances (at 25.9 per cent).[44]

Remittances have benefited from new technologies that have lowered the costs of sending small amounts of money privately from one country to another, but the impact of the war on terror and concerns about money flows to groups and individuals associated with terrorism have created numerous obstacles for Africans wishing to send money home. Furthermore, it still costs more to remit money to sub-Saharan Africa than any other region globally. Moving money between neighbouring African countries is even more expensive.

Modelling increased FDI, aid and remittances: The External Support scenario

In this section, I model the impact of an External Support scenario on the continent's medium- to long-term development trajectory. This consists of modest increases in aid, FDI and remittances.

Against the backdrop of a global focus on the achievement of the SDGs by 2030, the aid component of the External Support scenario envisions an increase in the amount of development aid to Africa in the run-up to the 2030 target year that then tapers down to the Current Path forecast by 2040. In the External Support scenario, Africa would receive a total of US$127.9 billion more aid (cumulatively over the forecast horizon) than in the Current Path forecast.[45] Most of the additional funds would go to low-income countries. The intervention in the External Support scenario increases the levels of FDI inflows to almost 4.4 per cent by 2040 (instead of 3.7 per cent in the Current Path), which is significantly higher than the 1.7 per cent of GDP (or US$116.1 billion) from aid that Africa would receive in 2040. Such inflows would only be possible with improved levels of stability and policy certainty, but would still constitute a relatively small portion of global FDI flows. The final intervention is on remittances.

The IFs Current Path forecast is that remittances will increase modestly by about US$3 billion to US$50 billion by 2040. Since the total African economy is significantly larger by then, remittances drop from 1.6 per cent of GDP in 2020 to 0.7 per cent by 2040. In the External Support scenario, remittances to Africa increase to US$54.5 billion by 2040. The largest portion of the increase in remittances goes to Nigeria, followed by Egypt, Morocco, Ghana, Senegal, Tunisia, Somalia, Libya and Lesotho.

Figure 14.1 presents the contribution from remittances, aid and FDI in the Current Path compared to the External Support scenario for 2020 and 2040. In addition to a modest increase in remittances, the bulk of the increase comes from FDI. Whereas the three components contribute roughly equal amounts in 2020, by 2040 FDI contributes almost two-thirds of the total in the External Support scenario. Had I included an additional column for 2030, the reader would have seen that aid peaked at US$113 billion in the External Support scenario versus US$100 billion in the Current Path, reflecting an expected increase in aid in the run-up to the final year of the SDGs. Thereafter levels of aid revert to the Current Path forecast.

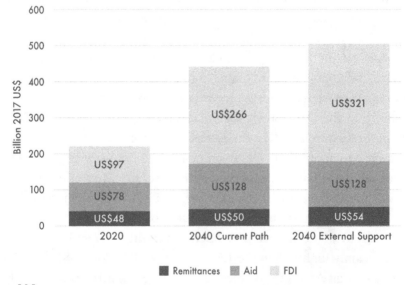

Figure 14.1: Contribution of remittances, aid and FDI in 2020 and 2040 in the Current Path and External Support scenarios[46]

The financial pool from which FDI is able to draw is so large that it necessarily needs to be prioritised as a source of growth and development for Africa. Hence the importance of measures such as trade facilitation (through Aid for Trade and other measures), ease of doing business and efforts to establish SEZs as vehicles to attract FDI, all of which are discussed in Chapter 8.

The impact of the combined External Support scenario

By 2040, Africa benefits from a total additional inflow of almost US$60 billion in the External Support scenario – the difference in the column heights for the Current Path and External Support in Figure 14.1. The majority of aid goes to low-income countries, remittances are spread across countries in line with historical levels, and most FDI goes to lower-middle-income countries.

The combined impact of the External Support scenario is to increase total government revenues in Africa by almost US$40 billion in 2040. The cumulative increase in government revenues from 2020 to 2040 is much more impressive, coming to US$405 billion. Although the interventions in all three areas are aggressive, the impact of FDI is significantly larger than that from aid and remittances as its contribution grows much more rapidly than that of the others, as is reflected in Figure 14.1.

The increase in government revenues translates into tangible outcomes, although generally only towards the end of the forecast horizon. For example, in 2040 African governments would be able to spend US$7.6 billion more on education, US$4 billion more on health and almost US$6 billion more on infrastructure. Initially, more children attend primary school in the External Support scenario compared to the Current Path, peaking at 638 000 in 2029. Then more children attend lower secondary, peaking at 768 000 more in 2033, and then upper secondary (568 000 more students in 2035). The reason for the staggered impact follows generally improved levels of education, with the additional funds allocated to where the need is the most acute.

Since health expenditure increases in the External Support scenario, death rates from communicable and non-communicable diseases decline, and average life expectancy by 2040 for Africa's total population of

2.081 billion people is, on average, a month longer. Also, by 2040 Africa experiences 0.5 fewer infant deaths per thousand live births in the External Support scenario than in the Current Path forecast. This may sound small, but bear in mind that in 2040 there would be almost 53 million births. So 0.5 fewer deaths per thousand live births equates to 26 500 more live births in that year!

Increased external support means that the total Africa economy is US$137 billion larger in 2040 than it would have been, and that GDP per capita increases by almost US$90. Inequality does not really change.

Beyond these findings, the External Support scenario reminds us that more aid, although important, would make only a modest additional contribution to reducing the levels of extreme poverty in Africa. By 2030 the External Support scenario reduces the number of Africans living in extreme poverty by only two million. By 2040 the number has increased to 25 million, of which two-thirds are in low-income countries. This is in spite of the fact that the bulk of additional aid goes to low-income countries, where most extremely poor people are to be found.

Conclusion: Unlocking foreign assistance

China's footprint in Africa has grown enormously in recent years, but Europe, and the EU in particular, remains Africa's most important partner in goods, stock of FDI and aid. It provides 36 per cent, 40 per cent and 54 per cent, respectively, of these three categories (with the UK included as part of the EU). For the 2017–2020 EIP, the EU budgeted €32.5 billion in grants to Africa, and its 2021–2027 budget provides for €40 billion. In addition, the EU budgeted for €3.7 billion in grants for blending and guarantees in its current plan. These amounts exclude bilateral aid from individual EU member states.[47]

In this context, the Belt and Road Initiative serves as the means to connect China with the resources for growth and development with a large potential future market, while Chinese peacekeepers and arms help to secure its investments. At the same time, Africa needs to realise that the focus of the Belt and Road Initiative is largely on connecting China to its immediate neighbourhood in Asia, and the impact in Africa is bound to be quite limited. In fact, Africa may already have experienced peak

Chinese interest and may increasingly have to look elsewhere for future investment growth.

The claim of the demise of aid is still premature. Together with remittances, aid will remain important for many poor African countries into the future. The growth of private capital flows from outside Africa has benefited only a few countries although it will grow in importance. African countries will have to learn to manage the associated volatility. Generally, FDI is conservative and follows rather than leads other sources of investment. Remittances have become significantly more important for some countries but their impact is limited. Infrastructure development in Africa will largely depend upon investment decisions from its own governments, which need to focus on sectors and segments (such as water and sanitation infrastructure) for which financiers have little appetite. FDI generally tracks investment decisions by locals, requires policy stability, and provides a limited answer to the continent's infrastructure backlog.

That said, the continent needs to work much harder to unlock investment from the wall of money searching for returns in Europe, North America, China and eventually India. FDI boosts economic growth and is key in contributing to knowledge transfer, and hence to Africa's economic transformation. But the inadequate technical, governance and implementation capacity in African countries requires a dedicated effort to strengthen domestic legislation, institutions and policies governing investment, as well as the ability to negotiate and oversee the associated agreements. If the international community wants to help Africa, it needs to give serious consideration to attracting private investment through tax benefits, de-risking foreign investment in Africa, and building African capacity to negotiate, manage and evaluate projects.

The rise of China is certainly the most noteworthy feature of the 21st century, and China's demand for natural resources played a big part in the story of Africa's growth from the mid-1990s. This is also evident from the extent to which commodity exports from Africa increased more rapidly than the global average (see Figure 11.1). As a result, Africa's broad pattern of increased dependence on commodity exports to earn foreign exchange, and continued deindustrialisation from already low levels, has continued unabated. Meanwhile, the Chinese economy is rebalancing and its once-insatiable appetite for commodities has tempered. As the hubris around the Belt and Road Initiative calms down, China has limited interest in maintaining the breakneck speed of investment growth in Africa.

Africa should therefore not rely on China's hunger for raw materials, nor on its loans and future investment in infrastructure projects. At the 2018 Forum on China-Africa Cooperation meeting in Beijing, China scaled back its forecast of future partnership with Africa, expressed its concern about rising debt levels, noted that projects need to be subject to cost-benefit analysis, and warned that it intends to pull back on vanity projects.[48]

If China stumbles, it will have a massive impact on Africa. According to Bloomberg, China's credit boom has been 'the largest factor driving global growth' in the decade from 2010, and debt is rising fast.[49] Over the same period, China's debt-to-GDP ratio has risen from about 140 per cent to more than 250 per cent. China has defied expectations before, but it is unlikely to do so indefinitely. In an important recent book, Nicholas Lardy argues that China's growth prospects are now being shadowed by the spectre of resurgent state domination.[50] Whereas it is China's private sector that is responsible for much of its economic growth, attention has shifted to ailing, underperforming and indebted state-owned companies. Inefficiencies are mounting. Additionally, the country's debt problem has been accelerated by the large stimulus project that Beijing launched in 2008, in response to the global financial crisis. Normally, countries experience growth problems when the debt-to-GDP ratio is in excess of 60 per cent. Chinese debt, now at more than 250 per cent of GDP, may already be responsible for a loss of up to two percentage points of economic growth, opines Lardy.

Looking to the future, Africa has significant scope to improve matters by investing in the capacity of its institutions to oversee and manage trade, FDI and aid, and to develop formal remittance processes. The sources of aid and investment support are less important, except to ensure that African countries are not forced to choose particular partnerships or alliances, as during the Cold War, but rather to encourage collaboration and mix-and-match. In this vein, the recent trend towards funding large projects is positive, and involves combining a basket of funding, such as from the World Bank, the African Development Bank, the European Investment Bank and the Bank of China, and a collaborative approach to project implementation – perhaps with a German engineering company to oversee technical compliance, American project management and Chinese construction capacity for the heavy lifting.

Ultimately, there is little difference between Africa's old and new partners. Each inevitably puts its own interests first, as should Africa. But, this time around, Africans should work more diligently to set the terms for how best it can benefit from aid, FDI and the flow of remittances. Africa needs to become a rule-maker and to assume a larger role in its own destiny, particularly in the mode of development that it pursues. The West and China have developed at the cost of others in terms of the impact on the global climate. Africa, the region that will be the development latecomer, has little option but to pursue a different pathway, namely, that of sustainable and green development, the topic of the next chapter.

15
Climate change

You are not mature enough to tell it like it is . . . We have
run out of excuses and we are running out of time.
– Greta Thunberg, UN Climate Change
COP24 Conference Summit, December 2018

Many scientists believe that the world is in the midst of its sixth mass extinction event, known either as the Holocene or Anthropocene extinction. Human activity may not have caused the Anthropocene extinction but humanity has clearly accelerated its onset compared to the previous five mass extinction events. That message was set out starkly in a statement released in November 2018 by several thousand scientists from 184 countries: '[W]e have unleashed a mass extinction event, the sixth in roughly 540 million years, wherein many current life forms could be annihilated or at least committed to extinction by the end of this century.'[1] The statement went on to include 12 'examples of diverse and effective steps humanity can take to transition to sustainability', none of which have been implemented.

Six months later, in May 2019, the UN released the summary findings of a sweeping, 1 500-page assessment, compiled by hundreds of international experts, that provides the most exhaustive look yet at the decline in biodiversity on earth. Among the various depressing findings was that the average abundance of native plant and animal life has fallen by 20 per cent or more over the last century and that many species are being pushed closer to extinction.[2]

This chapter presents the challenge of climate change and Africa's role within that global issue. It does not present a separate scenario but instead reviews the impact of four scenarios from previous chapters that have the greatest impact on carbon emissions, namely, demographics, manufacturing, leapfrogging and trade, and compares these with the Current Path forecast. The combined impact of all 11 scenarios, the Africa First! scenario, is presented in the concluding chapter. But before proceeding, it is important to underline that IFs is not a climate change model. It draws upon data such as that from the Intergovernmental Panel on Climate Change (IPCC) and the Carbon Dioxide Information Analysis Center to initialise its forecasts and then uses the output from its various submodules to estimate carbon emissions and the impact, such as on agricultural yields, on relationships taken from the academic literature.

Africa as a climate change taker

Africa is a climate change taker, even if it was not a climate change maker. Despite having very little to do with creating the problem, Africa is disproportionately vulnerable to the impacts of climate change – the most severe challenge facing life on earth today.

Although natural climatic variability is undoubtedly at play (an El Niño event was clearly a factor in Cape Town's 2018 water crisis, for example), the scientific consensus is that human activity, primarily the release of carbon dioxide (CO_2) and other greenhouse gases, has caused all global warming since 1970.[3]

The 2018 water crisis in Cape Town is a textbook example of the dangerous confluence of long-term anthropogenic climate change, natural variation in weather and poor planning. Cape Town has long been a water-stressed area, but it has been able to cope. That is, until temperatures got a little warmer, El Niño got a little worse, and national government failed to upgrade and maintain the necessary water infrastructure, or to invest in alternative water purification and treatment systems.

A three-year drought started in the Cape metropole in 2015 and peaked from mid-2017 to mid-2018, when dam water levels hovered between 15 to 30 per cent of total dam capacity. By late 2017 authorities were talking about 'Day Zero', a putative date when municipal water supplies would largely have to be switched off and residents would have to queue for a daily ration of water, much of which would need to be trucked in. Eventually, the City of Cape Town was able to implement significant water restrictions and, after good rains in June 2018, water restrictions were eased.[4]

The line between barely getting by and a national emergency can be very thin indeed. Cape Town managed to forestall a water crisis by the skin of its teeth, but in the future this 'new normal' will leave the city and surrounding area increasingly vulnerable, particularly as it is a destination for many poor South Africans who migrate from the Eastern Cape and for tourists from around the world. The result is extremely rapid urbanisation and intense pressure on infrastructure.[5]

The amount of CO_2 and other greenhouse gases that human activity has already released into the atmosphere has locked the world into a temperature increase of at least 1.2°C above pre-industrial levels.[6] The United Nations Environment Programme (UNEP) warns that on the current trajectory it is realistic to prepare for a 3°C increase. However, should emissions continue unmitigated and the levels of CO_2 continue to increase, warming of 3.4°C above pre-industrial levels will occur by the end of the century.[7]

In this world, 'the limits for human adaptation are likely to be exceeded in many parts of the world, while the limits for adaptation for natural systems would largely be exceeded throughout the world'.[8] Large portions of the Sahel and West Africa are likely to become unsuited for human habitation. This is a world that has moved beyond a tipping point, and it seems quite certain that much larger parts of Africa will mostly consist of desert than is currently the case.

The IPCC expects that the 'current cropping areas of crops such as maize, millet and sorghum across Africa could become unviable'.[9] In a report on a four-degree-warmer world, the World Bank notes some of the better-known foreseen consequences, such as 'the inundation of coastal cities; increasing risks for food production potentially leading to higher malnutrition rates; many dry regions becoming dryer, and wet regions wetter; unprecedented heatwaves in many regions, especially in the tropics; substantially exacerbated water scarcity in many regions; increased frequency of high-intensity tropical cyclones; and irreversible loss of biodiversity, including coral reef systems'.[10]

A 2018 special report from the IPCC found that an increase of 1.5°C is essentially inevitable and may be reached as early as 2030.[11] According to the report, limiting warming to this 1.5°C marker, as reflected in the Paris Agreement (2016), would require the entire world to cut greenhouse gas emissions by nearly half of 2010 levels by 2030 *and* to make an aggressive push to reach net-zero emissions by 2050.

Drawing on data provided by the Carbon Dioxide Information Analysis Center, the Current Path forecast is that global CO_2 in the atmosphere will increase from the current levels of just above 400 parts per million to 460 parts per million by 2040 and to 530 parts per million by 2100, translating to a 2.3°C warming by 2100.

Carbon can be released in many ways, but the three most important contributors to greenhouse gases are carbon dioxide (CO_2), carbon monoxide (CO) and methane (CH_4), with methane having the biggest negative impact. Since each gas has a different molecular mass, ie they have different weights (CO_2 weighs about four times more than CH_4), the unit of measure that is used when calculating carbon emissions is known as the carbon contribution, which means just the mass of the carbon component of each of the various greenhouse gases.[12]

Globally, carbon emissions are projected to increase from a current 9.5 billion tons per annum, to peak at 10.06 billion tons in 2037, and to decline to 5.3 billion tons per annum by 2100, as reflected in Figure 15.1, which also highlights the Current Path emissions from Africa. To be sure, this is a cataclysmic forecast.

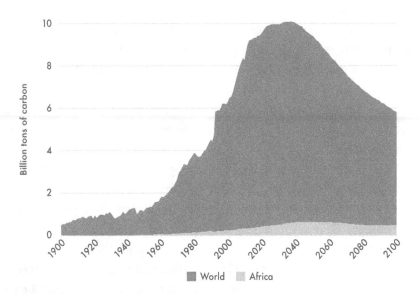

Figure 15.1: History and Current Path forecast of carbon emissions from Africa and the world, 1900 to 2100[13]

Most emissions are essentially locked into an expensive energy infrastructure. In Asia, the average coal plant is just 11 years old and has decades of operational life left. Coal plants in the US and Europe, meanwhile, are roughly 40 years old on average.[14] By implication, countries like China and India would have to be willing to prematurely decommission a very large number of recently built coal plants for the world to make progress towards global sustainability. In the absence of an extraordinary technological breakthrough, there is no other sustainable pathway, and all regions and countries, including Africa, will have to contribute to the best of their ability, although the largest contributions inevitably have to come from the biggest polluters.

Climate change might be taking place at a slow pace, but it has lots of momentum. Even if we were to magically cease adding more greenhouse gases to the atmosphere today, the climate would still warm for a few hundred years before slowly returning to pre-industrial levels of atmospheric carbon concentrations.[15] A world that sees temperatures rise by 1.5°C above pre-industrial levels is one in which the natural environment and resources upon which all life depends are highly unpredictable and severely degraded.

Extended droughts, heatwaves and other extreme weather events will become the norm; the sea will continue to rise and acidify, killing off vast numbers of marine species; and biodiversity is increasingly threatened. Already, research done by the University of Melbourne has found that extreme winds in the Antarctic Ocean have increased by 1.5 metres per second over the past 30 years and extreme waves have increased by 30 centimetres.[16]

In the short term, these impacts pose grave threats to 'health, livelihoods, food security, water supply, human security, and economic growth'.[17] And the IPCC has acknowledged that their previous risk assessments likely understated the risks from a 1.5°C to 2°C temperature increase.

Even limiting warming to 2°C would require dramatic action. Meeting that target would involve a reduction in global greenhouse emissions of about 25 per cent by 2030 and a net-zero world by 2070. This seems highly unlikely when one looks at the Current Path global forecast of emissions to 2100 in Figure 15.1.

The global energy transition

Just as fossil fuels shaped the geopolitical map over the last two centuries, so 'the energy transformation will alter the global distribution of power, relations between states, the risk of conflict, and the social, economic and environmental drivers of geopolitical instability'.[18] Whereas fossil fuels are concentrated in specific geographic locations and are vulnerable to disruption, renewable energy resources are distributed in one form or another in most countries. This means that renewables are better suited to decentralised forms of energy production and consumption.

Some countries, such as the US, are already close to being self-sufficient in terms of energy, largely due to the shale oil and gas revolution. Energy self-sufficiency will likely accelerate the international withdrawal and isolation of the US, while China's determined investment in connecting Asia through the Belt and Road Initiative, its leadership in research and development, and its investments in renewables are likely to improve its geopolitical standing.[19]

Once the energy storage problem is resolved, countries and populations across Africa will benefit greatly from the dispersed nature of renewables, particularly through reduced fossil fuel imports. Actually, most African countries have a unique opportunity to leapfrog the fossil-fuel-centred development model and move to renewables. Some, such as Libya, the Republic of Congo, Angola, Equatorial Guinea, South Sudan and Gabon, will suffer since they are extraordinarily dependent on the foreign exchange earnings from their fossil fuel exports. Others with large fossil fuel import bills, such as Tanzania, Côte d'Ivoire, Guinea and Senegal, will benefit.

High energy bills transfer large amounts of wealth abroad and make countries vulnerable to price swings. Renewables have none of these risks. Some countries, such as Ethiopia, Namibia and Lesotho, could obtain all or most of their electricity from hydropower. Others, such as Kenya, could achieve similar results using a mix of renewables, such as hydro, geothermal, wind, biomass and solar power.[20]

Most CO_2 is emitted by the energy sector, followed by transport, agriculture and forestry, residential and commercial, and industry. Most CH_4 comes from agriculture and energy production, and most nitrous oxide (N_2O) emissions come from agriculture.[21]

Data on emissions is often, and quite misleadingly, presented on the basis of emissions per country. A much more appropriate comparison would be to calculate emissions per person per annum. On average, Africans produce around 1.2 tons of CO_2 per annum, compared to more than 16 tons by Americans, almost 12 tons by Russians, more than 9 tons by Japanese and around 7 tons by Chinese. The global average is about 4.8 tons. In other words, the average African produces less than eight per cent of the emissions of the average American. Few numbers better illustrate the stark differences in responsibility for global emissions – and these numbers do not account for the stock of carbon emitted by the populations of these different countries over time.[22]

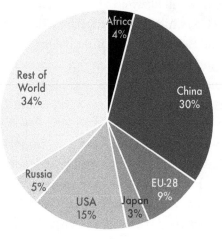

Figure 15.2: Carbon emissions by countries or region as a percentage of the total, 2018[23]

The IFs Current Path forecast for world energy production is presented in Figure 15.3 in billion barrels of oil equivalent from coal, oil, gas, nuclear, hydro and other renewables.[24] In this forecast, the production of coal, oil and gas dominate to 2050, although renewables start growing strongly beyond 2030. The forecast is that the contribution made by renewables will be larger than that from coal in 2038 and bigger than that from oil in 2040 and will surpass natural gas in 2046. Clearly, this forecast is nowhere near the target of keeping global warming to even 2°C by the end of the century.

Globally, the energy transition path in high-income countries is typically from coal to oil and then to natural gas (gas has emission levels 50 to 60 per cent below those from burning coal) and then to renewables.

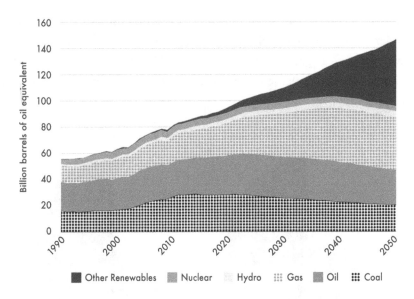

Figure 15.3: Current Path forecast of world energy production, by type[25]

Carbon emissions and energy in Africa

Apart from the uninhabited Antarctic, the continents that are most vulnerable to the impact of climate change are probably Africa and Australia. Yet Africa contributes very little to global carbon emissions, as can be seen from Figure 15.1. In 2018 Africa produced a mere four per cent of global carbon emissions, as shown in Figure 15.2.

The Current Path forecast is that, by 2040, Africa will be responsible for 6.1 per cent of carbon emissions. Its relative contribution would moderately increase thereafter as emissions in the rest of the world decrease. Emissions from Africa will increase for several subsequent decades in the Current Path forecast given increased populations and more industry, to peak at below eight per cent of the global total towards the end of the century.

On the Current Path, most African countries will, by 2040, be releasing more than one million tons of carbon each year. Figure 15.4 presents the five African countries that release the most carbon per year in 2018 and 2040. South Africa's current contribution dwarfs that of others given its dependence upon coal for electricity generation. As expected, Nigeria is projected to experience the largest increase in carbon emissions over 2018 levels by 2040. In South Africa, total emissions will decline as older coal-fired electricity plants are retired and the country shifts to renewables. Together with Egypt and Algeria, Nigeria and South Africa consistently release the most carbon in Africa across the forecast horizon.

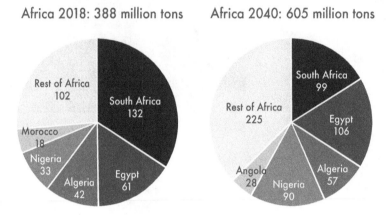

Africa 2018: 388 million tons   Africa 2040: 605 million tons

Figure 15.4: Current Path carbon emissions, Africa in 2018 and 2040 in million tons[26]

The Current Path forecast for African energy production is presented in Figure 15.5. Gas production will be greater than oil in 2026. Coming off a very low base, renewables overtake coal in 2034 and gas in 2050. Africa is well positioned for a much earlier transition to renewables than other regions. It also has some of the most valuable solar, hydro and wind real estate on the planet. Wind and solar (other renewables) are both becoming increasingly price-competitive, and electricity storage and efficiency are also improving. The contribution of nuclear energy, on the other hand, is hardly visible.

Although gas features prominently in Figure 15.5, it is important to note that this is a graph of *production* by type, often for export, not in-country use by type. African countries with big proven natural gas reserves are Nigeria, Algeria, Mozambique, Egypt, Tanzania and Libya. Given its under-explored status, Africa is likely to be a source of considerable additional gas discoveries. However, even in gas-producing countries there is very little installed gas infrastructure that would allow for domestic use. Instead, since demand for gas is expanding particularly

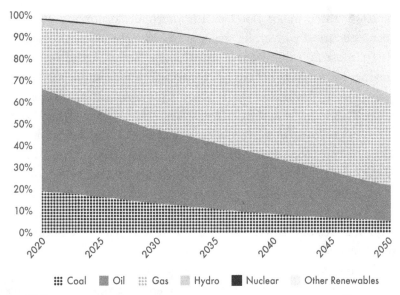

Figure 15.5: Current Path forecast of African energy production, by type[27]

rapidly in Asia, it is very likely that the vast majority of Africa's natural gas production (like its oil) will end up as exports to feed demand in China, India and elsewhere.

Oil is currently the largest source of energy produced in Africa and is likely to remain central to the economies of Nigeria, Angola, Algeria, Libya, Egypt, the Republic of Congo, Equatorial Guinea, Gabon, Chad, Ghana and Cameroon. Most of that oil is exported rather than refined, and then the refined product is imported again.

An energy transition would be the most difficult for South Africa (see Figure 15.4), which produces the most energy but from a highly polluting, coal-dominated energy sector.

The impact of climate change

Chapter 6 showed that agricultural yields in Africa are low by comparative regional standards, but that production can be improved considerably by increasing the amount of land under irrigation, using more fertilisers and genetically modified seeds, and improving farming practices. However, climate change poses a major threat and will constrain such improvements, particularly in North and West Africa, as the impact of higher temperatures and shifting rainfall takes its toll.

In 2006, three major flood events (normally occurring every 10–20 years) occurred within the space of two months in East Africa, displacing almost 200 000 people in Ethiopia, Somalia and Kenya and destroying thousands of hectares of cropland.[28] Maize and wheat production have already been affected in many countries, including fisheries in the Great Lakes region and fruit trees in the Sahel.[29] Droughts and floods are likely to become more frequent and more difficult to predict and could exacerbate food security issues and migratory push factors. In 2017 in Sierra Leone, weeks of heavy rain led to catastrophic mudslides that killed more than 600 people outside Freetown.[30] In 2018, extreme flooding in Niger killed more than 80 people, displaced 50 000 more, and wiped out 400 hectares of farmland and 26 000 head of livestock. Meanwhile, these countries have some of the fastest-growing populations in the world.

Africa has already experienced some of the most severe effects of climate change to date. The IPCC has identified the Sahel and West Africa as climate change 'hot spots' that are projected to experience unprecedented effects of climate change, owing to their existing hot and dry climate, high rates of poverty and profound dependence on rain-fed agriculture, before anywhere else in the world. In typically antiseptic language, the IPCC notes that during the 1970s and 1980s, the Sahel region 'experienced the most substantial and sustained decline in rainfall recorded anywhere in the world within the period of instrumental measurements' – in other words, the worst drought in recorded history. Initially, it was thought that the drought was caused mainly by human modification of the surrounding landscape, ie desertification. However, it has subsequently become clear that rising sea temperatures were the primary driver, reflecting the extent to which climate change is a truly global problem.[31]

While vulnerable populations are the most susceptible to the direct effects of climate change, such as flooding and drought, there are other impacts, such as the incidence and distribution of infectious diseases, including malaria. Increased temperatures will enable malaria to develop in regions where it was previously absent, such as in the highlands of Ethiopia, Uganda and Kenya.[32] Heavy rainfall in parts of Central Africa, particularly in areas with limited access to improved sanitation and proper waste management, is again likely to drive an increase in the transmission of water- and vector-borne diseases.[33]

The increased desiccation of arid climates such as the Sahel and parts of Southern Africa may also affect groundwater recharge rates. Combined with cyclical weather phenomena such as droughts or El Niño events, it will further exacerbate water security issues. In more affluent communities, this could mean higher prices or even restrictions on the use of basic services, but in poor communities this could lead to an inability to access these fundamental rights, with dire consequences. These trends threaten to negate the progress Africa has made in reducing the burden of communicable diseases and the associated maladies of undernutrition and chronic hunger.

In March 2019, Cyclone Idai smashed into Mozambique, unleashing hurricane-force winds and rain that flooded swathes of this poor country before battering eastern Zimbabwe. More than 700 people died in the two countries, leaving some 1.85 million people in need of assistance in a catastrophe that UN Secretary-General António Guterres said rang 'yet another alarm bell about the dangers of climate change'.[34] As if to emphasise the point, Cyclone Kenneth arrived a few days later, first smashing its way across the Comoro Islands before making landfall in northern Mozambique. Kenneth was reportedly the strongest cyclone ever to hit Africa.

Climate change makes things worse in areas that are already struggling with high levels of poverty and poor governance. With climate change, grazing lands have shifted, forcing herders in Nigeria to move southward. This has led to competition and violence between farmers and herders. In the first half of 2018, farmer-herder conflict led to more than six times as many fatalities as have been attributed to terrorist group Boko Haram.[35] In Mali, the situation has escalated to the point where '[m]ass repression based on faulty generalisations, and ethnic tensions between farmers and pastoralists are at the core of the ongoing insecurity'.[36]

West Africa is home to diverse climates that range from rainforests to hyper-arid deserts. In a sense, it is a microcosm of the continent. Its arid regions are likely to get significantly warmer and drier, with droughts becoming more severe and frequent. This will harm agricultural production and could in turn drive large internal and international displacement.

Rising temperatures are likely to have the greatest negative effect on agricultural production, with many crops already at their tolerance limits.

This problem will be exacerbated by the increasing variability of rainfall, which is most pronounced in Eastern and Southern Africa. These regions experience year-to-year variations exceeding 30 per cent around the mean, a rate much greater than in the temperate climates of Europe and North America. High seasonal variability compounds these effects, causing droughts and floods.[37] High inter- and intra-annual rainfall variability explains the unpredictable, and relatively low, seasonal and annual flows in many African rivers.

The IPCC is pessimistic about the prospects and expects that agricultural production could decline by more than 20 per cent across sub-Saharan Africa by 2050, with South Africa and Zimbabwe experiencing reductions of around 30 per cent or more.[38]

The negative effects are likely to be most severe in semi-arid regions, many of which are in North and West Africa. In the Current Path forecast the countries that would be most affected by 2050 would be Mauritania (at 7.5 per cent loss in agricultural yield compared to 2015), Mali, Eritrea, Sudan, South Sudan, Senegal, Burkina Faso and Djibouti (at 6 per cent loss). Countries that will suffer a yield loss of between 6 and 5 per cent are Egypt (at 5.8 per cent), Niger, Gambia, Namibia, Chad, Botswana, Algeria, Benin, Guinea and Morocco (at 5.1 per cent).

Although Africa's climates will generally become more arid, Central and Eastern Africa will experience heavier rainfall, especially after mid-century.[39]

Comparing the carbon emission in different scenarios

In this section, I compare the results of the Current Path with the four scenarios in this book that have the greatest positive and negative impact on carbon emissions, namely, the implementation of the Africa Free Trade (Chapter 11), Made in Africa (Chapter 8), Demographic Dividend (Chapter 3) and Leapfrogging (Chapter 10) scenarios.

Africa has roughly the same population size in 2040 in all scenarios, except for the Demographic Dividend scenario, which results in 100 million fewer people than in the other ten scenarios.

Just as development elsewhere in the world increased carbon emissions in the past, Africa, with its burgeoning population and huge demands for improved livelihoods, will also increase its carbon contribution, even if relatively marginally compared with the development path of other regions. Consequently, even the Current Path forecast of solid but unspectacular economic growth would see Africa's annual carbon emissions increase from the current level of roughly 388 million tons per year before plateauing from 2045 at roughly 625 million tons annually for a decade.

Thereafter, emissions start to decline. At that point, Africa will be responsible for roughly seven per cent of global emissions. By the end of the century, Africa's emissions along the Current Path forecast are projected to reach 456 million tons annually, roughly eight per cent of global carbon emissions.

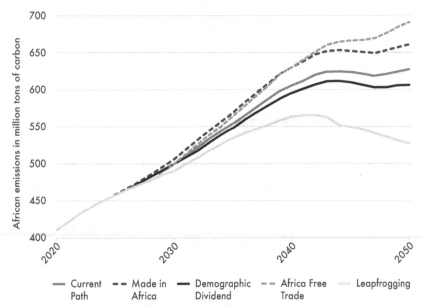

Figure 15.6: Africa's carbon emissions under different scenarios[40]

Generally, one would expect that carbon emissions would follow rates of economic growth, but this is not evident in Figure 15.6. In addition to the Current Path, each of the four scenarios depicted in Figure 15.6 presents an aggressive but reasonably positive development pathway. In other words, average economic growth rates are above those in the Current Path. However, in two scenarios, the Demographic Dividend and Leapfrogging, carbon emissions are actually *below* the Current Path forecast. In the

Leapfrogging scenario, growth rates increase largely because of the impact of digitisation in reducing the size of the informal economy and the more rapid transition to renewable energy. In the case of the Demographic Dividend, a smaller population translates into lower carbon emissions.

Cumulatively, the Agriculture Revolution (Chapter 6) and Made in Africa scenarios (Chapter 8) release the most carbon emissions over the time horizon 2020 to 2040. Previously, I noted that the agricultural sector is responsible for almost a quarter of global emissions, so it comes as no surprise that a larger agricultural sector increases emissions above the Current Path. Manufacturing is by nature more energy-intensive than other sectors, and hence in the Made in Africa scenario, carbon emissions increase above the Current Path.

A different and perhaps more useful measure is to see which scenario provides the highest GDP per capita for the lowest carbon emissions. Social Grants for Africa (Chapter 7) shows the least improvement while Leapfrogging (Chapter 10) again gives the best results.

Responding to climate change

The previous set of comparisons demonstrates how the nature of economic growth and the associated policy decisions impact on Africa's carbon emissions. In responding to this environmental challenge, we can either adapt our way of life or resort to mitigating actions. Such efforts focus on reducing emissions and stabilising the levels of greenhouse gases in the atmosphere. In this way, mitigation is a long-term climate change response as its benefits will only emerge during the second half of the century.

The Paris Agreement represents a global effort to mitigate the future impacts of climate change by trying to reduce greenhouse gas emissions now. And under the Kigali Amendment to the Montreal Protocol (the 1987 agreement to protect the stratospheric ozone layer), which came into force in January 2019, all countries will gradually phase down the production and consumption of hydrofluorocarbons (HFCs) and replace these with more environmentally friendly alternatives.

A second possible reaction is to adapt to life in a changing climate, that is, to the change that is already locked into the climate system. For example, in June 2018 Tanzania completed 2.4 kilometres of seawalls at a cost of US$8.34 million in an effort to protect Dar es Salaam and surrounding areas from rising sea levels. According to USAID, the country is estimated to suffer about US$200 million per year in lost land and infrastructure damage due to sea level rise.[41]

On the other side of the continent, Lagos is one of the largest and fastest-growing cities in the world, but much of the city is less than one metre above sea level.[42] Lagos is, and has always been, a city oriented towards the sea. In fact, it is expanding into the Atlantic through expensive developments on newly reclaimed land on the one hand and overpopulation in slum settlements on the other. With many of its slum communities literally built in the sea, vulnerable communities in Lagos are already highly exposed to rising sea levels and more severe storm activity caused by climate change.

Seventy per cent of the population of Lagos live in slums, with a population density ten times that of New York City, so a powerful storm would affect millions. Furthermore, average sea level rise is projected at 30 centimetres by 2050 and between 30 centimetres and 1.8 metres by 2100 (rising an additional 30 centimetres or more after each decade).[43] Against this backdrop, the 'Great Wall of Lagos' promises to offer protection from climate change, but only for those Nigerians who can afford to live in Eko Atlantic – a massive Dubai-style city under construction. The 8.5-kilometre seawall will 'protect the shoreline of Victoria Island and early phases of Lekki (a city on a peninsula to the east of Lagos) from coastal erosion. What will happen to the people of Makoko and other slum areas is, of course, an entirely different matter.

And then there is the Great Green Wall. For more than a decade, affected countries in the Sahel and elsewhere have advanced and promoted the Great Green Wall of the Sahara and the Sahel Initiative (Grande Muraille Verte pour le Sahara et le Sahel), which aims to halt the southward spread of the Sahara and to constrain the impact of climate change. The original concept, which dates from colonial times, is for a belt of trees 50 kilometres wide (now reduced to 15 kilometres) to be planted to help contain the desert.

The project has subsequently evolved into an integrated rural development effort to respond to the detrimental social, economic and environmental impacts of land degradation and desertification straddling 8 000 kilometres from Senegal in the west to Djibouti in the east.[44] In 2017, it was adopted as a flagship project by the UN Conference on Sustainable Development and now involves more than 20 countries.

But, apart from a minimum effort in Burkina Faso and Senegal, little progress has been made. In July 2019, Ethiopia claimed to have planted more than 353 million trees in just 12 hours as part of a wider reforestation campaign, 'Green Legacy', as an example of what could be possible.[45] This is the kind of effort that will be required to realise the Great Green Wall, possibly including moving away from the idea of a narrow band of trees along the southern edge of the Sahara, indeed across much of sub-Saharan Africa.

Africa's forests could actually be a game-changer in terms of tackling climate change. Approximately 2.6 billion tons of carbon dioxide, one third of the CO_2 released from burning fossil fuels, is absorbed by forests each year. 'Halting the loss and degradation of forest ecosystems and promoting their restoration,' according to the International Union for Conservation of Nature (IUCN), 'have the potential to contribute over one-third of the total climate change required by 2030 to meet the objectives of the Paris Agreement.'[46] According to the Global Forest Watch, tree-cover loss peaked in 2016 but the overall trend is still upward. The DRC is now the country with the second-largest losses by area, and Madagascar lost two per cent of its entire primary forest in 2018. Ghana and Côte d'Ivoire showed the highest rise in percentage losses of primary forest.[47] Most of this increase, particularly in Ghana, is likely due to small-scale gold mining. There has also been an expansion of cocoa farming, which has led to forest loss.

Africa does have some ability to mitigate climate change – massive tree planting is just one example – but needs to direct significant effort at adaptation. The AU acknowledges as much in Agenda 2063, which states: 'Africa shall address the global challenge of climate change by prioritizing adaptation in all our actions . . . for the survival of the most vulnerable populations . . . and for sustainable development and shared prosperity.'[48]

Development as coping mechanism

Developed countries with carbon-intensive economies have, by definition, more capacity to adapt to climate change and are also more responsible for mitigating it. A good proxy with which to measure the mitigation capacity of a country is to look at its average income levels or GDP per capita – a well-known yardstick for measuring and comparing technological sophistication and well-being across countries. Generally, the higher a country's GDP per capita, the more developed its infrastructure, the larger its carbon emissions and the greater its ability to adapt to climate change.

Countries that provide safe drinking water to the majority of their citizens through appropriate piped systems, and that have developed, waterborne sewerage systems, have more capacity to absorb the impact of climate change, including responding to severe weather events. Conversely, countries with large poor communities have much more limited mitigation capacity. Only 3.5 per cent of Africa's agricultural land is equipped for irrigation, consisting of some seven million hectares concentrated in a handful of countries. Expanding land under irrigation makes countries less susceptible to the impact of climate change.[49]

The provision of improved water is particularly critical in the context of climate change. In Central Africa, for example, only around 60 per cent of the population is estimated to have access to an improved water source (piped supplies, boreholes, protected wells and springs, and collected rainwater) – the lowest regional access rate on the continent. Across all of Africa, an estimated 290 million people are living without access to improved water owing to poor physical water infrastructure.

On the Current Path, the number of people without access to improved water is projected to grow for the next five to ten years in all African regions except North Africa, although that region will face increasing water scarcity and likely deteriorating water quality as well.[50] More rapid development, the outcomes of various scenarios, will therefore mitigate some of these effects. The scenarios with the largest impact on improving access to safe water are Improved Health (Chapter 4) and Leapfrogging (Chapter 10). Actually, by 2040, the impact of the Leapfrogging scenario outpaces that of any other scenario. For example, in this scenario access to piped water is 14 percentage points higher by 2040 than in the Current

Path forecast. The outcome is the same in respect of access to improved sanitation, where the Leapfrogging scenario drives more rapid improvement from 2035 than any other.

Conclusion: Finding an environmentally sustainable pathway

On its current development trajectory, the world is headed for serious climate change trouble. More CO_2 emissions will affect all of humanity, and with its low adaptation capacity, Africa is particularly at risk.

There are some leaders, such as US president Donald Trump, who argue that humans have not contributed to climate change and that what we are seeing is a natural change in the global system. Their denialism is based on short-term, self-serving political considerations. The recognition of the role of humanity in accelerating climate change means that leaders have to make difficult choices that will impact upon their election prospects. But politics is supposed to be about leadership, not only about attaining and retaining power. Many of our children will be alive by 2100. Theirs may be a world of technological wonders but could also be one of environmental disasters.

Africa is a small player in this unfolding drama. However, it can play an important role in combating deforestation and forest degradation. The impact of climate change upon the continent will be huge, and African leaders should therefore seize every opportunity to prepare and to make their voices heard. With a large, vulnerable population, Africa has more to lose than almost any other world region. Climate change is also a potential long-term accelerator of violent resource competition. Shifts in precipitation patterns are likely to have negative impacts on regions that are already water-stressed. Coupled with a growing population, this is becoming a lethal combination. Decreases in agricultural yields may impact on both human development and governmental legitimacy. Increases in carbon in the atmosphere are driving more intense weather patterns, which leads to more and greater threats from famine, drought and plague. These disruptive climate and weather conditions will change migration patterns. with possibly significant impacts.

Africa needs faster demographic change, higher productivity (but at lower levels of emissions), better education, a functioning health system, investment in basic infrastructure such as the provision of potable water, expansion of agricultural land under irrigation, and good governance to drive development and to provide improved living conditions and security. However, these development gains will need to be weighed against the long-term goal of mitigating and adapting to climate change. Good governance and long-term planning in Africa are now more important than ever. Mitigation and adaptation to climate change should be an intrinsic part of the African development agenda, such as the purposeful choice to transition to renewable energies and away from fossil fuels.

Africa's leadership is fully aware of the challenges that the continent faces in respect of climate change, but action is limited. A purposeful response is required if Africa is to embark upon a sustainable development pathway. This includes insisting that its development projects and those of its partners, China in particular, are based on the requirements of an environmentally sustainable development pathway. Hence, when looking at the combined impact of the various scenarios that have been modelled in the book, it is important to weigh the costs associated with an environmentally unsustainable development pathway.

The next and final chapter includes the combined carbon emissions from all of the scenarios modelled in this book and outlines the possibilities for African countries to close the gap with the rest of the world.

16
Africa First!

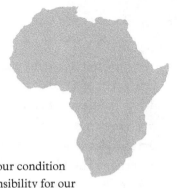

No longer shall we seek to place blame for our condition
elsewhere or to look to others to take responsibility for our
development. We are the masters of our own fate . . .

– Nelson Mandela[1]

In this book I have taken the reader on a journey across a variety of
improvements that are required to help reverse the growing gap between
Africa and the rest of the world on key indicators of human well-being.
In Chapter 1, I presented the gap by comparing the average GDP per
capita in Africa with that in the rest of the world. Figure 1.1 shows the
extent to which the gap has grown incrementally with each passing decade
since independence in the 1960s. The Current Path forecast is for that gap
to continue to widen to 2040 and beyond.

Things are improving in Africa, but more slowly than elsewhere.
Even at an average economic growth rate of 4.3 per cent from 2020 to
2040 (significantly faster than global growth rates) Africa will fall further behind even though the continent's economy will increase in size by
more than 130 per cent. But, because Africa's population will have
increased by 82 per cent by then, GDP per person (in purchasing power
parity, or PPP) will increase by only 30 per cent. Contrast this with the
expected increase of almost 150 per cent in the rest of the world.

To this end, successive chapters have looked at the impact of 11
scenarios to reverse the trend of growing divergence: achieving a Demographic Dividend; Improved Health; a Rejuvenation in Education; an
African Agriculture Revolution; rolling out Social Grants for Africa; a
manufacturing transition through the Made in Africa scenario; Leapfrogging through various technologies; trade integration through the
implementation of the African Continental Free Trade Area (AfCFTA);
a rapid decline in violence and insecurity by Silencing the Guns; continuing progress in a Fourth Wave of Democracy; and gaining from
External Support.

I have taken care to benchmark the interventions used in each of the 11 scenarios to ensure that the impact of each is aggressive but realistic. More detail on benchmarking is available at www.jakkiecilliers.org. It provides a degree of confidence that the various scenarios represent rates of progress comparable to what has been historically achieved in countries and regions at similar levels of development.

In addition, I reviewed the future of work in Africa (Chapter 9) and provided an overview of the effects of climate change (Chapter 15). These two chapters compared the impact of some of the 11 scenarios.

Forecasts and scenarios are not predictions, and it is certain that the future will unfold quite differently to what is set out in this book. It is also unlikely that all of Africa will be able to simultaneously advance on all 11 of these transitions. That caveat aside, the next section looks at the impact of a combined Africa First! scenario that includes all 11 scenarios.

Prospects in the Africa First! scenario

When discussing the combined Africa First! scenario, it is important to emphasise that in the world of scenario planning, one plus one does not necessarily equal two. The IFs forecasting platform is highly integrated, meaning that improvements in education, for example, will positively impact on human and social capital (and hence economic growth) and therefore improve productivity in the Made in Africa scenario on manufacturing.

This holds true across various dimensions. It means that some improvements could have an unexpected or greater than foreseen impact, although it is equally true that some interventions also compete with each other. For example, while more social grants reduce poverty, they eventually detract from economic growth prospects.[2] But, generally speaking, all good things come together in the Africa First! scenario and the combined impact of the 11 positive scenarios presents a step change in Africa's development prospects.

GDP per capita in the Africa First! scenario
Figure 16.1 presents the same information as presented in Figure 1.1 in Chapter 1, but includes the results from the combined Africa First!

scenario. It shows the dramatic change in fortunes that could follow from the combined effect of the various scenarios. From the middle of this century, Africa could actually start to catch up with the rest of the world, although even then Africa would have to maintain a positive trajectory for several decades to do so.

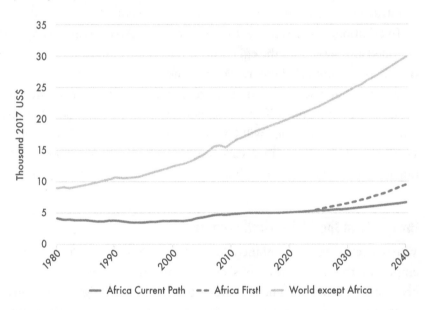

Figure 16.1: GDP per capita, Africa vs rest of the world[3]

If we consider progress in GDP per capita in each of Africa's five regions, Central Africa performs the worst and North Africa the best. The most important reason for this divergence is the very rapid population growth in Central Africa as compared to North Africa. Economic growth will simply be insufficient to impact substantially on the incomes of the rapidly growing populations in Central African countries.

Central Africa also faces another challenge when it comes to development in that it does not have locomotive states (such as Nigeria in West Africa and South Africa in Southern Africa) in which the size of a single national economy provides a sufficiently large market to boost the region as a whole.

Figure 16.2 presents the increase in GDP per capita for selected countries in Africa in 2020 to 2040 in the Current Path and the *additional* average incomes each country would gain from the Africa First! scenario.

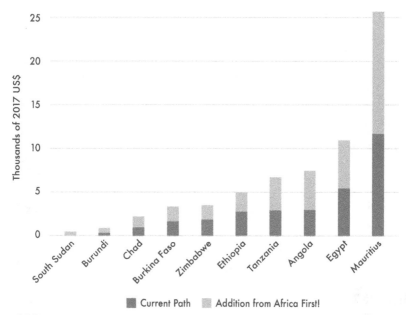

Figure 16.2: Improvement in GDP per capita in Current Path and Africa First! scenarios for selected countries, 2018 to 2040[4]

Mauritius, Libya (provided it ends its civil war soon), Seychelles, Botswana, Equatorial Guinea, Gabon, Egypt, eSwatini, Namibia and Tunisia are the ten countries that would, potentially, gain the most from the Africa First! scenario. The inclusion in this list of Equatorial Guinea, one of the most odious dictatorships in Africa, points to the importance of further analysis, and to the potential that income from oil revenues could have in improving future prospects.

With the exception of Sudan, which is a lower-middle-income country, the ten bottom countries (the others are South Sudan, Burundi, Somalia, DRC, CAR, Nigeria, Liberia, Comoros and Chad) are all very poor and categorised as low income by the World Bank. Almost all are in conflict.

Size of economies in the Africa First! scenario

Figure 16.3 compares the size of the total Africa economy in 2018 with the Current Path and the Africa First! scenarios in 2040 and 2063, the final year of the AU's Agenda 2063. It demonstrates the accelerated impact of the Africa First! scenario.

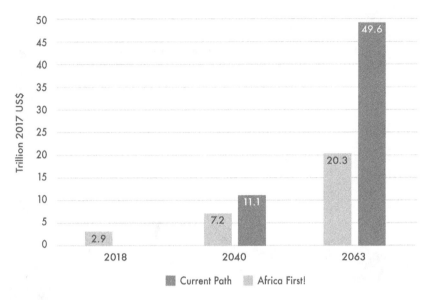

Figure 16.3: Size of the African economy in market exchange rates in Current Path vs Africa First! scenario[5]

An important dynamic is the way in which the Demographic Dividend combines with the Rejuvenation in Education scenario to reduce total fertility rates quite rapidly. As a result, Africa's total economy could be US$11.1 trillion in size in 2040 in the Africa First! scenario instead of US$7.2 trillion in the Current Path, despite (or because) of a population that is 137 million smaller.

The impact accelerates over time. In 2063 in the Africa First! scenario, Africa would have a population of 463 million *fewer* people, but its economy will be 2.5 times *larger* than in the Current Path forecast (US$49.6 trillion instead of US$20.3 trillion). If this were to occur, it would ensure a truly remarkable change in various other indices.

Africa's largest economies – Nigeria, South Africa, Egypt, Angola, Ethiopia and Tanzania – will gain the most in absolute terms, ie when the increase in the size of these economies is measured in billions of dollars. But it is the smaller economies, such as São Tomé and Príncipe, Comoros, The Gambia, Guinea-Bissau and Liberia, that will see the biggest increases in the percentage growth in the size of their economies over time.

Extreme poverty in the Africa First! scenario

The Africa First! scenario has an even more impressive impact on poverty than on economic size and GDP per capita. Figure 16.4 provides a forecast of the number of extremely poor people in Africa using the combined totals from three of the four measures of extreme poverty income announced by the World Bank in 2018 – US$1.90 per person per day for low-income countries, US$3.20 for lower-middle-income countries and US$5.50 for upper-middle-income countries.

Whereas Africa will have 658 million extremely poor people in 2020, in the Africa First! scenario this number could be reduced to 420 million people in 2040 and a mere 100 million in 2063. In the Current Path forecast, the numbers of extremely poor people would be 786 million in 2040 and 564 million in 2063.

Still, even in the Africa First! scenario, Africa will miss the SDG target of eliminating extreme poverty by 2030 by a very large margin. Using the US$1.90 extreme poverty line, 468 million Africans will still be extremely poor in 2030. Using a combination of US$1.90, US$3.20 and US$5.50, the number of extremely poor people would be more than 600 million, as reflected in Figure 16.4.

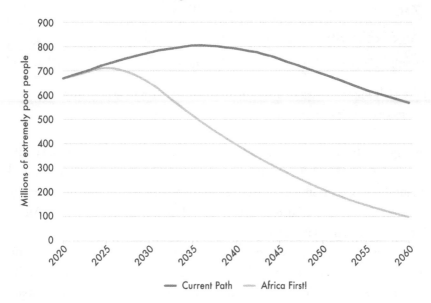

Figure 16.4: Extremely poor people[6]

These changes represent a potential seismic shift in Africa's fortunes and are perhaps the single most important measure of improved well-being.

Table 16.1 presents the difference, in millions, of extremely poor people between the Current Path and Africa First! in 2040. For illustrative purposes the table includes four low-income, three lower-middle-income and two upper-middle-income countries.

Country and relevant poverty line	Difference between Current Path and Africa First! scenario in 2040 in the number of extremely poor people
Ethiopia ($1.90)	-11 million
DRC ($1.90)	-42 million
Tanzania ($1.90)	-15 million
Nigeria ($3.20)	-47 million
Côte d'Ivoire ($3.20)	-5 million
Zambia ($3.20)	-9 million
Algeria ($5.50)	-8 million
South Africa ($5.50)	-7 million

Table 16.1: Impact on key countries in millions fewer extremely poor people in 2040, difference between Current Path and Africa First! scenarios[7]

In Nigeria, the absolute number of extremely poor people will inevitably increase from 2020 due to that country's rapid population growth and relatively slow economic growth rates. But, instead of 212 million extremely poor people in 2040 (Current Path), it would have only 164 million (Africa First!), which still is about 10 million more than in 2020.

Nigeria currently has around 200 million people. By 2040 its population is forecast to be 330 million in the Current Path but only 314 million in the Africa First! scenario as fertility rates decline, largely due to the impact of the Demographic Dividend scenario and better education. The percentage of its population living in extreme poverty will therefore decrease from 76 per cent in 2020 to 64 per cent in the Current Path, or only 50 per cent in the Africa First! scenario.

Carbon emissions in the Africa First! scenario

The improvements in Africa's development prospects in the Africa First! scenario come at a cost, even if it is a low cost by comparison to trends in the rest of the world. In the Africa First! scenario, Africa would release 40 million tons more carbon into the atmosphere by 2040 than in the Current Path. This may sound like a lot but by 2040 annual global emissions would be close to 10 billion tons, meaning that the additional emissions from Africa are quite modest. Had it not been for the reduction in Africa's total population as it progresses more swiftly through its demographic transition, the increase in annual carbon emissions would be larger.

Therefore, in the Africa First! scenario, Africa would by 2040 contribute six instead of seven per cent to global carbon emissions. This means that the continent would have added just over 370 million tons of additional carbon to the atmosphere (ie more than in the Current Path) over the preceding 20 years.

Thereafter, the impact of Africa's smaller population and the changed structure of the African economy reduce annual carbon emissions to such an extent that by 2053 the annual carbon emissions in the Africa First! scenario are similar to those in the Current Path. While the African economy is significantly bigger in the Africa First! scenario than in the Current Path, Africa eventually releases less carbon from mid-century. This is astounding, since the entire transformation of Africa only 'costs' around 720 million tons of additional carbon emissions by 2063.

Still, the increased emissions in Africa occur at a time when the world needs urgently to reduce carbon emissions if it is to constrain global warming to below two degrees by the end of the century. Climate change is real and these forecasts indicate that even greater efforts are needed to transition to a greener economy and a sustainable planet, including in Africa.

Structural change of economies in the Africa First! scenario

The transitions modelled in this book are intended to emulate a future in which Africa is able to reverse its growing commodities dependency and succeed with economic diversification. All six economic sectors in Africa's 2040 economy will be larger in the Africa First! scenario than in the Current Path scenario, as reflected in Figure 16.5.

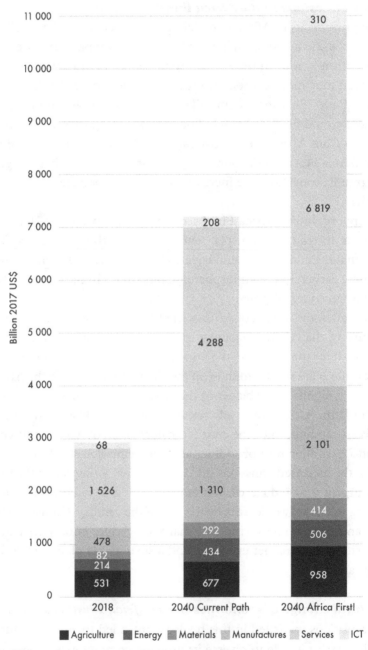

Figure 16.5: Value added by sector, in US$ billions[8]

The Africa First! scenario incentivises more growth in the manufacturing sector across the forecast horizon compared to the Current Path, while the contribution of the energy sector declines in the Africa First! scenario compared to the Current Path.

Figure 16.5 reflects the structural transition of African economies to become more productive (the key contribution that flows from a larger manufacturing sector). In line with global trends, the services sector will grow exponentially. It already constitutes the single largest share of the African economy, although, as I pointed out in Chapter 8, the traditional distinction between services, manufacturing and the like is really of limited value in the modern world.

Again, a word of caution is appropriate. Even with the best will and good fortune, it is unlikely that all countries in Africa would be able to achieve similar success in advancing across all dimensions. In addition, the reforms required to advance from low levels of development are quite different from those required at middle-income level. Eventually, only much more detailed individual country studies can indicate the potential growth that determined and far-sighted leadership can achieve.

Comparing the impact of individual scenarios over time

The preceding section presented the remarkable impact of the Africa First! scenario on key indicators. In this section, I compare the individual impact of key scenarios on GDP per capita.

Scenario comparison using income per person as key indicator

The impact of the various scenarios differs between countries and between low-, lower-middle and upper-middle-income country groups, and also changes over time. So, what contributes most to income growth for a first decade (to 2030) for low-income countries may change during a second (by 2040) and third decade (to 2050). For example, in low-income countries the Agriculture Revolution and Leapfrogging initially contribute the most to GDP per capita income growth. Then, from about 2031, Leapfrogging contributes more to income growth as income growth from agriculture starts to level off. As from around 2045, the implementation of the AfCFTA overtakes Leapfrogging. So, on average, by 2050 the Africa Free Trade, Leapfrogging and Agriculture Revolution scenarios are the most impactful (in that order) for low-income Africa.

A similar story holds for the group of lower-middle-income countries. Initially, agriculture contributes most to income growth but loses momentum over time. At around 2035 the income growth from the Made in Africa and Leapfrogging scenarios are roughly similar and the largest. But beyond 2040 the implementation of AfCFTA outpaces all others and continues to accelerate.

The average differences in the impact of the various scenarios across Africa's group of upper-middle-income countries is less pronounced, simply reflecting the fact that, as countries become more wealthy, it becomes more difficult to achieve rapid income growth from any set of interventions. That said, until around 2036 this group of countries gains most from the Leapfrogging scenario but thereafter the implementation of the AfCFTA is most impactful.

So, because intra-African trade comes off such a low base, by 2050 the AfCFTA scenario generally outpaces all other scenarios across all country income categories by a significant margin. This is why the African Development Bank, Uneca, the World Bank and development economists are excited about the progress being achieved with the implementation of the AfCFTA and its future potential.

The contribution of the Demographic Dividend remains constant as the fourth or fifth most powerful scenario to 2050 and beyond. It serves as a timely reminder of how important it is for Africa to move rapidly through its demographic transition. Even then, the impact is underplayed, as the Demographic Dividend scenario is a kind of force multiplier on all other scenarios. It reduces the number of children who need to be educated (and increases the money available for those children already in school), reduces the demand for basic infrastructure such as water and sanitation, and increases the proportion of working-age adults relative to dependants.

The Social Grants for Africa scenario contributes the least to average income growth in all scenarios. This is not surprising, as it deals largely with the symptoms of low growth and high inequality. Social protection against livelihood risks and to reduce the economic and social vulnerability of poor and marginalised groups is extremely important on a continent where the vast majority of the labour force does not have social insurance or related protection. However, social protection increases spending on recurring items rather than on investments for long-term growth. This is an important lesson for a country such as South Africa, which has, since the end of apartheid, generally focused its attention on redistribution rather than on investing for growth. Although social protection is important, it should generally be seen as a short- to medium-term transitory programme while investing in appropriate education and appropriate infrastructure that will eventually unlock more rapid growth.

In the medium term, the provision of jobs in the formal sector can structurally shift inequality and reduce poverty at a much greater rate than education can. But, in the long term, improvements in appropriate education are an indispensable requirement if countries are to go up the productivity curve. But it takes a very long time. By 2050 education makes only the sixth-largest contribution to income growth in low-income countries, fourth-largest in lower-middle-income countries and third-largest in upper-middle-income countries. In the very, very long term, education is the great leveller in providing improved opportunities to poor people, and the relationship between better education and improved levels of income is strong and well established in the academic literature. A rapidly growing low-income country such as Ethiopia cannot progress into low-end manufacturing (its stated goal) in spite of the large amounts of money that it spends in this sector since the language policies that it pursues in schools mean that kids do not understand what they are being taught by teachers who barely speak English themselves. Ethiopian children are currently taught in their mother tongue in Grades 1 to 4, then in Amharic until, in Grade 8, education switches to English.[9]

As I discussed in Chapter 5, the continent needs to change the way in which it rolls out education. The traditional methods of rote learning will not keep pace with the demand, never mind reducing the backlog in education, and bold innovation and hard work are required in this domain. Governments need to fix education from the bottom upward, starting with ensuring literacy and investing in primary-school enrolment and completion. Once progress is achieved there, the priority should shift to improving enrolment and completion in lower secondary schools, after which investment needs to shift to fixing upper secondary and, eventually, tertiary education. Not all countries do this, and some, such as Malawi, spend inordinate portions of their budget on tertiary education while neglecting primary and secondary education.

Generally, quality is more important than quantity when it comes to education. Simply pushing children through school is not a solution if the education that is provided does not comprehensively and fundamentally address the basics of reading, writing and arithmetic, never mind the skills required for the fourth industrial revolution. At the same time, much greater attention needs to be paid to vocational and technical training, as opposed to the singular focus on academic teaching so evident across many African countries.

As with education, improvements in general indices of health take time and translate very slowly into improved human capital, in which school pupils, students at technical colleges and universities, and workers are better nourished and healthier, and therefore more productive.

The apparently limited impact of democracy also needs to be placed in context. In Chapter 13, I note that democracy is not a prerequisite for economic growth at low levels of development and that it should rather be viewed as a general or inherent good in its own right. Yet, democracy is clearly the most desirable system of government. For example, with the exception of countries with high fossil-fuel exports, democratic countries are richer than others and they are also healthier, particularly when using a key indicator such as rates of child mortality. Furthermore, citizens of democracies are generally happier. Without exception, people across the world aspire to have a say in who governs them, particularly in Africa, where the alternatives have generally proven disastrous, with the admitted modern exceptions of Rwanda and Ethiopia.

Scenario comparison using progress with the HDI, inequality and extreme poverty

Using the HDI as an alternative measure of progress, the Rejuvenation in Education scenario consistently performs better than any other scenario. It raises HDI scores across the forecast horizon to 2040 and even beyond. Since the HDI includes a substantial education weighting in its basket of indicators, this is to be expected.

The Agriculture Revolution scenario has the largest positive impact in reducing inequality, using the Gini index, followed by Social Grants for Africa. However, by around 2050 the positive impact of the Agriculture Revolution, Social Grants for Africa and Leapfrogging scenarios in reducing inequality are generally similar.

Another useful measure of progress that is used extensively in almost all chapters is rates of extreme poverty. Figure 16.6 compares the increase or decrease in poverty rates for key scenarios with the forecast in the Current Path for Africa's current group of 24 low-income countries. Most visible is that the portion of Africans in extreme poverty increases initially by about two per cent by 2030 in the Made in Africa scenario. A manufacturing development pathway implies the use of scarce resources for more capital-intensive and less labour-intensive activities. The result is that poverty and inequality increase initially before stronger economic growth begins to reduce both.

On the other hand the Agriculture Revolution scenario is significantly more powerful in reducing the percentage of extremely poor Africans until shortly before 2040. Thereafter its impact declines, and by 2050 the implementation of the AfCFTA is more impactful.

The provision of social grants as a means to reduce extreme poverty is a strategy that is particularly well suited to poor countries that discover new mineral resources, such as Tanzania and Mozambique. In these countries, the idea of ring-fencing natural resource income for distribution as cash grants rather than through subsidies on fuel and food, which are more prone to corruption, wastage and inefficiencies, would have a salutary impact on levels of extreme poverty.

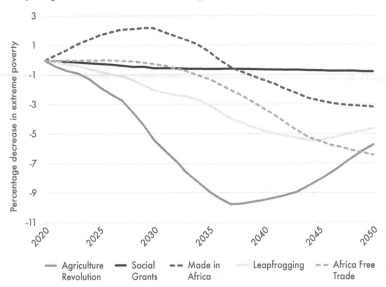

Figure 16.6: Comparison of key scenarios for low-income Africa, percentage reductions in people living below US$1.90 per person per day[10]

Figure 16.6 reinforces the traditional sequencing of development discussed in Chapter 14, namely, a governing elite that is strongly committed to economic growth that starts the developmental transformation process with a focus first on agriculture (to provide sufficient nutrition and food security), basic education and literacy (to improve human capital), and ensures a rapid demographic transition (through more rapid urbanisation and the provision of basic health care and modern contraceptives) while embarking on low-end industrialisation, even as the educational focus shifts to secondary, vocational and tertiary education. Entry into manufacturing requires participation in regional and global value chains and the need to attract FDI and foreign companies with clear incentives for them to build local capacity and ensure technology transfer. This can be termed the 'standard model' of development.

The role of government is crucial at low and middle levels of development. Then, as countries go up the income ladder, economic growth in the 21st century is increasingly dependent on the role of the private sector – as much in China and India as in Africa. Even then, the role played by government remains crucial, although it should shift to a predominantly regulatory and compliance function while ensuring inclusive growth through progressive tax policies, competition and other measures of redistribution.

As countries go up the manufacturing value chain, the spillovers from manufacturing facilitate and incentivise a more productive agricultural sector and the development of higher-end services such as finance until, in some instances, services drive growth.

What is possible? A comparison with China

Africa is young and rapidly urbanising, and its population and economy will grow quite quickly. The levels of energy that are available on the continent remind one of China 25 years ago, but with important differences.

First, technology can allow Africa to leapfrog faster than even China, but the quality and nature of governance is likely to inhibit this potential. To date, politics in Africa has often served as a constraint on development, and we have to find ways to make democratic accountability on the continent real.

While China is a single country with a centralised, authoritarian government, the African continent consists of 55 countries, each jealously guarding its independence and with large disparities in governance systems and traditions. Continental ambitions for regional economic integration are therefore likely to progress slowly, and regions such as Southern, North and East Africa should simultaneously move ahead with trade integration in their respective neighbourhoods (North Africa has had no success at any type of regional integration). As we saw in previous sections, the contribution from the AfCFTA to growth, income and poverty alleviation is the biggest over longer time horizons and the same results will hold at subregional levels.

Second, while the fast development of China was hugely aided by the country's very rapid (and politically driven) demographic transition, including its high peak demographic dividend, growth in Africa will be constrained by the slow pace of its demographic transition and the low levels of its peak demographic dividend.

The continent needs to engage in constructive debate on the extent to which its youthful population serves as a drag on development and on how to encourage appropriate measures to reduce fertility rates in a responsible manner. An important step would be to invest in improving the education levels of its expanding labour pool, as well as to close the gender gap in education. And then some African countries, such as Tunisia, Mauritius and Libya, actually have to invest in maintaining their total fertility rate above the replacement level of 2.1 children per woman if they want to extend their time in the demographic sweet spot. That is a lesson that China has not fully grasped yet.

Unlike Asia, where industrialisation and democratisation generally occurred *sequentially*, Africa has to balance the *simultaneous* challenges of democratisation and development on top of many others. This requires a fine balancing act and consummate political leadership.

In developing Asia, industrialisation took place under autocratic but generally developmentally oriented regimes. Leaders could discount the popular discontent associated with the disruptive changes required for productivity improvements. They could implement subsidies for a specific purpose (for instance, to provide an import-substitution window for the development of local industry) without having to deal with the vested political-economic interests that inevitably develop.[11]

Furthermore, in an autocracy the ruling elite can introduce tariff protection to support a particular sector or industry and more easily phase it out once that goal has been achieved. This is more difficult in a democracy. Instead of becoming economically independent during the 1960s, African countries have willingly subjected themselves to a relationship of dependency, often looking to others rather than themselves for their development.

Aid has generally not worked in Africa because many African leaders seem to expect aid to do their work for them. In such instances, the result will always be the same. It is not that aid is bad. Aid is neutral. It is the purpose or end that we put it to that makes all the difference.

A passion for knowledge and development

On a structural level, many of Africa's challenges are rooted in the process of imposed state formation that started with imperialism and lasted through the colonial period and until very recently, when the end of the Cold War released Africa into an international state-based system while its own constituent states had not yet been consolidated. This is very different to the process through which the modern form of the state was established in 17th-century Europe and from which we often draw our examples.

Subsequently, Africa and its amalgam of unconsolidated 'states in name' has been poorly served by elites who often appear to place politics (largely independence) and their own pockets ahead of development. Eventually, neither Western donors nor China nor India will develop Africa – only Africans can. To do this, we need to understand where we come from but then also to accept responsibility for shaping our future, managing our debt levels and investing responsibly.

Africa needs strong, developmentally minded governments that regulate, empower and support the private sector, which is the primary wealth creator in the 21st century. In fact, experience from around the world highlights the need for industrial policy to place particular emphasis on institutions and policies that promote strategic collaboration between the government and the private sector.[12]

The private sector in Africa is showing steady growth. A recent study by McKinsey[13] reveals that some 400 companies in Africa earn revenues of US$1 billion or more, and that nearly 700 companies have revenues greater than US$500 million. Most have grown faster than their peers in the rest of the world in local currency terms and most are more profitable. Just over half are owned by Africa-based private shareholders, 27 per cent are foreign-based multinationals, and 17 per cent are state-owned enterprises.

The continent needs governments that consistently invest in knowledge creation. In his epic study of economic history, the Norwegian scholar and economic philosopher Erik Reinert captures what lies at the heart of development. 'The global economy,' he writes, 'can in many ways be seen as a pyramid scheme of sorts – a hierarchy of knowledge – where those who continually invest in innovation remain at the apex of welfare.'[14] Reinert points to the importance of 'going up the productivity and technology curve'.

In a different context, the McKinsey Global Institute makes the same argument in concluding that 'all global value chains are becoming more knowledge-intensive'.[15] The associated response could take many forms, such as developing modern industrial policies, but only deliberate efforts to unlock the promise of digitisation and the fourth industrial revolution will achieve this in the 21st century.

In the aftermath of the great global recession of 2007/08, globalisation is again deepening, but growth and trade within regional trading blocs (as opposed to between these blocs) have become more important.[16] Global value chains now appear to be shortening as production moves closer to consumers. This seems to be partly the result of efforts to improve the speed of getting goods to market, but it is also a reaction to global tensions caused by a growing sense of nationalism – as seen in the very visible efforts by Europe and the USA to constrain technology transfer to and competition from China. In the past, the cost of labour was a deciding factor in the location of manufacturing, but in the last two to three decades non-labour costs – including the costs of managing complex global value chains – have increased in importance. The trade war between China and the US is accelerating these trends.

Regional value chains and localised production that is closer to the end market have become more attractive in advanced and emerging economies alike, with some even talking about doing manufacturing on demand based on technologies such as 3D printing.[17] This is the emergence of the so-called Alibaba model of decentralised, cottage-industry industrialisation referred to in Chapter 8.

Africa needs to integrate regionally and into the global economy to facilitate knowledge transfer as China has done so successfully. It can do so by embarking on a digital and urban transition that has the combined potential to unlock other transitions in, for instance, education and the provision of basic infrastructure. It can also do so by actively encouraging foreign companies to invest and locate on the continent, as well as by attracting skilled foreigners. Technological knowledge transfer is crucial, in addition to steadily expanding local content requirements, to make sure that these companies are embedded in city and national value chains. Too narrow (or high) an area of specialisation often means that knowledge transfers do not occur. Over time, local value chains will allow African companies also to participate in and become part of international value chains.

Instead, many African countries – Nigeria, Kenya and Zambia are three examples – specialise in what I refer to as the 'foreign ambush'. Their primary orientation is not to attract and nurture foreign business, but rather to trap companies. Once a foreign company has been attracted by a liberal legal framework and various incentives to invest, the rules are changed in an effort to extract greater profits and possibly even to benefit particular nationals or families. Nothing scares private investment off more than uncertainty, and the threat of changes to their legal or tax status is often a very large disincentive. The result is that those companies that do invest eventually capitulate and leave, as many South African (and other) companies have done in Nigeria, Kenya and Zambia. South Africa, compounding its general shoot-itself-in-the-foot policies, has been working hard since the end of apartheid to keep skilled foreigners at bay, making it as difficult as possible for them to obtain work permits and to invest.

In this regard, there is much that Africa can learn from China, which has perfected the art of setting up a subtler 'ambush' by requiring foreign companies to partner and transfer technology to local partners. In the process China, not the West, has emerged as the global manufacturing hub. It has achieved these goals by making technology transfer and skills requirements law, including them in every agreement and then negotiating hard. China has set out its intention clearly to rival the USA as technology leader in a number of key areas, including artificial intelligence, and this has led to the efforts by President Donald Trump to reverse the flow of knowledge by engaging in a trade war.

Many of Africa's post-independence efforts at industrialisation failed because they effectively became islands of technological sophistication and prestige in a sea of low-technology, informal economies. Without forward and backward linkages to the domestic economy, such projects were dependent on government subsidies and handouts in terms of access to foreign markets, for example via AGOA. Some of the recent investments in heavy-duty infrastructure (as opposed to basic infrastructure) threaten to replicate these mistakes.

When these agreements came to an end, the investment proved unsustainable and the companies inevitably folded or left. It is for the same reason that highly capital-intensive projects such as gas and petroleum extraction provide little spillover effect to the wider economy in northern Mozambique, Angola, Nigeria, Equatorial Guinea and Gabon. All provide a stream of money to state coffers, and the fight for control of that money often determines who governs. But oil or gas income on its own does not develop a country. Development needs, above all, appropriate government policy and oversight that unlocks the one thing we have in abundance, our human capital.

Eventually, the transformation of Africa is less about grand schemes and ambitions (of which there have been many) and more about the mundane functions of empowering locals to become self-sufficient, ensuring a hassle-free and facilitative investment environment, and holding one another to account. It requires governments to facilitate foreign investment on clear terms. It requires a technical and bureaucratic process to resolve, where appropriate, any impediment to innovation, entrepreneurship and doing business. It requires governments to get behind success, offering support and helping to facilitate a potential growth sector, and not merely to shovel money in that direction.

Planning for the long term requires policy certainty, and there are many challenges in this domain as civil resistance campaigns against dictators and lifetime presidents mount. For investment, as opposed to war profiteering, stability is virtually a non-negotiable prerequisite. At the moment there is not enough stability on the continent, although as I explore in Chapter 13 instability is confined to an increasingly small number of countries.

In conclusion

Development is about countries empowering their citizens and helping them to learn how to help themselves. It is not about handouts. The absence of a sense of nationhood is a major distraction in many African countries, and it is a sad reality that many nations that have done well in recent times (Ethiopia, Rwanda, South Korea and China) did so only after suffering a national trauma such as war or genocide.

This book has presented a host of policy recommendations that seek to advance the development of Africa. The general theme that emerges from the analysis is the need to work from the bottom upward – to fix the basics. For example, the need to invest in basic infrastructure such as electricity, sanitation, water and roads and literacy and primary education. Leapfrogging should be seen within this context: how can Africa benefit from new technologies to do things more rapidly and cheaply, such as to provide electricity to citizens through decentralised mini-grids using renewables? Access to electricity and the global village (via the internet) offers enormous potential to embark on a rapid digitisation process, the potential of which was explored in the Leapfrogging scenario.[18] Large infrastructure projects are important, but the trade-off is really first to make sure there are enough paved roads before investing in hugely expensive railway lines, unless these are intended to service specific heavy-duty exports such as iron ore.

Underlying much of this is the need for Africa to progress more swiftly through its demographic transition by reducing fertility rates and effecting more rapid but planned and deliberate urbanisation. Although Africa is urbanising, the process is generally not planned or maximised. Some countries are already largely urban, but East Africa (including the Horn of Africa) is probably the most rural region in the world.

The solutions to Africa's urbanisation trap are well documented. The first is security of tenure: without clear legal rights and a formal property market that allows for the transfer of property rights, land cannot serve as a tradeable asset and investments are limited to those done by the state.

The second is the early installation of infrastructure such as roads, water, sewerage and electricity connections at low levels of density, as was done in China. And this serves as an opportunity to build in climate resilience.

Third, cities develop if they are able to formalise business practices, hence the need to increase the tax base and improve efficiencies and productivity. Cities that are overcrowded and congested also have higher costs of production and are generally unable to produce internationally traded goods.[19]

Basic infrastructure must largely be in place *before* people arrive. Once an informal settlement has reached the size of Khayelitsha in Cape Town or Kibera in Nairobi, it is very difficult to uproot populations to install plumbing or build proper roads. Providing water and sewerage connections for half a million people is a challenging enough task. However, if all these people must be relocated to provide that infrastructure, it is not only significantly more expensive but also more difficult on a political level. In the absence of clean water and adequate sanitation facilities, it remains to be seen to what extent modern medicine can continue to offset the absence of basic infrastructure.

Urbanisation, digital transformation and electrification should be adopted as deliberate strategies for providing basic services, better education and improved health care, as well as encouraging economic growth and mitigating the impact of climate change. The digital transformation of Africa will require huge investment to make the internet accessible, but there is potential from the likes of SpaceX or OneWeb, which promise global, satellite internet coverage within the next few years.[20]

Current forecasts indicate that the rise of India could again see a global resources boom from around 2028. Much as African economies need to diversify, it is unlikely that this will be possible by then. Nor is it a given that Africa will be the region to benefit most from this boom; according to the Fraser Institute, much of Africa ranks near the bottom in terms of mining and exploration attractiveness, with Kenya and Mozambique the least attractive and Ghana and Mali the most attractive.[21]

Resource extraction can, at best, provide an opportunity to invest in the efforts required to transform Africa's economies and education systems for greater productivity. This is only possible if Africa industrialises, trades much more with other African countries, and embarks on a manufacturing-led growth path, although the knowledge economy also unlocks opportunities in services.

For countries to develop and grow, they need to invest in knowledge creation, which is done by investing in education through knowledge transfers and by a focus on spurring innovation and entrepreneurship, and on domestic research and development.

African countries need to buy into the sometimes divisive notion of nation-building and determined leadership, as Rwanda and Ethiopia have done. Without a virtual revolution in the leadership and a social compact, it is difficult to see how countries such as the DRC and the CAR will manage to meet the demands from their citizens for improved livelihoods.

Apart from everything else, African countries need a modern leadership that is able to connect with the aspirations of its youth population, is prepared to move on after a set term, and is determined to look to the future, not the past. A leadership attuned to tomorrow, not yesterday. This is where Nelson Mandela's call to no longer 'seek to place blame for our condition elsewhere or to look to others to take responsibility for our development', but to become the masters of our own fate, becomes meaningful.

These, then, are the challenges and opportunities that confront Africa today as it aims to close the gap with the rest of the world.

Acknowledgements

Four of the sixteen chapters draw on previous published studies that I authored as head of the African Futures & Innovation (AFI) programme at the Institute for Security Studies (ISS). All have been extensively updated and rewritten, and I am indebted to the ISS for allowing me to draw upon this body of work. These are Chapters 3, 12 and 13. In addition, Chapter 14 draws on an ISS report I published on the future of aid. These publications were reviewed by academics and colleagues who are listed in the original studies.

Zachary Donnenfeld played an important role in vetting and benchmarking the 11 scenarios developed for this book and contributed to the first drafts of the chapters on health, education and agriculture.

Marlene Barnard, Annie Olivier, Zachel van Aswegen and Julia Bello-Schünemann have all worked extensively on the manuscript, and I owe them immense thanks. The result is a book that I hope is comprehensive, logically structured and easily readable. This would not have been the case without their help.

Institutionally, the support for our work on the future of Africa has come from the Hanns Seidel Foundation of Germany and the Swedish International Development Cooperation Agency (SIDA). Both have allowed AFI freedom in pursuit of our priorities, offering ongoing support during many visits to Munich, Stockholm and Addis Ababa.

Finally, my long-standing friends at the Frederick S Pardee Center for International Futures at the University of Denver, professors Jonathan Moyer and Barry Hughes, were gracious in again allowing me to use their forecasting platform, International Futures, extensively in this book. Barry, as always, provided detailed and meticulous commentary on an earlier version of the book and Jonathan reviewed the scenarios.

The views and analysis presented in these pages do not reflect the views of the ISS, its donors or the Pardee Center, but are my own.

Endnotes

1: The growing gap between Africa and the rest of the world

1. Amoako, KY, 2018. 'Kofi Annan's quest for a better Africa.' *African Arguments*, 10 September 2018. Available at africanarguments.org/2018/09/10/kofi-annan-quest-better-africa/. Accessed on 20 September 2019.
2. Cilliers, J, Bello-Schünemann, J, Donnenfeld, Z, Aucoin, C and Porter, A, 2017. 'African futures: Key trends to 2035.' Institute for Security Studies, 1 September 2017. Available at issafrica.org/research/policy-brief/african-futures-key-trends-to-2035. Accessed on 20 September 2019.
3. IFs 7.36, initialising from World Bank, World Development Indicators, 2018.
4. In On Africa, 2017. 'Africa's Top 10 most food-secure countries.' Available at www.inonafrica.com/2017/12/05/africas-top-10-food-secure-countries/. Accessed on 20 September 2019.
5. Japan bottomed out at a dependency ratio of 0.43 in 1992; China and the Asian Tigers bottomed out at 0.36 in 2010 and 2013, respectively. All experienced their most rapid economic growth in the years during which their dependency ratios were declining.
6. Sharma, R, 2016. *The Rise and Fall of Nations: Ten Rules of Change in the Post-Crisis World*. New York: Penguin Random House.
7. Manyika, J and Sneader, K, 2018. 'AI, automation and the future of work: Ten things to solve for.' McKinsey Global Institute, June 2018. Available at www.mckinsey.com/featured-insights/future-of-work/ai-automation-and-the-future-of-work-ten-things-to-solve-for. Accessed on 20 September 2019.
8. Atluri, V, Dietz, M and Henke, N, 2017. 'Competing in a world of sectors without borders.' *McKinsey Quarterly*, July 2017. Available at www.mckinsey.com/business-functions/mckinsey-analytics/our-insights/competing-in-a-world-of-sectors-without-borders. Accessed on 20 September 2019.
9. Krishnan, M, Mischke, J and Remes, J, 2018. 'Is the Solow Paradox back?' *McKinsey Quarterly*, June 2018.
10. Calculated by deducting total value of food exports from food imports within IFs 7.36.
11. See Arnoldi, M, 2019. 'Agricultural sector plan prioritises job creation, agro-processing.' *Engineering News*, 29 January 2019. Available at www.engineeringnews.co.za/article/agricultural-sector-plan-prioritises-job-creation-agroprocessing-2019-01-29. Accessed on 20 September 2019.
12. IPCC, 2018. *Working Group II Impacts, Adaptation and Vulnerability*. Available at www.ipcc.ch/working-group/wg2/?idp=403. Accessed on 20 September 2018.
13. United Nations Conference on Trade and Development (Unctad), 2019. *State*

of Commodity Dependence 2019. Available at unctad.org/en/pages/Publication-Webflyer.aspx?publicationid=2439. Accessed on 20 September 2019.

14. Manyika, J, Sinclair, J, Dobbs, R, Strube, G, Rassey, L, Mischke, J, Remes, J, Roxburgh, C, George, K, O'Halloran, D and Ramaswamy, S, 2012. *Manufacturing the Future: The Next Era of Global Growth and Innovation.* McKinsey Global Institute, November 2012. Available at www.mckinsey.com/business-functions/operations/our-insights/the-future-of-manufacturing. Accessed on 20 September.

15. Newman, C, Page, J, Rand, J, Shimeles, A, Söderbom, M and Tarp F (eds), 2016. *Manufacturing Transformation: Comparative Studies of Industrial Development in Africa and Emerging Asia.* UNU-WIDER Studies in Development Economics, Helsinki. Oxford: Oxford University Press, p 5. See also Bhorat, H, Kanbur, R, Rooney, C and Steenkamp, F, 2017. *Sub-Saharan Africa's Manufacturing Sector: Building Complexity,* Working Paper Series no 256. Abidjan: African Development Bank.

16. Asia is, of course, hugely diverse. It basically consists of four groups of countries, namely, a group of advanced economies (Japan, Singapore, Hong Kong, South Korea and Taiwan), the two giants (China and India), a group of large countries (Indonesia, the Philippines, Vietnam, Pakistan and Bangladesh) and a group of poorer countries such as Afghanistan, Bhutan, Cambodia, Laos, Myanmar, Papua New Guinea, Samoa, Sri Lanka, Thailand and Timor Leste [East Timor]. Economy Watch, 2019. 'Developing Asia (Emerging and developing Asia) Economic Statistics and Indicators'. Available at www.economywatch.com/economic-statistics/country/Developing-Asia/. Accessed on 20 September 2019.

17. For the 2020 fiscal year. See World Bank, 'World Bank Country and Lending Groups'. Available at datahelpdesk.worldbank.org/knowledgebase/articles/906519-world-bank-country-and-lending-groups. Accessed on 20 September 2019.

18. I have used a conversion of 1.10074 to convert the 2011 constant US dollar in the IFs system to 2017 values.

19. Where no data is available for 2018, I use the forecasts from the IFs forecasting platform (initialising from 2015 values) but make no distinction in the use of the term 'data' or 'forecast'. Since the IFs forecasts generally demonstrate a high level of continuity with historical trends, the forecasts are a close representation of reality and likely paint a more accurate picture than 'most recent data', which can often be three to five years old.

20. Within IFs, South America consists of Argentina, Bolivia, Brazil, Chile, Colombia, Ecuador, Guyana, Paraguay, Peru, Suriname, Uruguay and Venezuela. South Asia includes Afghanistan, Bangladesh, India, Iran, the Maldives, Nepal, Pakistan and Sri Lanka.

21. African Union Commission, African Development Bank, United Nations Economic Commission for Africa and African Capacity Building Foundation, 2017. *Strategy for the Harmonization of Statistics in Africa 2017–2026 (SHaSA 2).* Available at www.tralac.org/documents/resources/african-union/2031-strategy-for-the-harmonization-of-statistics-in-africa-shasa-2017-2026/file.htm. Accessed on 20 September 2019.

22. The 2019 rebase of Tanzania to 2015 found that its economy had increased by 3.8 per cent. See Reuters Africa, 2019. 'Tanzania rebases economy, 2015 GDP now 3.8 pct larger – stats office.' Available at af.reuters.com/article/investing-News/idAFKCN1Q91G0-OZABS. Accessed on 20 September 2019.

23. Sy, A, 2015. 'Are African countries rebasing GDP in 2014 finding evidence of structural transformation?' Africa in Focus, 3 March 2015. Available at www.brookings.edu/blog/africa-in-focus/2015/03/03/are-african-countries-rebasing-gdp-in-2014-finding-evidence-of-structural-transformation/. Accessed on 20 September 2019. See also Benghan, B and Noshie A, 2018. 'Ghana: Economy expands by 44.6 per cent after rebasing.' *AllAfrica*, 1 October 2018. Available at allafrica.com/stories/201810010595.html; and Musarurwa, T, 2018. 'Economy rebasing to grow Zim revenue.' *The Herald*, 10 December 2018. Available at www.herald.co.zw/economy-rebasing-to-grow-zim-revenue/. Accessed on 20 September 2019.

2: The continent's current path

1. From US$3 482 to US$4 685 in constant 2017 US dollars at PPP.

2. United Nations Development Programme (UNDP), 2010. *Human Development Report 2010*. New York: Palgrave Macmillan.

3. Ibid, p 3.

4. Ibid.

5. See, for example, Shah, A, 2013. 'Structural adjustment – a major cause of poverty.' *Global Issues*, 24 March 2013. Available at www.globalissues.org/article/3/structural-adjustment-a-major-cause-of-poverty. Accessed on 20 September 2019.

6. There is also evidence that the debt trajectory and rate of economic growth is more important than the size of the debt. See Pescatori, A, Sandri, D and Simon, J, 2014. *Debt and Growth: Is There a Magic Threshold?* IMF Working Paper (WP/14/34). Available at www.imf.org/external/pubs/ft/wp/2014/wp1434.pfd. Accessed on 20 September 2019.

7. World Bank, 2019. 'Debt in low-income countries: A rising vulnerability.' Blog post, Let's Talk Development, 25 January. Available at blogs.worldbank.org/developmenttalk/debt-low-income-countries-rising-vulnerability. Accessed on 20 September 2019.

8. World Bank, 2018. 'Heavily Indebted Poor Country (HIPC) Initiative'. Brief, 11 January. Available at www.worldbank.org/en/topic/debt/brief/hipc. Accessed on 23 September 2019.

9. Easterly, W, 2001. *The Effect of International Monetary Fund and World Bank Programs on Poverty*. Open Knowledge Repository, Working Paper no 2517.

10. African Development Bank Group, 2017. 'Introductory remarks: Promoting sustainable industrial policies.' In *Industrialize Africa: Strategies, Policies, Institutions, and Financing*. Abidjan: African Development Bank Group, p 74.

11. World Bank, 1992. *Governance and development,* Washington, DC: The World Bank.

12. World Bank, no date. *World Development Indicators*. Available at datacatalog. worldbank.org/dataset/world-development-indicators. Accessed on 23 September 2019.

13. Ibid.

14. See, for example, African Development Bank Group, 'Introductory remarks'.

15. United Nations, 2019. *The State of Commodity Dependence*. New York: Unctad, p 3.

16. Ibid. Unctad defines a country as 'dependent on commodities' when its commodity exports account for more than 60 per cent of its total merchandise exports in value terms and 'strongly commodity export dependent' when this share exceeds 80 per cent.

17. According to research by the Bank of Canada, the previous four commodity supercycles peaked in 1904, 1947 and 1978, and lasted for 33, 29 and 34 years, respectively, from trough to trough. Commodity prices subsequently declined to 1995. The most recent supercycle peaked in 2011. See Büyükşahin, B, Mo, K and Zmitrowicz, K, 2016. 'Commodity price supercycles: What are they and what lies ahead?' *Bank of Canada Review* (Autumn), p 37.

18. Due to having passed the peak relationship between working age and dependants (discussed in Chapter 3).

19. See Diamond, L and Mosbacher, J, 2013. 'Petroleum to the people: Africa's coming resource curse – and how to avoid it.' *Foreign Affairs* (September/October), pp 87–88.

20. Gylfason, T and Zoega, G, 2006. 'Natural resources and economic growth: the role of investment.' *The World Economy*, 29(8), pp 1091–1115.

21. Ibid.

22. International Monetary Fund, 2018. *Macroeconomic Developments and Prospects in Low-Income Developing Countries*. Washington, DC: IMF, pp 39–40.

23. International Monetary Fund, 2018. *Regional Economic Outlook. Sub-Saharan Africa: Capital Flows and the Future of Work*. Washington, DC: World Economic and Financial Surveys, p 6.

24. Yao, K, 2019. 'China in bid to allay fears of debt risk in its Belt and Road initiative.' *Business Day*, 25 April 2019.

25. See Moore, WG, 2018. 'The language of "debt-trap diplomacy" reflects Western anxieties, not African realities.' *Quartz*, 17 September 2018. Available at qz.com/1391770/the-anxious-chorus-around-chinese-debt-trap-diplomacy-doesnt-reflect-african-realities/. Accessed on 23 September 2019. See also 'Reckless in Lusaka: Zambia's looming debt crisis is a warning for the rest of Africa.' *The Economist*, 15 September 2018.

26. See Freedom House, 2018. *Freedom in the World 2018*. Available at freedomhouse. org/report-types/freedom-world. Accessed on 23 September 2019.

27. The American social scientist Barrington Moore popularised the notion of 'no bourgeois, no democracy', denoting the fact that minimum levels of economic development were required for democracy. See Moore, B, 1966. *Social Origins of Dictatorship and Democracy: Lord and Peasant in the Making of the Modern World*. Boston: Beacon Press. For more recent work, see Przeworski, A and

Limongi, F, 1993. 'Political regimes and economic growth.' *Journal of Economic Perspectives*, 7(3), pp 51–69.

28. Glaeser, EL, Ponzetto, G and Shleifer, A, 2006. *Why Does Democracy Need Education?* NBER Working Paper, Issue no 12128, pp 3–4.

29. Varieties of Democracy (V-Dem) distinguishes between five high-level indices of democracy ideals: electoral, liberal, participatory, deliberative and egalitarian, and collects data to measure these and numerous component indices and indicators. It is a large collaborative project, with headquarters at the V-Dem Institute in the Department of Political Science at the University of Gothenburg. In version 8 of its data release (June 2018), the project covers 201 political units with historical data from 1789 to 2017.

30. In addition to V-Dem, the Polity datasets (Center for Systemic Peace) now go back more than a century. Others, such as from the Economist Intelligence Unit, are more recent and less compelling.

31. Robinson, PT, 1994. 'The national conference phenomenon in Francophone Africa.' *Comparative Studies in Society and History*, 36(3) (July), pp 575–610. Available at www.cambridge.org/core/journals/comparative-studies-in-society-and-history/article/national-conference-phenomenon-in-francophone-africa/F20505B66CA65C8D71ACBB7919ADE1D0. Accessed on 23 September 2019; see also Banzet, A, 2017. '#CAFDO2017: The first Francophone African Conference on Open Data and Open Government.' Blog post, Open Government Partnership, 15 June. Available at www.opengovpartnership.org/stories/cafdo2017-the-first-francophone-african-conference-on-open-data-and-open-government/. Accessed on 23 September 2019.

32. Afrobarometer, no date. Available at afrobarometer.org.

33. Transparency International, no date. 'Seize Mobutu's wealth or lose your own money, Western governments told.' Available at www.transparency.org/news/pressrelease/seize_mobutus_wealth_or_lose_your_own_money_western_governments_told. Accessed on 23 September 2019.

34. Saadoun, S, 2017. 'The trial of one of Africa's most corrupt politicians shows that fighting graft is global.' Human Rights Watch, 10 July 2017. Available at www.hrw.org/news/2017/07/10/trial-one-africas-most-corrupt-politicians-shows-fighting-graft-global. Accessed on 23 September 2019.

35. Wroughton, L, 2012. 'IMF finds most of Angola's missing $32 bln.' *Reuters*, 25 January 2012. Available at www.reuters.com/article/ozatp-imf-angola-20120125-idAFJOE80O00O20120125. Accessed on 23 September 2019.

36. Wolters, S, 2018. 'Will this election change the DRC?' *ISS Today*, 15 January 2019. Available at issafrica.org/iss-today/will-this-election-change-the-drc. Accessed on 23 September 2019.

37. Love, D, 2018. 'China threatens sovereignty of several African nations as it takes over their resources to cover debt.' *Atlanta Black Star*, 16 September. Available at atlantablackstar.com/2018/09/16/china-has-tightened-its-grip-on-africas-resources/. Accessed on 23 September 2019.

38. Roxburgh, C, Dörr, N, Leke, A, Tazi-Riffi, A, Van Wamelen, A, Lund, S, Chironga, M, Alatovik, T, Atkins, C, Terfous, N and Zeino-Mahmalat, T, 2010.

*Lions on the Move: The Progress and Potential of African Economie*s. Report, McKinsey Global Institute, June, p 19. Available at www.mckinsey.com/featured-insights/middle-east-and-africa/lions-on-the-move. Accessed on 23 September 2019.

39. Ravallion, M, Chen, S and Sangraula, P, 2007. 'The urbanization of global poverty.' *World Bank Research Digest*, 1(4).

40. By 2030 Africa will host six of the world's 41 megacities. Cairo, Lagos, Kinshasa, Johannesburg, Luanda and Dar es Salaam will have more than 10 million inhabitants each and 17 African cities will have more than five million each. See Leke, A, Chironga, M and Desvaux, G, 2018. 'Africa's overlooked business revolution.' *McKinsey Quarterly*, November 2018.

41. African Development Bank, 2016. *African Economic Outlook 2016*. Abidjan: African Development Bank Group.

42. Collier, P, 2016. *African Urbanisation: An Analytic Policy Guide*, London: International Growth Centre.

43. Auerswald, P and Joon, Y, 2018. 'As population growth surges, populism grows.' *The New York Times*, 22 May. Available at www.nytimes.com/2018/05/22/opinion/populist-populism-fertility-rates.html. Accessed on 23 September 2019.

44. Ibid.

45. IFs 7.36, initialising from UN Population Division medium-term forecast, 2017 revision.

46. Ibid.

47. IFs 7.36, initialising from IMF, *World Economic Outlook 2017*.

48. Carolina, R and Jahangir, M, 2018. 'Measuring multidimensional poverty for leaving no one behind.' United Nations Development Programme, Human Development Reports, 6 November 2018. Available at hdr.undp.org/en/content/measuring-multidimensional-poverty-leaving-no-one-behind. Accessed on 23 September 2019.

49. See Oxford Poverty and Human Development Initiative, Global Multidimensional Poverty Index. Available at ophi.org.uk/multidimensional-poverty-index/. Accessed on 23 September 2019.

50. Ferreira, F and Sánchez-Páramo, C, 2017. 'A richer array of international poverty lines.' Worldbank Blogs, 13 October. Available at blogs.worldbank.org/developmenttalk/richer-array-international-poverty-lines. Accessed on 23 September 2019.

3: Getting to Africa's demographic dividend

1. African Union Commission, 2017. *AU Roadmap on Harnessing the Demographic Dividend Through Investment in Youth*. Addis Ababa: African Union, p 36.

2. African Union Commission, 2006. *African Youth Charter*. Available at www.un.org/en/africa/osaa/pdf/au/african_youth_charter_2006.pdf. Accessed on 23 September 2019.

3. African Union, 2011. *African Youth Decade 2009–2018 Plan of Action*. Available at www.un.org/en/africa/osaa/pdf/au/african_youth_decade_2009-2018.pdf. Accessed on 23 September 2019.

4. African Union Commission, *AU Roadmap*.
5. Canning, D, Sangeeta, R and Abdo, YS (eds), 2015. *Africa's Demographic Transition: Dividend or Disaster?* Africa Development Forum series. Washington, DC: World Bank, pp 6–7.
6. Sharma, *The Rise and Fall of Nations*, pp 6–7, 19.
7. Roser, M, 2019. 'Economic Growth.' Our World in Data. Available at ourworldindata.org/economic-growth. Accessed on 23 September 2019.
8. Pearson, CS, 2015. *On the Cusp: From Population Boom to Bust.* Oxford: Oxford University Press.
9. A second definition is that a favourable 'demographic window' opens when children (ie, below age 15) make up less than 30 per cent of the population and those 64 or older make up less than 15 per cent. According to the third definition, the window opens when the median age is above 25.5 years and below 36 to 41 years. See Cincotta, R, 2017. 'Opening the demographic window: age structure in sub-Saharan Africa'. New Security Beat, 26 October. Available at www.newsecuritybeat.org/2017/10/opening-demographic-window-age-structure-sub-saharan-africa/. Accessed on 23 September 2019.
10. This is also known as the first dividend, since there are also second and third dividends, which are the result of savings and investments, and improvements in productivity.
11. Chad has the lowest life expectancy in Africa, at 52 years in 2018.
12. According to the World Report on Child Labour, one in four children (aged 5 to 17) in least-developed countries are involved in child labour. See International Labour Organization, 2018. *Women and Men in the Informal Economy: A Statistical Picture.* Geneva: International Labour Office; see also International Labour Organization, 2015. *World Report on Child Labour 2015: Paving the Way to Decent Work for Young People.* Geneva: International Labour Office.
13. The replacement fertility rate is generally accepted as 2.1 children per woman. Without inward migration, below that populations start to decline.
14. See Eloundou-Enyegue, P, Giroux, S and Tenikue, M, 2017. 'African transitions and fertility inequality: A demographic Kuznets hypothesis.' *Population and Development Review*, 43(S1), pp 59–83.
15. The averages are for the top and bottom quintile. Institute for Health Metrics and Evaluation, 2019. Global Health Data Exchange. Available at ghdx.healthdata.org/series/demographic-and-health-survey-dhs
16. Canning et al, *Africa's Demographic Transition*, p 18.
17. Roser, M, 2017. 'Fertility Rate.' Our World in Data. Available at ourworldindata.org/fertility-rate. Accessed on 23 September 2019.
18. Ibid.
19. Ibid.
20. International Labour Organization, 2018. *World Employment and Social Outlook: Trends 2018.* Geneva: International Labour Office, pp 11–12.
21. Canning et al, *Africa's Demographic Transition*, p 19.
22. United Nations Department of Economic and Social Affairs, 2018. Estimates and Projections of Family Planning Indicators 2018. Available at www.un.org/

en/development/desa/population/theme/family-planning/cp_model.asp. Accessed on 23 September 2019.

23. For example, three low-income countries (Rwanda, Ethiopia and Malawi) achieved a 13–19 per cent increase in contraceptive use over 15 years (2000–2015) and 22–27 per cent over 30 years (1985–2015). Three lower-middle-income countries (eSwatini, Lesotho and Zambia) achieved an 11–12 per cent increase in contraceptive use over 15 years (2000–2015) and 22–23 per cent over 30 years (1985–2015).

24. IFs 7.36, based on historical data from UN Population Division, World Population Prospects, 2017 revision.

25. Calculated using US$1.90 for low-income countries, US$3.20 for lower-middle-income countries and US$5.50 for upper-middle-income countries.

26. The HDI is made up of life expectancy, average levels of education measured by mean number of school years in the population over the age of 15 and average incomes.

27. IFs 7.36, initialising from United Nations Population Division medium-term forecast and Barro-Lee educational attainment dataset.

28. Canning et al, *Africa's Demographic Transition*, p 17.

29. Barro, RJ, 1996. *Determinants of Economic Growth: A Cross-Country Empirical Study.* NBER Working Paper no 5698, August. See also Rothman, DS, Irfan, MT, Margolese-Malin, E, Hughes, BB and Moyer, JD, 2014. *Patterns of Potential Human Progress, Volume 4: Building Global Infrastructure.* Boulder: Paradigm Publishers.

30. Woetzel, J, Madgavkar A, Ellingrud, K, Labaye, E, Devillard, S, Kutcher, E, Manyika, J, Dobbs, R and Krishnan, M, 2015. 'How advancing women's equality can add $12 trillion to global growth.' Report, McKinsey Global Institute, September. Available at www.mckinsey.com/featured-insights/employ-ment-and-growth/how-advancing-womens-equality-can-add-12-trillion-to-global-growth. Accessed on 23 September 2019.

4: Health, water, sanitation and hygiene

1. Deaton, A, 2013. *The Great Escape: Health, Wealth, and the Origins of Inequality.* Princeton: Princeton University Press, p 147.

2. For the most recent findings, see Harvati, K, Röding, C, Bosman, AM, Kara-kostis, FA, Grün, R, Stringer, C Karkanas, P, Thompson, NC, Koutoulidis, V, Moulopoulos, LA, Gorgoulis, VG and Kouloukoussa, M, 2019. 'Apidima Cave fossils provide earliest evidence of *Homo sapiens* in Eurasia.' *Nature*, 10 July. Available at www.nature.com/articles/s41586-019-1376-z. Accessed on 23 September 2019.

3. Aydon, C, 2007. *The Story of Man.* Philadelphia: Running Press, p 71.

4. Reader, J, 1998. *Africa: A Biography of the Continent.* New York: Penguin Books, p 234.

5. Diamond, J, 2015. *Guns, Germs and Steel: The Fates of Human Societies.* New York: WW Norton & Company, p 386.

6. Aydon, C, 2009. *A Brief History of Mankind: An Introduction to 150 000 Years of Human History.* Philadelphia: Running Press, p 125.

7. John Reader argues that this relates to the poor and hard soils of great parts of the continent, which would not have allowed ploughing. See Reader, *Africa*, p 99.

8. Wolfe, ND, Dunavan, CP and Diamond, J, 2007. 'Origins of major human infectious diseases.' *Nature*, 447, pp 279–283.

9. Alchon, SA, 2003. *A Pest in the Land: New World Epidemics in a Global Perspective.* Albuquerque: University of New Mexico Press, p 21.

10. Bollyky, TJ, 2018. *Plagues and the Paradox of Progress: Why the World Is Getting Healthier in Worrisome Ways.* Cambridge: MIT Press.

11. Wolfe et al, 'Origins of major human infectious diseases'; see also Reader, *Africa*, p 242.

12. World Health Organization, 2019. 'Lymphatic filariasis.' WHO factsheet, 12 April. Available at www.who.int/news-room/fact-sheets/detail/lymphatic-filariasis. Accessed on 23 September 2019; World Health Organization, 2019. 'Yellow fever.' WHO factsheet, 7 May. Available at www.who.int/news-room/fact-sheets/detail/yellow-fever. Accessed on 23 September 2019.

13. World Health Organization, 2018. *Global tuberculosis report 2018.* Geneva: World Health Organization.

14. For a helpful timeline, see Pickrell, J, 2006. 'Timeline: HIV and AIDS.' *New Scientist*, 4 September. Available at www.newscientist.com/article/dn9949-timeline-hiv-and-aids/. Accessed on 23 September 2019.

15. Dolgin, E, 2010. 'Ancient origin for monkey version of HIV.' *Nature*, 21 May. Available at www.nature.com/news/2010/100521/full/news.2010.259.html. Accessed on 23 September 2019.

16. Iliffe, J, 2006. *The African AIDS Epidemic: A History.* Oxford: James Currey, pp 4–5, 158–159.

17. IFs 7.36, using UN Population Division and Institute for Health Metrics and Evaluation data.

18. IFs uses three main ICD categories – communicable, non-communicable and injuries. The calculations were done as a portion of the total of all three. See also Narayan, K and Donnenfeld, Z, 2016. *Envisioning a Healthy Future: Africa's Shifting Burden of Disease.* Pretoria: Institute for Security Studies.

19. United Nations, Department of Economic and Social Affairs/Population Division, 2018. *World Urbanization Prospects 2018.* Available at population.un.org/wup/. Accessed on 23 September 2019.

20. Collier, *African Urbanisation*, p 23.

21. Map Kibera Trust, 2019. 'Mapping'. Available at mapkibera.org/work/tools/. Accessed on 23 September 2019.

22. United Nations, General Assembly, 2010. 'Resolution adopted by the General Assembly on 28 July 2010: 64/292, The human right to water and sanitation.' United Nations, 28 July. Available at www.un.org/en/ga/search/view_doc.asp?symbol=A/RES/64/292. Accessed on 23 September 2019.

23. Unicef, 2015. 'How WASH relates to health, education and development.' Available at www.unicef.org/wash/index_healthandeducation.html. Accessed on 23 September 2019.

24. WHO/Unicef Joint Monitoring Programme for Water Supply, Sanitation and Hygiene (JMP), 2012. *WASH Post-2015.* Washington, DC: JMP.

25. Defined as when a child's height-for-age ratio is more than two standard deviations below the WHO's Child Growth Standards median. See World Health Organization, 2006. *WHO Child Growth Standards.* Geneva: WHO Press.

26. World Health Organization, 2015. 'Stunting in a nutshell.' Available at www. who.int/nutrition/healthygrowthproj_stunted_videos/en/. Accessed on 23 September 2019.

27. A study from Malawi, for instance, found that only 46 per cent of girls who reached menarche before age 14 completed primary school, compared to 70 per cent who reached it after 16 years of age. This was due to a lack of appropriate menstrual hygiene management resources. See Sommer, M, 2013. 'Menarche: A missing indicator in population health from low-income countries.' *The National Center for Biotechnology,* 128(5), pp 399–401.

28. Gonsalves, GS, Kaplan, EH and Paltiel, AD, 2015. 'Reducing sexual violence by increasing the supply of toilets in Khayelitsha, South Africa: A mathematical model.' *PLOS One,* 29 April. Available at journals.plos.org/plosone/article?id= 10.1371/journal.pone.0122244. Accessed on 23 September 2019.

29. Markle, A and Donnenfeld, Z, 2016. *Refreshing Africa's Future: Prospects for Achieving Universal WaSH Access by 2030.* African Futures Paper, June.

30. This average is calculated using a bivariate regression with GDP per capita as the independent variable, fitted to a log distribution to obtain an expected value for a given level of income.

31. The category 'other communicable diseases' excludes diarrhoeal diseases, HIV/ Aids, malaria and respiratory infections.

32. The vaccine triggers the immune system to defend against the first stages of malaria shortly after the parasite enters the bloodstream after a mosquito bite. See Deutsche Welle, 2019. 'Africa begins world's biggest anti-malaria vaccine campaign.' Available at www.dw.com/en/africa-begins-worlds-biggest-anti-malaria-vaccine-campaign/a-48436460. Accessed on 23 September 2019.

33. Pavlakis, GN and Felber, BK, 2018. 'A new step towards an HIV/AIDS vaccine.' *The Lancet,* 392(10143) (21 July), pp 192–194.

34. More specifically, mortality from malaria is reduced by 95 per cent by 2030, Aids deaths are reduced by 75 per cent by 2030 and other communicable diseases are reduced by 25 per cent by 2030. There is also improved access to sanitation (up from 40 per cent in 2020 to 67 per cent in 2030) and safe water (up from 78 per cent in 2020 to 97 per cent in 2030).

35. Yu, K, 2018. 'Why did Bill Gates give a talk with a jar of human poop by his side?' Goats and Soda, NPR, 9 November 2018. Available at www.npr.org/ sections/goatsandsoda/2018/11/09/666150842/why-did-bill-gates-give-a-talk-with-a-jar-of-human-poop-by-his-side. Accessed on 23 September 2019.

36. This is calculated using US$1.90 for low-income Africa, US$3.20 for lower-middle-income Africa and US$5.50 for upper-middle-income Africa.

37. Murray, CJ and Lopez, AD, 1997. 'Global mortality, disability, and the contribution of risk factors: Global Burden of Disease Study.' *The Lancet,* 349(9063) (17 May), pp 1436–1442.

38. The measure is actually designed in reverse, where 1 represents a state of perfect health and 0 represents a state equivalent to death, which makes more sense

logically, but it is inverted for the purposes of accounting. See Murray and Lopez, 'Global mortality, disability, and the contribution of risk factors'.

39. Bloom, CE, Canning, D and Sevilla, J, 2004. 'The effect of health on economic growth: A production function approach.' *World Development*, 32(1), pp 1–13.

40. United Nations Economic Commission for Africa, 2014. *Socio-economic Impacts of Ebola on Africa*. Addis Ababa: Economic Commission for Africa.

5: Rejuvenating education

1. Mandela, NR, 2003. 'Lighting your way to a better future.' Launch of Mindset Network, Johannesburg, 16 July.

2. Hanushek, EA and Woessmann, L, 2010. 'Education and Economic Growth.' In P Peterson, E Baker and B McGaw (eds). *International Encyclopedia of Education, Volume 2*. Oxford: Elsevier, pp 245–252.

3. Morris, P, 1996. 'Asia's four little tigers: A comparison of the role of education in their development.' *Comparative Education*, 32(1), pp 95–109. The last datapoint for Ethiopia is for 2007. See, for example, UNESCO Institute of Statistics, no date. 'Ethiopia.' Available at uis.unesco.org/country/ET. Accessed on 23 September 2019.

4. Education in China has evolved so rapidly that today it is the second most popular destination for African students studying abroad (after France). Mo Ibrahim Foundation, 2019. *Africa's Youth: Jobs or Migration?* London: Mo Ibrahim Foundation.

5. Lutz, W, Cuaresma, JC, Fürnkranz-Prskawetza, A, Kebede, E and Striessnig, E (forthcoming). 'Education rather than age-structure brings demographic dividend.' *Proceedings of the National Academy of Sciences of the United States of America*.

6. See, for example, Roser, M and Ortiz-Ospina, E, 2018. 'Literacy.' Our World in Data. Available at ourworldindata.org/literacy. Accessed on 23 September 2019.

7. Reinert, ES, 2010. *How Rich Countries Got Rich and Why Poor Countries Stay Poor*. London: Constable, p 113.

8. Ibid, p 191.

9. Sanny, JA-N, Logan, C and Gyimah-Boadi, E, 2019. *In Search of Opportunity: Young and Educated Africans Most Likely to Consider Moving Abroad*. Afrobarometer Dispatches no 288.

10. This is the view advanced by Swedish economist and Nobel laureate Gunnar Myrdal. His work pre-empted that of John Maynard Keynes.

11. Carrol, B, Barrow, K and Wils, A, 2005. *Educating the World's Children: Patterns of Growth and Inequality*. Washington, DC: Education Policy and Data Center. Available at www.epdc.org/education-data-research/educating-worlds-children-patterns-growth-and-inequality. Accessed on 23 September 2019.

12. World Bank, 2018. *World Development Report 2018: Learning to Realize Education's Promise*. Washington, DC: The World Bank Group.

13. Ibid, p 16.

14. IFs 7.36, initialising from Barro-Lee educational attainment dataset.

15. At the primary level, the completion rate is calculated as the number of children

who are completing the final grade as a percentage of the population of the age a child would be who began first grade and progressed without repetition or interruption through to the final grade. See Dickson, JR, Hughes, BR and Irfan, MT, 2010. *Patterns of Potential Human Progress, Volume 2: Advancing Global Education.* New Delhi and Oxford: Paradigm Publishers and Oxford University Press.

16. IFs 7.36, initialising from UN Population Division medium-term forecast and Barro-Lee educational attainment dataset.

17. Roser and Ortiz-Ospina, 'Literacy'.

18. United Nations, 2018. *Sustainable Development Goal 4.* Available at sustainable development.un.org/sdg4. Accessed on 23 September 2019.

19. Hanushek, EA and Woessmann L, 2007. *Education Quality and Economic Growth.* Washington, DC: The World Bank Group.

20. Ibid, p 1.

21. A recent dataset has created a common measurement system for 163 countries, including 30 in sub-Saharan Africa. See Altinok, N, Angrist, N and Patrinos, HA, 2018. *Global Data Set on Education Quality (1965–2015).* World Bank Group Policy Research Working Paper 8314, January.

22. Ibid, p 5.

23. Ibid, p 23.

24. Ortiz-Ospina, E, 2018. 'Global education quality in 4 charts.' Our World in Data. Available at ourworldindata.org/edu-quality-key-facts. Accessed on 23 September 2019.

25. World Bank, *World Development Report 2018.*

26. Sow, M, 2017. 'Figures of the week: Africa, education, and the 2018 *World Development Report.*' Africa in Focus, 6 October. Available at www.brookings. edu/blog/africa-in-focus/2017/10/06/figures-of-the-week-africa-education-world-development-report-2018/. Accessed on 23 September 2019.

27. African Development Bank Group, Asian Development Bank, European Bank for Reconstruction and Development, Inter-American Development Bank, 2018. *The Future of Work: Regional Perspectives.* Washington. DC: Co-Publishers.

28. African Center for Economic Transformation, 2018. *The Future of Work in Africa: The Impact of the Fourth Industrial Revolution on Job Creation and Skill Development in Africa,* p 2. Report provided to author by Dr Julius Gatune of the African Center for Economic Transformation.

29. World Bank, *World Development Report 2018,* p 4.

30. Global Commission on the Future of Work, 2019. *Work for a Brighter Future.* Geneva: International Labour Office, p 13.

31. World Bank, *World Development Report 2018,* p 154.

32. Ibid, p 155.

33. Federal Ministry of Education and Research, no date. 'The German Vocational Training System.' Available at www.bmbf.de/en/the-german-vocational-training-system-2129.html. Accessed on 25 September 2019.

34. World Bank, *World Development Report 2018,* pp 9 and 157.

35. African Development Bank Group, 'Introductory remarks'.

36. IFs 7.36, initialising from UN Population Division medium-term forecast and Barro-Lee educational attainment dataset.

37. These numbers are all at market exchange rates.
38. See Lutz, W and Klingholz, R, 2017. *Education First! From Martin Luther to Sustainable Development.* Stellenbosch: Sun Media.
39. Diamandis, PH, 2018. 'A model for the future of education.' Singularity Hub, 12 September 2018. Available at singularityhub.com/2018/09/12/a-model-for-the-future-of-education-and-the-tech-shaping-it/. Accessed on 25 September 2019.
40. Hausmann, R, 2017. *Is South Africa About to Make an Historic Mistake?* Centre for Development and Enterprise, June 2017. Available at cde.org.za/wp-content/uploads/2018/06/CDE-Insight-Professor-Ricardo-Hausmann-Is-South-Africa-about-to-make-a-historic-mistake.pdf. Accessed on 25 September 2019.

6: Wanted: A revolution in agriculture

1. McNamara, R, 1973. *Address to the Board of Governors by Robert S McNamara.* Washington, DC: World Bank.
2. Reader, *Africa*, p 99; see also Diamond, *Guns, Germs and Steel*; Tignor, R, Adelman, J, Brown, P, Elman, B, Liu, X, Pittman, H and Shaw, B, 2010. *Worlds Together, Worlds Apart: A History of the World: Beginnings Through the Fifteenth Century.* Third edition. New York: WW Norton & Company. A 1997 study by the US Department of Agriculture concludes: 'Fifty five per cent of the land in Africa is unsuitable for any kind of agriculture except nomadic grazing.' See Eswaran, H, Almaraz, R, Reich, P and Zdruli, P, 1997. 'Soil quality and soil productivity in Africa.' *Journal of Sustainable Agriculture*, 10(4), pp 75–90.
3. Aydon, *A Brief History of Mankind*; Diamond, *Guns, Germs and Steel*; Reader, *Africa*.
4. Shahadah, A, 2017. 'Arab Slave Trade.' African Holocaust, 10 April. Available at www.arabslavetrade.com/. Accessed on 25 September 2019.
5. Lewis, T, 2018. 'Transatlantic slave trade.' Available at www.britannica.com/topic/transatlantic-slave-trade. Accessed on 25 September 2019.
6. Frankema, E, 2015. 'How Africa's colonial history affects its development.' WEF Regional Agenda, 15 July. Available at www.weforum.org/agenda/2015/07/how-africas-colonial-history-affects-its-development/. Accessed on 25 September 2019.
7. See Jochen Kraske with with William H. Becker, William Diamond and Louis Galambos, *Bankers with a Mission: The Presidents of the World Bank*, 1946-91, Oxford University Press, 1996, pp 159 to 211.
8. Rowen, H, 1980. 'McNamara to step down at World Bank next year.' *The Washington Post*, 10 June 1980.
9. These are, in ascending order of productivity, Eritrea, Botswana, Namibia, Somalia, Lesotho, Niger, Western Sahara, Zimbabwe, Sudan, Libya, the DRC, Mozambique, the Republic of Congo, Gambia, Chad, the CAR and Angola. The geographical spread highlights the breadth of the problem.
10. Veras, O, 2017. 'Agriculture in Africa: Potential versus reality.' How We Made it in Africa, 21 February 2017. Available at www.howwemadeitinafrica.com/agriculture-africa-potential-versus-reality/57635/. Accessed on 25 September 2019.
11. Historical data from the FAO. Forecast in IFs 7.36.

12. World Bank, 2018. *Agriculture in Africa: Telling Myths from Facts*. Available at www.worldbank.org/en/programs/africa-myths-and-facts. Accessed on 25 September 2019.

13. Hengl, T, Leenaars, JGB, Shepherd, KD, Walsh, MG, Heuvelink, GBM, Mamo, T, Tilahun, H, Berkhout, E, Cooper, M, Fegraus, E, Wheeler, I and Kwabena NA, 2017. 'Soil nutrient maps of Sub-Saharan Africa: Assessment of soil nutrient content at 250 m spatial resolution using machine learning.' *Nutrient Cycling in Agroecosystems*, 109(1), pp 77–102.

14. Fleshman, M, no date. 'Boosting African farm yields.' *African Renewal*, 2014. Available at www.un.org/africarenewal/magazine/special-edition-agriculture-2014/boosting-african-farm-yields. Accessed on 25 September 2019; and AGRA, 2016. *Africa Agriculture Status Report 2016: Progress Towards Agriculture Transformation in Sub-Saharan Africa*. Nairobi: Africa Fertilizer and Agribusiness Partnership.

15. Jayne, T and Ameyaw, DS, 2016. 'Africa's Emerging Agricultural Transformation: Evidence, Opportunities and Challenges.' In AGRA, *Africa Agriculture Status Report 2016*.

16. World Bank, no date. *Droughts Dominate Africa's Risk Environment*. Available at www.worldbank.org/en/programs/africa-myths-and-facts/publication/droughts-dominate-africas-risk-environment. Accessed on 25 September 2019.

17. AGRA, 2017. 'To ensure food security, keep soils healthy.' Available at agra.org/news/to-ensure-food-security-keep-soils-healthy/. Accessed on 25 September 2019.

18. Africa Food Security Leadership Dialogue, 2019. *Communique: Africa Food Security Leadership Dialogue*. 5 August. Available at allafrica.com/view/resource/main/main/id/00121601.html. Accessed on 25 September 2019.

19. Adegoke, Y, 2018. 'Why Europe dominates the global chocolate market while Africa produces all the cocoa.' *Quartz*, 4 July. Available at qz.com/africa/1320998/where-does-chocolate-come-from-europe-and-africas-roles-in-the-valuable-market/. Accessed on 25 September 2019.

20. Fofack, H, 2019. 'Overcoming the colonial development model of resource extraction for sustainable development in Africa.' Africa in Focus, 31 January. Available at www.brookings.edu/blog/africa-in-focus/2019/01/31/overcoming-the-colonial-development-model-of-resource-extraction-for-sustainable-development-in-africa/. Accessed on 25 September 2019.

21. Stunting in particular, which affects roughly 20 per cent of Africans, reduces cognitive development and can negatively impact the productivity levels of those that are affected by it for their entire lives.

22. The recommended daily caloric intake is about 2 500 calories a day for men and about 2 000 for women. See NHS, no date. 'What should my daily intake of calories be?' Available at www.nhs.uk/common-health-questions/food-and-diet/what-should-my-daily-intake-of-calories-be/. Accessed on 25 September 2019.

23. Hughes, BB, Kuhn, R, Peterson, CM, Rothman, DS and Solorzano, JR, 2011. *Patterns of Potential Human Progress, Volume 3: Improving Global Health*. Denver and Oxford: Paradigm Publishers and Oxford University Press.

24. World Bank, *Agriculture in Africa*.

25. World Bank and International Labour Organization, 2019. 'Employment in agriculture.' Available at data.worldbank.org/indicator/SL.AGR.EMPL.ZS?end=2018&locations=ET-CI&start=1991&view=chart. Accessed on 25 September 2019.
26. IPP Media, 2019. 'Value add in Africa: First steps in a long journey.' *Financial Times*, 23 January 2019. Available at www.ippmedia.com/en/business/value-add-africa-first-steps-long-journey. Accessed on 25 September 2019.
27. Losch, B, 2016. *Structural Transformation to Boost Youth Labour Demand in Sub-Saharan Africa: The Role of Agriculture, Rural Areas and Territorial Development.* Employment Working Paper no 204. Geneva: International Labour Office.
28. Ibid, p 2.
29. Fleshman, 'Boosting African farm yields'.
30. Tignor et al, *Worlds Together*.
31. Food and Agriculture Organization, 2019. 'Government expenditure on agriculture.' Available at www.fao.org/economic/ess/investment/expenditure/en/. Accessed on 25 September 2019.
32. In contrast to the tripling in growth cited earlier, this was an improvement across the entire country, so is understandably much smaller. See Lin, JY, 1988. 'The household responsibility system in China's agricultural reform: A theoretical and empirical study.' *Economic Development and Cultural Change*, 36(S3).
33. Simoes, AJG and Hidalgo, CA 2011. 'The economic complexity observatory: An analytical tool for understanding the dynamics of economic development.' Workshop at the 25th AAAI Conference on Artificial Intelligence, Menlo Park, California.
34. Galford, GL, Soares-Filho, B and Cerri, CEP, 2013. 'Prospects for land-use sustainability on the agricultural frontier of the Brazilian Amazon.' *Philosophical Transactions of the Royal Society B*, 368(1619) (5 June).
35. Meldrum, A, 2005. 'Mugabe turns back on west and looks east.' *The Guardian*, 19 April 2005.
36. Latin America and the Caribbean achieved a more rapid increase between 2000 and 2010, moving from roughly 6.9 tons per hectare to about 9.6 tons.
37. This intervention also includes a ten per cent increase in demand to stimulate domestic consumption
38. Food and Agriculture Organization, 2014. 'Aquastat: Did you know . . .?' Available at www.fao.org/nr/water/aquastat/didyouknow/index3.stm. Accessed on 25 September 2019.
39. By 93 million in low-income African countries, 32 million in lower-middle-income countries and 3 million in upper-middle-income countries, respectively, using the US$1.90, US$3.20 and US$5.50 poverty lines.
40. Numbers in market exchange rates (MER) except for GDP per capita, which is in purchasing power parity (PPP).
41. Historical data from the FAO. Forecast in IFs 7.36.
42. Some of these constraints can be overcome through technology, such as the use of precision irrigation and more precise application of fertiliser. Then there

is the potential of vertical farming, which could produce 180 million tons of food globally, according to some estimates.

43. World Economic Forum, 2017. *The Future of Jobs and Skills in Africa: Preparing the Region for the Fourth Industrial Revolution.* Geneva: World Economic Forum.

44. Ibid, p 4.

45. Abboud, L, 2018. 'The robot revolution down on the farm.' *Financial Times,* 5 December, 2018.

46. World Bank, *Agriculture in Africa.*

47. See farmdrive.co.ke/. Accessed on 25 September 2019.

48. In most of rural Africa this is objectively unknown. FarmDrive determines location in relation to known landmarks, for example a primary school.

49. Edwards, R, no date. 'Finding our farmers; or, Shamba Iko Wapi?' Available at farmdrive.co.ke/insights/3. Accessed on 25 September 2019.

50. Bird, J, 2018. '"Smart" insurance helps poor farmers to cut risk.' *Financial Times,* 5 December 2018.

51. World Food Programme and Oxfam America, 2011. 'The R4 Rural Resilience Initiative.' Available at www1.wfp.org/r4-rural-resilience-initiative. Accessed on 25 September 2019.

52. Gebre, S, 2016. 'AGRA plans to invest $500 million in African seed companies.' *Bloomberg,* 8 September 2016. Available at www.bloomberg.com/news/articles/ 2016-09-07/agra-plans-to-invest-500-million-in-african-seed-companies. Accessed on 25 September 2019.

53. Food and Agriculture Organization, no date. 'Key facts on food loss and waste you should know!' Available at www.fao.org/save-food/resources/keyfindings/ en/. Accessed on 25 September 2019.

54. See www.inspirafarms.com/about-us/?lang=za. Accessed on 25 September 2019.

55. See agrocenta.com/ and www.zenvus.com/. Accessed on 25 September 2019.

56. Food and Agriculture Organization, 2003. 'Crop production and natural resource use.' In J Bruinsma (ed), *World Agriculture: Towards 2015/2030: An FAO Study.* London: Routledge.

57. The International Institute of Tropical Agriculture (IITA, www.iita.org/) does particularly impressive work in this regard.

7: Inequality and poverty

1. Hobbes, T, 1660. *Leviathan.* Available at www.ttu.ee/public/m/mart-murdvee/ EconPsy/6/Hobbes_Thomas_1660_The_Leviathan.pdf. Accessed on 25 September 2019.

2. Roser, M and Ortiz-Ospina, E, 2018. 'Literacy.' Our World in Data. Available at ourworldindata.org/literacy. Accessed on 25 September 2019.

3. This analysis uses US$1.90 as the extreme poverty line.

4. Ruchir Sharma refers to before and after the 2007/08 financial crisis. In Europe, the region with the highest average income, the national income share of the top ten per cent is only 37 per cent. It is highest in the Middle East, at 61 per cent. The average for sub-Saharan Africa is 54 per cent, marginally below

the average for Brazil and India, at 55 per cent each. See Sharma, *The Rise and Fall of Nations*, p 5.

5. Roser, M, 2016. 'Global Economic Inequality.' Our World in Data. Available at ourworldindata.org/global-economic-inequality. Accessed on 25 September 2019.

6. Kozul-Wright, R, 2017. *The Trade and Development Report 2017. Beyond Austerity: Towards a Global New Deal.* New York and Geneva: United Nations Conference on Trade and Development.

7. Oxfam, 2018. *The Commitment to Reducing Inequality Index 2018.* Development Finance International and Oxfam report. Available at oxfamilibrary.openrepository.com/bitstream/handle/10546/620553/rr-commitment-reducing-inequality-index-2018-091018-en.pdf. Accessed on 25 September 2019.

8. Kwasi, FA, 2011. *Growth, Inequality, and Poverty Reduction in Developing Countries: Recent Global Evidence.* Helsinki: WIDER Working Paper 2011/001; UNU-WIDER and Ostry, JD, Berg, A and Tsangarides, CG, 2014. *Redistribution, Inequality, and Growth.* Washington, DC: International Monetary Fund.

9. Hughes, BB, 2007. *Forecasting Global Economic Growth with Endogenous Multifactor Productivity: The International Futures (IFs) Approach.* Working Paper 2007.12.31, Pardee Center for International Futures, Josef Korbel School of International Studies, University of Denver, p 2, note 2.

10. The IFs forecast on poverty levels uses the average levels of income and a log-normal distribution as indicated by the Gini index. Since the internal calculation using those variables will, however, almost inevitably produce a rate of poverty at odds with those provided by national surveys, the system computes an adjustment in the first year for the subsequent forecast years.

11. Edward, P and Sumner, A, 2013. *The Future of Global Poverty in a Multi-Speed World: New Estimates of Scale and Location, 2010–2030.* Center for Global Development, Working Paper 327.

12. Ravallion, M and Chen, S, 2007. 'China's (uneven) progress against poverty.' *Journal of Development Economics*, 82(1), pp 1–32; see also World Bank, 2019. 'The World Bank in China'. Available at www.worldbank.org/en/country/china/overview. Accessed on 25 September 2019.

13. Express News Service, 2018. 'UNDP report lauds India's strides in reducing poverty in past decade.' *The Indian Express*, 25 September 2019. Available at indianexpress.com/article/india/undp-report-lauds-indias-strides-in-reducing-poverty-in-past-decade/. Accessed on 25 September 2019. Still, 650 million people (49 per cent) on the Indian subcontinent continue to live in debilitating conditions (using the US$3.20 poverty line for low-middle-income countries).

14. The difference was about 19 percentage points.

15. In 1970 Botswana's average GDP per capita was US$1 246 below that of Ghana. Within four years, average income levels in Botswana surpassed those of Ghana, and by 1999 GDP per capita in Botswana was four times higher (or US$7 167) than in Ghana.

16. The MPI measures multiple deprivations in the same households in education, health and living standards across ten indicators ranging from nutrition and

child mortality to assets. In 2010 the UNDP also launched its Inequality-adjusted Human Development Index (IHDI) and Gender Inequality Index (GII).

17. Currently IFs initialises its poverty forecasts from US$1.90 and uses a lognormal Gini distribution for its estimates and forecasts at other levels. Its estimations and forecasts of poverty should therefore be treated with care.

18. IFs 7.36, initialising data from UN Population Division World Population Prospects medium-variant life expectancy.

19. Sharma, D, 2018. 'Why the World Bank is taking a wide-angle view of poverty.' Future Development, 14 November. Available at www.brookings.edu/blog/future-development/2018/11/14/why-the-world-bank-is-taking-a-wide-angle-view-of-poverty/. Accessed on 25 September 2019.

20. If I were to use US$1.90 for all of Africa and not distinguish between the three income groups, the 2018 poverty rate would be 36 per cent and would decline to 28 per cent by 2040.

21. IFs 7.36, initialising from UN Population Division World Population Prospects medium-variant life expectancy.

22. Algeria, another upper-middle-income country, barely escaped inclusion in the list with a poverty rate of 49 per cent, although a large portion of its extremely poor population is likely to cross the US$5.50 poverty threshold in the near future.

23. The top 1 per cent of South Africans own 70.9 per cent of the country's wealth, while the bottom 60 per cent control only 7 per cent of the country's assets. See Sulla, V and Zikhali, P, 2018. *Overcoming Poverty and Inequality in South Africa: An Assessment of Drivers, Constraints and Opportunities*. Johannesburg: International Bank for Reconstruction and Development/The World Bank.

24. Cilliers, J, Hughes, B and Turner, S, 2015. *Reasonable Goals for Reducing Poverty in Africa: Targets for the Post-MDGs and Agenda 2063*. Pretoria: Institute for Security Studies.

25. Using the US$5.50 poverty line for upper-middle-income countries.

26. *BusinessTech*, 2017. 'This is who is paying South Africa's tax.' Available at businesstech.co.za/news/finance/207631/this-is-who-is-paying-south-africas-tax/. Accessed on 25 September 2019.

27. StatsSA, 2015. *A Statistical Summary of Social Grants in South Africa*. Pretoria: Strategic Monitoring Branch, Strategy and Business Development; see also Zembe-Mkabile, W, 2017. 'Social grants: More than just money at stake.' Available at www.news24.com/Columnists/GuestColumn/social-grants-theres-more-than-just-money-at-stake-20170314. Accessed on 25 September 2019.

28. BBC, 2019. 'Kenya's controversial biometric project.' [Sound recording]. Available at www.bbc.co.uk/programmes/p078gm18. Accessed on 25 September 2019.

29. *The Economist*, 2018. 'African governments let too many taxpayers off the hook.' Available at www.economist.com/finance-and-economics/2018/08/18/african-governments-let-too-many-taxpayers-off-the-hook. Accessed on 25 September 2019. See also Coulibaly, SB and Gandhi, D, 2018. *Mobilization of Tax Revenues in Africa: State of Play and Policy Options*. Brookings Institution, 17 October

2018. Available at www.brookings.edu/research/mobilization-of-tax-revenues-in-africa/. Accessed on 25 September 2019.

30. Ibid.

31. For example, in India the fertiliser subsidy alone is about 0.8 per cent of GDP and is hugely distorting.

32. World Bank, 2018. 'The story of Takaful and Karama cash transfer program.' Feature story, 15 November 2018. Available at www.worldbank.org/en/news/feature/2018/11/15/the-story-of-takaful-and-karama-cash-transfer-program. Accessed on 25 September 2019.

33. Schreiber, L, 2018. *Funding Development: Ethiopia Tries to Strengthen its Tax System, 2007–2018.* Innovations for Successful Societies, Princeton University.

34. A cumulative additional amount of US$1 549 billion is transferred over the 20 years from 2020 to 2040.

35. Libya and Equatorial Guinea will potentially also do so, but the IFs system does not yet fully capture the impact of the civil war in Libya, while the data on Equatorial Guinea is highly suspect. According to IFs, extreme poverty in Libya in 2017 was at 25 per cent (using the US$5.50 poverty line). Previously, using the US$1.90 poverty line for all African countries, eight countries were on track to meet the World Bank target of less than three per cent of people living below the poverty line by 2030, namely, Gabon, Tunisia, Egypt, Algeria, Morocco, Libya, Mauritius and Equatorial Guinea.

8: Changing the productive structures

1. Bhorat et al, *Sub-Saharan Africa's Manufacturing Sector.* See also Newman, C, Page, J, Rand, J, Shimeles, A, Söderbom, M and Tarp, F 2016. 'The Pursuit of Industry: Policies and Outcomes.' In *Manufacturing Transformation: Comparative Studies of Industrial Development in Africa and Emerging Asia.* Oxford: Oxford University Press; and Fox, L, Thomas, AH and Haines, C, 2017. *Structural Transformation in Employment and Productivity: What Can Africa Hope For?* Washington: International Monetary Fund.

2. World Bank Open Data, data.worldbank.org/.

3. Newman et al, 'The Pursuit of Industry', p 5.

4. The challenge, notes Carol Newman and her co-authors, is that 'services have been absorbing workers faster than output in the sector has been increasing. The relative productivity of African market services fell from 3.0 times the economy-wide average in 1990 to 1.8 in 2010, suggesting that the marginal productivity of new services workers is low and possibly negative'; see Newman et al, *Manufacturing Transformation*; see also Bhorat et al, *Sub-Saharan Africa's Manufacturing Sector*, p 5.

5. Chang, H-J, 2003. *Kicking Away the Ladder: Development Strategy in Historical Perspective.* London: Anthem Press, p 43.

6. Newman et al, 'The Pursuit of Industry', p 5.

7. Banga, R, Kumar, D and Cobbina, P, 2018. *Identifying and Promoting Regional Value Chains in Leather and Leather Products in Africa.* Geneva: United Nations Conference on Trade and Development.

8. Lund, S, Manyika, J, Woetzel, J, Bughin, J, Krishnan, M, Seong, J and Muir, M, 2019. 'Executive Summary.' In *Globalization in Transition: The Future of Trade and Value Chains*. New York: McKinsey Global Institute; see also Dollar, D, 2019. 'Executive summary.' In *Technological Innovation, Supply Chain Trade, and Workers in a Globalized World*. Geneva: World Trade Organization.

9. Szirmai, A, 2009. 'Is manufacturing still the main engine of growth in developing countries?' Blog post, Wider Angle, May 2009. Available at www.wider.unu.edu/publication/manufacturing-still-main-engine-growth-developing-countries. Accessed on 25 September 2019.

10. Monga, C, 2017. 'Industrialization: A Primer.' In *Industrialize Africa: Strategies, Policies, Institutions, and Financing*. Abidjan: African Development Bank Group.

11. Freemantle, S and Stevens, J, 2010. 'Lessons for Africa inherent in India's meteoric economic ascent.' *Economics: BRIC and Africa*, Standard Bank, 9 June 2010, p 5.

12. Baldwin, R, 2016. *The Great Convergence: Information Technology and the New Globalization*. Cambridge: Harvard University Press.

13. McKinsey Global Institute, 2016. *Digital Globalization: The New Era of Global Flows*. New York: McKinsey & Company.

14. McKinsey Global Institute, 2017. 'What's now and next in analytics, AI, and automation.' Executive briefing. Available at www.mckinsey.com/featured-insights/digital-disruption/whats-now-and-next-in-analytics-ai-and-automation. Accessed on 25 September 2019.

15. African Development Bank Group, 'Introductory remarks'. Ethiopia, Kenya, Morocco, Seychelles, South Africa and Tanzania have managed to make strides into global value chains (GVCs). Manufacturing leads the integration into GVCs, ahead of agriculture and business services.

16. Ibid, pp 16 and 20.

17. African Center for Economic Transformation, *The Future of Work in Africa: The Impact of the Fourth Industrial Revolution on Job Creation and Skill Development in Africa*.

18. De Backer, K and Flaig, D, 2017. *The Future of Global Value Chains: Business As Usual or 'A New Normal'?* OECD Science, Technology and Innovation Policy Papers No 41, July 2017. Paris: OECD Publishing, p 21.

19. Simons, B, 2019. 'Africa's unsung "industrial revolution".' Blog post, Center for Global Development, 21 March 2019. Available at www.cgdev.org/blog/africas-unsung-industrial-revolution. Accessed on 25 September 2019.

20. Newman et al, 'The Pursuit of Industry'.

21. Ibid, p 18.

22. Ibid, p 19.

23. Ibid.

24. Newman C, Rand, J, Page, J, Shimeles, A, Söderbom, M and Tarp, F. 'Can Africa Industrialize?' In *Manufacturing Transformation: Comparative Studies of Industrial Development in Africa and Emerging Asia*. Oxford: Oxford University Press, 2016.

25. Mills, G, 2019. *A Tale of Two Free Zones: Learning from Africa's Success*. The Brenthurst Foundation Discussion Paper 01/2019, February, pp 17–20.

26. Ibid, p 12.

27. Manyika et al, *Manufacturing the Future*.

28. World Bank Open Data. Note: no data for Burundi, Eritrea, Libya, Somalia, South Sudan.

29. Bhorat et al, *Sub-Saharan Africa's Manufacturing Sector*. This understanding consists of the diversity of firms and productive capabilities described as non-tradeable networks of collective know-how, such as logistics, finance and supply and knowledge networks.

30. Ibid, pp 9–10.

31. Leke, Chironga and Desvaux, 'Africa's overlooked business revolution'.

32. Jayaram, K, Kassiri, O and Sun, IY, 2017. *The Closest Look Yet at Chinese Economic Engagement in Africa*. McKinsey & Company report, June 2017. Available at www.mckinsey.com/featured-insights/middle-east-and-africa/the-closest-look-yet-at-chinese-economic-engagement-in-africa. Accessed on 25 September 2019.

33. Ibid.

34. Ibid.

35. Oosthuizen, M, Linde, E, Durrant, K-L and Gopaldas, R, 2018. *The Future of Energy and Power Utilities in Africa*. Johannesburg: Gordon Institute of Business Science, p 65.

36. Bhorat et al, *Sub-Saharan Africa's Manufacturing Sector*, p 92.

37. Page, J, 2017. 'Industrial Policy in Africa: From State Leadership to the Investment Climate.' In *Industrialize Africa: Strategies, Policies, Institutions, and Financing*. Abidjan: African Development Bank Group, p 81.

38. Newman et al, 'The Pursuit of Industry', p 5.

39. African Development Bank, 2017. *Industrialize Africa: Strategies, Policies, Institutions, and Financing*. African Development Bank Group, p 46.

40. Newman et al, 'Can Africa Industrialize?', p 258.

41. Gelb, A, Meyer, C, Ramachandran, V and Wadhwa, D, 2017. *Can Africa Be a Manufacturing Destination? Labor Costs in Comparative Perspective*. Center for Global Development Working Paper 466, 15 October, p 8.

42. Newman et al, 'Can Africa Industrialize?', p 259. Gelb and his co-authors question some of these conclusions: '[F]or any given level of GDP, labour is more costly for firms that are located in sub-Saharan Africa. However, we also find that there are a few countries in Africa that, on a labour cost basis, may be potential candidates for manufacturing – Ethiopia in particular stands out'; see Gelb et al, 'Can Africa Be a Manufacturing Destination?'.

43. IFs uses the Fraser Institute's economic freedom index as a proxy for the level of economic freedom. The intervention means that Africa converges to the level of South Asia by 2030.

44. IFs 7.36, initialising from IMF, *World Economic Outlook 2017*.

45. Ibid.

46. Bughin, J, Chironga, M, Desvaux, G, Ermias, T, Jacobson, P, Kassiri, O, Leke, A, Lund, S, Van Wamelen, A and Zouaoui, Y, 2016. *Lions on the Move II: Realizing the Potential of Africa's Economies*. New York: McKinsey & Company.

47. Ibid, p 14.
48. Manyika et al, *Manufacturing the Future.*
49. Actually, levels of peak manufacturing employment have declined with each wave of industrialisation. See Bhorat et al, *Sub-Saharan Africa's Manufacturing Sector.*

9: The future of work in Africa

1. Global Commission on the Future of Work, *Work for a Brighter Future.*
2. African Development Bank, 2017. *Growth and Job Creation: Policy Options for Pro-Employment Growth.* Abidjan: African Development Bank Group.
3. Abdychev, A, Alonso, C, Alper, E, Desruelle, D, Kothari, S, Liu, Y, Perinet, M, Rehman, S, Schimmelpfennig, A and Sharma, P, 2018. *The Future of Work in Sub-Saharan Africa.* Washington, DC: International Monetary Fund.
4. International Labour Organization, *World Employment and Social Outlook: Trends 2018.*
5. Kapsos, S, 2005. *The Employment Intensity of Growth: Trends and Macroeconomic Determinants.* Geneva: International Labour Office.
6. World Bank, 2019. 'Human Capital Project.' Available at www.worldbank.org/en/publication/human-capital. Accessed on 25 September 2019.
7. International Labour Organization, *World Employment and Social Outlook: Trends 2018*, p 2.
8. See, for example, Joseph Stiglitz's keynote address, 'Beyond manufacturing export-led growth', to the UNU-WIDER Development Conference in Helsinki, 13–15 September 2018, Available at www.wider.unu.edu/plenary-session/beyond-manufacturing-export-led-growth. Accessed on 25 September 2019. See also Newfarmer, RS, Page, J and Tarp, F (eds), 2018. *Industries Without Smokestacks: Industrialization in Africa Reconsidered.* Oxford: Oxford University Press. Available at www.wider.unu.edu/publication/industries-without-smokestacks-2. Accessed on 25 September 2019. And see also Page, J. no date. 'How industries without smokestacks can address Africa's youth unemployment crisis.' In *Harvesting Africa's Youth Dividend: A New Approach for Large-Scale Job Creation.* Available at www.brookings.edu/wp-content/uploads/2019/01/BLS18234_BRO_book_007_CH3.pdf. Accessed on 25 September 2019.
9. Smith, N, 2019. 'Africa could become the new China if it plays to its industrial strengths.' *ThePrint*, 4 June. Available at theprint.in/opinion/africa-could-become-the-new-china-if-it-plays-to-its-industrial-strengths/245303/. Accessed on 25 September 2019.
10. According to the ILO, a person is unemployed if he/she is not in employment, is actively seeking work, and is available to take up work. International Labour Organization, 2013. *Resolution I Adopted at the 19th International Conference of Labour Statisticians.* Geneva: International Labour Office.
11. International Labour Organization. *Women and Men in the Informal Economy*, p 49.
12. International Labour Organization, 2019. 'Decent work.' Available at www.ilo.org/global/topics/decent-work/lang--en/index.htm. Accessed on 25 September 2019.
13. International Labour Organization, *World Employment and Social Outlook:*

Trends 2018, pp 11–13. Moderate and extreme poverty would include the share of workers living in households with income or consumption per capita below US$3.10 per day.

14. International Monetary Fund, 2017. 'Chart of the week: the potential for growth and Africa's informal economy. Blog post, IMF Blog, 8 August 2017. Available at blogs.imf.org/2017/08/08/chart-of-the-week-the-potential-for-growth-and-africas-informal-economy/. Accessed on 25 September 2019.

15. International Labour Organization, 2018. *Women and Men in the Informal Economy: A Statistical Picture*. Third edition. Geneva: International Labour Office, p 3. Available at www.ilo.org/global/publications/books/WCMS_626831/lang--en/index.htm. Accessed on 25 September 2019.

16. International Labour Organization, *World Employment and Social Outlook: Trends 2018*, p 14. The gender gap in informal employment (the rate at which women are more unemployed than men) in some parts of sub-Saharan Africa is more than 20 per cent and increases among the youth.

17. And 36 per cent when employment in agriculture is excluded; see International Labour Organization, *Women and Men in the Informal Economy*, p 29.

18. African Center for Economic Transformation, 2017. *African Transformation Report 2017: Agriculture Powering Africa's Economic Transformation*, p 1. Available at acetforafrica.org/publications/african-transformation-report-2017/african-transformation-report-2017/. Accessed on 25 September 2019.

19. Fox et al, *Structural Transformation in Employment and Productivity*, p viii.

20. Bhorat et al, *Sub-Saharan Africa's Manufacturing Sector*.

21. Abdychev et al, *The Future of Work in Sub-Saharan Africa*, p 1.

22. *The Economist*, 25 May 2019. The feature is entitled 'The great jobs boom'.

23. Sharma, *The Rise and Fall of Nations*, p 56.

24. Monga, 'Industrialization: A Primer', p 10. See also United Nations Conference on Trade and Development, 2017. *Trade and Development, Beyond Austerity: Towards a Global New Deal*. Geneva: United Nations Conference on Trade and Development, p ix.

25. Manyika, J, Chui, M, Miremadi, M, Bughin, J, George, K, Willmott, P and Dewhurst, M. 2017. *Harnessing Automation for a Future that Works*. Report, McKinsey Global Institute. Available at www.mckinsey.com/featured-insights/digital-disruption/harnessing-automation-for-a-future-that-works. Accessed on 25 September 2019.

26. McKinsey estimates that across 46 countries (a mixture of developing and developed economies) it looks as if by 2030 a range with a midpoint of 16 per cent of occupations will have been automated and dislocated by automation. McKinsey podcast, 'What is the Future of Work?', 1 December 2017.

27. African Center for Economic Transformation, *African Transformation Report 2017*, p 2.

28. European Commission, 2016. *The Future of Work Skills and Resilience for a World of Change*. EPSC Strategic Notes, Issue 13, p 11.

29. Ibid, p 4.

30. Ibid, p 2.

31. Africans in the informal sector do not have much job security, and global devel-

opments such as the gig economy appear to shift the risk of employment steadily to the employee; see European Commission, *The Future of Work Skills*, p 2.

32. Mo Ibrahim Foundation, *Africa's Youth*, p 46.
33. *The Economist*, 25 May 2019.
34. World Bank, 2019. *Identification For Development (ID4D) Global Dataset*. Available at datacatalog.worldbank.org/dataset/identification-development-global-dataset. Accessed on 25 September 2019.
35. See 'My Digital Address' at www.ghanapostgps.com/.
36. The intelligence Box (iBox) is a home-grown proprietary technology for the delivery of premium, curricular-specific, educational content for high schools and non-formal and skills training; see B&FTonline, 2018. 'Out of the Box.' Available at thebftonline.com/2018/opinions/investing-in-human-capital-innovation-and-knowledge-with-the-ibox/. Accessed on 25 September 2019.
37. Dean, J and Cisse, M, 2018. 'Google AI in Ghana.' Blog post, Google Africa Blog, 13 June. Available at africa.googleblog.com/2018/06/google-ai-in-ghana.html. Accessed on 25 September 2019.
38. This was done by using labinformshrm and gdpinformlabshr within the IFs forecasting system.
39. Ng'weno, A and Porteous, D, 2018. *Let's Be Real: The Informal Sector and the Gig Economy are the Future, and the Present, of Work in Africa*. Available at www.cgdev.org/publication/lets-be-real-informal-sector-and-gig-economy-are-future-and-present-work-africa. Accessed on 25 September 2019.
40. Ibid.
41. Ibid.
42. Mo Ibrahim Foundation, *Africa's Youth*, p 44.

10: Technological innovation and the power of leapfrogging

1. As quoted in Goodell, J, 2011. 'Steve Jobs in 1994: The *Rolling Stone* Interview.' *Rolling Stone*, 17 January 2011. Available at www.rollingstone.com/culture/culture-news/steve-jobs-in-1994-the-rolling-stone-interview-231132/. Accessed on 25 September 2019.
2. The IMF estimates that Africa's deficit in physical infrastructure reduces growth by two percentage points a year; see International Monetary Fund, 2014. 'Is It Time for an Infrastructure Push? The Macroeconomic Effects of Public Investment.' In *World Economic Outlook: Legacies, Clouds, Uncertainties*. Washington, DC: IMF, pp 75–114.
3. Within IFs, multifactor productivity is composed of physical, social, human and knowledge capital.
4. International Monetary Fund, 'Is It Time for an Infrastructure Push?', pp 75–114.
5. Bivens, J, 2014. *The Short- and Long-Term Impact of Infrastructure Investments on Employment and Economic Activity in the US Economy*. Washington, DC: Economic Policy Institute.
6. Frey, T, no date. 'The Curse of Infrastructure.' Available at foresightfordevelopment.org/featured/infrastructure-v?ct=t(FFD_Aug_2018_Future_of_Infrastructure). Accessed on 25 September 2019.

7. Originally by Eole Water.

8. ZLM Project Engineering, 2019. 'The case for offshore energy in KwaZulu-Natal.' 26 April. Draft IRP released by the South African Department of Energy.

9. See Sculpteo, 2018. '3D printing for construction: What is Contour Crafting?' Blog post, 27 June. Available at www.sculpteo.com/blog/2018/06/27/3d-printing-for-construction-what-is-contour-crafting/. Accessed on 25 September 2019; and Saunders, S, 2018. 'Contour crafting will develop concrete 3D printer for disaster relief, thanks to DoD contract.' Available at 3dprint.com/222125/contour-crafting-dod-contract/. Accessed on 25 September 2019.

10. Volkswagen, 2018. 'Rwanda's mobile revolution.' Available at www.volkswagenag.com/en/news/stories/2018/07/rwanda_s-mobile-revolution.html. Accessed on 25 September 2019.

11. Rapier, R, 2017. 'How the shale boom turned the world upside down.' *Forbes*, 21 April. Available at www.forbes.com/sites/rrapier/2017/04/21/how-the-shale-boom-turned-the-world-upside-down/#13052ef77d24. Accessed on 25 September 2019.

12. Ibid; and Crooks, E, 2018. 'Opec strikes a deal, CO2 emissions rise but Shell targets cuts, historic US oil exports and the positives of electric scooters.' *Financial Times*, 8 December.

13. Crooks, E, 2018. 'US energy independence is not the shining prize it seems.' *Financial Times*, 29 December.

14. USAID, 2018. *Power Africa 2018: Annual Report*. Available at www.usaid.gov/sites/default/files/documents/1860/2018-Annual_Report1015_508.pdf. Accessed on 25 September 2019; ZLM Project Engineering, 'The case for offshore energy in KwaZulu-Natal'.

15. Coony, J, Jaffe, AM and Lewis, JI, 2018. *Event: The Future of Renewable Energy*. Available at www.cfr.org/event/future-renewable-energy. Accessed on 25 September 2019.

16. Patel, S, 2018. 'Power in Africa: Prospects for an economic foothold.' *Power*, 6 January. Available at www.powermag.com/power-in-africa-prospects-for-an-economic-foothold/. Accessed on 25 September 2019.

17. African Development Bank Group, 2013. *The High Cost of Electricity Generation in Africa*. Available at www.afdb.org/en/blogs/afdb-championing-inclusive-growth-across-africa/post/the-high-cost-of-electricity-generation-in-africa-11496/. Accessed on 25 September 2019.

18. Hill, JS, 2018. 'China installs 24.3 Gigawatts of solar in first half of 2018.' CleanTechnica, 6 August. Available at cleantechnica.com/2018/08/06/china-installs-24-3-gigawatts-in-first-half-of-2018/. Accessed on 25 September 2019. See also Enerdata, 2018. 'China's installed capacity grew by 7.6% in 2017 to nearly 1800 GW.' Available at www.enerdata.net/publications/daily-energy-news/chinas-installed-capacity-grew-76-2017-nearly-1800-gw.html. Accessed on 25 September 2019.

19. The project is controversial due to the lack of an environmental impact assessment and a lack of stakeholder consultation with downstream riparian states, Egypt in particular. See International Crisis Group, 2019. *Bridging the Gap in*

the Nile Waters Dispute. Africa Report no 271, 19 March. And Flamik, M, 2018. 'Grand Ethiopian Renaissance Dam causes turbulence within East Africa.' Available at www.americansecurityproject.org/grand-ethiopian-renaissance-dam/. Accessed on 25 September 2019.

20. International Rivers, no date. 'Grand Inga Hydroelectric Project: An overview.' Available at www.internationalrivers.org/resources/grand-inga-hydroelectric-project-an-overview-3356. Accessed on 25 September 2019.

21. Clowes, W, 2018. 'Congo to start $13.9 billion hydropower project this year.' *Bloomberg*, 13 June. Available at www.bloomberg.com/news/articles/2018-06-13/congo-plans-to-start-13-9-billion-hydropower-project-this-year. Accessed on 25 September 2019.

22. Bii, B and Kimuge, S, 2018. 'Lake Turkana wind power project set to come on line by September.' *Daily Nation*, 3 June. Available at www.nation.co.ke/business/Lake-Turkana-wind-power-project-set-to-come-/996-4593956-x16b1fz/index.html. Accessed on 25 September 2019. Installed capacity in Chad is 130 MW and Liberia 126 MW, according to USAID's Power Africa; see USAID, 2018. *Chad Power Africa Fact Sheet.* Available atwww.usaid.gov/powerafrica/chad. Accessed on 25 September 2019.

23. Ibid.

24. United Nations, 2018. *UN Support Plan for the Sahel: Working Together for a Prosperous and Peaceful Sahel*, New York: United Nations.

25. Donnenfeld, Z, Cilliers, J, Kwasi, S, Shah, SR and Welborn, L, 2018. *Shaping the Future: Strategies for Sustainable Development in Kenya.* Report, 20 June. Pretoria: Institute for Security Studies. Available at issafrica.org/research/east-africa-report/shaping-the-future-strategies-for-sustainable-development-in-kenya. Accessed on 25 September 2019.

26. Crooks, E, 2018. 'The year in energy.' *Financial Times*, 23 December.

27. Bloomberg NEF estimates that the capital costs of a utility-scale lithium-ion storage system will fall by 52 per cent by 2030.

28. Christian, J, 2018. 'New details about Tesla's gargantuan 'megapack' power storage unit.' Available at futurism.com/the-byte/new-details-teslas-gargantuan-megapack. Accessed on 25 September 2019.

29. Robitzski, D, 2018. 'China is building its first huge battery storage facility.' Available at futurism.com/the-byte/china-battery-storage-facility. Accessed on 25 September 2019.

30. Crooks, 'The year in energy'.

31. Sanderson, 'Hydrogen power'.

32. Mo Ibrahim Foundation, *Africa's Youth*, p 75.

33. Ibid.

34. Johnson, O, 2019. *United Nations Economic Commission For Africa Conference of Planning, Economic and Finance Ministers Adebayo Adedeji Lecture 2019.* Marrakech: United Nations Economic Commission for Africa.

35. 'Eureka moment.' *The Economist*, 26 September 2009.

36. Czernich, N, Falck, O, Kretschmer, T and Woessmann, L, 2011. 'Broadband infrastructure and economic growth.' *The Economic Journal*, 121(552).

37. Houser, K, 2018. 'Alphabet will bring its balloon-powered internet to Kenya.' *The Byte*, 19 July. Available at futurism.com/the-byte/balloon-powered-internet-alphabet-kenya. Accessed on 26 September 2019.

38. Suri, T and Jack, W, 2016. 'The long-run poverty and gender impacts of mobile money.' *Science*, 354(6317), pp 1288–1292.

39. Leke, A, Chironga, M and Desvaux, G, 2018. *Africa's Business Revolution: How to Succeed in the World's Next Big Growth Market*. Brighton: Harvard Business School Press.

40. Open Society Justice Initiative, 2010. *Corruption and Its Consequences in Equatorial Guinea*. Briefing paper. Available at www.opensocietyfoundations.org/publications/corruption-and-its-consequences-equatorial-guinea. Accessed on 26 September 2019.

41. Dugmore, H. 2010. 'The impact of new media on recent sub-Saharan Africa elections (and African Democracy in general).' PowerPoint presentation shared with the author, 26 November.

42. Gilbert, P, 2018. 'Rain will launch 5G in early 2019.' *ITWeb*, 13 November. Available at www.itweb.co.za/content/6GxRKqY8n3LMb3Wj. Accessed on 26 September 2019.

43. United Nations Economic Commission for Africa, 2019. *Fiscal Policy for Financing Sustainable Development in Africa*. Addis Ababa: Uneca, p 113.

44. Ibid, p xiii.

45. The average potential for improvements for emerging economies is roughly six per cent of GDP in 2030; see McKinsey Global Institute, 2019. 'The value of digital ID for the global economy and society' [Video]. Available at www.mckinsey.com/featured-insights/innovation-and-growth/the-value-of-digital-id-for-the-global-economy-and-society. Accessed on 26 September 2019.

46. International Monetary Fund, 'Chart of the week'.

47. International Labour Organization, *Women and Men in the Informal Economy*, p 3.

48. According to *The Economist*, 2017. See 'China's embrace of a new electricity-transmission technology holds lessons for others.' 14 January.

49. All GDP per capita figures are in purchasing power parity.

50. IFs 7.36, initialising from IMF, *World Economic Outlook 2017*.

51. Von Haldenwang, C, 2018. *Trade Investment and Tax Cooperation: Tax Competition*. T20 Argentina 2018. Available at t20argentina.org/wp-content/uploads/2018/05/GSx-TF-7-Tax_competition-DEF_vf-1.pdf. Accessed on 26 September 2019.

52. Grow Global, 2018. 'Jack Ma launches new global e-trading platform in Kigali, Rwanda.' Available at www.growglobal.com/jack-ma-launches-new-global-e-trading-platform-in-kigali-rwanda/. Accessed on 26 September 2019.

11: Trade and growth

1. As quoted in Tralac, 2018. 'AEC2018: Africa must focus on its big resource –

its young people, experts urge.' Blog post, Trade Law Centre, 2 December. Available at www.tralac.org/news/article/13768-aec2018-africa-must-focus-on-its-big-resource-its-young-people-experts-urge.html. Accessed on 26 September 2019.

2. United Nations Comtrade. Note: includes intra-African trade.

3. See World Trade Organization, no date. 'Trade facilitation'. Available at www.wto.org/english/tratop_e/tradfa_e/tradfa_e.htm. Accessed on 26 September 2019.

4. Adopted under the Tokyo Round of GATT in 1979.

5. Agreed on at the UN World Trade Conference (Unctad II) in 1968 as a non-reciprocal facility that countries such as the EU and the US bestow on least-developed countries.

6. Trade under AGOA quadrupled in value from 2002 to 2008, a year when it reached US$100 billion, but fell back in 2017 to US$39 billion, according to figures compiled by USAID. The US Congress determines annually which countries are eligible for AGOA. As opposed to Everything But Arms, AGOA is based on progress in meeting criteria such as the establishment of a market-based economy, rule of law, elimination of barriers to US trade and investment and protection of workers' rights.

7. Fernandes, AM, Maemir, H, Mattoo, A and Rojas, AF, 2018. *Are Trade Preferences a Panacea? AGOA and African Exports.* Policy Research working paper no WPS 8753. Washington, DC: The World Bank, pp 4, 21–22. See also World Trade Organization, no date. 'Textiles Monitoring Body (TMB): The Agreement on Textiles and Clothing.' Available at www.wto.org/english/tratop_e/texti_e/texintro_e.htm. Accessed on 26 September 2019.

8. Fernandes et al, *Are Trade Preferences a Panacea?*, pp 41–42.

9. European Commission, *List of GSP Beneficiary Countries (as of 01 January 2019).* Available at trade.ec.europa.eu/doclib/docs/2019/may/tradoc_157889.pdf. Accessed on 26 September 2019.

10. European Commission, 2019. 'Generalized Scheme of Preferences (GSP).' Available at ec.europa.eu/trade/policy/countries-and-regions/development/generalised-scheme-of-preferences/. Accessed on 26 September 2019.

11. Schmieg, E, 2019. *EU and Africa: Investment, Trade, Development.* SWP Comment. Berlin: Stiftung Wissenschaft und Politik.

12. European Commission, 2018. 'Economic Partnership Agreements (EPAs) September 2018.' Available at trade.ec.europa.eu/doclib/docs/2017/february/tradoc_155300.pdf. Accessed on 26 September 2019.

13. Botswana, Lesotho, Mozambique, Namibia, South Africa and eSwatini. Angola has an option to join the agreement in future.

14. Mevel, S, Valensisi, G and Karingi, S, 2015. *The Economic Partnership Agreements and Africa's Integration and Transformation Agenda: The Cases of West Africa and Eastern and Southern Africa Regions.* Draft conference paper, 12 May. Available at www.gtap.agecon.purdue.edu/resources/download/7649.pdf. Accessed on 26 September 2019.

15. European Commission, 'Economic Partnership Agreements (EPAs) September 2018'.

16. AFP, 2019. 'US-African trade lagging despite free access.' AGOA.info, 8 August. Available at agoa.info/news/article/15638-us-african-trade-lagging-despite-free-access.html. Accessed on 26 September 2019.
17. Analysis based on UN Comtrade data.
18. Freemantle, S and Stevens, J, 2010. 'Placing the BRIC and Africa commercial partnership in a global perspective.' Standard Bank, 19 May, pp 2, 6–7.
19. United Nations Conference on Trade and Development; see also Eurostat, 2018. 'Africa-EU – international trade in goods statistics.' Available at ec.europa.eu/eurostat/statistics-explained/index.php/Africa-EU_-_international_trade_in_goods_statistics#Africa.E2.80.99s_main_trade_in_goods_partner_is_the_EU. Accessed on 26 September 2019. Note: Figure 11.2 excludes intra-African trade; EU-28 includes the UK.
20. Mureverwi, B, 2016. *China-Africa Trading Relationship*. Tralac Trade Brief, July 2016. Available at www.tralac.org/resources/our-resources/9174-china-africa-trading-relationship.html. Accessed on 26 September 2019.
21. Stevens, J, 2019. 'China-Africa trade expanded by 20% in 2018.' *Inside China*, Standard Bank, 16 January. Original data provided to author by email dated 5 April 2019. Available at ws15.standardbank.co.za/ResearchPortal/Report?YYY2162_FISRqWkWXsic7FKgCjGcLn4JFQVBznDhsEVWcAqZhonSB-CWKRZHtiYtASPMgyIUm/xoiITm+eZxvGcE6UxHkpQ==&a=-1. Accessed on 26 September 2019.
22. Wenjun, C, 2018. 'Twenty years on, China-SA relations embrace a new chapter.' Available at www.businesslive.co.za/bd/world/asia/2018-09-25-twenty-years-on-china-sa-relations-embrace-a-new-chapter/. Accessed on 26 September 2019.
23. Stevens, 'China-Africa trade expanded by 20% in 2018'.
24. Fernandes et al, *Are Trade Preferences a Panacea?*, p 20.
25. Most European trade is with North Africa, with Spain, France, Italy and Germany being the top four countries trading with Africa; see Eurostat, 'Africa-EU – international trade in goods statistics'.
26. Fernandes et al, *Are Trade Preferences a Panacea?*, pp 17–18.
27. Mold, A, 2018. 'The case for an integrated African market – the costs of "non-AfCFTA".' Op-ed, *The East African*, 12 August. Available at www.theeastafrican.co.ke/oped/comment/Integrated-African-market--the-costs-of--non-AfCFTA/434750-4709126-3el6hjz/index.html. Accessed on 26 September 2019.
28. Stoffaës, C, 2016. 'The Mediterranean Solar Plan.' Available at www.plan-solairemediterraneen.org/. Accessed on 26 September 2019.
29. European Commission, 2010. *Energy Infrastructure Priorities for 2020 and Beyond: A Blueprint for an Integrated European Energy Network*. Luxembourg: Publications Office of the European Union.
30. The Euro-Mediterranean Partnership (previously the Barcelona Process) was relaunched in 2008 as the Union for the Mediterranean.
31. The EU's Common Agricultural Policy (CAP) provides direct payments to European farmers in the form of a 'basic income support'. It is therefore decoupled from production, and payments amount to 72 per cent of the EU farming budget. This effectively amounts to a blanket subsidy for farming, even in the absence of targeted subsidies for specific product categories.

32. Edwards, C, 2018. 'Agricultural subsidies.' Blog post, Downsizing the Federal Government, 16 April. Available at www.downsizinggovernment.org/agriculture/subsidies. Accessed on 26 September 2019.

33. Although the launch of a SADC free trade area in 2008 was an important stepping stone towards the goals of a SADC common market by 2015 and a common currency by 2018, both goals have been missed by a large margin. Overall progress towards more economic integration is slow, although there is some movement via other processes such as a regional power pool, transport corridors and integrated payment systems.

34. A recent study, combining various macro datasets and variables, purports to show that integration in sub-Saharan Africa is more extensive than generally believed. See Arizala, F, Bellon, M, MacDonald, M, Mlachila, M and Yenice, MY, 2018. 'Trade and remittances within Africa.' Blog post, IMF Blog, 1 August. Available at blogs.imf.org/2018/08/01/trade-and-remittances-within-africa/. Accessed on 26 September 2019.

35. Based on data from UNCTADstat (unctadstat.unctad.org/EN/).

36. Institute for Security Studies, 2018. 'The African free trade area could be a reality by March next year.' PSC Insights, 23 November. Available at issafrica.org/pscreport/psc-insights/the-african-free-trade-area-could-be-a-reality-by-march-next-year. Accessed on 26 September 2019.

37. Lund et al, *Globalization in Transition*, p 1.

38. African Development Bank Group, 2018. *Eastern Africa Regional Integration Strategy Paper 2018–2022*. Abidjan: African Development Bank Group.

39. African Development Bank, 2018. *African Economic Outlook 2018*. Abidjan: African Development Bank Group, Chapter 3, p 63. Available at www.afdb.org/fileadmin/uploads/afdb/Documents/Publications/2018AEO/African_Economic_Outlook_2018_-_EN_Chapter3.pdf. Accessed on 23 September 2019.

40. Ashurst, 2016. 'Road infrastructure in Africa.' 1 June. Available at www.ashurst.com/en/news-and-insights/insights/road-infrastructure-in-africa/. Accessed on 23 September 2019.

41. African Union, 2018. *PIDA Implementation through Good Governance – Realizing Smart Infrastructure for Africa's Integration*. 26–28 November. Available at www.tralac.org/documents/news/2406-pida-week-2018-concept-note/file.html. Accessed on 23 September 2019.

42. Concept Note for the Second Ordinary Session of the African Union Specialized Committee on Transport, Transcontinental and Interregional Infrastructure, Energy and Tourism, Cairo, Egypt, 14–18 April 2019. Available at au.int/sites/default/files/newsevents/conceptnotes/36272-cn-ie24177_e_original-concept_note.pdf. Accessed on 23 September 2019.

43. The WTO is trying to address these barriers through the Technical Barriers to Trade Agreement (TBT Agreement) and a separate agreement on food safety and animal and plant health standards (Sanitary and Phytosanitary Measures Agreement).

44. Grinsted, J and Sandrey, R, 2015. *The Continental Free Trade Area – A GTAP assessment*. Trade Law Centre, 17 April. Available at www.tralac.org/publica-

tions/article/7287-the-continental-free-trade-area-a-gtap-assessment.html. Accessed on 23 September 2019.

45. See COMESA, EAC and SADC, no date. 'Non-Tariff Barriers to Trade.' Available at www.tradebarriers.org/ntb/non_tariff_barriers. Accessed on 23 September 2019.

46. ECA, ATPC, AU, Unctad and AfDB, 2018. *Concept Note. Assessing Regional Integration in Africa IX: Next Steps for the African Continental Free Trade Area.* Available at www.tralac.org/documents/news/2405-concept-note-assessing-regional-integration-in-africa-ix-report-uneca-2018/file.html. Accessed on 23 September 2019.

47. Ighobor, K, 2018. 'Africa set for a massive free trade area.' *African Renewal,* August–November 2018. Available at www.un.org/africarenewal/magazine/august-november-2018/africa-set-massive-free-trade-area. Accessed on 23 September 2019. See also AU, Uneca and ATPC, 2018. *African Continental Free Trade Area: Questions & Answers.* Addis Ababa: Uneca.

48. The dispute resolution mechanism does not, however, provide for private parties.

49. African Union, 2019. *Agreement Establishing the African Continental Free Trade Area.* Addis Ababa: AU, pp 20, 26 and 52.

50. Akeyewale, R, 2018. 'Who are the winners and losers in Africa's Continental Free Trade area?' WEF Regional Agenda, 17 October. Available at www.weforum.org/agenda/2018/10/africa-continental-free-trade-afcfta-sme-business/. Accessed on 23 September 2019.

51. AU, Uneca and ATPC, *African Continental Free Trade Area.*

52. Saygili, M, Peters, R and Knebel, C, 2017. *African Continental Free Trade Area: Challenges and Opportunities of Tariff Reductions.* Unctad Research Paper no 15.

53. Ibid, p 4.

54. Ibid.

55. Tralac, 'AEC2018'.

56. United Nations, 2019. *World Economic Situation and Prospects 2019.* Available at www.un.org/development/desa/dpad/publication/world-economic-situation-and-prospects-2019/. Accessed on 23 September 2019. See p 124.

57. Only five African countries have a GDP of more than US$100 billion (Nigeria, South Africa, Egypt, Algeria, Morocco).

58. Lund et al, *Globalization in Transition,* p 2.

59. Ogunniyi, A, Mavrotas, G, Olagunju, K, Adedoyin, R, Adewale, A and Ayodeji, O, 2018. *African Economic Conference 2018: Regional Economic integration, Governance Quality and Tax Revenue in Sub-Saharan African Countries: Linkages and Pathways.* Draft report. Kigali: UNDP, ECA and AfDB, p 12.

60. Somé, J, 2018. *African Economic Conference 2018: Industrial Policy, Institutions and Performance of the Manufacturing Sector in Africa.* Kigali: UNDP, ECA and AfDB, p 5.

61. Zahonogo, P, 2016. 'Trade and economic growth in developing countries: Evidence from sub-Saharan Africa.' *Journal of African Trade,* 3(1–2), pp 41–56.

62. Somé, *African Economic Conference 2018,* p 5.

63. See Erasmus, G, 2019. 'Where does the AfCFTA Process stand and what happens next?' Blog post, 23 January. Available at www.tralac.org/blog/article/

13855-where-does-the-afcfta-process-stand-and-what-happens-next.html. Accessed on 23 September 2019.

12: Prospects for greater peace

1. Pinker, S, 2012. *The Better Angels of Our Nature: Why Violence Has Declined.* London: Penguin Books, p xxii.
2. African Union, no date. *Agenda 2063: The Africa We Want.* Available at au.int/ agenda2063/overview. Accessed on 26 September 2019.
3. Hegre, H, Ellingsen, T, Gates, S and Gleditsch, NP, 2001. 'Toward a democratic civil peace? Democracy, political change, and civil war, 1816–1992.' *The American Political Science Review*, 95(1), pp 33–48.
4. See Pinker, *The Better Angels of Our Nature.*
5. See, for example, the discussion in Bowlsby, D, Chenoweth, E, Hendrix, C and Moyer, JD, 2019. 'The future is a moving target: Predicting political instability.' *British Journal of Political Science*, pp 1–13.
6. See, for example Institute for Security Studies, 2016. *Mali's Young "Jihadists": Fuelled by Faith or Circumstance?* Institute for Security Studies, Policy Brief 89. Available at issafrica.s3.amazonaws.com/site/uploads/policybrief89-eng-v3.pdf. Accessed on 26 September 2019.
7. See Uppsala Conflict Data Program, no date. 'UCDP: Department of Peace and Conflict Research.' Available at ucdp.uu.se/. Accessed on 26 September 2019. See also ACLED, no date. 'The Armed Conflict Location & Event Data Project.' Available at www.acleddata.com/. Accessed on 26 September 2019.
8. Gates, S, Nygård, HM and Trappeniers, E, 2016. *Conflict Recurrence.* PRIO Conflict Trends 02.
9. Ibid.
10. Goldstone, JA, Bates, RH, Epstein, DL, Gurr, TR, Lustik, MB, Marshall, MG, Ulfelder, J and Woodward M, 2010. 'A global model for forecasting political instability.' *American Journal of Political Science*, 54(1), pp 190–208. See also Hegre, H, Nygård, HM, Karlsen, J and Strand, H, 2013. 'Predicting armed conflict, 2010–2050.' *International Studies Quarterly*, 57(2), p 7.
11. World Bank, 2011. *World Development Report 2011: Conflict, Security, and Development.* Washington, DC: International Bank for Reconstruction and Development, p 5.
12. Hegre et al, 'Predicting armed conflict, 2010–2050', p 7.
13. Gates, et al, *Conflict Recurrence.*
14. Africa Center for Strategic Studies, 2018. 'Militant Islamist groups in Africa show resiliency over past decade.' [Infographic]. Available at africacenter.org/ spotlight/militant-islamist-groups-in-africa-show-resiliency-over-past-decade/. Accessed on 26 September 2019.
15. Alda, E and Sala, JL, 2014. 'Links between terrorism, organized crime and crime: The case of the Sahel region.' *Stability: International Journal of Security and Development*, 3(1).
16. Joshi, M and Quinn, JM, 2017. 'Implementing the peace: The aggregate implementation of comprehensive peace agreements and peace duration after

intrastate armed conflict.' *British Journal of Political Science*, 47(4), pp 869–892.

17. UCDP Georeferenced Event Dataset (GED), Global edition, version 19.1; population from UN Population Division in IFs 7.36.

18. The UCDP defines such events as 'an incident where armed force was used by an organised actor against another organised actor, or against civilians, resulting in at least one direct death at a specific location and a specific date'; see Sundberg, R and Melander, E, 2013. 'Introducing the UCDP Georeferenced Event Dataset.' *Journal of Peace Research*, 50(4), pp 523–532. See also Croicu, M and Sundberg, R, 2017. *UCDP GED Codebook version 17.1, Department of Peace and Conflict Research*. Uppsala: Uppsala University.

19. Egypt was added to the UCDP region of Africa for this calculation.

20. For more on the wars in the DRC, see Thompsell, A, 2019. 'The Second Congo War.' Available at www.thoughtco.com/second-congo-war-43698. Accessed on 26 September 2019.

21. Cilliers, J and Hedden, S, 2014. *Africa's Current and Future Stability*, Pretoria: Institute for Security Studies, p 16.

22. According to the ACLED codebook, a protest is 'a non-violent, group public demonstration, often against a government institution. Rioting is a violent form of demonstration.' See Raleigh, C and Dowd, C, 2015. *Armed Conflict Location and Event Data Project (ACLED) Codebook*. The Armed Conflict Location & Event Data Project, p 9.

23. See the analysis in Cilliers, J, 2018. *Violence in Africa: Trends, Drivers and Prospects to 2023*. Pretoria: Institute for Security Studies, p 10.

24. In respect of the latter, Hughes found that 'a 1.0 per cent drop in a moving average of economic growth (carrying 60 per cent of the moving average forward) is associated with a 0.04 point increase on a 0–1 scale for the rate of internal war'. See Hughes, BB, 2019. *International Futures: Building and Using Global Models*. Cambridge: Academic Press, p 180; see also Ianchovichina, E, Mottaghi, L and Devarajan, S, 2015. *Inequality, Uprisings, and Conflict in the Arab World*. New York: The World Bank.

25. See, for example, Buhaug, H, Gleditsch, NP and Theisen, OM, 2008. *Implications of Climate Change for Armed Conflict*. Washington, DC: Social Development, The World Bank. See also Andrews-Speed, P, Bleischwitz, R, Boersma, T, Johnson, C and Kemp, G, 2012. *The Global Resource Nexus: The Struggles for Land, Energy, Food, Water, and Minerals*. Washington, DC: Transatlantic Academy, pp 3–4.

26. Hendrix, CS and Salehyan, I, 2012. 'Climate change, rainfall, and social conflict in Africa.' *Journal of Peace Research*, 49(1), p 36.

27. Maslin, M, 2018. 'Politics and poverty caused past conflicts in East Africa – not climate change.' The Conversation, 23 May. Available at theconversation.com/politics-and-poverty-caused-past-conflicts-in-east-africa-not-climate-change-96372. Accessed on 26 September 2019.

28. Hegre et al, 'Toward a democratic civil peace?'

29. Paine, J, 2019. 'Ethnic violence in Africa: Destructive legacies of pre-colonial states.' *International Organization*, 73(3), pp 645–683.

30. United Nations and World Bank, 2018. *Pathways for Peace: Inclusive Approaches to Preventing Violent Conflict*. Washington: International Bank for Reconstruction and Development, p xviii.

31. Ibid, p 6.

32. On the Polity score, a mixed/intermediate regime type(s) has a score from +5 to -5 in an index that ranges from +10 to -10. V-Dem distinguishes between different types of democracy, each with its own index. Its electoral democracy index is closest to the Polity IV index.

33. Marshall, MG and Elzinga-Marshall, GC, 2017. *Global Report 2017: Conflict, Governance, and State Fragility*. Vienna: Center for Systemic Peace, p 30.

34. Ibid, p 12; Goldstone et al, 'A global model for forecasting political instability', p 195; Knutsen, CH and Nygård, HM, 2015. 'Institutional characteristics and regime survival: Why are semi-democracies less durable than autocracies and democracies?' *American Journal of Political Science*, 59(3), pp 656–670; Hegre et al, 'Toward a democratic civil peace?', pp 33–48.

35. Urda, H, 2011. *Demography and Armed Conflict: Assessing the Role of Population Growth and Youth Bulges*. Centre for Research on Peace and Development, Working Paper no 2; World Bank, World Development Report 2011, p 6.

36. Hegre et al, 'Predicting armed conflict', p 6.

37. Ibid, p 5.

38. Although the size of the youth bulge is often considered an important factor in the Arab Spring, the size of the bulge in North Africa is considerably lower than in the rest of Africa, pointing to the role played by other factors, most likely the low levels of political, economic and social inclusion in the region. See Brown, C, 2014. 'The Tunisian exception.' *Informed Comment*, 14 October. Available at www.juancole.com/2014/10/the-tunisian-exception.html. Accessed on 26 September 2019.

39. Ethiopia's youth bulge is coming down more rapidly than most other low-income countries in Africa due to the successful provision of water, sanitation and other basic health measures, and the availability of contraceptives that have, in combination, resulted in a rapid decline in total fertility rates in recent years. Ethiopia is expected to experience a decline in fertility rates from 4.6 children currently to 3.7 by 2030. See Donnenfeld, Z, Porter, A, Cilliers, J, Moyer, J, Scott, A, Maweni, J and Aucoin, C, 2017. *Ethiopia Development Trends Report*. Pretoria: Institute for Security Studies, pp 16–17.

40. See, for example, Idris, I, 2016. 'Youth unemployment and violence: Rapid literature review.' GSDRC, University of Birmingham, 1 November.

41. Mo Ibrahim Foundation, 2018. Ibrahim Index of African Governance (IIAG). Available at mo.ibrahim.foundation/iiag/. Accessed on 26 September 2019.

42. Rates of infant mortality are widely used as an indicator of poor service delivery and even as a short-term indicator of impending problems, including a violent rupture.

43. Donnenfeld, Z and Akum, F, 2017. *Gathering Storm Clouds: Political and Economic Uncertainty in Central Africa*. Pretoria: Institute for Security Studies, p 11.

44. See Center for Systemic Peace, 2017. *Global Conflict Trends: Assessing the Qual-*

ities of Systemic Peace. Available at www.systemicpeace.org/conflicttrends.html. Accessed on 26 September 2019.

45. IFs 7.36, initialising from IMF, *World Economic Outlook 2017.*

46. Calculated using the US$1.90, US$3.20 and US$5.50 poverty lines for low-income, lower-middle-income and upper-middle-income countries. The average income difference is GDP per capita in PPP.

47. See, for example, Commins, S, 2018. *From Urban Fragility to Urban Stability.* Washington, DC: Africa Center for Strategic Studies.

48. Bello-Schünemann, J and Aucoin, C, 2016. *African Urban Futures.* Pretoria: Institute for Security Studies.

49. Of the 15 current UN peacekeeping missions, five are in sub-Saharan Africa.

13: Good governance, democracy and development

1. Sharma, *The Rise and Fall of Nations*, p 75.

2. See University of Gothenburg, 2019. 'V-Dem: Global Standards, Local Knowledge.' Available at www.v-dem.net/en/. Accessed on 26 September 2019.

3. As used by V-Dem in their codebook v8, April 2018, pp 38–39. See University of Gothenburg, 2018. *Varieties of Democracy Codebook v8.* Available at www.v-dem.net/media/filer_public/e0/7f/e07f672b-b91e-4e98-b9a3-78f8cd4de696/v-dem_codebook_v8.pdf. Accessed on 26 September 2019.

4. V-Dem, v8.

5. According to the 2017 V-Data the average quality of electoral democracy in Africa is 0.45 and for liberal democracy it is less, at 0.31, both in relation to a possible maximum of 1.

6. Wike, R, Silver, L and Castillo, A, 2019. 'Many across the globe are dissatisfied with how democracy is working.' Available at www.pewglobal.org/2019/04/29/many-across-the-globe-are-dissatisfied-with-how-democracy-is-working/. Accessed on 26 September 2019.

7. The Economist Intelligence Unit, 2015. *Democracy Index 2015: Democracy in an Age of Anxiety.* Available at www.eiu.com/public/topical_report.aspx?campaignid=DemocracyIndex2015. Accessed on 26 September 2019.

8. Ibid; see also Foa, RS and Mounk, Y, 2016. 'The danger of deconsolidation: The democratic disconnect.' *Journal of Democracy*, 27(3), pp 5–17.

9. Ibid, p 6.

10. Based on survey data from the World Values Survey (conducted from 1995 to 2014).

11. The Economist Intelligence Unit, 2018. *Democracy Index 2018: Me Too? Political Participation, Protest and Democracy*, see p 4. Available at www.eiu.com/public/topical_report.aspx?campaignid=Democracy2018. Accessed on 26 September 2019.

12. Ibid, pp 3, 6.

13. Okello, C, 2019. 'No opposition, no internet: Benin election raises fears of authoritarianism.' Available at en.rfi.fr/africa/20190429-benin-parliamentary-election-no-opposition-no-internet-raises-fears-authoritarianism. Accessed on 26 September 2019.

14. Freedom House uses 25 indicators, with each country and territory assigned

a score from 0 to 4, for an aggregate score of up to 100. These scores are used to determine two numerical ratings, for political rights and civil liberties, with a rating of 1 representing the most free conditions and 7 the least free. See Freedom House, *Freedom in the World 2016*, and the chapter on survey methodology.

15. See afrobarometer.org/online-data-analysis.

16. Ibid.

17. This analysis is largely taken from the Polity IV project. See Center for Systemic Peace, 2018. 'The Polity Project.' Available at www.systemicpeace.org/polityproject.html. Accessed on 26 September 2019.

18. The Commission électorale nationale indépendante (CENI) has yet to release the results per polling station as required by law. The results announced by CENI were vastly at odds with the findings from the 40 000 observers deployed by the Catholic Church, which established a large and comprehensive parallel compilation process.

19. Cheeseman, N, 2015. *Democracy in Africa: Successes, Failures, and the Struggle for Political Reform.* Cambridge: Cambridge University Press. See also Cheeseman, N, 2015. *The State of Democracy in Africa.* Available at democracyinafrica. org/the-state-of-democracy-in-africa/. Accessed on 26 September 2019.

20. See Moore, *Social Origins of Dictatorship and Democracy*; and Przeworski and Limongi, 'Political regimes and economic growth'.

21. Glaeser et al, *Why Does Democracy Need Education?* Tunisia is a good example of the impetus that high levels of education provide to democratisation.

22. The World Bank, 2016. 'Access to electricity (% of population).' Available at data.worldbank.org/indicator/EG.ELC.ACCS.ZS?locations=ET. Accessed on 26 September 2019.

23. Human Rights Watch, no date. 'Ethiopian Protests.' Available at www.hrw.org/tag/ethiopian-protests. Accessed on 26 September 2019. Human Rights Watch, 2016. 'Ethiopia: Events of 2016.' Available at www.hrw.org/world-report/2017/country-chapters/Ethiopia. Accessed on 26 September 2019.

24. Al Jazeera and Agencies, 2016. 'Ethiopia state of emergency arrests top 11 000.' Available at www.aljazeera.com/news/2016/11/ethiopia-state-emergency-arrests-top-11000-161112191919319.html. Accessed on 26 September 2019.

25. Jeffrey, J, 2017. 'Hundreds of thousands of displaced Ethiopians are caught between ethnic violence and shadowy politics.' Available at www.pri.org/stories/2017-12-15/hundreds-thousands-displaced-ethiopians-are-caught-between-ethnic-violence-and. Accessed on 26 September 2019.

26. Glaeser et al, *Why Does Democracy Need Education?*, p 16.

27. Ibid, p 23.

28. See United Nations, no date. *What is Good Governance?* Bangkok: UNESCAP.

29. Booth, D, 2012. *Development as a Collective Action Problem: Addressing the Real Challenges of African Governance.* London: Africa Power and Politics Programme, Overseas Development Institute.

30. Ibid.

31. Englebert, P and Dunn, KC, 2013. *Inside African Politics.* Cape Town: UCT Press, p 191.

32. Cheeseman, *Democracy in Africa*, p 200.
33. Booth, *Development as a Collective Action Problem*.
34. Ibid, p 48. At a global level, China is the most enduring example.
35. Cheeseman, *The State of Democracy in Africa*.
36. Miguna, M, 2012. *Peeling Back the Mask: A Quest for Justice in Kenya*. Nairobi: Arrow Press. On Zimbabwe, see Thys Hoekman, 2013. 'Testing ties: Opposition and power-sharing negotiations in Zimbabwe.' *Journal of Southern African Studies*, 39(4), pp 903–920; Raftapoulos, B, 2012. *Towards Another Stalemate in Zimbabwe*. Norwegian Peacebuilding Resource Centre (NOREF).
37. Ibid.
38. *The Economist*, 2016. 'Government by gesture: A president who looks good but governs impulsively.' Available at www.economist.com/middle-east-and-africa/2016/05/26/government-by-gesture. Accessed on 26 September 2019.
39. AFP, 2018. 'Tanzanian president seeks end to contraception.' *News24*, 9 October 2018. Available at www.news24.com/Africa/News/tanzanian-president-seeks-end-to-contraception-20180910-2. Accessed on 26 September 2019.
40. Marks, Z, Chenoweth, E and Okeke, J, 2019. 'People power is rising in Africa.' *Foreign Affairs*, 25 April 2019.
41. See Hughes, BB, Joshi, DK, Moyer, JD, Sisk, TD and Solórzano, JR, 2014. *Patterns of Potential Human Progress, Volume 5: Strengthening Governance Globally: Forecasting the Next 50 Years*. New York: Routledge, Frederick S. Pardee Center for International Futures, University of Denver.
42. IFs 7.36, initialising from Polity IV data and using a five-year moving average.
43. GDP is in market exchange rates. Extreme poverty levels are calculated at US$1.90, US$3.20 and US$5.50 for low-, lower-middle- and upper-middle-income countries.
44. Leftwich, A, 1993. 'Governance, democracy and development in the Third World.' *Third World Quarterly*, 14(3), p 620.
45. See the World Values Survey, www.worldvaluessurvey.org/wvs.jsp.

14: External support: Aid, remittances and foreign direct investment

1. Khanna, P, 2019. *The Future Is Asian: Global Order in the Twenty-first Century*. New York: Simon & Schuster.
2. In constant 2017 dollars.
3. This is true irrespective of the way in which aid is calculated, ie as a total amount, percentage of GDP or per capita.
4. As opposed to official aid, most private money flows to Africa (and elsewhere) go to health and reproductive health in middle-income countries such as Nigeria and South Africa. See OECD, 2018. 'Private philanthropy funding for development modest compared to public aid, but its potential impact is high, says OECD.' Available at www.oecd.org/dev/private-philanthropy-funding-for-development-modest-compared-to-public-aid-but-its-potential-impact-is-high.htm. Accessed on 26 September 2019. See also aid data taken from Uneca and WTO, 2019. *An Inclusive African Continental Free Trade Area: Aid for Trade and the Empowerment of Women and Young People*. p 6. Available at www.tralac.org/documents/

resources/cfta/2892-an-inclusive-afcfta-aid-for-trade-and-the-empowerment-of-women-and-young-people-eca-wto-july-2019/file.html. Accessed on 26 September 2019.

5. Aid has a modestly positive effect on growth with an average internal rate of return of around ten per cent.

6. Ritchie, H and Roser, M, 2018. 'Now it is possible to take stock – did the world achieve the Millennium Development Goals?' Our World in Data, 20 September. Available at ourworldindata.org/millennium-development-goals. Accessed on 26 September 2019.

7. This number is for gross disbursement and is in 2016 constant values. The net disbursement amount is US$51.8 billion. See OECD, 2019. *Development Aid at a Glance: Statistics By Region. 2. Africa 2019 Edition.* p 2. Available at ww.oecd.org/dac/financing-sustainable-development/development-finance-data/Africa-Development-Aid-at-a-Glance-2019.pdf. Accessed on 26 September 2019.

8. Kitano, N, 2017. *A Note on Estimating China's Foreign Aid Using New Data: 2015 Preliminary Figures.* Tokyo: JICA. See also OECD, 2017. *Development Co-operation Report 2017: Data for Development.* Paris: OECD Publishing; and China Africa Research Initiative, 2019. *Data: Chinese Foreign Aid.* Available at www.sais-cari.org/data-chinese-foreign-aid-to-africa. Accessed on 26 September 2019.

9. OECD, 'Private philanthropy funding for development modest'.

10. The Federal Democratic Republic of Ethiopia, Ministry of Health, 2015. *Ethiopia Health Sector Transformation Plan.* Available at www.globalfinancingfacility.org/sites/gff_new/files/documents/HSTP%20Ethiopia.pdf. Accessed on 26 September 2019.

11. Alley, I, 2017. *Capital Flow Surges and Economic Growth in Sub-Saharan Africa: Any Role For Capital Controls?* African Development Bank Group Working Paper Series 252, March.

12. United Nations, no date. 'Goal 17: Revitalize the global partnership for sustainable development.' Available at www.un.org/sustainabledevelopment/global-partnerships/. Accessed on 26 September 2019.

13. These numbers are in 2017 values and are for net disbursements. See OECD, *Development Aid at a Glance.*

14. The EU and its member states provide 54 per cent of aid to Africa and the US 27 per cent. European Commission, 2018. 'Africa-Europe Alliance.' Available at ec.europa.eu/commission/africaeuropealliance_en. Accessed on 26 September 2019.

15. The BUILD Act replaces the Overseas Private Investment Corporation (OPIC), which was created in 1971.

16. See Runde, DF and Bandura, R, 2018. 'The BUILD Act has passed: What's next?' Available at www.csis.org/analysis/build-act-has-passed-whats-next. Accessed on 26 September 2019.

17. Airey, J, 2018. 'Bolton: New Africa strategy is tough on China, Russia, UN.' Available at www.dailywire.com/news/39347/watch-bolton-new-africa-strategy-tough-china-jacob-airey. Accessed on 26 September 2019.

18. Runde, DF and Bandura, R, 2019. *US Economic Engagement in Africa: Making*

Prosper Africa a Reality. Washington. DC: Center for Strategic & International Studies.

19. See Gavas, M and Timmis, H, 2019. *The EU's Financial Architecture for External Investment: Progress, Challenges, and Options*. CGD Policy Paper 136, pp 1–2. See also European Commission, no date. 'Joint Africa-EU Strategy.' Available at ec.europa.eu/europeaid/regions/africa/continental-cooperation/joint-africa-eu-strategy_en. Accessed on 26 September 2019.

20. The Aid for Trade Initiative was formally launched at the Sixth WTO Ministerial Conference in Hong Kong in 2005. See World Trade Organization, 2019. 'Aid for Trade.' Available at www.wto.org/english/tratop_e/devel_e/a4t_e/aid4trade_e.htm. Accessed on 26 September 2019.

21. Calculated from Uneca and WTO, 2019. *An Inclusive African Continental Free Trade Area: Aid for Trade and the Empowerment of Women and Young People*. p 6. Available at www.tralac.org/documents/resources/cfta/2892-an-inclusive-afcfta-aid-for-trade-and-the-empowerment-of-women-and-young-people-eca-wto-july-2019/file.html. Accessed on 26 September 2019.

22. See, for example, Bjorvatn, K, Kind, HJ and Nordas, HK, 2002. 'The role of FDI in economic development.' *Nordic Journal of Political Economy*, 28, pp 109–126.

23. Rabah, A, Bolton, P, Peters, S, Sanama, F and Stiglitz, J, 2017. 'From global savings glut to financing infrastructure.' *Economic Policy*, 32, pp 221–261.

24. In 2017 China provided 23.8 per cent of Africa's infrastructure commitment. See Prinsloo, C, 2019. *The Pitfalls of Private Sector Investment in Infrastructure Financing*. South African Institute of International Affairs, Policy Briefing no 197, June. Available at saiia.org.za/research/the-pitfalls-of-private-sector-investment-in-infrastructure-financing/. Accessed on 26 September 2019.

25. Zawadzki, S, 2019. 'Anadarko approves $20 billion LNG export project in Mozambique.' Reuters, 18 June. Available at www.reuters.com/article/us-mozambique-anadarko-lng/anadarko-approves-20-billion-lng-export-project-in-mozambique-idUSKCN1TJ2DI. Accessed on 26 September 2019.

26. United Nations Conference on Trade and Development, 2018. 'Regional Fact Sheets.' Available at unctad.org/en/Pages/DIAE/World%20Investment%20Report/Regional-Factsheets.aspx. Accessed on 26 September 2019.

27. A further 13 countries were rated by two of the three agencies, namely, Botswana, Republic of Congo, Cameroon, Cape Verde, Ghana, Kenya, Namibia, Nigeria, Rwanda, Senegal, Tunisia, Uganda and Zambia. See Country Economy, no date. 'Sovereign ratings list.' Available at countryeconomy.com/%20ratings. Accessed on 26 September 2019.

28. European Commission, 'Africa-Europe Alliance'. This data would still include the UK as a member of the EU.

29. Unctad, 2018. *World Investment Report: Investment and New Industrial Policies*. New York and Geneva: United Nations Publications. Available at unctad.org/en/PublicationsLibrary/wir2018_en.pdf. Accessed on 26 September 2019. Unctad, 2019. *World Investment Report: Special Economic Zones*. p x. New York and Geneva: United Nations Publications. Available at unctad.org/en/PublicationsLibrary/wir2019_en.pdf. Accessed on 26 September 2019.

30. American Enterprise Institute, 2019. 'China Global Investment Tracker.' Available at www.aei.org/china-global-investment-tracker/. Accessed on 26 September 2019. See also Jayaram et al, *The Closest Look Yet.*

31. Jayaram et al, *The Closest Look Yet.*

32. Oya, C and Wanda, F, 2019. *Working Conditions in Angola: Infrastructure, Construction and Building Materials Factories.* Angola Research Brief, SOAS, University of London. Available at www.soas.ac.uk/idcea/publications/reports/file141347. pdf. Accessed on 26 September 2019. See also Schaefer, F and Oya, C, 2019. *Employment Patterns and Conditions in Construction and Manufacturing in Ethiopia: A Comparative Analysis of the Road Building and Light Manufacturing Sectors.* IDCEA Research Report, SOAS, University of London. Available at www. soas.ac.uk/idcea/publications/reports/file141205.pdf. Accessed on 26 September 2019.

33. Neuweg, I, 2018. 'What types of energy does China finance with its development aid?' Available at www.lse.ac.uk/GranthamInstitute/news/china-energy-development-aid/. Accessed on 26 September 2019.

34. Partington, R, 2019. 'Fears grow in Africa that the flood of funds from China will start to ebb.' *The Guardian*, 5 January.

35. African Development Bank, *African Economic Outlook 2018*, Chapter 3, pp 63–93.

36. Jayaram et al, *The Closest Look Yet.*

37. Reinhart, CH, 2018. 'Exposing China's overseas lending.' Project Syndicate, 31 October. Available at www.project-syndicate.org/commentary/china-opaque-foreign-development-loans-by-carmen-reinhart-2018-10. Accessed on 26 September 2019.

38. Neuweg, 'What types of energy does China finance?'; International Monetary Fund, 2018. 'Regional economic Outlook. Sub-Saharan Africa.' Washington, DC: International Monetary Fund. See also Brautigam, D, 2019. 'Is China the world's loan shark?' *The New York Times*, 26 April. Available at www.nytimes. com/2019/04/26/opinion/china-belt-road-initiative.html. Accessed on 26 September 2019.

39. Reinhart, CM and Rogoff, KS, 2010. 'Growth in a time of debt.' *American Economic Review: Papers & Proceedings*, 100, pp 573–578.

40. Kazeem, Y, 2018. 'Nigeria has taken its first steps in adopting China's yuan as a reserve currency.' *Quartz Africa*, 2 August 2018. Available at qz.com/africa/ 1346766/chinas-yuan-trades-in-nigeria-africa-top-economy/. Accessed on 26 September 2019.

41. Nantulya, P, 2019. 'Chinese hard power supports its growing strategic interests in Africa.' Available at africacenter.org/spotlight/chinese-hard-power-supports-its-growing-strategic-interests-in-africa/. Accessed on 26 September 2019.

42. African migrants (including refugees, regular and illegal migrants, and short and long-term migrants) represent about 14.1 per cent (or 36.3 million) of the global migrant population. An estimated nine-tenths of African migrants stay within the continent, moving to neighbouring countries or elsewhere within their region. See Mo Ibrahim Foundation, *Africa's Youth*, pp 13–15.

43. World Bank Group, 2017. *Migrations and Remittances: Recent Developments and Outlook*. Special Topic. Return Migration. Migration and Development Brief 28, October, p 10.

44. Ibid. Remittance flows in North Africa mostly go to Egypt (at US$18.2 billion). Other large recipients are Morocco (US$7.1 billion) and Senegal (US$2.3 billion).

45. At its peak in 2030, Africa would receive US$113.3 billion instead of US$100.1 billion.

46. IFs 7.36, initialising from IMF, *World Economic Outlook 2017*, and other sources.

47. European Commission, 'Africa-Europe Alliance'.

48. Staff reporter, 2019. 'China's Xi offers another $60 billion to Africa, but says no to "vanity" projects.' Reuters, 3 September. Available at www.reuters.com/article/us-china-africa/chinas-xi-offers-another-60-billion-to-africa-but-says-no-to-vanity-projects-idUSKCN1LJ0C4. Accessed on 26 September 2019.

49. Orlik, T, Chen, F, Wan, Q and Jimenez, J, 2018. 'Sizing up China's debt bubble: Bloomberg Economics.' Available at www.bloomberg.com/news/articles/2018-02-08/sizing-up-china-s-debt-bubble-bloomberg-economics. Accessed on 26 September 2019.

50. Lardy, NR, 2019. *The State Strikes Back: The End of Economic Reform in China?* Washington, DC: Peterson Institute for International Economics.

15: Climate change

1. Ripple, WJ, Wolf, C, Galetti, M, Newsome, MT, Alamgir, M, Mahmoud, EC, Mahmoud, MI and Laurance, WF, 2017. 'World scientists' warning to humanity: A second notice.' *Bioscience*, 67(12), pp 1026–1028.

2. Díaz, S, Settele, J and Brondízio, E, 2019. *Summary for Policymakers of the Global Assessment Report on Biodiversity and Ecosystem Services of the Intergovernmental Science-Policy Platform on Biodiversity and Ecosystem Services*. Bonn: Intergovernmental Science Policy Platform on Biodiversity and Ecosystem Services.

3. IPCC, 2014. *Climate Change Synthesis Report Summary for Policymakers*. Available at www.ipcc.ch/site/assets/uploads/2018/02/AR5_SYR_FINAL_SPM.pdf. Accessed on 26 September 2019.

4. City of Cape Town, 2018. *Water Outlook Report*. Cape Town: Department of Water and Sanitation.

5. Republic of South Africa, Department of Water and Sanitation, 2019. *National Integrated Water Information System*. Available at niwis.dws.gov.za/niwis2/Surface WaterStorage. Accessed on 26 September 2019.

6. 'Pre-industrial' is defined as the average for the period 1850–1900.

7. United Nations Environment Programme (UNEP), www.unenvironment.org/explore-topics/climate-change.

8. Warren, R, 2011. 'The role of interactions in a world implementing adaptation and mitigation solutions to climate change.' *Philosophical Transactions of the Royal Society A*, 369(1934).

9. IPCC, 2014. *The IPCC's Fifth Assessment Report: What's in it for Africa?* Climate

& Development Knowledge Network. Available at cdkn.org/resource/highlights-africa-ar5/?loclang=en_gb. Accessed on 26 September 2019.

10. As summarised by the GreenFacts initiative, no date. 'Impacts of a 4°C global warming.' Available at www.greenfacts.org/en/impacts-global-warming/l-2/index.htm. Accessed on 26 September 2019.

11. IPCC, 2018. *Global Warming of 1.5°C*. Special report, October 2018. Geneva: Intergovernmental Panel on Climate Change. Available at www.ipcc.ch/sr15/. Accessed on 26 September 2019.

12. What this means is that the mass of CO_2 is 44.01 grams per 22.4 litres at 25°C and at sea level. CO weighs 28.01 grams per 22.4 litres and CH_4 weighs 16.04 grams per 22.4 litres. However, the carbon contribution for each is 12.01 grams per 22.4 litres.

13. IFs 7.36, initialising from the IPCC and Carbon Dioxide Information Analysis Center.

14. International Energy Agency (IEA), 2018. *World Energy Outlook*. Available at www.iea.org/weo2018/. Accessed on 26 September 2019.

15. University of Washington, College of the Environment, 2011. 'Projections of climate change: 2100 and beyond.' Available at www.atmos.washington.edu/academics/classes/2011Q1/101/Climate_Change_2011_part2.pdf. Accessed on 26 September 2019.

16. Young, IR and Ribal, A, 2019. 'Multiplatform evaluation of global trends in wind speed and wave height.' *Science*, 364(6440), pp 548–552.

17. IPCC, *Global Warming of 1.5°C*.

18. Global Commission on the Geopolitics of Energy Transformation, 2019. *A New World: The Geopolitics of the Energy Transformation*. Abu Dhabi: IRENA, p 12.

19. Ibid.

20. Ibid. Ironically, Kenya is building a coal-fired plant near the Lamu Port-South Sudan-Ethiopia Transport Corridor project that may even be dependent on coal imports. See Leithead, A, 2019. 'Row over Chinese coal plant near Kenya World Heritage site of Lamu.' Available at www.bbc.com/news/uk-48503020. Accessed on 26 September 2019.

21. Ritchie, H and Roser, M, 2017. 'CO_2 and Greenhouse Gas Emissions.' Our World in Data. Available at ourworldindata.org/co2-and-other-greenhouse-gas-emissions. Accessed on 26 September 2019. See also United States Environmental Protection Agency (EPA), no date. *Global Greenhouse Gas Emissions Data*. Available at www.epa.gov/ghgemissions/global-greenhouse-gas-emissions-data. Accessed on 26 September 2019.

22. Calculated from data available from the csv file on the chart CO_2 emissions per capita, see Ritchie and Roser, 'CO_2 and Greenhouse Gas Emissions'.

23. EPA, *Global Greenhouse Gas Emissions Data*.

24. The forecast from the International Energy Agency (IEA) *World Energy Outlook 2018* is that almost two-thirds of global capacity additions to 2040 will come from renewables, thanks to falling costs and supportive government policies. In the most recent forecast from the IEA, natural gas overtakes coal in 2030 to

become the second-largest fuel in the global energy mix. By 2040, the most likely IEA scenario is that the share of renewables in generation would have increased from its current 25 per cent to more than 40 per cent, but that coal is likely to remain the largest source of energy globally and gas the second largest.

25. IFs 7.36, initialising from International Energy Agency, *World Energy Outlook*.
26. IFs 7.36, initialising from Carbon Dioxide Information Analysis Center.
27. IFs 7.36, initialising from International Energy Agency, *World Energy Outlook*.
28. Swarup, A, 2007. 'Eastern Africa: worst floods in decades.' Available at www.ifrc. org/en/nouvelles/nouvelles/common/eastern-africa-worst-floods-in-decades/. Accessed on 26 September 2019.
29. IPCC, *The IPCC's Fifth Assessment Report*.
30. UNOCHA, 2017. 'West and Central Africa: 2017 flood impact.' [Infographic]. Available at reliefweb.int/sites/reliefweb.int/files/resources/OCHA-ROWCA%20 West%20and%20Central%20Africa%202017%20Flood%20Impact_18%20 Oct%202017.pdf. Accessed on 26 September 2019.
31. Giannini, A, Saravanan, R and Chang, P, 2003. 'Oceanic forcing of Sahel rainfall on interannual to interdecadal time scales.' *Science*, 302(5647), pp 1027–1030.
32. IPCC, *The IPCC's Fifth Assessment Report*, p 14.
33. Field, CB and Barros, VR, 2014. *Climate Change 2014. Impacts, Adaptation and Vulnerability: Part A Global and Sectoral Aspects*. New York: Cambridge University Press.
34. Rumney, E and Eisenhammer, S, 2019. 'Destructive Cyclone Idai rings "alarm bell" on climate change: UN chief.' Available at af.reuters.com/article/topNews/ idAFKCN1R80JJ-OZATP. Accessed on 26 September 2019.
35. International Crisis Group, 2018. *Stopping Nigeria's Spiralling Farmer-Herder Violence*. Report 262, 26 July.
36. Diallo, OA, 2017. 'Ethnic clashes, jihad, and insecurity in central Mali.' *Journal of Social Justice*, 29(3), pp 299–306.
37. Foster, V and Briceno-Garmendia, C, 2010. *Africa's Infrastructure: A Time for Transformation*. Africa Development Forum series. Agence Française de Développement and the World Bank. Available at openknowledge.worldbank.org/ handle/10986/2692. Accessed on 26 September 2019.
38. IPCC, The IPCC's Fifth Assessment Report.
39. Field and Barros, *Climate Change 2014*, p 762.
40. IFs 7.36, initialising from IPCC and Carbon Dioxide Information Analysis Center.
41. Cusick, D, 2018. 'New walls aim to hold back rising seas off Tanzania.' Available at www.scientificamerican.com/article/new-walls-aim-to-hold-back-rising-seas-off-tanzania/. Accessed on 26 September 2019.
42. The UNPD uses data from the state of Lagos that is then standardised.
43. Romm, JJ, 2015. *Climate Change: What Everyone Needs to Know*. Oxford: Oxford University Press.
44. See BBC *Newsnight*, 2017, 'Why is Africa building a Great Green Wall?' Available at www.youtube.com/watch?v=4xls7K_xFBQ. Accessed on 26 September 2019. See also BBC News, 'The Great Green Wall of Africa: Will it help fight climate

change?' Available at www.youtube.com/watch?v=HVOYN70scS8. Accessed on 26 September 2019.

45. Karasz, P, 2019, 'Ethiopia says it planted over 350 million trees in a day, a record.' *The New York Times*, 30 July 2019. Available at www.nytimes.com/2019/07/30/world/africa/ethiopia-tree-planting-deforestation.html. Accessed on 26 September 2019.

46. Rizvi, AR, Baig, S and Kumar, C, 2016. *Forests and climate change*. Gland: IUCN.

47. World Resources Institute, no date. *Global Forest Watch*. Available at www.globalforestwatch.org/. Accessed on 26 September 2019.

48. African Union, *Agenda 2063*.

49. Foster and Briceño-Garmendia, *Africa's Infrastructure*, pp 1–14, 272, 287.

50. Niang, I and Ruppel, OC, 2014. 'Africa.' In Cramer et al, *Climate Change 2014*.

16: Africa first!

1. Mandela, NR, 2002. 'Address by Nelson Mandela at gala banquet celebrating Africa's 100 best books of the 20th century.' 23 July. Available at www.mandela.gov.za/mandela_speeches/2002/020723_books.htm. Accessed on 26 September 2019.

2. On the other hand, over longer time horizons reductions in poverty would improve human capital and eventually have a positive impact upon economic growth.

3. IFs 7.36, initialising from World Bank, World Development Indicators, 2018.

4. Ibid.

5. IFs 7.36, initialising from IMF, *World Economic Outlook 2017*.

6. IFs 7.36, initialising from World Bank, PovCalNet.

7. Ibid.

8. IFs 7.36, initialising from IMF, *World Economic Outlook 2017*.

9. Donnenfeld, Z, Cilliers, J, Kwasi, S and Welborn, L, 2019. 'Emerging giant: Potential pathways for Ethiopia to 2040.' Institute for Security Studies (forthcoming).

10. IFs 7.36, initialising from World Bank, PovCalNet.

11. The large South African motor industry is often used as an example of an entire industry that has become addicted to concessionary tax breaks but serves as the locus of the country's manufacturing sector.

12. United Nations Economic Commission for Africa, 2013. *Making the Most of Africa's Commodities: Industrializing for Growth, Jobs and Economic Transformation.* Addis Ababa: United Nations Economic Commission for Africa.

13. Jayaram et al, *The Closest Look Yet*.

14. Reinert, *How Rich Countries Got Rich*, p 148.

15. Lund et al, *Globalization in Transition*, p 1.

16. McKinsey, *Digital Globalization*, p 3.

17. De Backer and Flaig, *The Future of Global Value Chains*, pp 8–9.

18. United Nations Economic Commission for Africa, 2019. *Fiscal Policy for Financing Sustainable Development in Africa*. Addis Ababa: United Nations Economic Commission for Africa, p xiii.

19. Collier, *African Urbanisation*, pp 23–25.
20. Moya, A, 2019. 'How Africa can tap into SpaceX's Starlink satellites.' *ITWeb*, 28 May. Available at www.itweb.co.za/content/KWEBbvyaw43vmRjO. Accessed on 26 September 2019.
21. See Stedman, A and Green, KP, 2018. *Annual Survey of Mining Companies: 2017.* Available at www.fraserinstitute.org/studies/annual-survey-of-mining-companies-2017. Accessed on 26 September 2019.

Index

378 — **AFRICA FIRST!**

social grants to relieve poverty 126-130, 133-135, 174, 296, 302-303, 312, 314-315
solar energy (see also renewable energy) 9, 178-182, 190, 192, 203, 287, 290
Soros, George 263
Southern African Customs Union (SACU) 204, 211
Southern African Development Community (SADC) 13, 181, 200, 204-205, 211, 216, 355
special economic zones (SEZ) 129, 145-146, 158, 198, 277
State of Commodity Dependence, The 23
Strategy for the Harmonization of Statistics in Africa (SHaSA) 14
sub-Saharan Africa 19, 22-23, 26, 45-49, 60-65, 67-68, 72, 77-81, 84-86, 88, 98, 101, 110, 113, 115, 120, 134, 137, 149, 159-162, 168-169, 182, 185-186, 192, 208, 214, 227, 233, 235, 237, 240, 263, 271, 274-275, 294, 298, 342, 347-348, 355, 360
Suri, Tavneet 187
Sustainable Development Goals (SDGs), Agenda for (United Nations) 5, 11, 17-18, 35, 67, 69, 71, 118, 121-123, 135, 162, 190, 199, 238, 265, 275-276, 298, 301, 307
Swedish International Development Cooperation Agency (SIDA) 263

Takaful and Karama cash transfer programme 130
Talon, Patrice 245
technical and vocational training (TVET) 88-89
telecommunications 15, 186
terrorism 218, 221, 228, 243, 266, 275
Thunberg, Greta 282
Tolstoy, Leo 218

Trade and Law Centre, Stellenbosch 208
Transparency International's Corruption Perception Index 259
transportation 5, 65, 97, 115, 127, 135, 138, 141, 158, 164, 175-177, 203, 207-210, 213, 269, 287, 355
Tripartite Free Trade Area 205, 209, 211, 216
Trump, Donald 197-198
Tshisekedi, Félix 29, 247
tuberculosis 60, 97, 193

unemployment, employment 9, 23, 25, 29-30, 39, 48-49, 75, 77, 88, 106-107, 111, 121-122, 127, 129-132, 137-138, 147, 149, 156-166, 168, 172-174, 190, 192, 211-212, 218, 226, 233, 264, 266, 347
United Nations Children's Fund (Unicef) 67
United Nations Conference on Trade and Development (Unctad) 23, 139, 211, 213, 329, 353, 356
United Nations Department of Economic and Social Affairs (Undesa) 212-213
United Nations Development Programme (UNDP) 16, 122, 263, 343
United Nations Economic Commission for Africa (Uneca) 73, 203, 206-208, 211, 213, 312, 363
United Nations Environment Programme (UNEP) 284
United Nations Food and Agriculture Organization (FAO) 101, 104, 108, 113, 115,
United Nations Population Division (UNPD) 49, 65, 369
Uppsala Conflict Data Program (UCDP) 218, 222, 358